CHURCHILL,
BY HIS CONTEMPORARIES

THE SUPREME TRIUMPH

Churchill broadcasts the news of Germany's
surrender—May 8th, 1945

CHURCHILL

By his Contemporaries

Edited by

CHARLES EADE

HUTCHINSON
Stratford Place
London

Hutchinson & Co. (Publishers) Ltd.

London   New York   Toronto

Melbourne   Sydney   Cape Town

First published 1953

Set in twelve point Monotype Bembo
one point leaded

Printed in Great Britain
by The Anchor Press, Ltd.,
Tiptree, Essex

CONTENTS

5

LIST OF ILLUSTRATIONS

ACKNOWLEDGMENTS

Charles Eade, the Editor of Churchill, *By His Contemporaries*, wishes to express his appreciation of the help and advice given by Lieut.-General Sir Henry Pownall in the compiling of this book.

The chapter "Churchill as an Ally in War" by President Eisenhower consists of edited extracts from *Crusade in Europe* by Dwight D. Eisenhower. Copyright 1948 by Doubleday and Company Inc.

"Churchill as a Guest" by Mrs. Roosevelt is extracted from her book *This I Remember*. Copyright Hutchinson and Co.

Extracts from the public speeches of Adolf Hitler which form the chapter "Churchill the Hated Enemy" were translated at the time they were delivered by members of the staff of Associated Newspapers Ltd.

Quotations from *Savrola*, by Sir Winston Churchill, used by Sir Compton Mackenzie in his chapter "Churchill the Novelist", and from *Great Contemporaries* and *Thoughts and Adventures*, both by Sir Winston Churchill, used by M. Paul Reynaud and other contributors, are by permission of Odhams Press Ltd., publishers and proprietors of the copyright.

Permission to include the chapter "Churchill the Man of Talent" by G. Bernard Shaw has been granted by the Public Trustee and the Society of Authors.

Quotations from Sir Winston Churchill's speeches and from *The Second World War* by Sir Winston Churchill are included by permission of Cassell and Co.

Copyrights of the photographs are owned by the Imperial War Museum (Churchill broadcasting the news of Germany's surrender, Churchill as a soldier in the First World War, and Churchill with Stalin); Associated Press Ltd. (Churchill with General Eisenhower, Churchill addressing the United States Congress, and Churchill painting at Madeira); Topical Press Agency Ltd. (Churchill with Prince Louis of Battenberg); Planet News Ltd. (Churchill arriving for his first day's work in the Second World War and Churchill with Colonist II); P.A.—Reuter Photos Ltd. (Churchill the Airman); and Sport and General Press Agency Ltd. (Churchill the Candidate).

INTRODUCTION

FOR more than half a century Sir Winston Churchill has been a personality of international interest and importance. From the adventurous days of his youthful escapades in the Boer War and the publication of his first controversial writings on the operations of the Malakand Field Force, Churchill has never for long been out of the public eye or the newspaper headlines. His dazzling and often stormy career has stretched from the solid, settled Victorian era to the new and hopeful promise of a second Elizabethan age. He has gloried in triumphs such as few men have achieved and he has suffered defeats, disappointments, humiliations and derision in a measure seldom experienced by any other man in public life. He has been mocked and isolated in Parliament and yet lived to see his critics hail him as the greatest parliamentarian of modern times—perhaps of all time. He was cheered as the architect of victory in the greatest war in history and then hurled from office by the very people he had led through the terror to triumph. Today he stands alone, pre-eminent among the great men of his age and high among all the giants of world history.

It is difficult, indeed, to find an historical parallel to the many-sided career of Sir Winston Churchill. His versatility and his achievements in so many different spheres of activity make him unique. There have been many statesmen who were also writers of high quality, many orators who were also men of action, many politicians who dabbled in the arts, many soldiers who experimented with the paint-brush and, no doubt, some historians who have also ridden to hounds, piloted an aeroplane or built a brick wall. But the existence of any other man who has done all these things—and many more besides—remains unknown. No one can be compared to Churchill in the wide range of his interests, the magnitude of his achievements and the number of roles he has played with distinction. He began his career as a soldier, soon turned to the more lucrative field of journalism, burst at an early age into national politics and rose to world eminence as a great war leader and elder statesman admired and respected by men and women throughout the Free World.

In Parliament he has, at various times, shouldered responsibility for the Army, Navy, Air Force, Finance, Colonies, Trade, Munitions, Home Affairs and National Defence as well as bearing the supreme burden of the Premiership with a vigorous interlude as Leader of the Opposition.

As a writer he has been a war correspondent, novelist, biographer, historian, reviewer, essayist and the contributor of innumerable topical articles on a wide range of subjects to newspapers and magazines throughout the world.

In his leisure hours he has embraced the delights of hunting, painting in oils, bricklaying, fencing, flying, polo, farming, horse-racing, shooting wild animals in Africa and collecting tropical fish.

His war speeches will live as long as the English language. He has a mastery of words, both written and spoken, attained by few men. He has displayed his skill as an organizer and administrator. He has given intelligent encouragement to the more practical forms of science. His theories on strategy have usually been justified by events. His prophecies, though occasionally derided, have, more often than not, been ultimately fulfilled; indeed it is given to few to see so clearly into the future as he can.

Much has been written about Sir Winston Churchill—some fifty books and some millions of words in magazines and newspapers the world over—but this book, which I have called *Churchill, By His Contemporaries*, is an attempt to describe and assess the man, his achievements, his personality, his public and private life in a manner never before attempted.

In the following pages nearly two score men and women, most of whom have known Sir Winston Churchill intimately, have joined together to write about him, each from a particular point of view. The writers include Earl Winterton, who sat in the House of Commons with Churchill longer than any other member; Admiral Sir William James, who was associated with him in naval matters for some thirty-five years; Sir Gerald Woods Wollaston, who was at Harrow with him; Mrs. Thompson, who was his Personal Private Secretary; President Eisenhower, who worked with him as a trusted ally in war; Detective-Inspector Thompson, who was his bodyguard on and off for over twenty years; Collin Brooks, who dined and travelled with him; Leslie Hore-Belisha, who sat in the War Cabinet with him; Professor Thomas Bodkin, who has talked pictures with him; Guy Eden, who stood by his side in the ruins of the bombed House of Commons; Colin Coote, who as an editor published his articles, and Beric Holt, who served under him when Churchill himself was an editor; Viscount Simon, his Cabinet colleague in many Administrations; Mrs. Roosevelt, who was his hostess; and Emanuel Shinwell, his opponent in innumerable House of Commons battles. All of them —and many others—have in this work contributed their stories and their assessments of this truly great Englishman.

Could a book like this be written about any other man? Is there another individual possessed of so many facets to his character and personality, so many achievements in so many different fields of endeavour? It is difficult to think of one. But this is not merely a collection of flattering, adulatory chapters about a man revered by millions. There is criticism too, since Churchill inspires controversy and opposition as well as respect and affection. It may well be that historians of the future will find some help in this collection of writings on Churchill by so many of his distinguished contemporaries.

Are there any conclusions to be drawn from these contributions so varied in their style and content? Is some single theme or trait, or characteristic or quality or secret, revealed by these personal analyses? Only the reader can decide that for himself when he reaches the end of the book. And, no doubt, different readers will reach different and possibly contradictory conclusions.

But this can be said with truth—Whatever his failings or weaknesses, whatever his reverses or errors, Sir Winston Churchill can be hailed, with more certainty than any other man of the age, as truly great, and as he nears his eightieth year as this book is completed there are few who can doubt that that will also be the final verdict of history.

CHARLES EADE.

CHURCHILL AT HARROW

Sir Gerald Woods Wollaston
K.C.B., K.C.V.O.

Sir Gerald Woods Wollaston was a contemporary of Sir Winston Churchill at Harrow and writes of the mark made in the School by "Spencer-Churchill (W.L.)" as a Harrow boy.

Sir Gerald was Garter King of Arms from 1939 to 1944 and has since been Norroy and Ulster King of Arms.

WINSTON CHURCHILL and I went to Harrow the same year. He preceded me by one term, entering the School in April 1888, while I went there in the following September. We both started in small Houses—he in Mr. Davidson's and I in Mr. Marshall's. It was not unusual for a boy to enter the School in one of the small Houses (consisting of about fifteen boys), either because his parents thought that initiation into the rough and tumble of Public School life would thus be somewhat cushioned, or because there was not at the time a vacancy in the large House for which he was entered. Churchill spent a year in Mr. Davidson's, and then moved into the Headmaster's House of some sixty boys.

At Harrow—as no doubt at other Public Schools where the House system prevails—there is competition between all the large Houses in most aspects of the School life, but particularly in games. Traditions have been established in them; and while, no doubt, they have their ups and downs and their better or worse periods respectively, these traditions of the older Houses are a source of pride to the boys in them, imparting to some, maybe, a sense of responsibility for their main- tenance, and affording to all an inspiration which, I think, must often extend to later life. However much, or little, Churchill profited during his years at Harrow from these feelings, I am sure that, consciously or unconsciously, they affected him in his life.

Had the spirit of prophecy not so long escaped us, no doubt we Harrovians of those days would have hailed the advent of Churchill to Harrow as a red-letter day in the history of the School, and we should have looked for any signs in the youthful prodigy of those characteristics which in after life have made him so renowned. Nor should we have been disappointed! But the facts compel me to record that he came to Harrow like any other small boy, and that no greater interest was taken in him than is wont to be taken in small boys at their first arrival at a Public School.

The only person perhaps who can be credited with vision was the Headmaster, Dr. Welldon, who admitted him to the School although at the entrance examination he returned a blank sheet of paper in Latin prose, having, after two hours' rumination, been unable to answer a single question! But I suspect that the Headmaster's vision was directed no further forward than to the inconvenience likely to be caused by the rejection of Lord Randolph Churchill's son, with the consolatory thought that the offspring of so distinguished a father could not fail somehow to make good, even if the immediate outlook seemed a little bleak.

Churchill was placed in the bottom form, in which he remained for a year, when he transferred to the modern side and thence to the Army class; but he never rose very far in the School. For some reason he had an aversion to Latin, and either could not or would not learn it. Although a "modern side" had existed at Harrow for some time, the classics were still then regarded as the principal scholastic fare, and the lack of them undoubtedly militated against Churchill's progress in the School. No doubt too he was handicapped by his own idiosyncrasies, for he resolutely refused to absorb anything that did not interest him, and was even selective in his choice of masters from whom he was willing to learn.

His long sojourn in the Fourth Form, however, was not unremunerative, for in it he acquired, under the tuition of Mr. R. Somervell, for whose methods of teaching he had a great regard, a complete knowledge of the elements of the English language, a knowledge which he extended later in the Army class, under Mr. L. M. Moriarty, and developed into that mastery of the language for which he is so conspicuous today. To these two masters must be added a third who made an impression on Churchill's brilliant but eclectic brain, Mr. C. H. P. Mayo, who taught him mathematics in the Army class. The combined efforts of master and pupil in this case enabled the latter— who for once worked with a will—to learn enough in six months to pass the entrance examination into Sandhurst.

If, as I have stated, no greater interest was evinced in Winston Churchill (more correctly known at the School as Spencer-Churchill and so described in the School lists) when he entered Harrow than is usually taken in small boys, his own reactions to school life did not allow this long to continue. He consistently broke almost every rule made by masters or boys, was quite incorrigible, and had an unlimited vocabulary of "back-chat", which he produced with dauntless courage on every occasion of remonstrance. He himself recalls that in his first term he one day pushed a Sixth Form boy into "Ducker" (the School swimming pool). The boy was Amery—afterwards to be one of his colleagues in the Cabinet—who retaliated with vigour. Churchill's excuse was hardly a classic example of tact—"I mistook you for a Fourth Form boy, you are so small!"—though he improved the situation somewhat by adding, "My father, who is a great man, is also small." Amery, if small, was endowed with prodigious strength and was champion gymnast of the School.

It is said (I do not vouch for the story) that the Headmaster on one occasion had to reprimand Churchill. "Churchill," he said, "I have very grave reason to be displeased with you." "And I, sir," replied the boy, "have very grave reason to be displeased with you!"

Although he remained throughout his time at Harrow in the lower forms, the capacity of his brain was indicated by his extraordinary powers of memory. While still in the bottom form he gained a school prize by reciting 1,200 lines of Macaulay's *Lays of Ancient Rome* without a mistake, and he could quote whole scenes from Shakespeare's plays and had no hesitation in correcting his masters if they misquoted. Contrary to all School rules, he kept dogs in a house in West Street, and used to walk them out accompanied by one of the townspeople with whom he had made friends. In his early days in the Headmaster's House Nugent Hicks (afterwards Bishop of Lincoln) was head of the School and of the House and Churchill was his fag. It was a privilege of heads of Houses and monitors to administer corporal punishment to junior boys who failed to fulfil their duties, or otherwise grievously offended against the rules of the House or the School. Hicks and Churchill met in these circumstances on more than one occasion. On the first, after receiving his "whopping", Churchill said to Hicks, "I shall be a greater man than you," to which Hicks promptly replied, "You can take two more for that," and gave them.

These and many other similar stories very soon went round the

School, to the detriment of the future Prime Minister. We who were in other Houses and had not met him personally soon heard about him, and what we heard created a somewhat unfavourable opinion.

There is one story which should be told to his lasting credit, though it was not so accounted to him in the School at the time. In his early home life, before he went to School, he had the inestimable advantage of a nurse, an old retainer in the family, one of those great and good women who in those days devoted their lives to the children whom they were engaged to look after. Many of us of that generation owe an immense debt to some such nurse, who was an integral part of the establishment and for whom we had a very real and lasting affection. In a "brave new world" they have gone, alas!, seemingly for ever, with many other benefits which modern childhood can ill afford to lose. Churchill had a great affection for his old nurse, and one day he brought her down to Harrow and showed her all over the School, to her immense delight; and not content with this, he marched arm-in-arm with her up the High Street for all who cared to see. Looking back now I will only make this comment on the story—and I believe most people will agree with me—I only wish I had had the courage, as a boy, to bring my old nurse to see the School as he did. But, at the time, the story of Churchill and his nurse went like wildfire through the School and did not then, I regret to say, add favourably to his schoolboy reputation.

Perhaps today we should not be disposed to credit the Prime Minister with having been an athlete in his young days, and he certainly was no good at the ordinary ball games when at Harrow. Yet he won the Public Schools fencing competition at Aldershot for the School, and he represented his House in the inter-House swimming competitions. As I also represented mine, I suppose I encountered him then, but I am afraid I do not remember it.

My only recollection of meeting him was in the School Rifle Corps, of which we were both members. The Corps, which was first formed in 1859 as a Company of the 18th Middlesex Rifle Volunteer Corps, was not well supported in the School when we first went there. The senior boys did not join it, and those who did were certainly less enthusiastic than they should have been. It was not until 1891 that its unsatisfactory state was taken up in the *Harrovian* (the School magazine), and by the combined efforts of Mr. M. C. Kemp (that eminent cricketer and Harrow master whose recent death we all regret) and Nugent Hicks (then head of the School) it was put on a proper basis, as a unit worthy to represent the School at field-days or in camp. We were then affiliated to the Middlesex Regiment, our uniform was grey with blue facings, and our badge was the crossed arrows which have since become the official badge of the School. There was daily drill in the Bill-Yard and periodical field-days. My chief recollection of the latter is that non-commissioned officers (I was a corporal and later an officer) had usually to carry the rifles of small boys to enable us to "retreat" with sufficient celerity—for some unexplained reason these field-days always seemed to involve retreat! I do not think that Churchill ever rose above the ranks in the Corps, perhaps because he was in the lower school, or maybe because in those days—though this is surprising—his martial instincts had not developed and the activities of field-days were not altogether to his liking.

It will not surprise many to learn that Churchill was a frequent contributor to the pages of the *Harrovian*. Amery has stated that as then schoolboy editor of that journal he had to blue-pencil many of these contributions. There is also an amusing story told of the Headmaster and Churchill on this subject; the Headmaster summoned him to his study and addressed him thus: "My boy, I have observed certain articles which have recently appeared in the *Harrovian*, of a character not calculated to increase the respect of the boys for the constituted authorities of the School. As the *Harrovian* is anonymous I shall not dream of inquiring who wrote those articles, but if any more of the same sort appear, it might become my painful duty to swish you." Though he wrote under a pseudonym, the articles which have been identified as his were on the gymnasium and the lack of interest displayed by the School therein, and on the nature of the assaults at arms given there; also on the use of one of the speech-room towers as a class-room, on which he wrote an amusing and clever skit emphasizing its unsuitability for the purpose.

These contributions prove that Churchill's long training in the English language in the Fourth Form was bearing fruit, and give early evidence of his great gifts as a master of both the spoken and the written word.

Churchill left Harrow at Christmas 1892, and after passing through Sandhurst obtained a commission in the Fourth Hussars. I must leave to others the record of his subsequent career, but I may perhaps mention here the occasions on which he has revisited his old School. The first of these was on October 26, 1900, when he gave a lecture to the School on his experiences after leaving Harrow and particularly those in the South African War, when he was the correspondent of the *Morning Post*, was taken prisoner and escaped from captivity. The next visit was forty years later, when, as Prime Minister, he came to Harrow, with Mrs. Churchill and some members of his Cabinet, and joined in singing the Harrow songs in Speech-room and addressed the boys. He has since made this an annual visit, and on November 7, 1952, he spoke in Speech-room for the thirteenth time and sang with the boys Harrow songs. Though, as he said then, he found it difficult to vary these annual speeches, Harrow boys will hope that, having passed the ill-fated number thirteen, he will repeat many times yet the occasions when they can accord to him that welcome which acclaims a great personality and a true friend of Harrow.

It is often said that one's schooldays are the happiest days of one's life. I have always been sceptical of this statement as one of general application. No doubt it is true in some cases. In a few it may be definitely untrue. These are the fringes. The vast majority of boys undoubtedly enjoy school life, but there are many restrictions, whether made by masters or boys, which temper its pleasures. A new boy at a Public School has to spend some considerable time learning his way about a world which is new to him, and troubles and anxieties may well beset him in the process. If, by his own ability and application, he in time attains high position in the school, at work or in games, he may still have anxieties, and perhaps some disappointments, before he achieves his ambitions. He is never quite master of his own destiny. It is just these very circumstances which make our Public Schools such great institutions for the formation of character, and enable them constantly to send forth a stream of boys qualified to take their places in the "wider life to be", who have learned by service to lead. But has that wider life no happiness to offer to them comparable to their schooldays? That is not my experience.

Sir Winston Churchill has himself said that his schooldays were not happy. "I was on the whole considerably discouraged by my school days. . . . I am all for the Public Schools but I do not want to go there again." Yet I think he will agree that our Public School days do influence us and go far to guide our later actions. In a long life I can say that on many occasions of difficult decision I have found myself wondering what those whose opinions I respected at School would have expected me to do in any such case.

Sir Winston, whatever his feelings may have been at Harrow, was certainly impressed by the Harrow songs, that great collection peculiar to the School which he is so happy to sing at his periodical visits to Harrow, and the words and music of which he still treasures in his wonderful memory. I feel sure that many of those songs must have recurred to him in his cases of difficulty, and perhaps not least the noble verse:

> So today—and oh! if ever
> Duty's voice is ringing clear
> Bidding men to brave endeavour
> Be our answer "We are here".

No one in his life has ever more completely fulfilled the spirit of that verse than Sir Winston Churchill.

CHURCHILL AND THE ARMY

Lieut.-General H. G. Martin
C.B., D.S.O.

Lieut.-General Martin, who has been Military Correspondent of the Daily Telegraph *since 1943, joined the Royal Artillery in 1906 and served in the First World War, the Afghan War (1919) and the Second World War. He was Instructor at the Staff College, Quetta, 1928–1931, and at the Imperial Defence College, 1936. He was Major-General in charge of Anti-Aircraft at the G.H.Q. British Expeditionary Force in France in 1940.*

TO describe his experiences in war Sir Winston Churchill himself has filled some sixteen volumes of history and reminiscences, and his collected speeches on warlike occasions fill nearly a dozen more. His personal experience of war is unique. He himself has served with no less than eight different regiments—the 4th Hussars, the 31st Punjabis, the 21st Lancers, the South African Light Horse, the Oxfordshire Yeomanry, the 2nd Battalion Grenadier Guards, the 6th Royal Scots Fusiliers and the Oxfordshire Artillery—and even before the two World Wars he had seen service in four campaigns. As a hussar with a roving commission he watched the Spanish Army fight the rebels in Cuba in 1895; as a war correspondent and, afterwards, attached to the 31st Punjabis he took the field with the Malakand Field Force in 1897; attached to the 21st Lancers he charged with them at Omdurman in 1898; again as a war correspondent and, later, attached to the South African Light Horse, he was among the first into Lady-smith on its relief; in 1915–1916 he was in the trenches in Flanders, first with the 2nd Grenadier Guards and later in command of the 6th Royal Scots Fusiliers; and, throughout both World Wars he repeatedly visited the fronts.

Moreover, this knowledge gained by personal experience he has supplemented vastly by research. The writing of his many books, and in particular of the four-volume life of his great ancestor, the first Duke of Marlborough, has necessitated a profound study of military history in general and, in particular, of the history of the British Army. His love of the Army and of soldiering shines out from all his writings.

Finally there is another and entirely different field in which Sir Winston Churchill has exercised a predominant influence on the Army. I refer, of course, to the part he has played as a statesman in the higher direction of two World Wars and in their aftermaths.

In the account that follows I propose to devote Part I to Churchill's personal experiences as a soldier; Part II to his higher direction of war and particularly of land operations.

THE SOLDIER

We have it on Sir Winston's authority that his toy soldiers, of whom he had a fine array, were responsible for his choice of a career. One day his father, Lord Randolph, had come to inspect these soldiers on parade; had seen; and had been so impressed that he had asked Commander-in-Chief Winston whether or not he would like to go into the Army. The reply had been favourable; whereupon Sandhurst became young Winston's goal.

To get there was to prove rather a business. After an extensive course at Captain James's incomparable cramming establishment— known as "Jimmy's" to generations of would-be officers—Churchill scraped into Sandhurst at his third attempt, but only high enough to qualify for a cavalry cadetship. The Sandhurst course brought to an end twelve years of schooling, on which period Sir Winston looks back as the least satisfactory of his life.

At Sandhurst, Gentleman Cadet Churchill was able to begin that study of military history and the art of war which he has continued all his life. Also, regarding horsemanship as one of the important things in life, he delighted in riding school. In December 1894 he passed out of Sandhurst with honours, eighth in his batch of 150, and was commissioned in the 4th Hussars at Aldershot.

There in the Long Valley he revelled in the cavalry training of the 'nineties, with all its galloping and panache. Yet, even in that epoch when the *Arme Blanche* still reigned supreme, sometimes there would intrude a horrid doubt: in the next war, 2nd Lieutenant Churchill would wonder, what of Mr. Maxim with that gun of his that fired goodness knows how many shots a minute?

In November 1895 2nd Lieutenant Churchill and his friend Reginald Barnes sailed away to Cuba. It was the beginning of the leave season when all good cavalrymen settled down to hunt throughout five glorious winter months. Having spent all his money on polo ponies, however, Churchill had none left for hunting. A suitable alternative was a sniff of active service and in Cuba there was an insurrection in progress.

In due course the two young officers arrived. They found the Spanish regular forces involved in a guerilla war which, had Churchill but guessed it, was to be the pattern of many more that he was to know elsewhere later on—in South Africa, for instance, and in Ireland, in Malaya, Indo-China and Kenya. Up and down the land the Spanish Government had stretched its cordons of posts and blockhouses manned by regulars; while in the jungle between there wandered ponderously a dozen or so columns of regular troops. As these columns approached, the enemy melted away—melted, that is, till their chosen moment came to strike back savagely and with all the advantages of surprise. In the ensuing fight the regular troops, behaving with their traditional bravery, would drive home their attack, only to find the enemy flown and pursuit impossible in the jungle. It was a highly dangerous business and Churchill himself seems to have been extremely fortunate to return intact. From the point of view of the Spanish Government, the effort expended was plainly out of all proportion to the results achieved.

It was in Cuba, be it noted, that Churchill acquired the siesta habit. In after life he has found that by sleeping for an hour or so after luncheon he can add two hours to his working day. The Allies of World War II are thus indebted to the siesta for countless thousands of Churchill-hours worked on their behalf. The debt is incalculable. The only sufferers have been those Chiefs of Staff and others who, in conformity with the siesta, have banished sleep to endure in conference far into the small hours. They have the consolation that they could have suffered in no better cause.

In 1896 2nd Lieutenant Churchill went with the 4th Hussars to the India that so many of us used to know and love so well. He had two ambitions: to go on active service somewhere—anywhere; and to help the 4th to win the Inter-Regimental, supreme among polo tournaments. By dint of infinite pertinacity he was to achieve both ambitions.

In the annals of North-West Frontier warfare, '97 is a vintage year. In that year those peerless warriors, the Independent Tribes, staged what was perhaps their finest performance. When the outbreak began Churchill was at home on leave. Needless to say, no sooner had the news reached him than he hurried back to India; called in at Bangalore in the far south to placate his Colonel and brother officers; set out on the 2,028-mile railway journey to Nowshera, railhead of the Malakand Field Force, and joined the Commander of the Field Force, General Sir Bindon Blood.

September 16, 1897, was a day ever memorable in Frontier warfare. On it one of Sir Bindon's brigades entered the Mamund Valley on what was designed to be a punitive operation. Churchill, ever in search of trouble, accompanied this brigade—and again he was lucky to return intact.

The Mamunds, a redoubtable tribe, struck back: the Brigade Commander lost control of his far too widely dispersed brigade; there ensued a soldiers' battle in which the courage and staunchness of the troops alone saved the day. But losses, British and Indian, were heavy, and the news of that day's and night's fighting spread like wildfire along the Frontier. Hearing it, that most formidable of all the tribes, the Afridis of the Tirah, joined in the fun.

It was his experiences of those days that gave Churchill an understanding of the Indian soldier and an appreciation of his worth. At this stage he was posted temporarily to the 31st Punjabis, who had lost nearly all their British officers: an episode that he was to recall with pride forty-four years later when honouring the Indian forces who had won so fine a fight at Keren in Eritrea.

Shortly afterwards Churchill was recalled to his regiment in Bangalore. Understandably perhaps, his Commanding Officer took the view that it was time he did a bit of regimental soldiering. Churchill's heart, however, was still on the North-West Frontier, where greatly extended operations against the Afridis had now begun: return there he would by hook or crook.

At first all his efforts—whether pursued by himself in person at Army Headquarters in Calcutta or on his behalf by his mother in London—failed. All the world seemed banded against him. Never take no for an answer: that has ever been the Churchillian motto. There was one last hope. Putting fate to the touch with sublime audacity, he presented himself at the headquarters of the Commander-in-Chief,

Sir William Lockhart, in Peshawar: either he must melt Sir William's heart or else he must return to Bangalore to answer a charge of absence without leave. Fortune smiled; Sir William's heart was melted; he appointed Churchill an extra orderly officer on his personal staff. But fortune had smiled too late: this war, it proved, was over.

Conveniently, however, another was about to begin—this time in the Sudan; so off went Churchill home to London to arrange matters. To get to the Sudan, however, was to prove even more difficult than to get to the Tirah. The Commander-in-Chief in the field, Sir Herbert Kitchener—afterwards Lord Kitchener—was grimly determined that 2nd Lieutenant Churchill should not join his force. Even when Churchill had mobilized Lord Salisbury, that great Prime Minister, to intervene on his behalf, Kitchener refused to be cajoled. A stroke of luck or genius won the day. By chance Churchill learnt that Sir Evelyn Wood, the Adjutant-General to the Forces, greatly resented Kitchener's interference with the posting of officers, which he regarded as his own prerogative as Adjutant-General. Taking full advantage of this, 2nd Lieutenant Churchill succeeded in an appeal to Sir Evelyn and so attained his desire at last; he found himself attached to the 21st Lancers for the Sudan Campaign.

On the eve of the Battle of Omdurman Lieutenant Churchill had his first meeting with Kitchener: it was the first of many that these two were to have in war. Churchill had been out on reconnaissance with the 21st and had been sent back to report the advance of the Dervish Army. He found Kitchener riding at the head of his force, a striking figure, and to him personally he made his brief report.

Next day was fought the Battle of Omdurman that broke the power of the Dervishes. In the 21st Lancers' famous charge, of which he has given a most vivid account, Churchill commanded the troop second from the right of the line. His troop and that on the extreme right overlapped the mass of two or three thousand Dervishes who awaited the charge in a dry water-course: these two troops were thus able to increase their pace and to curve inwards to take the mass in flank. Moreover, they were able also to keep moving, whereas the troops on their left were brought to a standstill in the swarm of packed humanity and had many of their number hacked to pieces. In two or three minutes the 21st thus lost five officers, sixty-five men and 120 horses. As for the Dervishes, they left thirty or forty corpses behind. It was a poor advertisement for the *Arme Blanche*.

In November 1898 Churchill rejoined the 4th Hussars in India. Having found life in his polo-playing regiment too expensive for him, he had already decided to leave the Army and to support himself by writing—with the possibility of going into Parliament later on—but before he sent in his papers there was still the Inter-Regimental to be won. That tournament used to be played in the month of February at Meerut. And Meerut lies 1,400 miles to the northward of Bangalore. No regiment from Southern India had ever yet won the Inter-Regimental.

Having dislocated his shoulder, Churchill played throughout the tournament with his right elbow strapped to his side. In the final the 4th Hussars met the 4th Dragoon Guards. As No. 1 Churchill had to mark the opposing back, the redoubtable Captain Hardress Lloyd, afterwards an international player against the United States. Throughout the game Churchill hustled Lloyd unmercifully. In the breathless outcome the 4th Hussars won 4 to 3, and of these four goals Churchill, despite his crippled arm, had scored all but one. Surely the story of that game is fit to rank with the saga of the Maltese Cat or with that Battle of Titans described by Bengal Lancer. Thus it was in a blaze of glory that Churchill left the 4th and the Army.

It was not long, however, before he was off to the wars once more. In the first days of October 1899 Paul Kruger in Pretoria sent an ultimatum to the British Government. Three days later the South African War began. On October 11 Churchill—now war correspondent to the *Morning Post*—sailed for South Africa in the *Dunotter Castle* along with Sir Redvers Buller and the staff of our one and only army corps.

Though later he joined the South African Horse without pay, Churchill's experiences in South Africa were not those of the orthodox soldier. Largely on account of the dual role which he himself had played on the North-West Frontier and up the Nile, the War Office had now ruled that there was to be no more doubling of the roles of soldier and war correspondent. Thus the part played by Churchill in

CHURCHILL THE SOLDIER

Major Churchill, wearing a French shrapnel helmet, at
a French H.Q. during the First World War

South Africa can best be described as that of an extremely belligerent war correspondent.[1]

Perhaps it was what Churchill, the young war correspondent, saw of Sir Redvers Buller's generalship that conditioned the attitude of Sir Winston Churchill, the statesman, to general officers in later life. There was no more gallant gentleman than Sir Redvers, but he had long lost all conception of the value of time. The ineptitude of his ponderous and dilatory operations for the relief of Ladysmith exceeded belief. In Hitler's war, on the other hand, time was to be the sole commodity that Churchill would grudge to his commanders in the field. Well does he understand Napoleon's *cri du cœur*, "Ask me for anything but time!"

When at last Ladysmith was relieved, Churchill was among the first into the town, beaten to it only by Hubert Gough and his Composite Horse. At this stage Churchill decided to transfer his allegiance from Sir Redvers to Lord Roberts, who was then advancing into the Orange Free State in what was now the main theatre of war. There was no difficulty. Having obtained indefinite leave from the South African Light Horse, away Churchill went.

That he survived the advance on Pretoria was a dispensation from Heaven. When his insatiable zest for adventure, coupled with his warm sense of comradeship with those in danger, had placed him once more in an apparently hopeless position—alone, on foot, a thousand yards from the nearest cover and under close-range Boer fire—succour appeared from nowhere in the form of a lone scout: a scout, moreover, prepared to draw rein, pick Churchill up behind him on his horse and carry him to safety. Afterwards Churchill was at pains to obtain for the scout in question, Corporal Roberts, the award of the Distinguished Conduct Medal.

Almost his last adventure in South Africa was to bicycle in plain clothes through Johannesburg while that town was still in possession of the Boers. He thus risked trial by court martial and summary execution as a spy. Fortunately, however, the bicycle ride ended uneventfully. With the fall of Pretoria came the end of military operations on a major scale. True, a devastating guerilla war of two

---

[1] Fully dealt with in the chapter "Churchill the War Correspondent", by G. Ward Price.

years' duration was about to begin, but none could foresee this calamity. Resuming civilian status, Churchill went home to England, in time to be returned as Conservative Member for Oldham in the General Election of 1900. As Lord Dufferin said of him shortly afterwards, when introducing him to an audience at the Ulster Hall: "This young man—at an age when many of his contemporaries have hardly left their studies—has seen more active service than half the general officers in Europe."

Before Churchill next saw service sixteen years were to elapse.

In 1915 he was the chief protagonist of the campaign at the Dardanelles. It was his advocacy of this assault on what even in those days he thought of as the "underbelly" of Europe that led to his return to the Army. In retrospect we can see clearly enough that in his determination to open the Dardanelles, supply Russia, and knock out Turkey he was a hundred per cent right. In those days, however, we had not yet mastered the technique of inter-Service planning. Even so, it was only by an almost unbelievable concatenation of mishaps that, time after time, victory eluded us when already in our grasp.

When, in November 1915, the British Government finally determined to evacuate Gallipoli, Churchill decided that his place was with the Army in the field. His intention was to rejoin his regiment, the Oxfordshire Yeomanry, who were then serving in France.

We have been given a glimpse of the reactions of those nearest to him when he set off for the front. His mother was overcome with grief and anxiety, but his wife remained calm. In the years to come Lady Churchill was to have many more occasions to exercise the same iron self-control. Typical of such occasions—if we may pause for a moment to look ahead—there was to be Churchill's mission of June 11, 1940, when Reynaud's Government on its flight from Paris had paused at the Château du Muguet on the Loire. France was tottering, and Churchill was determined to see Reynaud once more before it was too late; but the R.A.F. had declared that weather conditions that day made flying impossible. His colleagues were dismayed—and, approaching his wife, begged her to dissuade him. "There is a battle on," said she, "other men are flying: he must go." And fly he did, despite weather and Luftwaffe.

So much for a later war. On his arrival in France on that autumn day of 1915, Churchill found awaiting him a car sent by Sir John French, the Commander-in-Chief, to bring him to G.H.Q. near St. Omer. There French offered him the command of a brigade—a command which, on account of his wide experience of war and affairs, Churchill felt himself well fitted to exercise. But first, he stipulated he must have a month or so in the trenches to learn local conditions, for which purpose there could be no better school than the Guards. So it was to the 2nd Battalion, Grenadier Guards, in the trenches near Laventie, that Sir John French sent him.

Churchill has described his frigid reception. His Colonel had not been consulted about his posting—and made it abundantly plain that he resented the omission. His brother officers were determined to put the politician in his place. It took Churchill no more than forty-eight hours, however, to win their confidence and respect. To this fact Haig's Diary bears impartial witness: on December 16, 1915, Haig notes that Churchill's Commanding Officer "speaks highly of his keenness". About this time, too, when the battalion second-in-command went on leave, his Commanding Officer invited Churchill temporarily to take over the appointment: one of the greatest honours, Churchill holds, that he has ever received. The regard was mutual: the admiration that Churchill himself felt for those "magnificent Grenadiers"—to borrow his phrase—was intense.

When his month's apprenticeship with the Grenadiers had run its course Churchill felt ready for his promised brigade. French, too, was anxious to fulfil his promise. It appeared, however, that there were now two obstacles in the way. The first, according to Lord Beaverbrook's account,[1] took the form of a veto imposed by Asquith, the Prime Minister, who went in fear of those who still blamed Churchill for the failure at the Dardanelles. But the second was even more insurmountable: it took the form of a blank refusal of French's request by Haig, who had now succeeded French as Commander-in-Chief. Churchill, Haig ruled, must ascend the military ladder rung by rung. With his hopes thus dashed, Churchill left the Guards in January 1916 to take command of the 6th Royal Scots Fusiliers in the 9th Division near "Plugstreet". The Divisional Commander, Major-General Tudor, was an old friend.

[1] *Politicians and the War*, Vol. II.

The 6th Royal Scots Fusiliers, as Churchill found them, had all the magnificent qualities of Kitchener's First Hundred Thousand but inevitably lacked the polish of the Guards. It was against lice that Churchill had to fight his first action, and he won a signal victory. His Lowland Scots were immensely impressed by the arrival of so famous a figure to command them: his word was law. He set a personal example of meticulous performance of duty, never failing to carry out his day and night inspections of the trenches. The change that he wrought in his battalion was remarkable. His Adjutant gives us a glimpse of him while whizzbangs were swishing close overhead during an enemy bombardment. "At that moment," the Adjutant writes, "I profoundly hated war. But at that and every moment, I believe, Winston Churchill revelled in it. There was no such thing as fear in him."

Churchill, however, was not long to enjoy the fruits of his labours. Already, thanks to Asquith's reluctance to introduce an adequate National Service Bill, the shortage of manpower was acute. Perforce, the 6th Royal Scots Fusiliers had to be amalgamated with another battalion, and it was Churchill who, as the junior of the two battalion commanders, lost his command.

Meanwhile his friends at home had been urging him to return to the House, and to join a strong Opposition pledged to prosecute the war relentlessly. He obtained leave of absence accordingly and returned in May 1916, only to find himself engaged for nearly a year in the proceedings of the Statutory Committee of Enquiry into the Operations at the Dardanelles.

So ended Churchill's personal experiences in the Army. With his going, a soldier with a great future was lost to the Army, but his destiny was elsewhere.

THE STATESMAN AND THE ARMY

Sir Winston Churchill himself has written the full record of his part in the higher direction of the two World Wars. Here I can attempt to touch only on the outstanding episodes which concern the Army in particular.

Let us go back to autumn, 1914. In August the Admiralty had become responsible for the air defence of Great Britain. To carry out its role it had established air squadrons on the coast of Belgium and France, and to protect these squadrons it had employed armoured cars. The enemy had riposted by cratering the roads. Thus the need had arisen for a cross-country armoured vehicle. It was in this manner that Churchill, then First Lord, first had his mind directed to the conception of the tank. His interest was soon to be quickened by the need to find a way to penetrate the enemy's ever-growing trench systems and to overcome his machine-guns. Already it was plain that, as 2nd Lieutenant Churchill had foreseen in the Long Valley twenty years earlier, the machine-gun dominated the battlefield.

In October 1914 Admiral Bacon, Manager of the Coventry Ordnance Works, produced, at Churchill's request, the design of a caterpillar tractor that would cross trenches. In May 1915 the War Office subjected the prototype of this caterpillar to a test of achievement so exacting that it was never to be attained by any tank throughout the Kaiser's War. Understandably, Bacon's caterpillar failed—whereupon the War Office rejected the whole project summarily.

Meanwhile Colonel E. D. Swinton, better known perhaps as "Ole Luk Oie", who was then attached to G.H.Q. as Eye Witness or Official Correspondent, had formulated a similar project quite independently. Colonel Hankey, now Lord Hankey, who was then Secretary of the War Council, embodied Swinton's project in a paper which, early in January 1915, Churchill brought to the attention of the Prime Minister. The Prime Minister in turn enlisted the help of Kitchener, who sent the paper to the Master-General of Ordnance with his blessing. The Master-General promptly pigeon-holed it—and so for the second time the tank perished in the womb.

Later in January, suspecting that the War Office was stalling, Churchill ordered his own Director of the Air Division at the Admiralty to carry out certain experiments. For mechanical reasons, however, this third attempt was also abortive.

Here again, however, Churchill was true to his principle: never take no for an answer. These vexatious obstructions merely made him the more determined to carry his project through in some form or another. To this end, on February 20, 1915, he created the Land Ships

Committee of the Admiralty under the presidency of Mr. Tennyson-d'Eyncourt, the Chief Constructor of the Navy. A month later Mr. Tennyson-d'Eyncourt reported that he had evolved two practicable types of "land ship", the one wheeled, the other tracked. On his personal responsibility, Churchill promptly ordered eighteen of these at an estimated cost of £70,000. So at long last the tank was born.

The tank had no one inventor. As early as 1903, Mr. H. G. Wells had developed the idea in fictional form, and in 1914 the components of the tank—that is to say, high-grade steel plating, the internal combustion engine and the caterpillar track—were all ready to hand. The British Army owed the help which—at long last—it was to get from the tank on the later battlefields of the Kaiser's War to two distinct persons or groups. First, there was the authority who took the responsibility for ordering tank production to go ahead, and who drove the project through to completion. Secondly, there was the technical expert who executed this order, solving the extremely intricate mechanical problems involved in the process of production. It was Churchill who took upon himself the personal responsibility for ordering those eighteen land ships at a time when no demand for them whatever had come from France, and it was Mr. Tennyson-d'Eyncourt who executed the order with matchless skill. To them the Army's gratitude is due.

The story of the use or abuse of the tank in action is as chequered as that of its production. As early as December 3, 1915, Churchill drew up a prescient paper termed "Variants of the Offensive", in which he advocated the surprise use of tanks in large numbers to destroy enemy wire. Despite his protests, however, and those of Mr. Lloyd George, the first twenty tanks were frittered away uselessly in the Battle of the Somme, and the element of novelty thus lost. Again at the Battle of Passchendaele our tanks were thrown in in penny packets, to be swallowed up in a sea of mud. It was not till the Battle of Cambrai on November 20, 1917, that General Byng used his tanks in mass and with the advantage of tactical surprise, to achieve a brilliant success.

Cambrai, according to Churchill, was the ideal battle, which should have been the model for all the great Allied offensives—so slow and costly—that had gone before. There is this to be said, however: Byng had an advantage which none of his predecessors had enjoyed. In this battle advances in the science of gunnery at last permitted his artillery to dispense with preliminary registration and to open accurate, predicted fire at H-hour. Thus, for the first time, Byng could make surprise complete.

So much for Churchill's all-important part in developing the tank. In July 1917 he became Minister of Munitions in Lloyd George's Government. In the Ministry he found 12,000 officials organized in fifty departments, each of which claimed direct access to himself. To remedy this over-centralization he grouped the fifty departments in ten large groups, each under a head of outstanding capacity. These ten heads formed a Munitions Council, and they alone were directly responsible to himself. The Council's reports were so masterly that he had rarely to alter a word. Thus relieved of detail, Churchill was able to concentrate on matters of policy.

The pre-eminent success which his Ministry achieved is recorded in Haig's final Dispatch. In 1916 there had still been a shortage of shells; in 1917 the supply of guns had caused anxiety. "Only in 1918," Haig wrote, "was it possible to conduct artillery operations independently of any limiting consideration other than that of transport."

Great though his services had been as Minister of Munitions, however, it was after the Kaiser's War had ended that Churchill put the Army deepest in his debt. On the morrow of the General Election of January 1919 Lloyd George transferred him from the Ministry of Munitions to the War Office. He took up his new post only just in time to save the Army from dissolving in widespread mutiny. Before taking it up he had wisely stipulated that in all matters affecting the discipline of the troops his authority should override that of civilian departments.

The cause of the trouble was this: after November 11, 1918, demobilization had begun according to a scheme prepared in 1917 under civilian auspices. This scheme had the highly commendable object of restarting industry as quickly as possible, but it paid no regard to discipline or to the feelings of the troops themselves. The first to be released were to be the "key men"—that is to say, those men whose return had been asked for by their employers.

The injustices of such a system were patent enough. The more highly skilled men were generally those who had been kept at home the longest at their jobs. Yet now these same key men were to be the first to go home.

Churchill was prompt with his remedies. Release was to be by age and length of service only; Army pay was to be increased to more than double the War-time rate; 80,000 young lads then training in depots at home were to be retained for two years' service overseas. His one concern was lest these remedies should be too late. By extraordinary efforts, which involved obtaining the assent of many important persons including Lloyd George himself, who was absent in Paris, Churchill achieved the issue of the necessary Army Orders and Royal Warrants by January 29—that is, within fourteen days.

During these fourteen days, however, and during the further time that must elapse before the new dispensation could be made known to the troops, armies of nearly 4,000,000 men remained poised on a knife-edge between their allegiance and chaos. In one week there were more than thirty cases of insubordination, some of these very grave. No sooner had they had these new and equitable regulations explained to them, however, than those armies became orderly and disciplined bodies of men once more, content to await their turn.

Haig, who was not always an admirer of Churchill, makes it amply clear in his Diary for January 21 and 22 that it was Churchill and Churchill alone who realized the true gravity of the situation, and who was wholly responsible for the prompt action which saved the country from a disaster that does not bear contemplation.[1]

It is in May 1926 that we shall make our next brief pause. Stanley Baldwin is now Prime Minister; Churchill is Chancellor of the Exchequer; the miners' strike is on; the General Strike is beginning. Churchill, who has held almost every one of the great Offices of State other than that of Prime Minister, has unique understanding of how all departments interlock, and dominates the proceedings of the Cabinet in consequence, imbuing it with his own determination to govern. When decisions have to be taken—such, for instance, as the decision to use the Territorial Army as auxiliary police—he inevitably takes the lead. It is at this time that a young Indian cavalryman, Assistant Secretary to the Committee of Imperial Defence, first finds himself

---

[1] Churchill's handling of the 1919 demobilization problem is more fully dealt with in the chapter "Churchill and the Ex-Servicemen", by Sir Ian Fraser, M.P.

carrying out Churchill's instructions. His name is Hastings Ismay, and to him it is that Churchill will address the countless minutes that he will pen as Defence Minister during Hitler's War.

So we come to September 3, 1939, when Hitler's War began. Having asked for the immediate resignation of his Cabinet colleagues, Neville Chamberlain formed his War Cabinet, numbering eleven, and Churchill returned as First Lord of the Admiralty. The Chiefs of Staff Committee became the War Cabinet's main policy committee. Major-General Ismay—now General Lord Ismay—who the year before had succeeded Lord Hankey as Secretary to the Committe of Imperial Defence, became the War Cabinet's Deputy Secretary (Military); the Secretariat of the Committee of Imperial Defence became its Military Secretariat; the Joint Planning and Joint Intelligence Committee assumed all the functions of a combined staff. The transition from a peace to a war footing went with perfect smoothness—but the military resources available were as yet pitifully inadequate for our task.

Early in April 1940 Lord Chatfield, who had been Minister for the Co-ordination of Defence, resigned and was not replaced. In Lord Chatfield's place Churchill, as Senior Service Minister, became President of the Military Co-ordination Committee. In this capacity, however, Churchill had no more power to reach decisions than had Lord Chatfield before him; he could merely do his best to bring the other Service Ministers and their advisers to his point of view. Churchill's position, therefore, remained as anomalous as that of Lord Chatfield. Later, it is true, Chamberlain somewhat improved matters by empowering Churchill to convene and preside over the Chiefs of Staff Committee, and to give it "guidance and direction".

On the night of May 10, at the height of battle, Churchill became Prime Minister. Recalling, doubtless, Lloyd George's dictum that "effective war policy cannot be directed by a Sanhedrin", he formed a War Cabinet of five—afterwards six—Ministers, one of them without portfolio; and he assumed the additional title of Minister of Defence. His duties as Minister of Defence he was careful never to define. He made no constitutional change, and he created no Defence Ministry. The important point was that, as Minister of Defence with indefinite powers and supported by the authority of the War Cabinet, he took over the supervision and direction of the Chiefs of Staff Committee.

B*

His thus became the guiding hand—hitherto so conspicuously lacking —to formulate a unified defence policy for the three Services.

The Chiefs of Staff Committee, under the direction of the Prime Minister and Minister of Defence, became the authority responsible for preparing strategic plans, and for issuing unified operation instruction to Commanders-in-Chief in the field. The Service Ministers did not attend meetings of the Chiefs of Staff Committee, but remained responsible for their own Ministries.

Churchill set up also a Defence Committee of which he was Chairman and which met with decreasing frequency as the war progressed. Its members were the Deputy Prime Minister, the Foreign Secretary, the Minister of Production, the Service Ministers and the Chiefs of Staff. The Service Ministers kept in touch with the progress of the War through the medium of this Committee. Moreover, the Committee had a further use. On those rare occasions when Churchill found himself in fundamental disagreement with the Chiefs of Staff, he could refer the question to the Defence Committee and so obtain ministerial support for his views.

In his capacity of Minister of Defence Churchill used as his staff the Military Secretariat of the War Cabinet under Ismay, who was his Chief Staff Officer and representative on the Chiefs of Staff Committee.

This Secretariat arranged business, drafted reports and telegrams and maintained records not only for the Chiefs of Staff Committee but also for all the other committees and sub-committees that dealt with defence. It was not the duty of this Secretariat to give military advice to Churchill. Its duty was to obtain for him advice from those who would be responsible for action.

With the entry of the United States into the War, President Roosevelt was quick to perceive that what the United States lacked for the higher direction of war was a corporate Chiefs of Staff organization such as ours, served by a central military secretariat. In consequence he modelled the United States Joint Chiefs of Staff to our pattern. The way was thus prepared for the creation of the Anglo-U.S. Combined Chiefs of Staff—the instrument, that is, which made possible the continuous co-ordination of Anglo-U.S. strategy throughout the War. The close personal relations that developed between Churchill and

Roosevelt were to prove a further saving grace when formal methods of co-ordination came near to breaking down.

Churchill's and Roosevelt's periodical meetings were models for all time of the way in which the war effort of a coalition should be directed. At these meetings the Combined Chiefs of Staff would confer and submit their recommendations to the two heads of Government, who would then reach agreement. As President and Commander-in-Chief Roosevelt's constitutional powers in war-time were very wide. As Prime Minister, on the other hand, Churchill was scrupulous to seek the prior approval of the War Cabinet to all such agreements as he might reach. The War Cabinet's approval was invariably and immediately forthcoming, however; so decisions could be taken with the minimum of delay.

Such then was the machine for the higher direction of war that Churchill created. It was a machine designed to the specification of a particular driver. Another Prime Minister might not have assumed the office of Minister of Defence—but what other Prime Minister could have won the war? And, while Hitler's War lasted, only Churchill could have been Churchill's Minister of Defence. His great achievement was to establish the corporate authority of the Chiefs of Staff in the higher direction of war under his own personal guidance.

But where, we may ask, does the direction of war end and its conduct begin? Few will quarrel with Field Marshal Sir William Robertson's statement of principle that, while the direction of war is a matter for the Government, its conduct is a matter for the military authorities. Every improvement in the means of communication, however, obviously tends to expand the Government's province at the expense of that of the Commander-in-Chief. Moreover, their respective provinces will expand or contract with every change in the relationship between them. Thus a Government which accepts Clemenceau's dictum that war is too important a matter to entrust to soldiers will be inclined to leave its Commander-in-Chief very little latitude indeed. The greater the prestige of the Commander-in-Chief, on the other hand, or the greater the trust that he inspires in his Government, the larger will be his province. A Grant, for instance, enjoying the complete confidence of a Lincoln, may extend his province almost indefinitely at the Federal Government's expense;

whereas that same Government will strip a McClellan of almost all
initiative. A Haig enjoying immense prestige with the British public
can maintain the frontiers of his province against all the assaults of a
Lloyd George. Likewise a Montgomery with nearly two years of
victory behind him can go his own way in a manner that would have
been tolerated in few of his predecessors. Since, therefore, the frontiers
between direction and conduct are not fixed, Sir William Robertson's
statement does little to clarify matters for us.

How then does Churchill view this division of responsibility? His
wide experience of war and General Officers has inclined him, I suggest,
to share Clemenceau's view. Jeffrey's gallant but ill-directed leadership
in '97; Buller's procrastinations on the Tugela; the mishandling of the
tanks in 1914–16; Joffre's ponderous offensives, and the recurring
blood-baths of the Kaiser's War: looking back, he remembers them all.
"In truth," he wrote between the World Wars, "these high military
experts all belong to the same school." In Hitler's War, therefore, we
find him ever watchful of detail, ever grudging of time, and driving
his Commanders-in-Chief hard. Without his daemonic drive there
would have been no V-day.

CHURCHILL
THE WAR CORRESPONDENT

G. Ward Price

G. Ward Price is the doyen of British war correspondents. He has covered every major conflict for the Daily Mail *and* Sunday Dispatch *from the First Balkan War of 1912 to the campaign in Korea.*

"*HE has qualities which could make him almost at will a great popular leader, a great journalist or the founder of a great advertising business.*"

That was a daring prophecy for a young man of twenty-eight, in the closing years of the last century, to make about another of twenty-four . . . but two-thirds of it have been confirmed by subsequent history.

With penetrating foresight, G. W. Steevens of the *Daily Mail*, the most brilliant newspaper-writer that the British Press has ever produced, thus summed up the character of Winston Churchill in an article with the heading "The Youngest Man in Europe".[1] His forecast was based on no more than a shipboard-acquaintanceship that sprang up between them as two war correspondents travelling home after taking part in the campaign against the Mahdi that ended with the victory of Omdurman.

Little more than a year later, Steevens was to die of enteric fever in the siege of Ladysmith at the other end of Africa. Churchill was still close by, but he was with the army of General Sir Redvers Buller, which was making repeated efforts to raise the siege.

Young as they were when they first met, these two had already proved themselves the greatest masters of descriptive journalism that Fleet Street has ever known. Yet, so arbitrary are the dispositions of Destiny that one of them is completely forgotten, while the other, his junior by only four years, has survived to become the greatest national hero of his time.

Sir Winston Churchill has participated in no activity of life that he has not adorned—but there is none in which he attained more immediate mastery and universal recognition than in that of a war correspondent. His grasp of detail, bold enterprise and command of

[1] Reprinted as the next chapter in this book.

47

vivid prose enabled him to put before the readers of his dispatches a narrative so clear and convincing as to give them the impression of having personally taken part in the events that he records.

Although Leonard Jerome, his grandfather on the side of his American mother, was the owner of a newspaper in the United States, Winston himself might never have become a journalist but for financial compulsion.

As a child his instinct had led him towards a military career. As a schoolboy he made no progress in subjects that did not interest him, although the fact that he won a prize by reciting 1,200 lines of *Lays of Ancient Rome* without a mistake, shows that nature had endowed him with one of the most valuable characteristics of a war correspondent— a retentive memory. His boyhood games, too, in which he sought adventure and experiences, as his own writings show, all helped to mould his character into ideal form for the arduous task of reporting a campaign. It was typical of him that as a young officer he should go off, in the year 1895, to the long-drawn-out struggle between Spanish forces and guerilla bands in Cuba. Here, in the first enterprise among many by which he was to distinguish himself, Churchill took full advantage of his family background.

It is beyond dispute that throughout his career as a war correspondent he enjoyed preferential privileges that were not available for those Press colleagues who lacked such advantages as membership of the ducal house of Marlborough, and connections with relatives and friends holding positions of authority and influence in almost every branch of public life. His father, Lord Randolph, had been a close friend of Sir Henry Wolff, the British Ambassador in Madrid. To him Winston wrote, asking whether Sir Henry could obtain for him a permit from the Spanish military authorities to visit Cuba for the purpose of seeing something of the campaign. The request was granted with eagerness by the Minister of War in Madrid.

It was during this visit to Cuba that Churchill used for the first time his natural descriptive gifts for any other purpose than private letters. The campaign had only a mild interest for the British public but the *Daily Graphic* published some reports by him on this distant war. It was a humble but promising beginning to his career as a war correspondent. After his return from Cuba, he spent the next six months as an idle spell, almost the only one he has ever had. He played polo, dined out, and enjoyed by right of birth the amusements and interests of the brilliant closing years of the Victorian age.

But the young Churchill was no playboy. While entering with his natural impetuosity upon all the varied activities open to a young man of good family, inexhaustible energy and high intelligence, he had his vision firmly fixed on the future. The contacts he was making in that golden summer of 1896 were to serve him in good stead later on.

One of them was General Sir Bindon Blood, a distinguished soldier of those days who was the senior commander on the North-West frontier of India. He had just returned to England from conducting one of the small campaigns in that area which were certain to recur. Winston at once took advantage of this acquaintanceship and extracted a promise that—if ever the General commanded another expedition on the Indian frontier, he would let Churchill go with him.

At the end of that year the 4th Hussars arrived in India and there Churchill undertook a course of self-education by systematic reading of the English classics, history and philosophy. It is evidence of the dynamic force which in old age still enables Sir Winston Churchill to discharge such heavy responsibilities that, in the swelteringly hot afternoon of a day which began at dawn with cavalry drill and manœuvre, and ended in the cooler evening with polo practice, he was able to read and absorb such works as Gibbon's *Decline and Fall of the Roman Empire*, Plato's *Republic*, Schopenhauer and Darwin.

This intensive course of literature helped to fashion Churchill's own literary style. There are passages of Gibbonian pomposity in his early dispatches as a war correspondent that reveal this influence clearly—as, for instance, in describing the administration of the Sudan by Egyptian officials, he wrote: "If honour did not impede the achievement, mercy did not restrict the effects of their inglorious successes."

In May 1897, after barely a year in India, Churchill obtained leave and returned to England. He was on the racecourse at Goodwood when the news reached him of a Pathan rising on the North-West Frontier of India. It was announced that his friend General Sir Bindon Blood would be in command of the Field Force of three brigades that was to deal with it.

To this development Winston reacted with that promptitude that is one of the most indispensable assets of the war correspondent. He immediately sent a cable to General Blood, recalling his promise, and, without waiting for an answer, started on the return journey to India.

At Bombay the General's telegraphic reply was awaiting him. "Very difficult. No vacancies. Come up as a correspondent. Will try to fit you in," it ran.

That message marks the real opening of the journalistic phase of Churchill's career. On the strength of it he at once offered his services to *The Pioneer* newspaper of Allahabad, while in London Lady Randolph Churchill, his mother, at her son's cabled request, induced the *Daily Telegraph* to agree to publish Winston's letters from the front at the modest rate of £5 a column.

He arrived in time to accompany the march of the British troops against the Mamunds, and Churchill, on his first experience as a war correspondent, rode with the advance-guard.

Many as are the examples of brilliant descriptive work that came later from Winston Churchill's active pen, there was never one that surpassed the account he gave of this sideshow among the mountains of the North-West Frontier. Whether the account of the action that he subsequently sent to his newspapers *The Pioneer* and the *Daily Telegraph* is identical with the story as he relates it in his autobiography *My Early Life* cannot at this late stage be established—but certainly the story as it appears in his book is personal narrative at its very best.

The tribesmen watched the advance of their foes from the steep slopes looking down on the villages that the invaders were preparing to destroy. After penetrating some distance up the valley the cavalry dismounted to open fire at a range of about 700 yards. The party to which Churchill had attached himself was about fifteen strong.

They reached a village and lay down. Behind them were about eighty-five Sikhs, with four officers. Before long the captain in command of them decided to withdraw, leaving Churchill and the few men with him to cover their retirement. For about ten minutes nothing happened—then, suddenly, swords flashed and smoke-puffs broke from behind rocks in front of them. He has told how the enemy began to gather, evidently preparing for an assault. His subsequent description of the fight, the casualties suffered by his party and his personal combat with a tribesman showed that despite the desperate conditions

Churchill's mind could continue to register what was going on around him. That his talent for narrative should have enabled him to put the circumstances so dramatically on record is proof that one of the paths which his manifold genius might have taken was that of the finest descriptive writer of his age.

The losses suffered by Sir Bindon Blood's force were so great that Churchill was posted to the 31st Punjab Infantry, which had only three white officers, besides its Colonel, left. He got through three or four more skirmishes without mishap and dispatched accounts of the campaign to *The Pioneer* and the *Daily Telegraph*.

Churchill, energetically supported by his mother in London, tried hard to get permission to accompany the Tirah Expedition, which followed on the operation in the Malakand Pass, and was a more important campaign. But though authorities so high as Lord Wolseley and Lord Roberts were approached he found himself tied up to duty with his regiment at Bangalore.

During the winter he wrote his first book, having learnt that his letters to the *Daily Telegraph*, although written anonymously "From a Young Officer", had been well received.

Churchill accordingly devoted three or four hours in the middle of the day to the task of writing, in which he "found a real pleasure". The manuscript of the book was finished shortly after Christmas 1897 and sent home to Lady Randolph Churchill to sell. She arranged for its publication by Longmans. The title was *The Story of the Malakand Field Force 1897* and it bore on the dust-cover a photograph of a pensive young man wearing a silk-faced frock-coat, and already slightly bald, who looked like anything but the fighting soldier whose experiences it recounted.

The praise of the book was general. The Prince of Wales, afterwards King Edward VII, wrote a personal letter saying that he had read it "with the greatest possible interest", and that he "only heard it spoken of with praise".

The Pioneer attributed to its author "a wisdom and comprehension far beyond his years".

These compliments pointed the way to a literary career. Churchill found that this small book had earned him in two months the equivalent of two years' pay as a subaltern. A new way of making a living and of asserting himself was opening before him. He managed to get a staff appointment for the closing period of the Tirah campaign and, at its conclusion, moved to London, where his eager brain already perceived new opportunities in the form of an impending advance into the Sudan to recapture Khartoum, which for sixteen years had been held by the Mahdi.

Here fresh obstacles awaited him, as Lieut.-General Martin has related in the previous chapter. Sir Herbert Kitchener was a man of stubborn will, who objected to any "wire-pulling" in connection with appointments to his command. Nevertheless Churchill was successful in his efforts and as soon as he obtained permission to join the expeditionary force he lost no time in getting into touch with his friend Oliver Borthwick, son of the proprietor of the *Morning Post*, who agreed to take a series of letters on the campaign at £15 a column. Within a week Churchill was in Cairo, in the double capacity of soldier and war correspondent.

With the good fortune that has been the indispensable background for so adventurous a life, he arrived just in time for the final battle of Omdurman. He had missed the tedious experience of the advance up-country, with the difficulties of bringing material by river up the cataracts of the Nile, and he was with the cavalry advance-guard that first came in sight of the Mahdi's stronghold of Omdurman.

Though Steevens and Churchill were not yet acquainted, both of them were eye-witnesses of the final battle of the campaign, which restored the Sudan to Anglo-Egyptian administration—and it would be difficult indeed to decide which of their thrilling descriptions of that historic encounter is the more masterly piece of descriptive writing.

Churchill, in his capacity as an officer, went into action with the cavalry regiment to which he was attached. Steevens was with the infantry that swept away the fierce attacks of the Dervishes with relentless, well-aimed rifle-fire.

A week after he had charged with the Lancers at Omdurman, Churchill started for home. The financial rewards of journalism were by now beginning to make his Army pay of fourteen shillings a day appear ridiculous. His letters for the *Morning Post* had brought him more than £300 and there was *The River War*, his book about the

Sudan campaign, still to come. In addition he was negotiating with *The Pioneer* to write for them a regular weekly letter from London. So Winston decided to leave the Army and take up journalism.

The Boer War, which broke out in October 1899, was the climax of his journalistic career. The stirring adventures that awaited him in South Africa made his name, at the age of twenty-four, known throughout the world. The popularity with which they surrounded him prepared an easy and successful approach to the political arena in which the main efforts of his subsequent life have been exerted.

This time there was no question of doubling the role of combatant and journalist. Churchill's fame as a war correspondent had already placed him at the head of a calling which had produced such well-known figures as Archibald Forbes and Bennett Burleigh. The success of his book *The River War*, which was regarded almost as an official history of the Sudan campaign, had confirmed the prestige that *The Story of the Malakand Field Force* had won for him a year or so earlier.

This increase of his prestige was reflected in the conditions offered him by his friend Oliver Borthwick. Immediately on receiving the news of the Boer ultimatum Borthwick offered him an appointment as principal war correspondent of the *Morning Post* at a salary of £250 a month, plus expenses, and complete freedom as to movements and opinions. Churchill has since claimed that these terms were higher than any previously paid by a British newspaper to a war correspondent.

It was natural that a young man of such distinction and parts should be provided with a passage in the same steamship as carried Commander-in-Chief General Redvers Buller to the Cape, and that the Secretary of State for the Colonies, Mr. Joseph Chamberlain, should receive him for a half-hour's talk before he sailed.

In those days the passengers in a ship on the high seas were almost as cut off from news of the rest of the world as if they had been on another planet. The only bulletin that the Commander-in-Chief and his staff received during their voyage of a fortnight consisted of seven words scrawled on a blackboard hung over the side of a homeward-bound tramp steamer, which read: "BOERS DEFEATED. THREE BATTLES. PENN SYMONS KILLED".

The general opinion among Churchill's fellow-passengers was that the war would be over almost before they could reach South Africa. Winston, with his usual impetuosity, urged that a fast dispatch-vessel should have been sent to meet General Buller's ship, or that at least the tramp-steamer should have been stopped for more detailed interrogation about the situation in South Africa.

When he landed at the Cape, he saw at once that the first fighting would be in Natal, which province the Boers had already invaded. He accordingly set out, by train and then by small coastwise steamer, for Durban. From there he made his way up-country to Pietermaritzburg, where he found his friend and companion on the visit to Cuba, Reginald Barnes, in hospital, shot through the thigh.

It had been Winston's intention to get into Ladysmith, where he would have met his *Daily Mail* admirer, G. W. Steevens, but the Boers were already investing that town, in which General Sir George White was preparing his troops for a long siege.

Churchill proceeded to Estcourt, the nearest point to the advancing enemy, from where patrols were constantly sent out to locate Boer activities. In addition to these cavalry movements, it was decided to use an armoured train for a reconnaissance at a greater distance. The commander of this sortie was an old friend, and invited Churchill to accompany the expedition, which he did with alacrity.

Thus began the famous "incident of the armoured train", which, carrying two companies of infantry and a small naval six-pounder gun with its crew, was ambushed by the Boers, who derailed some of the six trucks and brought their occupants under a deadly accurate rifle-fire.

Though Churchill was technically a non-combatant, the danger that he shared with the crew of the train led him to take the leading part in the endeavour to clear the line. In this he succeeded so far as the engine was concerned, and it steamed back to Estcourt, laden with wounded.

Churchill was one of those left behind, and he was hurrying along a cutting to find the rest of the troops when he came under the close-range fire of two Boers. Another mounted man came galloping up and covered him with his rifle, forcing him to surrender. Not till three years later, when the war was over, and some of the enemy Generals visited England, did he discover that his captor had been Botha, the man who ended the war as the chief leader of the Boers.

Botha and Churchill became close friends in post-war years, and concerted their plans to meet the danger of a German attack, which Botha clearly saw approaching.

All these dramatic developments were hidden, however, from the gaze of Winston as he was marched sixty miles under pouring rain to Elandslaagte, and thence was conveyed by train, with other prisoners, to Pretoria, the capital of the Transvaal.

He had some misgivings as to what treatment he would receive. As a correspondent, his status was strictly non-combatant—yet he had taken and exercised command during the efforts that were necessary to get the engine of the armoured train away. It came as a relief when a Boer field-cornet said to him: "We are not going to let you go, old chappie, although you are a correspondent. We don't catch the son of a lord every day."

Arriving at Pretoria, Winston was lodged with some sixty other captured officers in the State Model Schools, where they set themselves with energy and ingenuity to concoct plans for escape.

During the next three weeks, Churchill kept up a steady protest against his internment, claiming that, as a Press correspondent, he should be released. Unfortunately for him, the survivors of the armoured train incident had given high praise to the part he played in dealing with that critical situation, and the Natal newspapers published glowing accounts of his activities. The Boer General Joubert therefore decided that, since he had contributed to the escape of the engine with its cargo of wounded, he had taken part in the operation, and was thus liable to be held as a prisoner-of-war.

The State Model Schools were surrounded by a ten-foot-high fence, patrolled on the inside by sentries fifty yards apart. Winston and two of his friends discovered that they could watch the movements of the sentries from a circular lavatory, so that, when their guardians' backs were turned, it would be possible for the escaping officers to clamber over the fence into a garden that abutted on it. After one abortive attempt, the correspondent of the *Morning Post* made good this feat, and landed in the garden outside the internment camp. There he waited for his two companions to join him, but they called out cautiously that this was impossible, as the sentry was now suspicious and on the *qui vive*.

Churchill therefore set out alone, walking boldly down the middle of the main street of Pretoria without being challenged. He made his way to the railway that runs due east from Pretoria into the neutral Portuguese territory of Delagoa Bay, and there clambered, with an effort, onto a passing goods train filled with empty coal-sacks, under which he found shelter. Not daring to remain on board the train by daylight, since it might be unloaded, he left it at dawn, and hid in a grove of trees.

Ultimately the fugitive found his way, or was led by Divine protection, to the only house in that part of South Africa that was still occupied by a Briton, who had been allowed to remain in charge of a coal-mine. There, at the bottom of a shaft swarming with rats, Churchill remained hidden for several days, till the hue-and-cry after him was beginning to die down. Posters offered a reward for his capture "dead or alive". Meanwhile his protector was making plans to smuggle him by train to Portuguese East Africa. Late one afternoon he reached the Portuguese port of Lourenco Marques, and reported his arrival to the British Consul.

From then onwards all was easy and enjoyable. The British residents of Lourenco Marques rallied round, provided a hot bath and clean clothes, even forming an armed guard to protect him against a possible attempt at recapture by Boer agents in the town. A steamer was leaving at once for Durban, and when he arrived there several days later Winston Churchill had become the most discussed and admired figure in the British Empire. The courage and resource that he had shown in escaping were a welcome antidote to the depression caused by the news of British defeats at Stormberg, Magersfontein and Colenso, which made up the grim "Black Week" of the South African War.

The Commander-in-Chief, Sir Redvers Buller, sent for Churchill as soon as he returned to the British front to question him about his observation of conditions in the Transvaal. The General expressed his admiration for his achievements, and asked, "Is there anything we can do for you?"

Churchill replied that he would like a commission in one of the irregular corps that was being raised in the British-held part of South Africa.

"What about the *Morning Post*?" asked the General. The answer was that he was under contract to them, which he could not break. Despite the rule, made since the Sudan campaign, that combatant officers could not act as war correspondents, Buller decided to make an exception in the case of Churchill, whom he had known for years. "All right," he said, "you can have a commission and will have to do as much as you can for both jobs, but you won't get any pay for ours."

Thus Winston became once more a soldier in the newly raised South African Light Horse, and continued to dispatch a stream of letters to the *Morning Post* until the relief of Ladysmith, which occurred at the end of February. He was one of the guests of the Headquarters staff that night, and has told how jealously-preserved bottles of champagne were uncorked in honour of the occasion.

As the campaign went on, however, Churchill began to find himself less welcome to the staff of Lord Roberts, who had come out to take over command. Some of his contributions to the *Morning Post* provoked resentment of the views he expressed on the proper policy to be adopted after the war. By the good offices of Winston's friends, of whom he had so many, these objections were overcome, and he ranged the war-zone equipped by his newspaper on a munificent scale.

The fall of Pretoria, the enemy's capital, decided Churchill to return home and enter politics. Henceforth that would be the sphere to which he would devote his brilliant abilities.

What were the outstanding qualities that within a few years brought Churchill, as a journalist, not only fame, but what was in those times the substantial little fortune of £10,000, which rendered him independent for some years after ceasing to collaborate with the Press?

He was favoured far beyond the less-privileged war correspondents who were his colleagues and rivals in the field. But, even apart from his aristocratic and far-reaching connections, Churchill, by his own merits alone, would have risen to the very front rank of that calling.

His chief asset as a journalist was an extraordinarily wide field of vision, which enabled him to take in the whole background of a complicated situation.

With this was allied a memory of unfailing retentiveness, and a gift for rapid and vivid expression. Supreme self-confidence and complete lack of sensitiveness to opposition or hostility were also valuable factors in the highest class of intellect that has ever put itself at the disposition of the daily Press. Future historians will look to Churchill's dispatches to the *Daily Telegraph* and the *Morning Post* for the most reliable and well-balanced records of the campaigns in which he served in the role of war correspondent.

Never has a young man lived more dangerously than did Winston Churchill in that capacity . . . and survived. He is a living embodiment of the theory, which he has himself enunciated, that *Free Will and Predestination are identical*. His daring led him into perils, which Destiny brought him through unscathed. Greatest and most frequent were the hazards that beset him during those early years when he combined military service with the status of a war correspondent. On the North-West Frontier of India; in the Omdurman campaign; and on countless occasions during the South African War, Winston Churchill, by all the laws of probability, should have lost his life. On patrol with the Malakand Field Force, in the charge of the 21st Lancers, and in desperate battles like that of Spion Kop—which devasted eminence he was one of the last to leave—men were falling all around him. On the first occasion that his brother Jack came under fire he was wounded by Winston's side.

Death casts his darts in vain at those whom fate reserves for higher things. By the time Churchill had renounced the fame he had achieved as a war correspondent, and embarked on his political career as M.P. for Oldham, he had been time and again in mortal danger. Most conspicuous of these occasions were:

Age 18—thirty-foot fall at Bournemouth.

19—swimming in the Lake of Geneva.

21—under fire in Cuba.

23—nearly cut off in the Mamund Valley.

24—Charge of the 21st Lancers.

25—the armoured train, followed by escape from Pretoria.

Age 26—Battle of Spion Kop.

      Incident of rescue under fire by mounted trooper.

      Frequent brushes with the enemy.

      Entry into Johannesburg in plain clothes before evacuation by enemy.

      Boers shell train taking him to coast.

The gallantry displayed by Churchill on these and many other occasions is only equalled by the modesty with which, in various autobiographical works, he has described them. His dispatches from the front, necessarily written sometimes under conditions of difficulty and discomfort, are so vivid, accurate and detailed that they constitute the most reliable account of every campaign with which he has dealt.

Not for him was the path made smooth by a Public Relations Department in the War Office. As Churchill, with characteristic tolerance, relates: "The hybrid combination of subaltern officer and widely-followed war-correspondent was not unnaturally obnoxious to the military mind."

But the British Press will take enduring pride in the fact that for a few years it was the medium of expression chosen by one of the very greatest figures in the national history.

"THE YOUNGEST MAN IN EUROPE"

G. W. Steevens

On his way back to England after the battle of Omdurman in 1898, Winston Churchill, then twenty-four years old, travelled with a remarkable personality only four years his senior. He was G. W. Steevens, the Daily Mail *war correspondent in the Sudan campaign. In his autobiography, written more than thirty years later, Churchill described Steevens as "the most brilliant man in journalism I have ever met". Steevens, too, was so impressed by his young friend that he wrote an article about him, prophesying a golden future and describing him as "the youngest man in Europe". Steevens was one of the first men to recognize Churchill's potential greatness and his article is a remarkable assessment of the young Winston's qualities and characteristics. It is reprinted here, fifty-five years after its original publication in the* Daily Mail, *and—as a character-sketch of Churchill in his early twenties—it forms a valuable contribution to this study of Churchill by his contemporaries.*

WINSTON SPENCER CHURCHILL is the youngest man in Europe. A gallery of young men's pictures could not possibly be complete without him, for there is no younger. In years he is a boy; in temperament he is also a boy; but in intention, in deliberate plan, purpose, adaptation of means to ends he is already a man. In any other generation but this he would be a child. Anyone other than he, being a junior subaltern of Hussars, would be a boisterous, simple, full-hearted, empty-headed boy. But Churchill is a man, with ambitions fixed, with the steps towards their attainment clearly defined with a precocious, almost uncanny judgment as to the efficacy of the means to the end.

He is what he is by breeding. He is the eldest son of Lord Randolph Churchill, and his mother is American. Lord Randolph was not so precocious as he was popularly supposed to be, but they begin early in America. From his father he derives the hereditary aptitude for affairs, the grand style of entering upon them, which are not the less hereditary in British noble families because they skip nine generations out of ten. Winston Spencer Churchill can hardly have seen much of Government and Parliament and forensic politics at twenty-four, but he moves in and out among their deviations with the ease, if not with the knowledge, of a veteran statesman. But that inheritance alone would not give him his grip and facility at twenty-four; with us hereditary statesmen and party leaders ripen later. From his American strain he adds to this a keenness, a shrewdness, a half-cynical, personal ambition, a natural aptitude for advertisement, and, happily, a sense of humour.

At the present moment he happens to be a soldier, but that has nothing whatever to do with his interest in the public eye. He may and he may not possess the qualities which make a great general, but the question is of no sort of importance. In any case, they will never be developed, for, if they exist, they are overshadowed by qualities which might make him, almost at will, a great popular leader, a great journalist, or the founder of a great advertising business.

He will shortly leave the Army; in the meantime his brief military career is interesting, mainly as an illustration of the versatility, the pushing energy, and—its complement—the precocious worldly wisdom of the man. Educated at Harrow, he passed, like anybody else, into Sandhurst, at eighteen, in 1893, passed out with honours in 1894, joined the 4th Hussars in 1895. From that till now is less than four years; yet in that time he has seen something of three campaigns—not an ungenerous allowance for a field-officer of more service than Winston Spencer Churchill counts years of life. He saw his service, it is true, more in the irresponsible way of a war correspondent than on the plodding grind of a subaltern with his regiment; but then that is the only way—bar miracles—in which a man can see three campaigns in four years. Having to give the first years of his manhood to war-making, he characteristically gave them in the way that was likely to prove most fruitful of experience for use afterwards.

Before he had been a year in the Army he was in Cuba, travelled over much of the island, saw a certain amount of service, got the Order of Military Merit from Marshal Martinez Campos, and wrote letters to the *Daily Graphic*. In the last frontier war in India he started as the correspondent of the *Daily Telegraph* and *The Pioneer*—to what other subaltern of twenty-two would it have occurred to syndicate himself thus fruitfully?—went on to the 31st Punjab Infantry, was mentioned for "courage and resolution" by Brigadier-General Jeffreys, and wound up as orderly officer to Sir William Lockhart. What other subaltern of twenty-two would have gone through so many phases? To top all he was author of the first book published on the series of campaigns—*The Story of the Malakand Field Force*—and the book was a decided success.

How many men had the combination of merit, energy, and luck to combine the Tirah clasps with Khartum? Very few, but among the few duly appeared Winston Churchill. He got up just in time to march from Fort Atbara with the 21st Lancers, to which he was attached—missed them, indeed, by a day, but rode out confidently at night, missed the track, lit matches and found it, had to turn miles out of his way for water, overtook the force next day. He finished the march, scouted in the reconnaissances, rode in the charge. Now—you will have guessed—he is writing a book. And yet he found time on his way home to prepare three political speeches.

It was not possible that a man who has done so much so well at twenty-four would be altogether popular. Enemies he has probably none, but precocious success is not the way to win facile friend-ship—even when joined with modesty—and Winston Churchill is, outwardly, not modest. In the Army especially, where the young are expected not to know better than their elders—or, at least, to keep their knowledge to themselves—his assurance has earned him many snubs. One general will delight in his light-hearted omniscience, the next, and the next, and the next will put a subaltern in his place. But Winston Churchill cannot be snubbed. His self-confidence bobs up irresistibly, though seniority and common sense and facts themselves conspire to force it down.

After all he is hardly to be charged with any but outward im-modesty. Chaff him about his self-satisfaction and he laughs and says, "I'm young." He knows he is not omniscient; but he knows it will pay to pretend to be.

He is ambitious and he is calculating; yet he is not cold—and that saves him. His ambition is sanguine, runs in a torrent, and the cal-culation is hardly more than the rocks or the stump which the torrent strikes for a second, yet which suffices to direct its course. It is not so much that he calculates how he is to make his career a success—how, frankly, he is to boom—but that he has a queer, shrewd power of introspection, which tells him his gifts and character are such as will make him boom. He has not studied to make himself a demagogue. He was born a demagogue, and he happens to know it.

The master strain in his character is the rhetorician. Platform speeches and leading articles flow from him almost against his will. At dinner he talks and talks, and you can hardly tell when he leaves off quoting his one idol, Macaulay, and begins his other, Winston Churchill. A passionate devotion to the matter in hand, an imper-turbable self-confidence, a ready flow of sonorous, half-commonplace, half-lofty English, a fine faculty of striking imagery—we shall hear more about this in the course of ten years. Out of the perfect stump orator's wallet he has taken everything but humour; his humour he is likely to keep for private moments; he is not yet the man who, like Lord Rosebery, will feel he can afford to smile at himself in public.

His face is square and determined rather than delicate, his body fitter for the platform than for the saddle; his colour reddish and sanguine. He looks a boy. As yet, naturally, he knows little more than many clever boys, whether of faces or of men. But for all that he has put himself in the directest way of learning. At present he calls himself a Tory Democrat. Tory—the opinions—might change; democrat—the methods—never. For he has the twentieth century in his marrow.

What he will become, who shall say? At the rate he goes there will hardly be room for him in Parliament at thirty or in England at forty. It is a pace that cannot last, yet already he holds a vast lead of his contemporaries. Meanwhile he is a wonder—a boy with a man's ambitions and—more wonderful yet—a very mature man's self-appreciation—knowledge of his own powers and the extent to which each may be applied to set him forward on his road.

CHURCHILL THE NOVELIST

Sir Compton Mackenzie

Early in his career as a writer, Churchill produced his only novel—Savrola, a Ruritanian story of politics and romance. In this chapter Sir Compton Mackenzie, whose own career as a best-selling novelist has stretched from the years before the First World War to the present time, tells the story of Savrola and writes of Churchill's qualities as a novelist at the age of twenty-three.

CHURCHILL'S only novel, *Savrola*, written in 1897 and "inscribed to the Officers of the IVth (Queen's Own) Hussars in whose company the author lived for four happy years", was first published serially in *Macmillan's Magazine*. To quote from the author's preface when it appeared in volume form: "Since its first reception was not unfriendly, I resolved to publish it as a book, and I now submit it with considerable trepidation to the judgment or clemency of the public."

When Churchill found time to write a novel of some 70,000 words between his adventures with the Malakand Field Force and the Tirah Expeditionary Force, which would be a surprising statement about almost anybody except Churchill, he was in his twenty-fourth year, and *Savrola* offers an opportunity, as it will seem to some of us, to pry into the dreams of a young man of destiny, not merely about his own political future but also about the political future of dictators and communists.

The scene is Laurania, a Mediterranean republic where five years after a Civil War President Antonio Molara is still ruling the country in a manner reminiscent of the Metaxas dictatorship in Greece. However, under the leadership of Savrola, a well-bred young Democrat of thirty-two, the National Party is on the up and up, and as the book opens President Molara has decided to make a concession to the popular will by agreeing to issue electoral writs, but in the fashion of dictators, with which we are so familiar nowadays, the President has given orders to mutilate the register of citizenship and thus disenfranchise half the electorate. The people massed in Constitution Square outside Parliament House are infuriated, and when the President enters his carriage an attempt is made by the mob to rush it. The assailants are charged by the Lancers of the Guard and fired on by the infantry. The

President drives on to the Palace; "forty bodies and some expended cartridges lay on the ground".

Savrola rebukes his friend Moret for prematurely rousing the anger of the populace by telling them about the Government's treatment of the register. Savrola's policy is to give tyranny enough rope to hang itself; he believes that within a few months this is what will happen. From an emergency meeting of the leaders of the Popular or National Party, at which Savrola calms the feelings stirred up by the violence of the Government while promising to devise a way of frightening the Dictator, we drive back with Savrola in a hackney-coach to a "small though not inelegant house, for he was a man of means, in the most fashionable quarter of the town.

"The apartments he lived in were on the second story—a bedroom, a bathroom, and a study. They were small, but full of all that taste and luxury could devise and affection and industry preserve. A broad writing-table occupied the place of honour. It was arranged so that the light fell conveniently to the hand and head. A large bronze ink-stand formed the centrepiece, with a voluminous blotting-pad of simple manufacture spread open before it. The rest of the table was occupied by papers on files. The floor, in spite of the ample waste-paper basket, was littered with scraps. It was the writing-table of a public man.

"The room was lit by electric light in portable shaded lamps. The walls were covered with shelves, filled with well-used volumes. To that Pantheon of Literature none were admitted till they had been read and valued. It was a various library: the philosophy of Schopenhauer divided Kant from Hegel, who jostled the Memoirs of St. Simon and the latest French novel; RASSELAS and LA CURÉE lay side by side; eight substantial volumes of Gibbon's famous History were not perhaps inappropriately prolonged by a fine edition of the DECAMERON; the ORIGIN OF SPECIES rested by the side of a black-letter Bible; THE REPUBLIC maintained an equilibrium with VANITY FAIR and the HISTORY OF EUROPEAN MORALS. A volume of Macaulay's Essays lay on the writing-table itself; it was open and that sublime passage whereby the genius of one man has immortalised the genius of another was marked in pencil. *And history, while, for the warning of vehement, high, and daring natures, she notes his many errors, will yet deliberately pronounce that among the eminent men whose bones lie near his, scarcely one has left a more stainless, and none a more splendid name.*

"A half empty box of cigarettes stood on a small table near a low leathern arm-chair, and by its side lay a heavy army revolver, against the barrel of which the ashes of many cigarettes had been removed."

In that arm-chair Savrola sat in meditation upon the day's events.

"His nervous temperament could not fail to be excited by the vivid scenes through which he had lately passed, and the repression of his emotion only heated the inward fire. Was it worth it? The struggle, the labour, the constant rush of affairs, the sacrifice of so many things that make life easy, or pleasant—for what? A people's good! That, he could not disguise from himself, was rather the direction than the cause of his efforts. Ambition was the motive force, and he was powerless to resist it. He could appreciate the delights of an artist, a life devoted to the search for beauty, or of sport, the keenest pleasure that leaves no sting behind. To live in dreamy quiet and philosophic calm in some beautiful garden, far from the noise of men and with every diversion that art and intellect could suggest, was, he felt, a more agreeable picture. And yet he knew that he could not endure it. 'Vehement, high, and daring' was his cast of mind. The life he lived was the only one he could ever live; he must go on to the end."

Whatever his contemporaries may have thought at the time, it is difficult for us today to keep from speculating whether Churchill himself in his twenty-fourth year might not have indulged in a comparable meditation, and indeed even have smoked cigarettes in those days.

Next day President Molara was moody and silent at breakfast and his beautiful young wife Lucile "tactfully refrained from irritating him by the laboured commonplaces of matutinal conversation".

The President was at work before nine o'clock and Lucile decided to take a drive because she felt it was her duty to display courage after the events of the previous day. "It might help her husband, for her beauty was such that an artistic people showed her respect."

Just as she was getting into her carriage Savrola arrived at the Palace to take part in a deputation of protest against the action of the Government's troops yesterday. It is clear that Her Excellency attracts the Democratic leader, of which Miguel, the President's Secretary, is aware. Molara was successful in appeasing the anger of the deputation by reading to them his reply to a Note from the English Government about a boundary dispute in Africa. It was couched in strong, indeed in insulting, terms.

" 'And that, Gentlemen,' said the President, when it was finished, 'is addressed to one of the greatest military and naval powers in the world.' " The rest of the deputation might feel their patriotism roused and their pride gratified, but Savrola 'smiled provokingly'. He did not feel as confident as the President that the English Government would not appeal to arms.

It may be noted that in the year of the Diamond Jubilee the Government was English, the Army was English, the Navy was English; only Her Majesty Queen Victoria was Britannic, and therefore her Ambassador British.

When the deputation had left him President Molara was worried. He foresaw gloomily that Savrola would be elected to the Senate, but he could not accept his Secretary's suggestion of an accident to the Democratic leader. He felt it would provoke a revolution at home and cause unpleasant repercussions abroad.

Miguel then suggested the possibility of compromising Savrola with Her Excellency and being discovered by her husband. The President snubbed his Secretary, but presently he was wondering what course the Opposition intended to pursue at the opening of the Senate.

" 'How can we induce Savrola to speak? He is incorruptible,' the President exclaimed."

Miguel returned to his former suggestion, only to be squashed again, but when the President went for a stroll in the Palace garden he saw his beautiful wife seated by the fountain, and after confiding to her his anxiety to know Savrola's intentions Lucile suggested sending a personal note from herself with an invitation to the State Ball, when she might hope to persuade Savrola to reveal his policy.

"Molara looked at her with admiration. At no time did he love her more than when he realised of what use she was to him. 'I leave it to you, then. I fear you will fail, but if you can do it, you may have saved the State. If not, no harm will have been done.'

" 'I shall succeed,' she answered confidently, and rising from her seat began to walk towards the house. She saw from her husband's manner that he would like to be alone."

When his friend Moret came to tell him that he had arranged for him to address a public meeting on Thursday night Savrola shocked his supporter with the news that he was going to the State Ball on that night. Moret dreaded the effect upon the Trade Unions. Savrola was unmoved and Moret had to agree to arrange the meeting for Friday instead.

Savrola was not worried about the Trade Unions, but he was worried about agencies at work in the party which he did not control.

" 'That secret society they call the League is an unknown factor. I hate that fellow, that German fellow, Kreutze, Number One as he styles himself. He is the source of all the opposition I encounter in the party itself; the Labour Delegates all seem to be under his influence. Indeed there are moments when I think that you and I and Godoy, all who are striving for the old Constitution, are but the political waves of a social tide that is flowing we know not whither. Perhaps I am wrong, but I keep my eyes open and their evidence makes me thoughtful. The future is inscrutable but appalling; you must stand by me. When I can no longer restrain and control, I will no longer lead.' "

There must have been moments when Churchill said to himself something not unlike that in considering the state of affairs in Yugoslavia, in Greece, and elsewhere during the Second World War.

And here surely is an anticipation in the description of Savrola composing a speech.

"His speech—he had made many and knew that nothing good can be obtained without effort. These impromptu feats of oratory existed only in the minds of the listeners; the flowers of rhetoric were hothouse plants.

"What was there to say? Successive cigarettes had been mechanically consumed. Amid the smoke he saw a peroration, which would cut deep into the hearts of a crowd; a high thought, a fine simile, expressed in that correct diction which is comprehensible even to the most illiterate, and appeals to the most simple; something to lift their minds from the material cares of life and to awake sentiment. His ideas began to take the form of words, to group themselves into sentences; he murmured to himself; the rhythm of his own language swayed him; instinctively he alliterated. Ideas succeeded one another, as a stream flows swiftly by and the light changes on its waters. He seized a piece of paper and began hurriedly to pencil notes. That was a point; could not tautology accentuate it? He scribbled down a rough sentence, scratched it out, polished it, and wrote it in again. The sound would please their ears, the sense improve and stimulate their minds. What a game it was! His brain contained the cards he had to play, the world the stakes he played for."

The State Ball follows the convention of the period as a piece of descriptive writing and the convention of the period in the development of the mutual attraction of Savrola and Lucile. The British and the Russian Ambassadors step straight out of the pages of Seton Merriman. The former, Sir Richard Shalgrove, is rather surprisingly a K.G., and the Spirit of Irony smiles to hear that H.M. battleship *Aggressor* (12,000 tons displacement and 14,000 horse-power, armed with four 11-inch guns) was steaming at eighteen knots towards the African port of the Lauranian Republic. "Aggressor" evidently had a less pejorative significance in the last decade of the nineteenth century than Churchill was to give the word forty years on.

The President was distressed to hear from French sources the news about the *Aggressor* because it meant that he would have to send the Lauranian Fleet of five ships to Africa at a moment when he was anxious for the support of Admiral de Mello against a possible revolutionary outbreak. He confided to his wife:

" 'I don't like the situation at all. They have a Jingo Government in power and have sent ships as an answer to our note. It is most unfortunate. Now I have to send the fleet away—at such a moment.' He groaned moodily.

" 'I told Sir Richard that we had to think of the situation here, and that the despatch was meant for domestic purposes,' said Lucile.

" 'I think,' said the President, 'that the English Government also have to keep the electorate amused. It is a Conservative ministry; they must keep things going abroad to divert the public mind from advanced legislation.' "

Once again the Spirit of Irony smiles.

Lucile made up her mind to attend the great meeting in the City Hall at which Savrola was to address nearly seven thousand people.

The audience was hostile at first because many people disapproved of the democratic leader's going to the State Ball. However, his oratory gradually bewitched them, and by the time he had finished speaking they were completely under his sway. Not quite all, however, for as early as this the Communist minority had realized that Savrola had no sympathy with the Cause. "What does he care about the community of goods?" one of them asked.

In the press of the crowd surging to acclaim the "great Democrat" Lucile was hurt and when she screamed Savrola hurried to rescue her from being crushed. As he was offering a glass of water to revive her he recognized her through her thick veil. With presence of mind he hailed her as "Mirette, my little niece!" and drove her back to his own house instead of the Palace, because his friend Moret insisted on escorting him. When an hour or two later the carriage came back Moret's servant brought back this message:

Code wire just received says, Strelitz crossed frontier this morning with two thousand men. The hour has come.

Laurania is so Ruritanian that its inhabitants have Portuguese, German, French and Italian names and are addressed as "señor".

Savrola left the message from Moret about the insurgent military leader on the table when he went downstairs to let out his servant and Lucile read it.

" 'So you will rise and murder us in the night—conspirator!'

"Savrola smiled suavely; his composure was again perfect. 'I have sent the messenger away on foot, and the carriage is at your disposal. We have talked long; it is now three o'clock; Your Excellency should not further delay your return to the Palace. It would be most imprudent; besides, as you will realize, I expect visitors.'

"His calmness maddened her. 'Yes,' she retorted; 'the President will send you some—police.'

" 'He will not know about the invasion yet.'

" 'I shall tell him,' she replied.

"Savrola laughed softly. 'Oh, no,' he said, 'that would not be fair.'

" 'All's fair in love and war.'

" 'And this——?'

" 'Is both,' she said, and then burst into tears."

Next morning at breakfast in the Palace the President was gloomy and when he told his wife that he had had bad news she was relieved to know that she should not have to tell him the secret she had learned.

" 'Has he started?' she asked incautiously.

" 'Yes, last night; but he will be stopped.'

" 'Thank heaven for that!'

"Molara looked at her in amazement. 'What do you mean? Why are you so glad that the Admiral and the fleet are prevented from carrying out my orders?'

" 'The fleet!'

" 'Good gracious! What did you think I meant?' he asked impatiently."

What was annoying the President was that a British collier had grounded in the Suez Canal after H.M.S. *Aggressor* went through and was thus preventing the Lauranian Fleet from reaching the African Colony. However, soon afterwards Miguel came in with a telegram which by the effect it had on the President's composure evidently brought news of what had happened on the frontier. When Molara was discussing the position with his Secretary, the latter brought up again the possibility of discrediting Savrola by compromising him with Her Excellency. The President in justice to him was not enamoured of the odious Miguel's plan, but when news came that the garrison on the frontier had gone over to the insurgents he became desperate.

" 'Lucile,' he said with unwonted tenderness, 'one chance remains. If you could find out what the leaders of the agitation in this city intend to do, if you can get Savrola to show his hand, we might maintain our position and overcome our enemies. Can you—will you do this?'

"Lucile's heart bounded. It was, as he said, a chance. She might defeat the plot, and at the same time make terms for Savrola; she might still rule in Laurania, and, though this thought she repressed, save the man she loved. Her course was clear; to obtain the information and sell it to her husband for Savrola's life and liberty. 'I will try,' she said.

" 'I knew you would not fail me, dearest,' said Molara. 'But the time is short; go and see him to-night at his rooms. He will surely tell you. You have power over men and will succeed.'

"Lucile reflected. To herself she said, 'I shall save the State and

serve my husband;' and herself rejoined, 'You will see him again.'
Then she spoke aloud. 'I will go to-night.' "

So Lucile went to Savrola's house that night, but after discussing
the future and the need for her to forget him "before she could frame
a resolution or even choose her mind, they had kissed each other. The
handle of the door turned quickly. Both started back. The door swung
open and the President appeared", followed by Miguel.

His Excellency pointed a revolver at the great Democrat.

" 'Down on your knees and beg for mercy, you hound; down, or
I will blow your face in!'

" 'I have always tried to despise death, and have always succeeded
in despising you. I shall bow to neither.'

" 'We shall see,' said Molara, grinding his teeth. 'I shall count five,
—one!' "

In view of his name the President might certainly be expected to
grind his teeth.

" 'Four,' he counted.

"Lucille sprang up, and with a cry threw herself in front of the
President, 'Wait, wait!' she cried. 'Have mercy!'

"Molara met her look, and in those eyes read more than terror.
Then at last he understood; he started as though he had caught hold of
red-hot iron. 'My God, it's true!' he gasped. 'Strumpet!' he cried, as
he pushed her from him, striking her with the back of his left hand in
the mouth."

Miguel, with an eye to his own future, knocked up the President's
arm when he fired, and Savrola with a leap bore him to the ground.
The meeting came to an end with the President's retiring on a promise
to come and arrest Savrola at the Mayoralty next day.

" 'You may take your mistress with you to hell,' were his parting
words."

Savrola decided that Lucile must stay in his house for the present.

"And so he departed to play a great game in the face of all the
world, to struggle for those ambitions which form the greater part of
man's interest in life; while she, a woman, miserable and now alone,
had no resource but to wait.

"And then suddenly the bells began to ring all over the city with
quick impatient strokes. There was the sound of a far-off bugle-call and

a dull report, the boom of an alarm-gun. The tumult grew; the roll of a drum beating the assembly was heard at the end of the street; confused shoutings and cries rose from many quarters. At length one sound was heard which put an end to all doubts,—*tap*, *tap*, *tap*, like the subdued slamming of many wooden boxes—the noise of distant musketry. The revolution had begun."

The description of the street fighting which follows is brilliant. The stock trappings of late Victorian romance vanish, and one feels that the young author having safely disposed of his heroine for the time is enjoying every sentence.

At last when the President with a small garrison was beleaguered in the Palace, Savrola sent his friend Moret to accept his surrender and guaranteed the lives of all the defenders. Colonel Sorrento, the War Minister, shot Moret, and the insurgents brought a gun into action at close range; the President recognized that the end was near.

"He called his last defenders around him. There were but thirty left, and of these some were wounded.

" 'Gentlemen,' he said, 'you have been faithful to the end; I will demand no more sacrifices of you. My death may appease those wild beasts. I give you back your allegiance, and authorise you to surrender.

" 'Never!' said Sorrento.

" 'It is a military order, Sir,' answered the President, and walked towards the door. He stepped through the shattered woodwork and out on the broad flight of steps. The courtyard was filled with the crowd. Molara advanced until he had descended half-way; then he paused. 'Here I am,' he said. The crowd stared. For a moment he stood there in the bright sunlight. His dark blue uniform-coat, on which the star of Laurania and many orders and decorations of foreign countries glittered, was open, showing his white shirt beneath it. He was bareheaded and drew himself up to his full height. For a while there was silence.

"Then from all parts of the courtyard, from the wall that overlooked it and even from the windows of the opposite houses, a ragged fusillade broke out. The President's head jerked forward, his legs shot from under him and he fell to the ground, quite limp. The body rolled down two or three steps and lay twitching feebly. A man in a dark suit of clothes, and who apparently exercised authority over the crowd, advanced towards it. Presently there was a single shot."

At this moment Savrola arrived with Lieutenant Tiro, who had managed by a breath-taking escape along the telegraph wires to reach him as the only man able to keep the mob in control.

"A man in a black suit was reloading his revolver; it was Karl Kreutze, the Number One of the Secret Society. The President had bled profusely from several bullet-wounds in the body, but it was evident that the *coup de grâce* had been administered by a shot in the head. The back and left side of the skull behind the ear was blown away, and the force of the explosion, probably at close quarters, had cracked all the bones of the face, so that as the skin was whole, it looked like broken china in a sponge bag.

"Savrola stopped aghast. He looked at the crowd, and they shrank from his eye; gradually they shuffled back, leaving the sombre-clad man alone face to face with the great Democrat. A profound hush overspread the whole mass of men. 'Who has committed this murder?' he asked in low hoarse tones, fixing his glance on the head of the Secret Society.

" 'It is not a murder,' replied the man doggedly; 'it is an execution.'

" 'By whose authority?'

" 'In the name of the Society.' "

Savrola was enraged by this reply and slashed Karl Kreutze across the face with his cane. The man sprang at him but was cut down by Lieutenant Tiro, which upset the mob. However, Savrola, who had been shot through the left arm when he was trying to reach the Palace and prevent a massacre, was able to change the mood with dramatic eloquence, and then just as the garrison were being marched off to the State Prison there was the sound of a "dull heavy boom from the sea-front; another and another followed in quick succession. The fleet had returned at last."

We are now given a thrilling description of the fleet running the gauntlet of the harbour forts at the end of which the Admiral brought his ships to anchor 500 yards from the shore.

To a couple of insurgent officers who came aboard under a flag of truce the Admiral gave his terms:

" 'The leader of the conspiracy—this man, Savrola—must be surrendered at once and stand his trial for murder and rebellion. Unless this is done by six o'clock to-morrow morning, I shall bombard the town and shall continue to do so until my terms are complied with.' "

This ultimatum caused consternation at the Mayoralty.

"The idea of a bombardment was repugnant to the fat burgesses who had joined the party of revolt as soon as it had become obvious that it was the winning side. It was also distasteful to the Socialists who, however much they might approve of the application of dynamite to others, did not themselves relish the idea of a personal acquaintance with high explosives."

The Committee of Public Safety resolved to reply that bombardment would entail the shooting of the Palace garrison and refused to listen to Savrola's protests. So he sent the prisoners off by a special train to the frontier. Miguel, who deserted the President to become Savrola's secretary, decided to betray him too, and told the Committee what the great Democrat had done. Savrola had decided to send Lucile away by carriage. She begged him to come with her, but he declared that he must remain and see it out. Half-way to the Mayoralty he sent a patrol of insurgent soldiers. The officer recognized him and having sent his men on warned Savrola that he had a warrant for his arrest.

" 'They will deliver you to the Admiral. Fly while there is time!' "

Savrola, with profound common sense, decided to accompany Lucile into exile.

"Those who care to further follow the annals of the Republic of Laurania may read how, after the tumults had subsided, the hearts of the people turned again to the illustrious exile who had won them freedom and whom they had deserted in the hour of victory. They may, scoffing at the fickleness of men, read of the return of Savrola and his beautiful consort, to the ancient city he had loved so well."

To the contemporary critic *Savrola* would have seemed merely one more example of the Ruritanian romance that *The Prisoner of Zenda* published in 1894 had made such a popular medium. For us *Savrola* is a significant revelation of Winston S. Churchill in his mid-twenties. It is the day-dream of a man of action, and if some accident or illness had deprived the author of the opportunity to remain a man of action that author might have written many more romances and left an eminent name as a romancer. As destiny ruled he remained hale and vigorous and there was neither leisure to dream in romances nor the urge of frustration to inspire him with stories of what he desired from life but could not attain through disability.

It would be idle flattery to claim more for *Savrola* than its author would claim for it, and the fact that he has allowed it to remain out of print for so many years suggests that he regards it now as a facet of his brilliant youth outshone by others. Still, *Savrola* deserves to be reprinted, so many coming events cast in its pages their shadows before. Not all the artificiality of Ruritanian romance can deprive this book of authentic vitality when it is read with the knowledge of what one day its author would become. The dreams of a great man are perdurable.

CHURCHILL THE PARLIAMENTARIAN

Earl Winterton, P.C.

Earl Winterton was a Member of Parliament for forty-seven years. He was "Baby" of the House of Commons when elected in 1904 and "Father" of the House when he retired in 1951. He has therefore been able to watch Sir Winston Churchill's career as a parliamentarian as no other man has been privileged to do. When Earl Winterton entered Parliament as Member for Horsham, Churchill, who had been elected four years earlier, was still a back bencher. Earl Winterton saw him rise from the modest, junior office of Under-Secretary for the Colonies to the Premiership. He knew him, too, during those years in the political wilderness when Churchill was denied a post in a Conservative Government and Earl Winterton worked with him then in the group which he led advocating rearmament. Later, when Churchill was Leader of the Opposition, having been defeated at the polls after leading the country to victory in the greatest war in history, Earl Winterton sat under him in the "Shadow Cabinet". So Earl Winterton can write of Churchill's parliamentary career in all its phases—its successes and its disappointments, its defeats and its triumphs.

Earl Winterton was Under-Secretary of State for India 1922–23 and again from 1924–29 and was Chancellor of the Duchy of Lancaster 1937–39 and a member of the Cabinet 1938–39. At the end of his parliamentary career he was created a Baron.

THE young, clever and ambitious M.P. who hopes in twenty or thirty years' time to fill the great Office of Prime Minister of Great Britain must find it hard to decide what course he should pursue and what attitude he should adopt in his first years in the Commons.

For the early careers of future Prime Ministers in that Assembly in the last 150 years present an astonishing set of contrasts.

Gladstone, for instance, was a hard-working Member from the start and each year improved his position by the substance and moral earnestness of his speeches. Balfour, on the contrary, gave the impression, in the first few years of his Membership, of indolence and flippancy, despite his intellectual brilliance and success as a debater. Asquith attracted favourable attention at the very beginning of his parliamentary career. Baldwin and Attlee were remarkably unobtrusive as Private Members and Junior Ministers; indeed, neither of them until they reached high Office made a single speech in the Commons which received or indeed merited attention. Lloyd George made an immediate impression on the House by the power of his invective directed in all his speeches against the Conservative Party, for whom he had a bitter and unconcealed hatred. Disraeli and Churchill in their very early years as Members were neither popular nor treated seriously. Indeed, they met with a considerable amount of ridicule and contempt. In Disraeli's case this was due to an extravagance in dress and affectation of manner which were jointly responsible for the failure of his maiden speech. In that of Churchill the reasons were more complex. They afford an interesting study to which insufficient attention has been paid in most of the books and articles about his career.

Today his bitterest opponents must, if they are honest, admit that no other British Prime Minister in history has occupied so great and pre-eminent a position as a producer of the written and spoken word. At their best Asquith, Lloyd George and F. E. Smith, among statesmen of living memory, had as great command over the House of Commons or a big mass meeting, through the brilliance alike of their speeches and their personality, as Sir Winston Churchill has today and has had for many years. But none of them possessed his talents as a writer.

During the 1900 Parliament, of which he was a Member, Churchill was already successful as a writer. His *River War* was a first-class description of the second Soudanese war; the biography of his father was brilliant. Many of the phrases and descriptions in it equal, in their clarity and beauty of expression, anything which he has written in recent years. But he had not in those days made a great reputation as a speaker in the Commons or on a platform.

He made many witty and some brilliant interventions in debate, especially after he severed his connection with the Conservative Party early in 1904. The harassed Balfour Government was a "sitting target" for anyone possessing Churchill's gifts. Nevertheless, his attacks on it, though they brought him almost as much publicity in the Press as he commands today, did not establish his parliamentary position on a satisfactory foundation. Quite wrongly, as I believe, his motives were impugned. He was charged with leaving the Conservative Party because Balfour had failed to give him Office.

The memory of the unhappy later years of Lord Randolph Churchill's career was still vivid. Members of Parliament said in private and some in public that he was like his father—brilliant but unstable and a dangerous man with whom to work.

Winston Churchill suffered, in those days, from a slight defect in speech which he has almost completely mastered in recent years. It consisted of a slurring of the pronunciation of the letter "s". The House of Commons is normally kind, but can, on occasions, be brutal to a Member who is not *persona grata* to it. I recollect one or two occasions in the 1900 Parliament when some ill-mannered Members on the Conservative Benches mocked this defect when Churchill was speaking. They did it in a *sotto voce* manner which made it impossible for the Speaker to detect and rebuke the offenders, but the incidents plainly disconcerted Churchill.

In the 1900 Parliament Churchill made no attempt to dispel the suspicion and dislike with which he was regarded by the majority of the House of Commons. He seemed to enjoy causing resentment. He appeared to have, in modern parlance, a "chip on his shoulder" when in the Chamber itself or in the Lobbies.

Some commentators in the Press at the time attributed this attitude to an excess of filial devotion. Lord Randolph Churchill had always been a rebel at heart. In the early years of his Membership he, like Disraeli before him, did most valuable service to the country and the Conservative Party by his emphasis on the need for closing the gap between classes and his insistence that the Conservative Party must be a National Party and not representative of any one section of the community. He met, as was to be expected, with opposition from some of his own Party. The vigour alike of his personal and political criticisms of those from whom he differed did not endear him to his colleagues, though they gained popularity for him in the country. At the time of his resignation from Office and quarrel with his Party his enemies, within that Party, as well as his political opponents, had full scope for showing their satisfaction at his misfortunes. Many who disliked him but had not dared to attack him at the zenith of his power now did so.

His son, so argued the commentators, was determined to carry on the fight against those individuals in public life and elements in the Conservative Party who, as he thought, had either brought about his father's downfall or failed to stand by him. His father had great ideals for which he was prepared to risk his career; so had he. His father was a rebel; so would he be. His father never cared if he caused offence in public or private; nor would he.

I think that most of Churchill's contemporaries would agree that there is a considerable measure of truth in the contention which I have described. It was, however, a phase in his career and in his attitude towards Parliament which disappeared after his selection for high Office and his marriage.

It is difficult when you are most happily married to an exceptionally beautiful and charming woman, and successfully hold high Ministerial Office at a very early age, to believe that it is your mission to fight the world in general or, at any rate, some of those few thousands in it with whom you come into contact because they treated your father badly and were not too friendly to you; resentment lessens as you climb the ladder of fame, especially in the case of a man with so generous a nature as Sir Winston Churchill. But before this attitude of mind disappeared and he attuned himself to the House, as he did from 1908 onwards with ever increasing success, he was to meet with a serious parliamentary set-back.

Early in the 1906 Parliament a Private Members' Motion by a supporter of the Liberal Government, Mr. Byles, M.P., which directly criticized the conduct of Lord Milner, in his capacity as High Commissioner for South Africa, for authorizing the flogging of Chinese labourers in South Africa, was debated in the House. Churchill, as Under-Secretary for the Colonies, was the Minister responsible for answering on behalf of the Government and he moved an Amendment, which was subsequently passed, which, while condemning the flogging of Chinese coolies, went on to say that "the House desires, in the interests of peace and conciliation in South Africa, to refrain from passing censure upon individuals". Churchill was in a very difficult position, since the Party of which he was a member had largely won its huge majority on the subject of Chinese labour. Unfortunately, he made that position worse by a bad speech in which he made use of several unfortunate phrases amid growing uproar in the House; his speech was torn to pieces by Balfour, who followed him. I remember even today how subdued and crestfallen he appeared to be at the end of the debate.

To a man of lesser genius than Churchill, so calamitous a beginning as Minister on the first occasion on which he had to handle a difficult situation might have easily meant the ruin of his hopes that he would ever be a success in Office; Churchill, however, profited by the painful lesson which he had learnt and the punishment which the House had given him by its attitude towards his first speech in Junior Office, so that in subsequent speeches he pleased the House and had it with him.

By 1914 Churchill had become a first-class parliamentarian. He had mellowed and matured to a degree which only those of his personal friends among his political opponents, of whom he had many, including myself, would have believed possible seven or eight years earlier. He had studied and learnt to recognize the varying moods of the House. He could be as formidably aggressive as ever when the occasion demanded it; but he made full use of the qualities of tact, persuasion and conciliation when the interests of the Government of which he was a member were thereby advanced.

His command of the beauty and imagery which reside in the English language was manifest. He delighted the House with his magnificent epigrams and great sense of humour and it did not resent his occasional outbursts of scowling rage even when they appeared unnecessary; for they were so soon followed by amiability and a cheerful grin.

Of course, the establishment of his position in the House would have been impossible without his great success in Ministerial Office. To discuss that success lies outside the scope of my contribution to this book. But impartial contemporary opinion accepted the fact that he was an excellent Home Secretary and that as First Lord of the Admiralty he did immeasurable service to the country before and at the outbreak of the 1914 war.

After his resignation from Office following the disasters in the Gallipoli campaign, for which he had to take Ministerial responsibility—though I, as one who fought in Gallipoli, do not believe he was morally responsible—Churchill's position in Parliament, naturally, suffered some decline. It was soon restored after his return to Office in the later stages of the war.

Sir Winston Churchill's parliamentary career, indeed, has presented a remarkable picture of rises and falls throughout its existence which has by no means always coincided with the changes of fortune of the Parties to which he has belonged. After he had been defeated in 1922 and he was unable to obtain another seat for some time it looked as if it might have ended; from 1924 to 1929 he not only occupied, as Chancellor of the Exchequer, one of the most powerful Offices in the State, but completely re-established his parliamentary position.

In the early 'thirties, after the formation of the National Government, of which he was not a member, there was a distinct decline in Churchill's prestige and influence over the Commons. The old, ill-natured criticisms and comments about his personality and character which were so prominent in the 1900 Parliament began to recur in the Lobbies and smoking-room of the House and in Fleet Street. He was an erratic genius; he was utterly unreliable; he had caused unnecessary trouble to the Prime Minister and to all his colleagues in every Cabinet in which he had served by his volubility and persistence in disregarding every opinion except his own; so ran the tale carefully fostered, I may say, by most of the leaders of the National Government.

By the mid-'thirties, as a result of the delivery of a series of some of the greatest speeches ever made in Parliament in peace-time on defence and foreign affairs, he had again reached a position of great power and influence in the Commons. Indeed, only Baldwin and Lloyd George could equal him in the attention which his speeches attracted.

Much has been written about Churchill's tremendous achievements as a statesman after he became Prime Minister in the darkest hour of this country's chequered history in 1940. Less has been said about his influence in Parliament and the joint contribution which he and the House of Commons made to national morale.

In the 1914 war Parliament did little in the first two years of it to sustain the spirit of the nation. The Government had small moral authority and Asquith, its leader, for reasons which were not altogether his fault, did not inspire confidence; there was a great improvement after the formation of Lloyd George's Government in 1916. He himself, in and out of Parliament, made a series of speeches which were an inspiration to the country; his energy and determination to win the war were manifest; but he and his administration, powerful as both were, suffered from certain defects. He had had no administrative knowledge of military matters before the war or any particular interest in them; though he had performed a public service in calling attention to the danger of Germany's foreign policy in his famous Mansion House speech after Agadir, he was known to have been hesitant about the entry of Britain into the war; some of his colleagues were converted pacifists in the sense that they had been generally opposed to defence measures before the war. All this resulted in an uneasiness between the Government and a number of its Conservative supporters in the Commons which even Lloyd George's great gifts of leadership could not wholly dispel. This uneasiness was increased by the number of pacifists on the Liberal and Labour benches. There were some unedifying debates and scenes in the House of Commons which annoyed and alarmed M.P.s on service like myself.

The fact that the House of Commons in the Second World War was far more helpful to the national war effort than its predecessor of the 1914–18 war was due to a happy combination of circumstances in which Churchill's personality played a great part.

Unlike Lloyd George, he had great knowledge and practical experience of national defence. He had warned Parliament and the country again and again before the war about the perils of the international situation and Britain's inadequate preparations for defending herself. He did not suffer the disadvantage under which Lloyd George suffered in his war Premiership of having always to confront a considerable number of pacifists in the Commons, for the opponents of the war in 1940 were a mere handful of M.P.s. Above all, he established his supremacy not only as leader of the national will but as a great parliamentarian by his magnificent first speech after taking Office. In that speech he clearly indicated that both Houses of Parliament had their part to play in the supreme test of the nation's will-power. In common parlance they would "stay put". It was known to most of us, though not to the public, that there were plans for evacuating both Houses to a distant and secluded town in the West Country. It was equally known that Churchill was opposed to the operation of such a plan. The arrangement which he and the Government made for alternative accommodation for Parliament in London should the Chamber be destroyed enhanced the respect and regard for both when the actual occurrence took place.

This mutual regard between Winston Churchill and Parliament did not result, of course, in a perpetual honeymoon. There were criticisms in some important debates of his leadership and the actions of the Government. It could not have been otherwise if Parliament was to do its duty, for failures and defeats must be discussed in a democratic legislature even in time of war. At first, Churchill appeared to resent this attitude. But, when some of us, including myself, used the argument that if we were to adopt the policy of saying that the leader was always right and must never be criticized we should be betraying the principle for which we were fighting and accepting that of Hitler and Mussolini, he did not, like the good parliamentarian he is, demur; for he has always accepted the principle that the Commons are entitled to express the views of the public which they represent, however misguided and dangerous they may be.

The general relationship between Churchill and Parliament during the Second World War was a credit to both. It played no small or unworthy part in the nation's war effort.

After the crushing defeat of his Government in the 1945 Parliament, Churchill's parliamentary position might easily have suffered a permanent or at least temporary eclipse. That this did not occur is striking evidence of his foremost place in world statesmanship. Indeed, it was as a world statesman, and not as the Leader of the Opposition, that he excelled in the 1945 and 1950 Parliaments. There were certain defects in his leadership of the Opposition. He was not as assiduous in his attendance at unimportant debates as occupancy of the post demands. To be wholly successful in leading the Opposition a man must resign himself to sitting long hours through dreary debates. He must watch and wait. He must watch especially the men and women on his own side so as to judge the capabilities of each of them who show promise for future Office; he must wait for any legitimate opportunity to intervene so as to hearten his own side and attack the Government. Such a task was plainly uncongenial to Churchill and, in view of his other important work, including the completion of his great book on the Second World War, would in any case have been difficult.

But not even in the period of his war Premiership did he do more to lead and inform public opinion, through his speeches in Parliament, on defence and foreign policy than he did whilst Leader of the Opposition. He, more than any statesman at home and abroad in the years from 1945 to 1951, prepared the ground plan for the defence, in a military, moral and psychological sense, of Western Democracy against the menace of Russian Communist Imperialism. One of the greatest of his achievements was that in the 1945 Parliament, though suffering from the disadvantage of having sustained as a Party leader a great electoral defeat, he nevertheless persuaded the House of Commons as a whole that his views on external affairs were right, despite the furious resentment with which they were met at first by the Labour Party. In fact, by the end of the Parliament, the Government were following the policy which he had advocated a few years earlier.

He attained this achievement by a series of speeches whose brilliance and hold on the House of Commons were as great as any which he has ever made. He did this when well over seventy and after having undergone a period of tremendous strain and terrific responsibility as Prime Minister in the previous five years. It cannot be disputed, I think, that no other British statesman has approached Churchill's record in this regard.

It is true that Lloyd George, between his fall from power in 1922 and his translation to the House of Lords, made a number of speeches in the Commons which, judged from the standpoint of oratory and the attention which a packed House paid to them, were very successful. Like Churchill in the 1945 Parliament, he could attract and thrill a greater audience than any Minister. But, unhappily, the main thesis of these speeches was almost invariably wrong and was usually very soon proved to be by events.

The success of Churchill's advocacy lay not only in the brilliance with which it was presented but in the indisputability of the facts upon which it was based. He persuaded the House and the Government to accept the disagreeable truth that a Third World War was possible and that, in consequence, all possible steps must be taken to try to prevent it and, if it could not be avoided, to fight it with reasonable hopes of victory. Never has Churchill's skill as a great parliamentarian been used to more beneficial effect than when he was Leader of the Opposition and since he has been Prime Minister for the second time.

His success in the latter capacity has been, indeed, extraordinary. When his Government was formed in 1951 many Conservatives, in private, doubted if, with its small majority, it could survive for more than a year or eighteen months. They were also dubious about Churchill's capacity, at his age, to stand the strain of leading an Administration with a tiny majority in the Commons which was also confronted with some of the gravest problems ever to beset this country. Events since October 1951 illustrate once again the difficulty of accurate prophecy about the future of a particular Government, House of Commons or Prime Minister. Contrary to all the accepted rules and precedents, the present Government has, at the time of writing in the summer of 1953, a stronger hold upon the House of Commons and, to judge from by-elections, the country than when it was formed. As for Sir Winston Churchill, his hand is as firmly as ever upon the rudder. Indeed, the Government at least owes some of its enhanced prestige to Churchill in two respects.

He chose the right men in both Houses to form his Government and left the right men out of it. It requires a very skilled and practised parliamentarian to do that. In the course of my forty-seven years[1] in the House of Commons, during which time I advanced from the position of its "Baby" to its "Father", I was a member of four separate Governments in Junior or Senior Office; so it is in no sense a case of "sour grapes" for me to state from my experience that I have seen some astonishing instances of men being put into Offices for which they were wholly unfit and thereby, by the ridicule and annoyance which they caused in either the Lords or the Commons, injuring the whole fabric of the prestige of the Government of the day.

No such mistake has been made by Sir Winston Churchill.

The other respect in which the Government has benefited from Churchill's Premiership is in his speeches and answers to questions in the House. His genius in both arts remains untarnished by age and undimmed by the immense strain which he has personally undergone in the huge tasks which he has undertaken in half a century. Never once has the most skilful Socialist swordsman got under his guard in the present Parliament, not even Aneurin Bevan, who did once hit him hard in a magnificent speech in a former Parliament. It was characteristic of Churchill that he grinned amiably throughout it and once interjected, "Don't spoil a good speech."

What is the secret of Sir Winston Churchill's great influence over and popularity in the House of Commons? It is unique in the sense that, in recent years in his bouts at Question Time with Morrison, Shinwell and Bevan, he has said things which, in the case of any other Leader of the Opposition or Prime Minister, would have led to such prolonged uproar that the House would have had to be adjourned, under the appropriate Standing Order, because of "grave disorder".

It is not solely due to his supreme gifts as a statesman, nor to the gratitude which the House, like the country, owes him for his leadership in the Second World War and its affection for the generosity of his character, nor does it result entirely from his superb oratory and his deep admiration for the House as an institution. To answer the question one must consider the composition of the House itself. It represents the amalgam of races and traditions which is Britain. In

[1] From 1904 to 1951.

some of its moods it reflects the emotional genius of Wales and the Western Highlands of Scotland; in others the stolid common sense of Northern England and Southern Scotland; in others again the vulgar humour and good-nature of the average Cockney. Its attitude in any debate cannot be predicted in advance; it is sometimes frivolous and even irresponsible when the subject is far too important for jesting; it occasionally treats an unimportant matter with undue solemnity. At its best it has no rival among the democratic legislative bodies of the world. Sir Winston Churchill is steeped in its atmosphere and traditions; he is familiar with all its varying moods; he knows its likes and dislikes; he has an instinctive understanding of what it will accept and what it will not accept; he prepares his speeches with great care because he very properly believes that the House has a right to expect that he shall give of his best.

To a man of Sir Winston's gifts and stature, with more than half a century's membership of the Commons, it is not surprising that all this should be so, or that he should share the great merits and some of the defects of the House. It is this, above everything else, which makes him the greatest living parliamentarian.

CHURCHILL AS A LIBERAL

Viscount Simon

Viscount Simon has been a close colleague of Churchill in politics for many years.

In the Liberal Government headed by Asquith, oj which Churchill was a member, he was Solicitor-General 1910–13, Attorney-General 1913–15 and Home Secretary 1915–16.

In the National Governments headed by Ramsay MacDonald, Stanley Baldwin and Neville Chamberlain he was Foreign Secretary 1931–35, Home Secretary and Deputy Leader of the House of Commons 1935–37 and Chancellor of the Exchequer 1937–40. Churchill, as Prime Minister, chose him to be Lord Chancellor 1940–45.

SIR WINSTON CHURCHILL is the leader of the Conservative Party, but at the root of his many-sided nature there remains the essence of liberalism. His tolerance, his sympathy with the oppressed and the underdog, his courage in withstanding clamour, his belief in the value of the individual and in self-government for communities sufficiently advanced to use it wisely, all derive from a heart and a head which made him in his early years of Ministerial office a Liberal statesman. This liberal outlook was sincerely adopted (and indeed in some sort inherited from his father) and his liberal views were embodied in well-argued speeches and were not a mere pose, so that he has carried this liberal temper with him throughout his life and has not hesitated to show it in the great offices which he has since occupied.

His biography of his father is a splendid book, which shows how deeply he has gone below the surface of contemporary politics and how he has studied the movement of the tide in the affairs of men. Lord Randolph Churchill proclaimed "Tory democracy" at a time when not every Conservative would have appreciated being called a democrat. Lord Randolph saw further; he was engaged in transforming Conservative policy. When he resigned, he wrote: "In inflicting on the old gang this final fatal blow, I have mortally wounded myself. But the work is practically done; the Tory Party will be turned into a Liberal Party, and in that transformation may yet produce a powerful governing force." How often must the Prime Minister have reflected on the difference it might have made to our political history if his father had not vanished from the scene so early. The son came to realize (what all true Liberals ought to understand) that a liberal outlook, which attaches so much importance to individual liberty, was increasingly threatened by a rival philosophy founded on the belief that state-regulation and state-ownership and state-control must more and more take charge of our lives. Could anyone, for example, put the case against Socialism in better terms than this?

"Liberalism has its own history and its own tradition. Socialism has its own formulas and aims. Socialism seeks to pull down wealth; Liberalism seeks to raise up poverty. Socialism would destroy private interests; Liberalism would preserve private interests in the only way in which they can be safely and justly preserved, namely, by reconciling them with public right. Socialism would kill enterprise; Liberalism would rescue enterprise from the trammels of privilege and preference. Socialism assails the pre-eminence of the individual; Liberalism seeks, and shall seek more in the future, to build up a minimum standard for the mass. Socialism exalts the rule; Liberalism exalts the man. Socialism attacks capital; Liberalism attacks monopoly."

Can any Liberal put it better than that? Churchill said it during the Dundee election on May 14, 1908, when he was newly appointed by Asquith to be the Liberal President of the Board of Trade. I will wager that, Conservative leader though he be, there is not one word in this finely phrased passage which he would wish to alter now.

But there is a second point. It is an essential part of the Liberal doctrine which inspired the Governments of Campbell-Bannerman and Asquith that the inequalities of human lot, the ill-health that strikes at the root of the lives of so many worthy citizens, the unemployment that bad times may bring about, the curse of sweated and underpaid labour, should be the constant concern of a democratic state and that, as we used to preach in the great days before the first German war, "the State should come to the aid of those who need help most". It was this principle which justified the establishment of old age pensions, and insurance against sickness and unemployment, and the unemployment exchanges and trade boards. Churchill, as a Liberal Minister, was in the thick of the fight for all of them and that at a time when they came in for much criticism from the short-sighted. It is not that Parliament can equalize human fortunes and can make the situation of the unfortunate equal to that of his happier neighbour, but by just taxation and wise assistance the extremes of misfortune can be lightened and legislation can be used to bring a measure of equality—not, as Lady Violet Bonham-Carter once said, to draw a line above which no one can rise, but to draw a line below which no one can fall.

Some who call themselves Liberals think it enough to recall the days when these proposals and policies were challenged and denounce the modern Conservative because some of his ancestors were among the challengers. They boast of the days when a Liberal Government (which contained Churchill) established social reform. But there is a much prouder boast which Liberals can make. The reforms in our domestic life which they framed and fought for and established as the rule of the community have passed from being the victories of a Party and have become part of the common stock of our people. They have been so worked into the warp and woof of the social fabric that ordinary folk do not recognize them as distinctively Liberal achievements at all. Whatever may be said of the past, the modern Conservative accepts and promotes such changes as essential to national well-being, and this, I think, is the real way in which Liberal policy is justified to mankind.

I am reminded of the speech which I heard Churchill make when he was commending to the House of Commons in 1906 the Government's scheme for granting self-government to the Transvaal and the Orange Free State—a speech inspired by as high a conception of the part which the Old Country had to play in relation to newer communities as the great speeches of Chatham on the independence of America. The young Under-Secretary, after explaining and justifying what the Liberal Government was doing, appealed to the Opposition to make the grant of self-government not the victory of a Party but the gift of a nation. He said:

"I address myself particularly to the right hon. gentlemen who sit opposite, who are long versed in public affairs, and who will not be able all their lives to escape from a heavy South African responsibility. They are the accepted guides of a Party which, though in a minority in this House, nevertheless embodies nearly half the nation. I will ask them seriously whether they will not pause before they commit themselves to violent or rash denunciations of this great arrangement. I will ask them, further, whether they cannot join with us to invest the grant of a free Constitution to the Transvaal with something of a national sanction. With all our majority we can only make it the gift of a Party; they can make it the gift of England."

Now that the ex-Liberal Minister has become leader of the Conservative Party, has he not carried into that body the reinvigorating spirit of English liberalism and so brought to fulfilment his father's notion that Toryism could be led into democratic channels? The content of national policy changes with time, but there is a profound sense in which Sir Winston Churchill, though a Conservative Prime Minister, is a Liberal still.

CHURCHILL IN HIGH OFFICE

Guy Eden

Guy Eden, one of Britain's leading political correspondents for a quarter of a century, is a former Chairman of the House of Commons Press Gallery and of the exclusive Parliamentary Lobby Journalists. In this chapter he writes of Sir Winston Churchill's career in some of the highest Offices of State, including his first Cabinet post—President of the Board of Trade—his controversial term as Home Secretary, his short but important stay at the Colonial Office, where he was responsible for negotiating the Irish Treaty, his five years as Chancellor of the Exchequer, and, finally, his supreme years as Prime Minister. Few political correspondents have enjoyed such close acquaintance with Churchill as Guy Eden, who wrote a successful book about the Prime Minister—Portrait of Churchill.

ON the morning of May 11, 1941, I stood with Winston Churchill amid the still-smoking ruins of the House of Commons, which had, a few hours earlier, been shattered by Nazi bombs.

The Prime Minister gazed silently, a long time. His eyes travelled sadly along the space where the floor of the Chamber had been, to the site of the Table from which he had delivered many a speech, up to the Galleries from which thousands had listened to him and finally to the place where the Press Gallery had been—the famous Press Gallery from which had gone to the world so many fateful pronouncements and announcements, many of which had come from Churchill himself.

His jaw-muscles were working tensely as he looked slowly around. The end of the walking-stick he carried was ground silently and savagely into the powdering cinders that had once been part of the doors leading from "behind the Speaker's Chair" and which—had they voices—might have told many a dramatic tale of intrigues and off-the-record understandings and misunderstandings between political friend and foe.

For a full five minutes, probably, he let his eyes rove. One could almost read his thoughts. Of his introduction into the House, as a young, arrogantly confident, red-haired man, after a sensational and sometimes boisterous election at Oldham. Of his maiden speech, soon afterwards, in which he had shown rare nervousness but which he had contrived to make go with a reasonable bang. Of his speedy climb to Ministerial office, first junior, and then, at the early age of thirty-four, the senior post of President of the Board of Trade. Of his rise through the various offices, in war and peace. Of his changes of Party. Of his wordy battles from the Opposition side of the House as Socialist Governments came and went. Of his acceptance of the surprise offer of the Treasury by Stanley Baldwin, and his Budget statements before a House crowded to the very ceilings. Of his years in the political wilderness, with everybody sadly or gleefully prophesying his political demise and even some of his friends freely saying that he was "finished". Of the coming of World War II and his return to the very office he had held when World War I had opened a quarter of a century earlier—the Admiralty. Of the personal and political difficulties that had preceded his arrival at the goal of all his political ambitions, the Premiership, but in circumstances that would have appalled most people.

All this one could almost see passing through his mind as he surveyed the wreckage of the place he had often described as being the very centre of his life. As I, too, looked around, I could feel something of his grief and pain. For I, too, had seen and experienced many of the occasions and events that passed in review through his mind.

At last he moved, and in the dim light I could see that tears were running unchecked down his cheeks. Turning abruptly to an official, he controlled his voice with an effort and said quietly: "This Chamber must be rebuilt—just as it was! Meanwhile, we shall not miss a single day's debate through this!"

Brushing the sleeve of his coat across his eyes with the gesture of the schoolboy rather shamefacedly hiding his tears from public gaze, Churchill strode off, back to his War Room, with its map-covered walls, back to his planning and scheming for the victory that was to make him, a few years later, for a brief time the most lauded and cheered man in the land—indeed, in the world—and to change the course of history.

As I watched him go, I could not help reflecting on the remarkable career of this man who had known ups and downs almost unprecedented, even in British political life. I could recall—even in my own relatively short political life—how he had been on the very topmost twig of the tree, and how he had been so "down" that a prophecy of his arrival in Downing Street would have seemed fantastic and laughable.

It would be absurd to suggest that he took his ten-years "down" period entirely philosophically. He clearly hated it and a bitterness crept into his speeches and his general attitude in political life which had not been there before and which has not been there since.

In the unfriendly—the hostile—atmosphere of his years deep in the wilderness, he would have needed to be more than human to have taken the snubs, the sneers and the patronizing nudgings and shruggings calmly, or even with unfailing good-temper. Political life is a merciless affair and the man who has been at the top of the tree is most ruthlessly "clawed"—to use one of Churchill's own favourite words—when he falls or even slips.

Most, I think, would have given in when faced with such a situation. His very seat in the Chamber had something symbolical of fallen greatness. He sat on the front bench on the Government side of the House . . . but "below the gangway". What a gap there is, what a vast, terrific chasm, between the Treasury Bench, seat of power, and that seat just two-feet-six-inches away, below the gangway!

From the seat *above* the gangway, his every word would be significant, conveying some possibly historic decision or recommendation. From that *below* the gangway, his words meant little or nothing, produced no more than sarcastic references to the fact that he who had uttered them was taking the fullest advantage of the circumstance that he was now "in a position of greater freedom and less responsibility".

Many a time I have seen Winston Churchill wince as that phrase was used or implied—and it was almost daily that someone would bring it forth.

No one who has really studied Churchill can honestly say that he enjoys being out of office. Every one of the relatively few years he has spent out of office, in the course of his long political life, he has hated. Every hour he has dreamed of the time when he could return, once more, to a position of power and authority.

One of the engaging things about him, I have always felt, is the frank and obvious enjoyment he has of the trappings of High Office. He loves to stump around the ranks of a Guard of Honour, stopping now and then to grunt a question at some man or woman wearing a row of medal ribbons. He enjoys the cheers of the crowds as he passes through the streets. He will play to the gallery in a manner, and with a skill, most men of the theatre would give their all to be able to emulate, putting his hat on the end of a gold-mounted ebony walking-stick and waving it with the abandon of an undergraduate.

And yet he has a strong sense of dignity and of the importance of his office and his own position in the life of the country. A good many people have found this when seeking to presume on some slight acquaintance and to be over-familiar with him. His method with such people—and they have come from all ranks and walks of life—is to gaze steadily at them for a few moments and then, as the subject of scrutiny reddens uneasily or decides that the Great Man is about to recall some incident shared with him, to grunt with mild disgust and walk firmly away, without so much as a single word.

I have seen men whose own claim to fame is considerable treated in this way, because they have been, in Churchill's view, presumptuous in their approach. I well recall an occasion, during the war, when a distinguished Conservative Member of Parliament had made a reference which Churchill took as casting a slight on a member of the Churchill family. He turned at once to cast a look of disdain and dislike at the speaker (who, to do him justice, had meant no such thing) and later, when the unfortunate man sought to explain in private, shook off his detaining hand, snarled that he had no room for him, and left him flat.

This brusqueness and often rudeness makes Churchill's rise to—and long retention of—the highest offices the more remarkable. I make the distinction between rising to office and retaining it, because I have seen many men rise to high office, only to lose it because they have failed to "handle" Parliament with sufficient skill and with kid gloves well enough padded.

Churchill has never bothered about kid gloves, in office or out. A stinging snub is just as likely to be administered to one of his own supporters as to an "honourable gentleman opposite".

Indeed, there was a time in the difficult periods of the war when his supporters were apt to complain—I am bound to say, with some justification—that his opponents and critics got a kinder reception from him than did his staunchest and most loyal friends.

Maybe because he has had so many years of High Office, he certainly does not suffer fools gladly, and he has his own very definite and specialized ideas as to who *are* fools. Nor does he enjoy being opposed in any way, although he can be magnanimous to those who oppose him—if they are on that somewhat exclusive list not classed as "fools". Anthony Eden and Lord Beaverbrook had the reputation of standing up to him in the War Cabinet. But Eden was in a very special relationship to the Prime Minister.

Sir James Grigg, for many years his Principal Private Secretary, was another who was privileged to "tell him where he got off". The two had many a row, in the course of which (so it was said) some very frank things were said—on personal, as well as public, affairs. But they always ended, sometimes after a few days of formal iciness, with mutual apologies. As often as not, they would end with Churchill, looking over his spectacles, saying softly, "*Why* are you so rough with me?" and the fiery-tempered but kindly "P. J." bellowing with the laughter which kills anger stone dead.

It is a strange fact that Churchill has so few confirmed enemies, in view of the number of offices he has held and the number of politicians and officials, high and low, with whom he has had personal contact. There are some, of course, who have not a good word to say for him, but there are many more who can recall some act of personal kindness which, perhaps, wiped out some smaller act of inconsiderateness committed in a moment of pique or in haste.

Beyond any question, Churchill likes power. I am convinced that —like almost every other man or woman I know in our public life— he cares not at all for the spoils of office and least of all for the financial side. But power he certainly likes, with all the deference and the ceremony that go with it. And, looking back over his crowded life, this is, after all, not surprising, for power is a heady drink.

Let us look back over some of the offices he has held.

Under-Secretary of State for the Colonies, 1905–08. A junior office, but gained in less than five years after he had become a Member of Parliament, and at the age of thirty-one or so. I was told by one who knew him when he held this office that he "certainly did not underestimate its (or his own) importance" and that his general attitude was "Ministerial" to a degree.

However, he seems to have done well enough, for, at the age of thirty-four—when most M.P.s are well content to be Junior Whips (unpaid)—he was given Cabinet rank as

President of the Board of Trade, even then a "key" office in the Government. In those days it was necessary to fight a by-election on taking Ministerial office, and Churchill had to fight North-West Manchester—by then his constituency—again. The Suffragettes made the contest a lively one, and so did his other political opponents, to such an extent that the ambulances had sometimes to be called out at over-exuberant meetings. And Liberal Churchill was defeated—by 492 votes—by William Joynson-Hicks, later to become, in the whirligig of politics, his close colleague in a Tory Cabinet.

His political opponents, in Party and Press, were overjoyed, and Churchill was correspondingly depressed. Why had he been rejected? Nobody seemed able to say. John Morley, his Ministerial colleague, expressed the view that it was because he had made too many promises to too many conflicting groups (including the Suffragettes, with whom he had pleaded, "Trust *me*, ladies!") and that some electors had felt that he had "no principles". Whatever the reason, the defeat must have seemed a bitter blow, but it was considerably assuaged by an invitation, on the very day of his Manchester defeat, to contest a by-election in Dundee. This time, he gained a majority of more than 7,000 votes—about as many as his two opponents polled between them. The Churchill Luck had held.

At the Board of Trade he established the Labour Exchanges, which took much of the humiliation out of the quest for employment, and Boards which did much to prevent sweated labour. This enabled him to wield the big brush which he has always preferred—as he does still— to the small detail of a Government office. These two important measures apart, his tenure of the Board of Trade does not seem to have made history, but it put him on the path to still higher office and greatly increased his standing in Parliament, without which no Prime Minister, however experimental his turn of mind, would dare promote a Minister. His "funny hats", and the fact that he was so often the target for the sometimes unconventional missiles of the militant ladies whose trust he had invited, ensured that he remained steadily in the eye of the Press and the public. He was also, probably, the most hated man in our public life because of the manner in which he provocatively sought battle on all occasions, and, in F. E. Smith's bitterly taunting words, "spent the best years of his life preparing impromptu speeches".

In 1910 Asquith offered him the post of Irish Secretary, the hoodoo job of the Cabinet. It must have been a worrying situation for the young politician, having to decide whether to accept the office, with all its risks, or take the risk of refusing. The Churchill Luck came into play again when he refused, for he was offered the office of Secretary of State for the Home Department, a job Churchill never failed to point out was that of the *Principal* Secretary of State.

One of his first tasks was to maintain public order during the long and bitter strikes of coal-miners in 1910.[1] He called the military to the aid of the civil police when there was trouble in Wales, and the decision aroused a storm. This move, incidentally, illustrates what his critics hold to be a weakness of his, the too-ready invocation of overwhelming force in dealing with a difficult situation. But when one reflects that it was this attitude which produced the landings in Normandy on D-Day, 1944, and which yielded such historic dividends, one may be permitted to wonder if it is a bad characteristic!

A high-ranking officer of the War Office was appointed to command the forces of law and order, both civil and military, and including a big party of police from London. The officer in charge "found an inclination" on the part of the Home Secretary to interfere in things that could be decided only by the man on the spot (how many officers have since noticed the same inclination?), but this "wore off" and Churchill supported him through thick and thin in anything he felt it necessary to do. The strikes passed off without any very serious trouble.

But Churchill found himself under criticism in 1911, over the notorious Sidney Street Affair. Some foreign anarchists murdered policemen in the course of a burglary and then barricaded themselves in a house in Sidney Street, in London's East End, then a very different place from its present-day appearance and atmosphere.

Churchill was in his bath—it is astonishing how many important decisions he has made in his bath—when he was asked by the chiefs of the police what should be done to dislodge the two desperadoes. Shots had already been exchanged between them and the police, and now the sanction of the Home Secretary was sought to the use of soldiers. With only a moist towel round him, Churchill heard the case and gave assent to the use of troops. Then, dressing hastily, he dashed off to the Home Office and—another characteristic touch—set up a battle headquarters, to which all concerned had to send frequent reports. But this G.H.Q. behind-the-lines stuff soon palled and the Home Secretary decided that his place was in the front line—so off he went (with the

---

[1] Dealt with more fully in the chapter "Churchill and the Trade Unions", by the Rt. Hon. George Isaacs, M.P.

photographers and reporters in close attendance) to the scene of the battle.

There, in top-hat and fur-collared coat, he took his place in an observation-post and provided the Press with one of the most dramatic pictures of his pictorially dramatic career, with heavily armed soldiers sniping around him. All this was greatly to his taste for action and he has admitted that his "conviction of duty was supported by a strong sense of curiosity".

But trouble of another kind lurked around the corner, and when he got to the House of Commons he found that body sitting with folded arms and a frown on its collective face. What, it asked, did the Home Secretary mean by interfering with the man on the spot?—the very complaint that had come from the military commander in Wales. And it is fair to say that Churchill himself had already realized that his somewhat impulsive action had put him and others in a serious difficulty, because the officers in command naturally looked to the Secretary of State—and the *Principal* Secretary of State, at that!—for a decision whether the anarchists should be burned out of the house or not. He did, in fact, order that the house be allowed to burn, but he was himself scorched a little in the subsequent debate in the Commons, when no less a critic than the great A. J. Balfour turned the withering fire of his sarcasm on him. He could understand, said A. J. B., what the Press photographers were doing—but not what the Home Secretary was doing, getting himself pictured standing in an East End doorway under fire.

But the Home Secretary survived and it was not long before he turned his attention to preparations for a much bigger battle than that of Sidney Street—World War I. The fact that these preparations were no direct concern of the Home Secretary (there were no Civil Defence plans to be made in those days) worried Churchill not at all, and he was soon up to his neck in investigations and planning. All this, as it happened, was to be very useful when he made his next move, to the office of

First Lord of the Admiralty,[1] which he did in 1911. Here, indeed, he had a post that gave him scope for his genius for what has been called

---

[1] Dealt with more fully in the chapter "Churchill and the Navy", by Admiral Sir William James.

CHURCHILL IN HIGH OFFICE

Churchill, as Chancellor of the Exchequer in 1927, discusses
the Budget with his Secretary, Mr. (later Sir) Edward Marsh

imaginative organization. The Admiralty has always been his favourite office in Government, but it is true to say that the Admirals have not always been so keen on their chief as he has been on the Royal Navy. However, as in many other posts he has held, he succeeded in impressing the holders of permanent office with his knowledge of their own professional duties and with his enthusiasm for the Department they served.

Churchill has a curious trait. He is not—all who have served with him seem to agree—a good "team" man, in that he does not co-operate readily with others, but he always wants to have a considerable say in the running of Departments other than his own. This has led, in the past, to some pretty sharp exchanges with fellow Ministers—but it has also produced some surprising, and often highly beneficial, "extraterritorial" results in other offices.

Churchill stayed at the Admiralty until 1915, when he spent a little time as a soldier in France before becoming, in 1917,

Minister of Munitions, another office which gave him scope for his gift for invention. Then, as now, there were many who believed that his talents were those of a man of war, rather than a man of peace, and there were a good many raised eyebrows when, after being Secretary of State for War and Air[1] from 1918 to 1921, he became

Colonial Secretary, in which office he played a considerable part in the conclusion of the agreement with Ireland which resulted in the setting up of the Irish Free State.[2] To those who can recall the atmosphere of those times, this was, in many ways, one of the great achievements of his life, for it was a situation in which force and forceful speaking were worse than useless, and in which diplomacy in its most difficult, subtle and persuasive form had to be employed with the extremely tough and intractable Irish negotiators. That is worth remembering when it is contended that Churchill knows nothing of the rapier, but only of the broadsword.

I well remember the consternation there was when, in the autumn of 1924, the MacDonald Government having crashed, Stanley

[1] Sir Winston Churchill's service as Secretary of State for War and Air are fully dealt with in the chapters "Churchill and the Army", by Lieut.-General H. G. Martin, and "Churchill the Airman", by Air Chief Marshal Sir Philip Joubert de la Ferté.

[2] Dealt with more fully in the chapter "Churchill and the Empire", by Sir Evelyn Wrench.

Baldwin, having won a heavy majority in the Commons, sent for Winston Churchill. Most people expected that he would be given one of the more or less ornamental posts in the Cabinet—and then it was announced that he had been made

Chancellor of the Exchequer. I recall telling a highly placed Conservative the news and receiving the reply, "Don't be so silly—why, he's not been in the Tory Party five minutes!"

There was, indeed, a story current at the time that Baldwin had said to Churchill, "I can offer you the job of Chancellor." To which Churchill replied, eagerly, "Of the Duchy?" [of Lancaster, a sinecure post]. Baldwin: "No, of the Exchequer!"

A good many Tories of very senior rank were unhappy and disgruntled at the appointment and they made it plain to Churchill in the House. But a man with his character and career is not easily put off, and he set to work with a will to prove that his father's lack of acquaintance with "those damned dots" (decimal points) had not descended to him.

He was apt to be somewhat by-and-large with figures, and to be over-optimistic about revenue, over-sanguine about economy drives.

He was apt to sweep aside—as his father had tended to do—the calculations and forecasts of the people he called the "technicians", with the result that some of his best-laid plans sometimes went seriously agley and never saw the light of parliamentary day. He was, according to those with whom he had to deal, sometimes over-assertive of his right to intervene in the financial affairs of other Departments, with occasional embarrassment to the easy-going Baldwin, called on to act as court of appeal. But he had ideas. He made mistakes, and got himself into trouble—as over the return to the Gold Standard—but even his best enemies did not deny that he had ideas.

I still think dizzily of that marathon speech in which he presented a Budget, including the de-rating plan for industry, and which took, I think, something like four hours to deliver, with a tea-interval halfway. It had in it a formula for the making of Government grants to local authorities, authorship of which Churchill blandly disclaimed, and which would, indeed, have defeated a mathematician of vastly superior skill to his.

But that did not worry him. He had launched the ship of De-rating, and somebody else—it turned out to be Neville Chamberlain—could do all the fiddling detailed work necessary. That is another characteristic of his: he likes to make the big plans and to leave the details to others.

It is not difficult to believe the various stories that were in circulation behind the political scenes at the time, that Churchill ploughed steadily through the list of Government Departments, battling in turn with the Minister at the head of each, and, more important, with the Civil Service head of each. But he also won himself some devoted admirers among the Civil Service, as in the House of Commons.

It was while he was Chancellor of the Exchequer that the General Strike occurred, in 1926. I was at No. 10 Downing Street very late one night when Churchill strode out to make his plans to meet and beat the strike, and which included the creation of the *British Gazette*, a weird and wonderful publication which served, at least, its aim of ensuring that the people got *some* newspaper.[1] There is no doubt that Churchill enjoyed this fleeting period as Editor of an extremely partisan newspaper and, perhaps even more, the fact that he was producing it in a cloak-and-dagger, Underground atmosphere which appealed to the incurably romantic, penny-blood strain in his make-up.

Considering the various upheavals he was reportedly causing behind the scenes, Churchill's tenure of the Treasury was remarkably unexciting from the public's angle.

It ended in 1929, when the Conservative Government went down before another electoral victory by the Labour Party. And the fall of the Tory Government marked the beginning of Churchill's decade in the wilderness, which did not end until the Second World War brought him back to office, again as First Lord of the Admiralty. He went quietly to the office, called for the maps he had had in the First World War, had them stuck on the walls, and got to work. He had accepted Neville Chamberlain's offer with a simple, "Certainly, I am at your service!"

I know something of the tension of life in "official circles" during the next few months, with disaster following disaster—after the period of the "phoney" war had ended—in seemingly endless procession. I

---

[1] Dealt with fully in the chapter "Churchill the Editor", by Beric Holt.

sat through every moment of the long debate in Parliament which resulted in the fall of the Chamberlain Government, and listened to the powerful, but vain, attempt of Churchill to save the situation and his chief, the Premier.

Chamberlain, broken-hearted, went, and Churchill became Prime Minister. His lifelong ambition had been achieved, but in what circumstances! I saw him at the time, naturally excited about his elevation, but realizing, perhaps more clearly than most, the magnitude of the task that lay before him and the nation. Him and the nation, certainly, in that order, for the war was, to him, something of a personal crusade against "that wicked man", as he usually called Hitler. For Mussolini, later, he had profound contempt—"that jackal", he called him—but for Hitler he had respect as a man of vision, even if it was distorted vision, and drive, even if it was a drive to evil.

In his tenure of office as war-time Prime Minister Churchill found the supreme satisfaction of being able to wield the broadest brush and to plan on a scale satisfying even to him. The egotism he never tries to conceal was given full play. Orders and objurgations, condemnations and encouragements flowed ceaselessly from his office, all bearing the firmly penned initials "W. S. C." at their foot. Generals and planners were told not to argue but to get the thing done. Ministers were sharply told that their job was to produce the plans and results asked for, and not to present the difficulties and complications of their tasks. Not for him, the Head of the Government, the niggling details. For him, only the Big Order and a report, in due course—"on one sheet of paper"— that it had been carried out by some subordinate, high or low. "Action This Day" was his watchword.

For anyone who, like myself, saw him constantly at close quarters during the war years, there is no doubting that this was, indeed, the supreme period of his life. He worked fantastically long hours, and drove himself as hard as he drove his aides—which was very hard indeed. He never let up, and he never forgot to follow up an order he had given. One relatively junior Minister received a 'phone call from the "Old Man" himself, brusquely inquiring "what had happened" about some almost unimportant order sent out a fortnight earlier, and was crisply told that, if he could not carry out the order, "someone else will".

THE START OF THE SECOND WORLD WAR

On the morning of Monday, September 4th, 1939, Churchill arrives at his office to begin his first day's work in the Second World War. His keys hang from the silver, snake-like chain described by Mr. Hore-Belisha in his chapter "How Churchill Influences and Persuades" and the early edition of an evening paper, his dispatch box, other cases, stick, gas mask and cigar complete his equipment

As always, Churchill loved making speeches, and was as delighted as a schoolboy when he was hailed as a star broadcaster.

Churchill loved the secrecy that had to surround his movements in war-time. He was thrilled by the thought that the enemy would give almost anything to be able to kill or—better—capture him. He delighted in the "security" that had to surround his leaving the country for the first meeting with President Roosevelt, including the taking of a photograph of himself outside No. 10 buying a flag from a beaming woman—for publication on the real flag day, which fell a week or more later. And he loved the thrill of moving through submarine-infested waters to the Atlantic meeting-place.

Churchill loved the pomp and circumstance of office as Head of the Government, and many of his Ministers complained that he seemed to think he *was* the Government. No doubt he did. To see him travelling in a flagged and guarded car, hurtling through the streets preceded by a police-car with a specially prearranged signal on the hooter, to ensure that the Great Man was not held up, was to realize what official travel can be in war-time.

Nothing on earth would have prevented his dash to the beaches of Normandy very soon after D-Day, and it took all the authority and diplomacy of the King himself to prevent his going over with the invading forces on the first day of the invasion of Europe.[1]

The way in which the Generals and the Admirals and the Air Marshals saluted and took their orders gave him undisguised pleasure. As always, he was convinced that he knew just what was needed and that he could best say how it was to be done or achieved.

When the war in Europe ended, nothing on earth would have prevented his making the triumphal—and much publicized—journey from Downing Street to the Houses of Parliament, through deliriously happy crowds or his smiling acceptance of their acclaim. The mere fact that the thronged House was waiting for him mattered not at all. He felt that he had earned the ovation, and he proposed to make the most of it.

He could scarcely credit the cruel blow the electorate dealt him only a few months later, when it hurled him brusquely from office and placed Attlee in power with a huge majority. But he took it fairly

[1] See the chapter "Churchill as an Ally in War", by President Dwight D. Eisenhower.

philosophically, after the first burst of pained anger the seeming ingratitude of the people aroused in him. It is said that, when the members of his Cabinet called to meet him for the last time as Prime Minister, he looked around and said quietly, "Well, gentlemen, this is our Dunkirk!" And thus he became, for the first time, Leader of the Opposition. Frankly, he was not a great success in this exacting role. He was inclined to make too much of relatively unimportant matters and to wrangle over trifles, while letting points of major political importance go unchallenged.

The 1951 General Election again gave him office, even though it was with a tiny majority. Without hesitation, he accepted the Premiership and set about the task of selecting his Government.

Not all his appointments were accepted with acclamation, and the Labour Party was particularly severe about his selection of "Co-ordinating Ministers" to oversee the work of the ordinary Departmental Ministers. There are still two views about the efficiency of this plan, but it accorded with his military "chain-of-command" ideas about the running of a Government, and his liking for an inner circle of Ministers, to be more or less permanently in conference with him.

But those immediately about him noted one difference in his general attitude. He was much more ready than formerly to delegate tasks and to allow Ministers to get on with their work without too much direct interference from him. Not that he kept out of any Department for long. He was still given to sending Ministers cut-and-dried plans which they were expected to adopt and put into effect, but he was a little more ready than before to accept their considered verdict that "it could not be done".

With this change of attitude has come, inevitably, some relaxation of his personal control of detail, and he is more ready to content himself with a general supervision.

A Great Prime Minister? In war-time, and in war conditions, yes, beyond any question. In peace-time? *That* story is still being told.

CHURCHILL
AS A POLITICAL OPPONENT

The Rt. Hon. Emanuel Shinwell, M.P.

Emanuel Shinwell has been for many years one of Sir Winston Churchill's most vigorous opponents in the House of Commons and in the country and writes of him entirely from that point of view. Shinwell entered Parliament in 1922 and has held high offices in Labour Governments. He was Secretary for Mines 1924 and 1930–31, Financial Secretary War Office 1929, Minister of Fuel and Power 1945–47, Secretary of State for War 1947–50, and Minister of Defence 1950–51. He has been Chairman of the National Executive of the Labour Party.

NOBODY in British politics during the early 'twenties inspired more dislike in Labour circles than Winston Churchill. His crowning sin was the fatuous declaration that Labour was unfit to govern, an accusation that gave the gravest offence to members of the Labour Party. "What right," it was asked, "had he to talk in this arrogant fashion", thus disparaging responsible Labour leaders like Arthur Henderson, George Barnes and J. R. Clynes, all members of the Coalition Government, whose ability and industry had won the respect of their Conservative and Liberal colleagues?

In those days criticism of Churchill was the outstanding feature at meetings organized by the Labour Movement. In every market-place Labour propagandists dwelt upon his eccentricities, quoted his fulminations against the Conservative Party when he was a Liberal and sought with impassioned oratory to expose the iniquities of this "wayward genius". Regarded as the principal impediment to Labour's progress, he became the target for almost every epithet in the English language.

When I entered Parliament in 1922, Churchill was not a Member. His sensational rejection by the electors of Dundee at the previous Election was hailed with unconcealed delight by the Labour Party throughout the country. This was the year in which a tremendous political transformation caused the return of the largest number of Labour Members of Parliament the House of Commons had ever known. Not less satisfactory was the defeat of Churchill, Labour's most dangerous opponent, and—there were few who would have dared to deny it—the most brilliant of them all. There were unprecedented scenes of enthusiasm at Election celebrations. Many thought that the day of revolution had arrived. "Give us another Election," they declared, "and we shall wipe both Conservatives and Liberals out of existence."

The Election of 1924 failed to bear out the promise of 1922. It was, for many of us, a tragic event. I lost my seat and did not return to Parliament until early in 1928. Meanwhile, Churchill, who had successfully fought Epping, had joined the Baldwin Government. His activities as Chancellor of the Exchequer and as the self-appointed defender of the Constitution during the General Strike served to embitter relations still further between him and the Labour Movement. He was accused of taking decisions that led to a sharp increase in unemployment, of raiding State funds in the interests of wealthy taxpayers, and of rejecting attempts to compromise in the General Strike, thus prolonging the dispute. Nor was his conduct as Editor of the official anti-strike paper, the *British Gazette*, calculated to enhance his reputation among the industrial workers. The mention of his name at Labour gatherings was the signal for derisive cheers; when a Labour speaker found himself short of arguments, he only had to say, "Down with Winston Churchill." This never failed to draw thunderous applause. Undoubtedly, he was our most valuable propaganda asset.

During Labour's second term of office—this time as the largest single Party in the House of Commons—Churchill seldom restrained his feelings. Nobody on the Front Opposition Bench assailed the Government with greater violence. His frequent bouts with Philip Snowden, Labour's Chancellor of the Exchequer, were the highlights of our debates. But Snowden, with his penetrating logic and vitriolic tongue, proved more than a match for the scintillating orator of the Tory Opposition.

It was otherwise with Ramsay MacDonald: he detested Churchill; his dislike of an opponent increased in the measure of the criticism directed against him. Churchill never ceased to jibe and sneer at MacDonald. One memorable passage sticks in my memory. After a reference to MacDonald's skill in falling without hurting himself he recalled a visit when a child to a circus which contained an exhibition of freaks and monstrosities. "The exhibit he most desired to see was the 'Boneless Wonder'. His parents objected to his taste in wishing to see such a revolting spectacle so he had to wait fifty years to see the 'Boneless Wonder' sitting on the Treasury Bench." This cruel jibe created considerable amusement on the Opposition Benches but caused MacDonald's followers to vent all their spleen on Churchill. The junior members of the Government, who were among MacDonald's ardent supporters, strained at the leash. They could not assail Churchill in the House—junior Ministers are only permitted to speak when instructed. They did, however, give full rein to their emotions in public about the man who was regarded as the Labour Party's most formidable opponent.

The economic crisis of 1931 brought further frustration. Our principal leaders, MacDonald and Snowden, had forsaken us and gone over to the enemy. Worse still, many of us lost our seats at the General Election when Conservatives and Liberals, with a few Labourists, combined against us. Once more we were thrust back into the wilderness.

I fully expected that Churchill would now become a member of the National Government. He had been the Labour Government's principal antagonist and had conspired to bring about its downfall. But while the ablest man in the Tory Party was placed on the shelf Baldwin appointed some of the stodgiest creatures that ever disgraced the Treasury Bench. No wonder Churchill regarded them with contempt.

Among his friends there was a general conviction that this was the twilight of his career, but the debates on the India Bill continued and some of Churchill's most powerful speeches were heard in Parliament —however unpalatable they were to those of us who rejected his imperialistic and reactionary opinions.

It was not until after the Election in 1935 that I made actual contact with Churchill. Once again I was on the Opposition Benches—this time as the Member for the Seaham Division. I had ousted my former Leader, MacDonald, in one of the most bitterly contested fights in the Election—and by a huge majority.

And then began that memorable series of speeches by Churchill where the case for rearmament was argued with a skill, lucidity and earnestness which, if it failed to convince the Labour benches, at least earned for the orator the admiration his qualities deserved. Among the Tories his advocacy of more adequate defence preparations, far from gaining unqualified support, created considerable confusion. Bitter exchanges ensued between Baldwin and his former Chancellor of the

Exchequer, while on the benches immediately behind Churchill sat a group of Tories who persistently interjected, treating his remarks with derision.

Churchill has often referred to differences in the Labour Party—no doubt with malicious intent. In turn, I have reminded him of his criticism of the Baldwin and Chamberlain Governments which angered all his colleagues, of the heated exchanges and of his long sojourn in the wilderness. It is no exaggeration to say that, while the Labour Party vehemently opposed him, they were more conscious of his gifts than many of those on his own side of the House. Here was this striking figure in our political life, this sparkling orator who had held the highest offices in the State, who presented his case with unquestionable sincerity, however misguided we regarded it—scorned by his former colleagues. One could, so it seemed to me, dispose quite easily of his arguments, yet his resolution, his marshalling of the facts and his industry, elevated him above his fellows, most of whom were political midgets in comparison.

How could Baldwin ignore Churchill's abilities in the sphere of defence by appointing Sir Thomas Inskip as the Minister for the Co-ordination of Defence, who yielded nothing but a weary collection of turgid utterances in our debates, and bored the House to such a degree that hardly anybody could be induced to stay and listen to him?

I must frankly admit that any admiration that I felt for Churchill seldom prevented me from indulging in sharp and no doubt irrelevant interjections, but these were inspired more by my anxiety to widen the cleavage in the Tory ranks than out of discourtesy. Often enough he gave me more than I had bargained for—but what of that? I was gaining experience in the Parliamentary cut-and-thrust of debate. Moreover it was his own technique. In Opposition, he maintained a constant stream of interjections, some audible and to the point, but often quite unintelligible.

What intrigued me above all else was the manner of his treatment by the Tory members. I have watched him, accompanied by a sole companion, walking broodingly through the corridors of the House, or conversing in the smoke-room with a few admirers like Brendan Bracken and Robert Boothby. But generally, Tory members gave him a wide berth.

Then we came to those fateful days when many of his predictions, far from being falsified, were justified in the event. The conflict broke upon us. Once again he was installed at the Admiralty. Two incidents come to my mind. While he was engaged in defending the Government against the general onslaught by members of all Parties, I interrupted him from the farthest seat on the top back bench. I had entered the Chamber during his speech. The Front Opposition Bench was full, so I made my way to the only seat available. My interjection caused him to pause in the argument and indulge in a slashing attack on the Member "skulking" and afraid to show himself. I was in no way abashed; by this time I was aware that the parliamentary rejoinder, however harsh, mattered less than ramming home the point. It was enough that I had ruffled him, upsetting his discourse; it was his own method—why not use it?

The second incident came not long after when I discovered how approachable he was. My interest in Merchant Shipping brought me into contact with the seafaring community, and I was asked to lead a deputation to the Admiralty on the arming of merchant vessels. He received us with the greatest cordiality, which I found distinctly embarrassing. This was heaping coals of fire on my head. I had expected a chilly atmosphere, instead of which he displayed the utmost charm. We had come to accuse him of neglect in the care of merchant seamen, but how can one rail against an opponent so pleasing and so responsive?

Churchill, while being a strong Party man, has a soft spot for coalitions, provided that he is at the head of the Government in power. He lost no time in forming such a Government in 1940 on the downfall of the Chamberlain administration. Attlee, the Leader of the Labour Party, with Greenwood, the Deputy Leader, were sent for and agreed to ask their colleagues in the Labour Party to join the Government. After the Labour Party Conference had accepted the recommendation of the leaders to join the Coalition, Churchill sent me a message to telephone him at Downing Street. He asked me to take over "the important post of looking after the Food Ministry in the House of Commons". Lord Woolton had been named as the Food Minister; he wanted me to take charge in the House. To his surprise, I declined the invitation. He expressed his regret and, in turn, I gave him the assurance that my anxiety for victory was equal to his own. I would cause him no embarrassment and would be glad to help in any way outside the Government. He thanked me and wished me well. Again in 1943 I was sounded on whether I cared to join as Minister of Fuel, but the ensuing discussion proved abortive.

Apart from a few dissentient voices, the British public were solidly behind Churchill in his efforts to bring victory to the Allies. This was recognized as a task transcending all others in importance. Despite the early reverses, and the obvious weakness of several of his Ministers, some of them appointed out of loyalty to old friends, he had reached a pedestal of popularity unprecedented in British history.

I was not among the dissenters. The war must be prosecuted with the utmost vigour; slackness in Government Departments must be ruthlessly eliminated; the loss of merchant vessels, which threatened to reduce the nation to starvation, the failure to produce a tank with striking-power comparable to those in the possession of the enemy, the stubborn attitude of the Prime Minister when proposals were made for the co-ordination of war transport, food and agriculture, with supply and production, provoked me into ceaseless criticism against the Government. More than one collision with the Prime Minister occurred when, with others in all Parties, I demanded that the Second Front be speedily organized. At first he showed his resentment, and indulged in sharp rejoinders at my expense. But persistence won in the end; he seemed to realize that this was not mere opposition designed to obstruct or weaken his administration, but was intended to be constructive and helpful. Harassed as he undoubtedly was, he succeeded in preserving a reasonably good temper during these exchanges, fighting back at us, with witty and sometimes caustic repartee, the members on the Government Benches roaring with laughter at our discomfiture.

Personal abuse of him, or taunts about his conduct of the war, provoked him into a torrent of vituperation in which he was more than a match for the critics. Towards those Members, who seemed to be less concerned about victory for the Allied Forces than they were about gaining notoriety, he vented all the force of his invective. He has a sneaking admiration for any Member who commands unusual debating ability, even when the argument is against him. One incident, in which I was involved, comes to my mind. It was during one of the darkest periods of the war. When everything was shrouded in gloom he delivered a massive oration on the course of the conflict. The House was profoundly impressed; it seemed that instead of suffering a reverse we had listened to a panegyric on victory. It was my task to follow him from the Front Opposition Bench and, in my speech, I used a familiar quotation by Macaulay on the younger Pitt.

"It may seem paradoxical to say that the incapacity which Pitt showed in all that related to the conduct of the war is, in some sense, the most decisive proof that he was a man of very extraordinary abilities. Assuredly, one tenth part of his errors and disasters would have been fatal to the power and influence of any Minister who had not possessed in the highest degree the talents of a Parliamentary leader. While his schemes were confounded, his predictions falsified, while the coalitions which he laboured to form were falling to pieces, his authority over the House of Commons was constantly becoming more and more absolute. If some great misfortune had spread dismay through the ranks of his majority, the dismay lasted only till he rose from the Treasury Bench, drew up his haughty head, stretched his arm with commanding gesture and poured forth in deep sonorous tones the lofty language of inexhaustible hope and inflexible resolution. Thus, through a long and calamitous period, every disaster that happened without the walls of Parliament was regularly followed by a triumph within them."

I asked him whether he recognized himself in that vivid and colourful description, at which there was loud laughter from all sides of the House. He enjoyed it as much as I did and showed no resentment at the implied criticism of his conduct.

Towards the end of the war criticism of the Government gained momentum. Victory was now dawning; the demand emerged for post-war reconstruction. Recollections of what had happened after the First World War fortified the activities of an all-Party Group who sought to extract from the Prime Minister assurances that plans were in course of preparation. It was strange that while in the tragic period of the war his popularity was undimmed, yet as the end drew near his prestige was less enhanced. Reconstruction became the principal topic of debate in the House. It was known that there existed dissensions in the Government. So under pressure the Prime Minister announced that a four-year plan was about to be promoted.

The appointment of Lord Woolton as Minister of Reconstruction was not too well received by the all-Party Group, who, by this time, were devoting their efforts to bringing pressure upon the Government. I recall a deputation which waited upon Woolton. It consisted of some of the younger Tories, a few Liberals and some members of my own Party. I was asked to act as spokesman. Woolton's response annoyed the deputation so much that a demand was made for his resignation. Churchill resisted this with his customary determination. It seemed to us that it was loyalty to a colleague rather than conviction which caused him to reject the proposal.

But from that time the Opposition in the House gathered strength. The attitude of the Prime Minister confirmed my opinion that with all his fine qualities as a war leader he never really appreciated the importance of domestic issues. The Opposition would have proved more formidable if it had not been for the esteem in which he was held by members of all Parties.

Churchill has always enjoyed knocking his opponents about, although he dislikes being subjected to similar treatment. To make fun at the expense of an opponent affords him the keenest satisfaction. He is a masterly exponent of the parliamentary art of evasion; when asked awkward questions he takes refuge either in silence or in a witticism, sometimes causing pain to the victim. Applause is essential to him; the approbation of his audience must be sought, if not by force of argument, then by resort to any other device, however unfair. In the present House of Commons he has seldom any anxiety on this score; the Tory claque can be invoked. It was otherwise when he was a lone figure speaking from the Bench below the Gangway with few supporters gathered around him. He resents abuse and vituperation, but nobody I have heard can use it with more devastating effect. When in this mood his words pour out in a torrent; he almost seems as if about to spring upon the enemy.

Yet how quickly the mood changes. One moment bristling with

anger, real or simulated, the next passing the incident off with a boyish grin, hugely delighted at being permitted to share in the fun, and marching out of the Chamber seeking the applause of his supporters, regardless of the jeers of his critics. I have witnessed the clownish spectacle of Churchill putting out his tongue at the Opposition Benches, thus showing his contempt, nor has he refrained from occasionally thumbing his nose at his assailants with a disdainful gesture that has convulsed the whole House.

Surely Churchill has run through the whole gamut of emotions: malicious, provocative and persuasive in turn, majestic one moment, the next displaying a capacity for rudeness which dismays his friends; resilient and stubborn, yet, it must be conceded, ready to show a kindliness towards an opponent that leaves one, at least momentarily, disarmed. Truly, with all his faults, a man of rare quality.

There is nothing static or rigid about him. I find him unpredictable. He will depart from his brief to lavish praise on a political opponent; then quite unexpectedly, and apparently without reason, he will turn upon the same person and smite him hip and thigh. During the war he paid me the most gracious compliments, but sometimes they were of the left-handed variety. "The Hon. Member," he said, "will never be a great Opposition leader because he cannot conceal his enthusiasm when we gain the victory." I have been the recipient of high praise from him which surprised the House, only to be accused of unpatriotic motives in advancing a proposition to which he took exception.

The Election results in 1945 undoubtedly shocked him; how could the electors treat him in this disgusting fashion? Apparently, dialectical displays, vicious assaults on members of the Labour Government, the constant defamation of Government policy, not only at home but abroad, together with his obvious appreciation when the Government found itself in trouble, consoled for his defeat. Now that he is again Prime Minister he has discovered that it is far easier to be destructive in Opposition than to resolve the manifold problems that beset modern society. He still talks as if solutions might be found more readily by an all-Party Government; yet loses no opportunity of discrediting the Labour Party. What he fails to understand is that in adjusting ourselves to the realities of the post-war world, old-fashioned ideas and policies are irrelevant. That he can remain unconscious of the need to inject

E

new ideas is incomprehensible. Perhaps it is difficult to teach an old dog new tricks? He has an unbounded confidence in himself. When he attacked the Labour Service Ministers for their alleged incompetency, I reminded him that during the war he had appointed as Secretary for War a Civil Servant; that when he formed his Government in 1951 it was a famous soldier he sent to the Ministry of Defence. Was this because he lacked confidence in his Tory colleagues? "But," as I have remarked elsewhere, "the Rt. Hon. Gentleman had no confidence in Baldwin or Chamberlain, nor does he seem to have much confidence in his friends on the Treasury Bench; the only person in whom he has any confidence is Winston Churchill."

I do my best to dislike Churchill; there is abundant reason why I should; indeed, as one of his political opponents, it is expected of me. His activities during the Labour Government's term of office from 1945 onward I found deplorable; his ideas are to me reactionary, he is out of touch with modern social trends. But he has served his country with the highest distinction; in moments of peril he was undaunted; in majestic phrases, which linger in the memory of those who heard them, he crystallized the resolution of the whole nation. Many blunders occurred in the war for which he must bear the responsibility; to me and to millions of our fellow countrymen his social ideas and activities are anathema. Yet, how can one work up an intense dislike for a man who has "borne the heat and burden of the day", whose abilities are unquestionable, even though directed into the wrong channels, and who concentrates in his person such varied and brilliant qualities?

CHURCHILL THE CANDIDATE

Rowland Arnison

Sir Winston Churchill has been Member of Parliament for Woodford (Essex) since it was formed in 1945 by the splitting of his old constituency, the Epping Division of Essex, into two Divisions. In this chapter Mr. Rowland Arnison, the Chairman of the Woodford Conservative Association, writes of Churchill as a Candidate. He has been assisted in the preparation of this section of the book by two other leading members of the Association, Alderman Donald L. Forbes (Mayor of Wanstead and Woodford) and Mr. A. E. Healey, both of whom have also taken prominent parts in Churchill's election campaigns.

NO man knows more about fighting a parliamentary election than Sir Winston Churchill, for there is no man living who has been a candidate as often as he has. He has fought in every General Election—and in several by-elections—since he first stood for Oldham in a by-election in 1899 and was soundly defeated. It certainly was without exaggeration that he could write in one of his brilliant essays—"If you want to know about elections I am the person to tell you."

His Oldham defeat was quickly avenged when he won the seat in the "Khaki Election" of 1900 and since then he has stood as a candidate in N.W. Manchester, Dundee, West Leicester, the Abbey Division of Westminster, the Epping Division of Essex and, finally, its southern portion, the Woodford Division.

It was after his defeats at Dundee, Leicester and Westminster that he came to our constituency in 1924. The man primarily responsible for inviting Churchill to be our candidate was Sir James Hawkey, Bt., my predecessor as Chairman of the local Conservative Association. Sir James acted as his personal representative in the constituency, supervised the minutest detail of every election campaign and remained, until he died in 1952, his champion and loyal, personal friend.

Many people might assume that Sir Winston Churchill's eminence as a world statesman makes his parliamentary election automatic, but although, of course, it is now unthinkable that the electors of Woodford would ever reject him, we never take his victory for granted. We are anxious for him to pile up as big a majority as possible and each campaign is planned with the utmost care not only by the members of the local Conservative organization but also by Churchill himself. All the workers in the constituency know that their candidate insists on the highest level of efficiency. One instance of this is the formation of a "contingency reserve" in the election expenses budget so that a last minute message can be circulated to the electorate.

The Election Address, always one of the most vital factors in a campaign, is written personally by Churchill, and revised time and again until he is satisfied that it is not only word perfect but conveys in the clearest, most vigorous manner his message to the voters. The revisions to the Election Address go on until the last possible minute and its final form is usually decided on at a late-night conference with the printers standing by waiting anxiously to set up the completed copy and produce it in accordance with a carefully arranged schedule.

But important as the Election Address is, the keystone to a successful campaign, in Churchill's view, is a complete door-to-door canvas. Throughout an election he follows this part of the fight with close attention. At the end of each day's work he studies a full account of the day's canvassing together with the cumulative totals, and as the result of these reports he frequently gives amended instructions to his Election Agent.

Once Churchill has satisfied himself that his organization is running efficiently and he has met the workers chosen to staff his Central Committee Rooms, he is content to rely on their ability to conduct the various stages of the campaign and does not interfere in detail.

Churchill has always displayed plenty of independence in his political career and never more so as a candidate than during the ten years from 1929, when he was outside the influence of the Conservative Party Central Office. During that period he was free to write his own election propaganda of all kinds. Even now that he is leader of the Party he still uses in his own constituency only that part of the Central Office propaganda which he considers particularly applicable to the Division. This is especially the case in the display of poster material. He is a firm believer in posters and insists on as wide a show as possible.

No candidate anywhere in the country enjoys his election meetings more than Churchill. He is always ready with his devastating wit to silence hecklers and would-be wreckers. When he has to address more than one meeting in an evening, a schedule which involves the use of supporting speakers, he always insists on the other man finishing his speech after the applause which has greeted his own entrance has subsided.

CHURCHILL THE CANDIDATE

Churchill, campaigning in the 1951 General Election which
returned him to power, speaks at an open-air meeting in his
constituency, the Woodford Division of Essex. His wife
is on his left

At these election meetings, many people in the audience have wondered what is contained in the large dispatch-box which invariably appears on the platform with Churchill. The secret is a very simple one. This dispatch-box, which he has had with him on many historic occasions, is specially designed to raise his notes to a convenient eye level—just an example of his attention to detail. In recent years the notes of his bigger election speeches have been a complete draft of what he is going to say—a necessary arrangement in view of the great measure of importance attached to all his public utterances.

Churchill does not attempt to hide his notes. On the contrary, he has, somewhere in his writings, advised young orators that if they use notes they should not be ashamed of them. Rather should they employ them as a sort of weapon to be flourished in the face of the audience if necessary as a method of giving emphasis to a point.

No one knows better than Sir Winston the great value of the Press and the publicity it can give to a candidate, but nowadays he finds it disturbing when photographers flash off their lamps while he is developing the main theme of a speech. Fortunately most Press photographers know this and respect his feelings in the matter.

At the end of a meeting, Churchill likes to have the first verse of "Land of Hope and Glory" sung before the National Anthem.

During an election campaign Churchill receives a big correspondence and innumerable good-luck souvenirs from well-wishers in all parts of the country. He appreciates these friendly gestures. The souvenirs are displayed for his inspection and everything is carefully listed so that acknowledgments and thanks can be sent after the election.

Just before Polling Day Churchill tours the district in an open car from which he can address meetings at many points in the constituency. We prepare routes and times with care but our schedules are invariably disorganized by the candidate himself as his mounting and infectious enthusiasm leads him to make many more stops and many more speeches than we plan. At almost any stop, too, he will single out small children for his special attention. His car is invariably followed by a great motor cavalcade consisting not, as many people seem to think, of his supporters but rather of representatives of the world's Press.

On Polling Day Churchill is in action from very early in the morning. He demands a summarized report of polling progress taken at two-hourly intervals. He also makes a tour of his Committee Rooms, where he expects his helpers to be at work and not forming reception committees in honour of his visit. During recent elections he has characteristically worn in his coat a "V" sign made of white heather. While his tour is in progress an endless stream of telegrams arrive, all of which have to be listed so that he may read them on his return. When the polling booths are closed and the count is being made, Churchill displays great restlessness and even though the canvass returns have predicted a substantial majority he watches with close attention the mounting stacks of voting papers divided between himself and his opponents. When the count is finished and the Returning Officer is completing formalities, Churchill chats with the scrutineers, the counters and all the other officials present. In past years nothing gave Churchill greater pleasure than to go, after the declaration of the result, to the house of Sir James Hawkey and from the balcony offer his thanks to the workers who had helped him to victory. This little ceremony, unhappily, will be no more and there will be many besides Sir Winston who will miss it.

Soon after the election Churchill insists that a letter of thanks be sent to all who have assisted in his victorious campaign, and these letters are far from being a mere formality. He takes a sincere interest in his workers and is truly grateful to them for their efforts.

As a candidate, Churchill is undoubtedly exacting and requires untiring efforts from those around him, but in all his career—even when he was out of favour with the electorate—he has never lacked willing helpers. His impish sense of humour, which is never far below the surface, makes it a real pleasure as well as an honour to work for him.

And finally, but of tremendous importance to Churchill as a candidate, is—Lady Churchill. As President of the Woodford Conservative Association she naturally takes a close interest in all constituency matters, but her most important role is at election time, when she plays a personal part in every phase of the campaign. In recent years Churchill has travelled the country to speak in support of other candidates and during his absences on these tours his wife has held the fort in Woodford. There is no doubt that she is a tower of strength to her husband then—as at all other times.

Many meetings in our Division finish up with a call for three cheers for Churchill, whereupon he will come forward and with his broadest smile will call for another one—for his wife. And it makes him very happy when that cheer is loudest of all.

CHURCHILL AND THE NAVY

Admiral Sir William M. James, G.C.B.

No man has a more intimate knowledge and understanding of the great effect of Churchill's influence on the Royal Navy than Admiral Sir William James. At the time of their first meeting, more than forty years ago, Churchill was First Lord and James First Lieutenant of the Home Fleet Flagship. In the Second World War Churchill was Prime Minister and Minister of Defence and Admiral James was Commander-in-Chief, Portsmouth, till October 1942, and afterwards Chief of Naval Information, and Member of Parliament for North Portsmouth. He was Director of the Royal Naval Staff College in 1925 and 1926, Naval Assistant First Sea Lord in 1928, Chief of Staff Home and Mediterranean Fleets 1929–30, Commanding Battle Cruiser Squadron 1932–34, and Deputy Chief of the Naval Staff 1935–38. He has written extensively on naval matters and his books include The British Navy in Adversity, Admiral Sir William Fisher, The British Navies in the Second World War *and biographies of Nelson and St. Vincent.*

IN the autumn of 1912 the Home Fleet, of seventeen dreadnoughts, was at its base at Portland. I was Gunnery Lieutenant of the Fleet Flagship, and when my Captain told me that the First Lord of the Admiralty, Winston Churchill, would be visiting the Fleet in a few days and intended to come to sea with us to watch a night firing, I looked forward eagerly to meeting the most provocative figure in public life.

But my interest was not shared by all my messmates. Though the Navy was then taking advantage of every new invention to increase its battle-power, it was at heart a conservative service, accustomed to a First Lord who had sufficient knowledge to present the Naval Estimates in Parliament but who abided by the advice of his professional colleagues on all technical matters, on strategy and on training.

Now, if rumour was true, the Board of Admiralty was presided over by a First Lord who exercised his prerogative for the appointment of senior officers and was extremely inquisitive about every naval activity, ashore and afloat.

Had he not rescued Beatty from retirement and appointed him his Naval Secretary, to the discomfiture of his naval colleagues; had he not forced on a reluctant Navy this new-fangled staff, a necessity in the Army but calculated to undermine the authority of the Admirals?

His curiosity about the service for which he was responsible seemed to many of the older officers almost indecent. They had no intention of putting themselves out when he came on board.

After the night firing was completed, I invited our visitor to the wardroom. It was now past midnight and we found only a sprinkling of officers who had been concerned with the night firing. We sat down by the fire and Churchill began to pepper me with questions about our system of control and what steps we were taking to improve the performance of the guns and searchlights. The wardroom gradually filled, and soon a large circle of officers was listening intently to the discussion, into which Churchill soon drew many of those who had hitherto avoided him.

Next morning I accused one elderly officer of having got out of bed and dressed when he heard that the First Lord was in the wardroom, and he did not deny the charge.

From that day the officers of the Fleet Flagship rejoiced that the affairs of the Navy, which, unless there was a great change of heart in Germany, would ere long be steaming to its war bases, were in the hands of Churchill.

Unbeknown to them their faith was already justified, as, by a brilliant stroke, he had assured adequate oil supplies for the Navy, whose mobility was now entirely dependent on oil. He had appointed a Royal Commission to examine the oil position. The proceedings were conducted in secret, but the result was the conclusion of a long-term contract between the British Government and the Persian Oil Company. Of Churchill's part Lord Greenway, the President of the Anglo-Persian Oil Company, wrote:

> "The credit of carrying through these extraordinarily favourable contracts is, of course, entirely due to him. . . . From the point of view of the Navy, it was a great feat of statesmanship for which the country should always be grateful."

Though the officers of the Fleet did not know at the time what was passing in Whitehall during those fateful weeks of July 1914, they had no doubt who was responsible for the measures that resulted in the Fleet being fully mobilized and at its war stations by August 4.

There had, that summer, been a test mobilization instead of the unusual manœuvres, and instead of the fleets dispersing to their ports on July 18 Churchill and the First Sea Lord, Prince Louis of Battenberg, cancelled the leave that was to follow the dispersal, and kept the reserve ships in commission and ordered the Home Fleet to concentrate at Portland.

On July 28 Churchill, on his own initiative and without Cabinet sanction, ordered the Fleet to its war stations, and on August 1, notwithstanding Cabinet decision to the contrary, he ordered complete mobilization and without the Royal Proclamation that should have been signed.

Next morning the Cabinet gave its formal assent to this unconstitutional procedure. The Navy's faith in their First Lord was being more than justified.

In the sailing era the First Lord was often a distinguished Admiral and, as there was then no staff, he conducted the strategy himself and issued orders to the fleets, but now there was Churchill's newly created staff and a machinery for controlling the movements of the numerous squadrons, flotillas and units deployed in the five oceans. Though a First Lord would be responsible to Parliament for the sins and omissions of his naval colleagues, it was not expected that he would interfere with the dispositions and instructions approved by them.

But this passive role did not suit Churchill, who had accumulated much knowledge about maritime war and the ways of ships on the sea, and if more attention had been paid to his strategical insight, at least two blunders, involving heavy loss of life, would have been avoided.

The three cruisers *Aboukir, Hogue* and *Cressy,* patrolling the Broad Fourteens and exposed to submarine attack, were sunk on September 22; on September 18 Churchill had written this minute:

"These cruisers ought not to continue on this beat. The risk to such ships is not justified by any services they can render."

On November 1 Cradock's squadron was sunk off Coronel on the West coast of South America by a far more powerful German squadron; on October 12 Churchill had minuted a telegram from Cradock giving the latest news of the German squadron and his own dispositions.

"In these circumstances it would be best for the British ships to keep within supporting distance of one another, whether in the Straits or near the Falklands, and to postpone the cruise along the West coast until the present uncertainty about the *Scharnhorst* and *Gneisenau* is cleared up."

Since the outbreak of war agitation against every one of German descent had been rising, and in October Prince Louis of Battenberg, First Sea Lord, resigned, and Churchill invited Lord Fisher to return to the Admiralty. Fisher had retired in 1910 after five years as First Sea Lord, during which he had carried through a vast programme of naval reforms against much hostile criticism.

Churchill had championed him against his critics, and had kept in touch with him since taking office as First Lord. Though Fisher was now seventy-three, the old fires were still burning brightly and there could not have been a stronger combination for a war of movement, a war in which strategical talent could be given play.

If there was any doubt about the smooth working of this formidable combination, it was whether Fisher would maintain his hostile attitude towards the staff system which Churchill had created, and whether he would try to exclude the First Lord from any direct part in the conduct of the sea-war.

Fisher had written in 1909, when he was First Sea Lord:

> "Wilson and I have talked a lot about our War Plan for the Navy. You know he told the Defence Committee that only he and I knew of the War Plan, which is quite true. He would sooner die than disclose it. God bless Sir Arthur Wilson!"

and his views on a staff were epitomized in "A Naval War Staff is an excellent organization for cutting out and arranging foreign newspaper clippings."

Wilson, Fisher's successor as First Sea Lord, was on leave when the Agadir crisis occurred, and a search of his room for the War Plan was fruitless; it was believed that it was in his pocket.

A few weeks after Churchill was installed at the Admiralty, Lord Haldane wrote to his mother:

> "Winston and Ll.G. dined with me last night and we had a very useful talk. Winston is full of enthusiasm about the Admiralty, and just as keen as I am on the war staff,"

but Churchill bided his time until Wilson retired, and then he went into action.

However much Fisher disliked sharing with the First Lord the responsibility for all orders sent out to the Fleet, and the new staff of naval officers, he was wise enough to accept the position, and we know

CHURCHILL AND THE NAVY

Centre of a 1914 controversy—Prince Louis of Battenberg, the First
Sea Lord, crosses Horse Guards Parade with Churchill, then the
First Lord of the Admiralty

that they worked in complete accord until a question of major strategy split them apart.

Fisher had not been many hours in his old room at the Admiralty before every department felt his presence. With the backing of the First Lord he at once put in hand a great building programme of special vessels for an amphibious operation in the Baltic and despatched two battle cruisers to the South Atlantic to bring von Spee's squadron to battle.

This was a colleague after Churchill's heart, and if the sea-war had remained fluid the master stroke that revenged the loss of Cradock's squadron would no doubt have been repeated in other waters, but the pattern of the war was inevitably becoming the same as it had been for the last three centuries.

In that familiar pattern the smaller warships protecting the trading vessels cruised under the wing of the main fleet, based so that it could contain the enemy main fleet, which would not put to sea until the pressure of blockade became unbearable.

This enforced inaction, which would only be relieved by an occasional bustle if the German high-speed ships attempted tip-and-run raids on our coast or shipping, was irksome to a man of Churchill's temperament, and even before the return of Fisher he had seriously contemplated seeking a new and more active outlet for his energy and experience.

Captain Richmond, then in Operations Division, wrote in his diary on October 24:

> "Last night, at 8 o'clock, when I was on my way upstairs to dress for dinner, a telephone message came from Churchill asking me to dine. He was in low spirits, oppressed with the impossibility of *doing* anything. The attitude of waiting, threatened all the time by submarines, unable to strike back at their fleet, which lies behind the dock-gates of the Canal, Emden, or Wilhelmshaven, and the inability of the Staff to make any suggestions seem to bother him. I have not seen him so despondent before."

But Richmond had to admit that he could suggest "nothing serious".

So at the end of October, shortly after returning from Antwerp, where by Sir Ian Hamilton's account he had "handled the Naval Division as if he were Napoleon and they were the Old Guard, flinging them right into the enemy's opening jaws", he asked the Prime Minister to relieve him of his office and permit him to seek a military command. Asquith entered an account of the interview in his diary. . . .

> "Having, as he says, tasted blood these last few days, he is beginning like a tiger to rave for more and begs that sooner or later, and the sooner the better, he may be relieved of his present office and put in some kind of military command. I told him that he could not be spared from the Admiralty. He scoffed at that, alleging that the naval part of the business is practically over as our superiority will grow greater and greater every month."

Incidentally, the impartial verdict in the official history on the effort to save Antwerp by the despatch of the Naval Division, which was entirely Churchill's idea, begins: "The British effort to save Antwerp had failed. Nevertheless it had a lasting influence on the operations."

In view of what happened later Churchill's opinion that the naval war was practically over may seem to indicate a lack of vision, but at that time no one foresaw the immense expansion of the German submarine fleet and the threat to our survival by a powerful and sustained submarine offensive.

Two months later there came an opportunity for a more active role for the Navy which Churchill was quick to seize. On January 2, 1915, Russia asked for a demonstration against the Turks to relieve the pressure on their forces in the Caucasus, and Kitchener wrote to Churchill that the only place that a demonstration might have some effect would be the Dardanelles.

Thus was set in movement an operation that was to bring down both the Titans at the Admiralty.

Churchill brought all his driving-power to bear on this operation which would strike at the point where the Central Powers were weakest and break the deadlock on the Western Front.

Fisher, too, supported the plan of opening up the Dardanelles and Bosphorus by a sudden strike, but later on when it became clear that the political situation in the Balkans and the available military force invalidated any prospect of success by a *coup de main*, he withdrew his support on the grounds that long and costly operations would ruin his plan for an offensive campaign in Northern waters. But this was a plan for the distant future and here, in Churchill's view, was a heaven-sent opportunity to turn the tide of war to flow in our favour.

Fisher carried his opposition to the point of resignation, and when he resigned, confidence in the Government, already sapped, broke, and a Coalition Government was formed.

The Conservatives in the new Government were unrelenting in their opposition to Churchill's remaining at the Admiralty, and though Balfour tried to overcome their opposition and Lloyd George fought to retain him in the Cabinet as Secretary of State for India, Asquith would go no further than offer him Chancellor of the Duchy of Lancaster.

The loss of the two men to whom the Navy owed its readiness for war seemed at the time to be a tragedy, and to be suddenly deprived of any control of events at such a critical moment in history must have been Churchill's most bitter experience, but Fisher was aging and losing grasp and, after the evacuation of the Dardanelles, Churchill would have once again had to endure inaction, enforced by the unalterable pattern of the sea-war.

After the abandonment of the Dardanelles operation, the maritime war offered fewer and fewer opportunities for enterprise; the sole objects became the maintenance of the Grand Fleet at adequate strength to meet the High Seas Fleet and the progressive building up of the defence of the trade-routes.

In this latter task, which was at a later stage to prove so difficult to achieve as to nearly land us in disaster, Churchill's driving-power and vision would no doubt have fortified and inspired the efforts of the ship-builders and scientists and his buoyancy would have dispelled the gloomy forebodings during what were called the black months, but I do not think that this was a field in which his full powers would have had as wide play as they did at the Ministry of Munitions.

Eight years passed before Churchill was again deeply involved in the business of the Navy, and now his role was reversed. Instead of driving forward a great ship-building programme, his task, as

Chancellor in a Government committed to reduce expenditure on armaments to a minimum, was to fight the Admiralty inch by inch for every penny of their estimates.

In this contest, which had followed every maritime war in the past, he encountered a worthy Admiralty champion in his old friend Beatty. On becoming Chancellor, he had written to Beatty:

"I am one of your greatest admirers, and I never cease to proclaim you as an inheritor of the grand tradition of Nelson. How I wish I could have guided events a little better and a little longer. Jutland would have had a different ring if the plans already formed in my mind after the Dogger Bank for securing you the chief command, had grown to their natural fruition. I live a good deal in those tremendous days."

In May 1917, when Beatty was seriously disturbed by the Admiralty's defensive attitude and lack of enterprise, he wrote:

"There is not a man that I know of who could go to the Admiralty and put it right, not one, unless it's Winston."

In these contests the Government, whose responsibility it is to keep under constant review the international stresses, must have the last word, but irreconcilable differences had in the past often perpetrated a crisis, and it was fortunate that, now, both protagonists greatly admired and respected their opponent's qualities.

At the height of the controversy Beatty was able to write:

"Yesterday I was vigorously engaged with Winston and I think on the whole got the better of him. I must say, although I had to say some pretty strong things, he never bears any malice and was good-humoured throughout the engagement."

Churchill's unrelenting efforts to cut the Naval Estimates below what the Admiralty held to be the irreducible minimum raised doubts whether the once-powerful advocate of sea-power had lost his faith in the "sure shield", but that was unjust, and how unjust was clear a few years later when he was fighting a lone battle against unilateral disarmament and appeasement, when, as he put it, our life was flowing placidly downstream.

The London Naval Treaty in which we abandoned our justifiable claim to have more trade-route protection ships than the other maritime powers who were not dependent on sea-borne imports, and agreed to unwelcome provisions governing future construction because the Government would not support the Admiralty to the point of any straining of relations with the other powers, aroused all Churchill's fears for our inability to gain command of the seas in the event of another war.

In the Commons he said:

> "What a disastrous instrument it (The Treaty of London) has been, fettering the unique naval knowledge we possess, and forcing us to spend our money on building wrong or undesirable ships; and condemning us to send out into deep waters and sink vessels like the four *Iron Dukes*, which would have been invaluable for convoying fleets of merchant ships to and from Australia and New Zealand in the teeth of hostile cruisers."

He was later to describe the Anglo-German Naval Agreement as "the acme of gullibility".

Though he held no office during the years between the Government's decision to rearm the nation and the outbreak of war, from 1936 onwards he was in constant touch with Admiralty affairs and took full advantage of opportunities to discuss naval matters freely with naval officers at the Admiralty.

In the hot dispute on the future of the Fleet Air Arm, he came out in strong support of the Admiralty contention that the aeroplane was as integral a Fleet weapon as the gun and torpedo, and that the existing dual control was hampering development.

The decision to mount 14-inch guns instead of 16-inch guns in the new battleships caused him grave concern, but after considerable correspondence with the First Lord and many discussions with the Sea Lords, he reluctantly agreed that, in view of the steadily mounting threat from Germany, we could not afford the delay involved in mounting the larger guns in the five battleships under construction.

So when, on September 5, 1939, he took charge of the Admiralty for the second time, he was familiar with all the preparations for a German war.

I have described the attitude of many naval officers to the First Lord in 1912; now there was only one attitude, and the Admiralty, in sending out a general signal "Winston is back", correctly interpreted the feelings of the Navy afloat.

It was a different Admiralty from that which he had left in "pain and sorrow" a quarter of a century earlier; the seed he had sown had grown into a large plant and there were now Planning and Operations Divisions, manned by officers who had studied war and been working on War Plans for several years, plans for a war in which for the first time in history there would be no great fleets glaring at one another across the narrow seas and moving majestically into battle, but instead encounters between high-speed vessels whose freedom would be severely restricted by the aeroplane, and the certainty that the enemy would exploit to the full the power of the submarine to harass our ocean life-lines, now more important to us than ever before.

When Churchill took office the operational orders to start up the convoy system, to establish patrols and to arrest German shipping, had been despatched, so he at once set to work on a project, not in the War Plan, of gaining the mastery of the Baltic so as to free Scandinavia from the menace of invasion and influence Russian policy and strategy. For this purpose he proposed to convert some older battleships for service in narrow waters, by giving them large anti-torpedo bulges, stronger armoured decks and many anti-aircraft guns.

He won the support of his naval colleagues but, in January, reluctantly had to abandon the project because the material for conversion was not forthcoming and the German air attack on ships was proving far more severe than had been anticipated. But he never could be content with the passive policy of Convoy and Blockade, and during his seven months at the Admiralty he was always seeking a means of striking at the enemy.

On September 19 he brought to the notice of the Cabinet the importance of stopping the flow of iron ore from Narvik to Germany by laying minefields to compel the German ships to leave territorial waters and lay themselves open to attack, but he was not able to overcome his colleagues' hesitation to infringe Norway's neutrality until April.

In November he prepared a plan for mining the Rhine with fluvial mines in retaliation for the indiscriminate laying of magnetic mines in our harbour approaches. Five months later the mines were ready, but the French Government objected on the grounds that such aggressive action would draw reprisals on France.

When Reynaud succeeded Daladier as Prime Minister, he agreed to the operation, but it was now too late as France was about to collapse.

Though these projects, all calculated to impair seriously the German war effort, were never implemented, I have given them prominence because they do illustrate Churchill's remarkable grasp of sea-warfare. This grasp can be seen in the numerous minutes he wrote on such matters as forming Units of Search to hunt down German warships and raiders in the oceans, on the design of ships to combat the sub-marines, on the laying of a Northern Mine Barrage between Scotland and Norway, on the influence of the German air attack on the freedom of the Main Fleet, on modifying the convoy system to increase the flow of sea-borne trade.

He also, and with great advantage, influenced the ship-building policy. On arrival at the Admiralty he withheld approval for the construction of new cruisers as we were now free of Treaty restrictions and could build more powerful vessels capable of fighting the new German 8-inch cruisers; a few days later he suspended work on battleships that could not be ready before the end of 1941, so that work could be concentrated on ships already well advanced. At a later date he pressed for a reduction in the size of destroyers, whose tonnage had been progressively mounting for some years past.

Despite his unflagging interest in the day-to-day conduct of the war and in long-distance planning, he found time to inquire into the welfare of the personnel. On his initiative a theatre and cinema ship was fitted out as "an important adjunct of naval life at Scapa". He suggested a routine that would give the hard-pressed destroyer crews more rest; and he cancelled the rule obliging a court martial when ships were damaged as it damped the ardour of the officers.

He found time, too, to visit the Home Ports and the Fleet at Scapa.

His visits to Portsmouth, where I was in command, were of incalculable benefit. His energy was remarkable, he seemed quite tireless, and long before he had seen all he wished to see, his companions, Beaverbrook or Harry Hopkins, had given up the struggle to keep up with him. He left us all, sailors and dockyardmen, more than ever determined not to flag.

As the French Navy was fighting with our Navy, it was necessary to co-ordinate their efforts, and Churchill crossed to France to confer with Admiral Darlan. He took with him an offer to fit every French anti-submarine vessel with Asdics and a request that the French would step-up the completion of all ships that could fight the submarines, and also the new battleship *Richelieu*.

Darlan agreed to this request and also to proposals for the disposition of French ships in the Atlantic.

The profit-and-loss account on the trade-routes was about evenly balanced during the first months; against the loss of the *Courageous*, *Royal Oak* and *Rawalpindi* we could place the conquest of the magnetic mine, and the sinking of the *Graf Spee* as well as the release of her prisoners in the *Altmark*, an episode that sent a thrill through the country, and which was the result of this minute by Churchill:

> "On the position as reported to me this morning, it would seem that the cruiser and destroyers should sweep northward during the day up the coast of Norway, not hesitating to arrest *Altmark* in territorial waters should she be found. The ship is violating neutrality in carrying British prisoners of war to Germany. Surely another cruiser should be sent to rummage the Skagerrack to-night? The *Altmark* must be regarded as an invaluable trophy."

The Twilight War ended on April 8 with the German invasion of Norway. The sinking of the destroyer *Glowworm* on that day was the first of a series of battles in Norwegian waters, during which our ships experienced the full blast of air attack.

Churchill could no longer devote all his attention to the Navy because four days earlier he had been asked by the Prime Minister to preside over the Military Co-ordination Committee and had thus become responsible for co-ordinating the operations of all three services, though without power of effective direction, and now all three services were to combine in an effort to check the German advance.

This is not the place to give an account of the Norwegian campaign, for which no well-considered War Plan had been made, and which was to a great extent conducted separately by the three services without guidance or direction from the Prime Minister or an effective representative of supreme executive power. Wider powers were given to Churchill in May, but by then the enemy, executing a long-prepared plan, had forced our troops out of Southern Norway. The bright spot in this tale of frustration and defeat was that though we lost an aircraft-carrier, two cruisers, a sloop and nine destroyers, and many ships were disabled but repairable, the Germans were left with only one large cruiser, two light cruisers and four destroyers fit for immediate service.

The disasters of the Norwegian campaign precipitated a Government crisis and on May 10 Churchill left the Admiralty to become Prime Minister and, what was more important to the Navy, also Minister of Defence.

If, in any previous war, the First Lord had become Prime Minister, he would not have attempted, nor would it have been necessary for him, to keep close touch with the conduct of the sea-war, but now the conditions were entirely different.

Churchill was now responsible for the over-all conduct of a global war, which could only be won if the three services combined to effect a landing in Europe and destroy the enemy armies.

It was Pitt, the greatest War Minister before Churchill, who first realized the importance of amphibious operations to an island power; now our future depended on our ability to mount and conduct amphibious operations on a vast scale, and to this task Churchill brought his wide knowledge of ships and sea-warfare.

Though the first great landing in Africa did not take place until November 1942, he had given instructions for designs of landing-craft to be prepared in July 1940 and had urged Roosevelt to commence building tank-landing craft in July 1941.

Shouldering such tremendous burdens he could no longer be so closely associated with the day-to-day business of the Admiralty, but

he had not been long in office before he had brought immense relie⌃
to the Admiralty by two masterstrokes.

When France collapsed, the future of the powerful French Navy
became a matter of grave concern to us, because if it was seized and
operated by the Germans, we would be hard put to it to protect our
vital sea-communications.

Darlan assured Churchill that he would never let the French Navy
fall into German hands, but he would not, as Churchill requested, order
the ships to a British or French or Colonial harbour. In a letter to
Churchill, shortly before he was assassinated, Darlan gave as his reason
that if the ships sailed the Germans would occupy all France and
North Africa.

By the terms of the Armistice the French Fleet was to be
demobilized and pass under German control, and with the promise
that it would not be used in the war. A promise by Hitler was not
worth the paper it was written on, and so Churchill took what he
called the "hateful decision" to seize all French ships at our Home
Ports and Alexandria and sink those lying at Oran if the Admiral would
not proceed to a French West Indian Port. To Vice-Admiral Somerville,
commanding the force for Oran, he sent this message:

> "You are charged with one of the most disagreeable and diffi-
> cult tasks that a British Admiral has ever been faced with, but we
> have complete confidence in you and rely on you to carry it out
> relentlessly."

And so the Admiralty were freed to make their plans without the
possibility of a sudden accession of strength to the German and
Italian fleets.

The other masterstroke, obtaining the loan of fifty destroyers from
the American Navy, brought even greater relief to the Admiralty, who,
owing to very heavy losses in the Channel and on the trade-routes,
were pitifully short of escort vessels to meet the steadily mounting
submarine attack.

Though, during the early years of his Premiership, Churchill must
have spent many hours looking at the flags and discs on the maps of
North Africa, Greece and Crete, his thoughts can never have been far

away from the Atlantic, because it was there that the war would be lost unless their domination could be wrested from the German submarines.

In March 1941 he said to the First Sea Lord, Sir Dudley Pound: "We have got to lift this business to the highest plane, over everything else. I am going to proclaim the 'Battle of the Atlantic'."

Six months earlier he had overcome Admiralty resistance to establishing a Western Approaches command at Liverpool, a measure that was already proving its value, and now he threw all the weight of his authority and driving-powers into building up an adequate defence against the submarines.

For the next two years the fierce struggle was waged between the submarines, whose tactics and weapons were continually improving, and the escort and hunting vessels and aircraft, whose powers of destruction were also progressively increased, and always, behind every endeavour of the ship-builder, scientist and seaman was the understanding, the imagination and the buoyancy of the Defence Minister.

It was in April 1943 that something like a miracle happened. Up to the end of March there was a real danger of the enemy severing our sea-lines of communication, but after that the defence forces slowly but steadily acquired dominance over the U-boats.

As the menace faded Churchill was able to turn to the great amphibious operation against Sicily, for which nearly 3,000 vessels of many types had been assembled, and to the mounting of the still greater operation planned to land a large army on the Normandy coast, and which would require over 5,000 vessels. The task of finding all these ships was not made easier by the heavy losses on the Russian Convoy route and the large number of ships required to guard the convoys, but Churchill, despite Stalin's ingratitude and brusqueness, would not break his promise to help the Russians to our utmost ability.

I have not found it easy to write this digest of Churchill's work for the Navy because he was at the helm during the most critical years in our history, when every day brought some new and perplexing problem. If I was asked to name his most notable contributions to our victory at sea in the two wars, they would be the Oil Agreement that secured our fuel for the first war, the measures that ensured the readiness of the Fleet for that war, the decision to immobilize the French Fleet and the reinforcement of our dwindling destroyer force by fifty American destroyers in the second war; but by far his greatest contribution was his inspiring leadership, which was felt on every bridge and lower deck; his driving power, which was such a powerful support to his naval colleagues; and his vision, which informed all the long-distance planning.

CHURCHILL THE AIRMAN

Air Chief Marshal Sir Philip Joubert de la Ferté,
K.C.B., C.M.G., D.S.O.

*Sir Winston Churchill has maintained a close association with
the growth and development of flying—both civil and military—
since those early years when a cross-country "hop" of a few miles
was a hazardous adventure to the trans-ocean jet flights of the
present day. He has piloted a 'plane, travelled many thousands of
miles as a passenger and, as Secretary of State for War and Air
Minister, borne political responsibility for British aviation.*

*Air Chief Marshal Joubert, the author of this chapter, has held
many high posts in the Royal Air Force, and while in the Air
Ministry and as Officer Commanding-in-Chief of R.A.F. Coastal
Command was frequently in contact with the Prime Minister
during the critical war years 1940 to 1943.*

WHEN Churchill went to the Admiralty as First Lord in 1911 he was soon brought into contact with that small band of adventurous naval officers who were the pioneers of naval flying. As a result of this experience he resolved to develop and extend the air arm and in particular the naval air service by every means in his power. He was given ample opportunity to carry out this intention, since, except for the year 1916, he was in control of one or the other branch of the air arm during the first eleven years of their existence.

At the Admiralty from 1911 to 1915 he was responsible for the creation and development of the Royal Naval Air Service; from July 1917 to the end of the war, while he was at the Ministry of Munitions, he was in charge of the design, manufacture, and supply of all kinds of aircraft and air material needed for the war. During the later years of the Kaiser War he was the prime mover in the political discussions that resulted in the appointment of the Smuts Committee, which recommended the formation of the Royal Air Force from the R.N.A.S. and R.F.C. From 1919 to 1921 he was Air Minister as well as Secretary of State for War. In a sense this dual role was a disadvantage to the Royal Air Force, and if another Minister had been in this position the results might have been unfortunate. But with his immense energy and industry Churchill found time, not only to direct the fortunes of the War Office, but those of the Air Ministry as well. His dual loyalty did not lead him into the error of accepting the War Office theory (stoutly supported by the Admiralty) that now the war was over the air arm should once more be divided between the two older services.

Thus it fell to his lot to have witnessed, and to a considerable extent have shaped, the whole of this new arm, which was destined to revolutionize war by land and sea, and to play an ever-increasing part in our national defence.

To a man of Churchill's temperament the fact that some men had learned to fly was a challenge to his enterprise and courage. He was fascinated by the idea of flying, but he admits that side by side with desire was also a dread of going into the air for the first time, and it was probably some months after he met the pioneer airmen of the Royal Navy that he made his first flight. There had already been several accidents and he felt a very keen sympathy with the young officers who were risking their lives. In addition to his personal interest in the art he realized that it would be a stimulus to progress generally if he, as First Lord, participated to some extent. So, early in 1913, he commenced instruction with the late Commander Spenser Grey and subsequently with Lieutenant Jack Sedden, R.N., and resigned himself to what was in those days at once a novel and a thrilling experience.

Jack Sedden describes with feeling one most exciting flight with Churchill. He says: "I well remember a flight that Churchill made with me when I and G. V. Fowler, each in our own seaplane, both Short 100's, flew Churchill and his secretary, Edward Marsh, from Gravesend to Grain. This flight was made against a strong south-easterly or easterly wind in rapidly deteriorating weather. In fact the wind almost reached gale force before we got to Grain. Indeed, after landing Churchill safely, my seaplane 'took off' again, landing trolley and all, over the sea wall as it was being brought up the slipway, and was more or less wrecked. G. V. Fowler, with Marsh, flew high to avoid the bumps. If my memory serves me he took nearly three hours for the sixteen or so miles from Gravesend, whilst I, by keeping within a few feet of the river surface, was only about forty-five minutes. It was so rough that if I had been my own passenger I should have been quite seasick—or airsick if you prefer it. Churchill was a much better sailor than I was and never mentioned it."

At this time the Royal Navy possessed perhaps a dozen aircraft and a similar number of pilots whose skill was in proportion to their experience, which was not very extensive. The aircraft were frail, and the engines unreliable, while each manœuvre in the air had to be worked out by trial and error. A serious error usually had fatal consequences, so that progress was slow.

A new vocabulary was being coined to describe the equipment and its usage, and Churchill claims to have invented the terms "seaplane"

CHURCHILL THE AIRMAN

A memory of the early days of flying. Churchill
arrives at Portsmouth by air in June 1914

and "flight", the latter representing a given number of aircraft—usually four.

At first he was astonished by what is now a commonplace of flying: the absence of vertigo or dizziness produced by flying at height. The explanation of this phenomenon seems to be that there is nothing to guide the eye of the aviator from his aircraft to the ground, and without this aid to perspective height has little meaning. He also realized that his expectation of life was not a good insurance risk and, like most people with a vivid imagination, conjured up gruesome pictures of a possible crash.

In spite of these fears he continued to fly on every possible occasion, becoming a very fair pilot once he was in the air, but more than uncertain in his take-off and landing. His instructors usually took over the controls to make the final approach and touch-down. Of all the pilots he flew with he seems to have been most impressed by Gustav Hamel, the world-famous monoplane pilot of the early years.

Churchill's description of Hamel's mastery of the controls of his aircraft likens him to "the most perfect skater on the rink, but the skating was through three dimensions and all the curves and changes were faultless, not by rote or rule, but by native instinct. As for the grim force of gravity—it was his slave. In all his flying there was no sense of struggle with difficulties or effort at a complicated feat; everything happened as it could not have happened in any other way. . . ."

As his knowledge of flying increased, Churchill's apprehensions of the hazards of the art became more acute. He observed the minor damage that followed almost every flight with a sharply observant eye, and his sympathy for those engaged professionally in the business became deeper. At the same time he was vividly conscious of the changes which aviation was to bring to almost every human activity in peace and war, a consciousness that was to be made more vivid by the threat of war in 1914. His experiences in actual operations in France, though perforce confined to the ground, were to enhance still more his appreciation of air power.

He had little time to fly while he was First Lord during the war, but as Minister of Munitions in 1917–18 he had to be alternately on each side of the Channel, and he usually travelled by air, landing at the

F

nearest point on the front to the place where he had to meet someone or where he wished to witness particular operations.

His pilot in these days was a young officer who had been very severely wounded at Gallipoli and on the Somme, with the result that he could not endure shellfire. He was not worried by any other form of danger, and as a pilot he was exceptionally skilful.

At this time, the crucial years of the Kaiser War, all the best machines were, of course, needed for the Front, and few mechanics could be spared for non-operational aircraft. Returning by air from General Headquarters one afternoon to London, where he had an important engagement, Churchill was imperilled twice by engine failure at most awkward moments. The first time was over the Channel, when a valve broke. Only 2,000 feet up and five miles out from the French shore, and with a failing engine the aircraft lost height quickly. It was a dull afternoon and the grey Channel lay below. If the engine did not pick up again, a forced landing in the sea was inevitable. Usually the Channel is crowded with traffic, but as always happens at a critical moment, not a steamer, not a trawler, not a fishing-smack could be seen. In those days flotation jackets and rubber dinghies had not yet been devised, and the pilot threw up his hands in a despairing gesture. For a long minute, extinction seemed certain. It was impossible to keep afloat in thick clothes and heavy boots, but suddenly the engine began to cough and splutter again, picking up enough power to enable the pilot to swing the aeroplane back towards the coast of France, and after ten anxious minutes to pass over the headland of Gris Nez. The aerodrome of Marquise was reached with about a hundred feet of height to spare.

The resources of Marquise soon provided another aeroplane of uncertain quality and once again Churchill and his pilot took off with about an hour of daylight in which to cross the Channel. The wind was against them and the engine pulling poorly. Forty minutes later they reached the English shore, but shortly afterwards there was another engine failure which led to a repetition on the part of the pilot of these gestures which indicated that they had no choice but to descend. Side-slipping artistically between two tall elms and just avoiding the branches on either side, the pilot made a beautiful landing in a small field.

Churchill, like so many other air passengers before and since, missed his engagement in town.

During the time he combined the roles of Secretary of State for War and Air Minister, Churchill flew very frequently. His work took him much abroad, particularly during the Paris Peace Conference. His pilot on almost every occasion was Group-Captain Scott, who at the time was also his Private Secretary. Jack Scott, badly injured in an air crash in the early part of the war, was an exceptionally fine pilot in whom Churchill had great confidence. Many of these journeys were accomplished uneventfully and with the speed and convenience attendant on successful air travel. But occasionally things went wrong, as when low clouds and mist made the passage most hazardous. Jack Scott's knowledge of bad weather pilotage saved the situation on several occasions, but there were anxious minutes when the freezing breath of fear must have chilled their nostrils. Nothing is more terrifying than flying below low cloud, surrounded by mist-enshrouded hills and without certain knowledge of the aircraft's position. The situation is made worse if an earlier attempt to climb over the bad weather has failed and the glide down to clear air has been made with the expectation that at any moment the ground will be found before visibility returns. This was Churchill's experience on at least one occasion. He also met that other terror of the air—fire on board. There again Jack Scott was master of the situation and put out the flames before disaster could ensue.

The event which may have finally extinguished Churchill's ambition to become a qualified pilot (though not his ardour for flying in general) occurred in the summer of 1919. Again flying with Jack Scott, he took off from Croydon for a local flight. Scott handed over the controls and at first all went well. But most unfortunately, the pupil pilot allowed the aircraft to stall on a turn low down and only by the utmost good fortune did the subsequent crash not result in a fatality. Scott broke both his legs, but Churchill escaped with a severe bruising. After this sad affair he confined himself to the administrative and policy aspects of aviation, though he continued to use aircraft as a means of transport on every occasion where urgency justified their employment.

One of the major problems of Imperial Defence with which

Churchill was concerned when he was Chancellor of the Exchequer was that which was very hotly debated between the Army and the Royal Air Force. In 1925 the decision was taken to create a major naval base in Singapore and a large sum was voted for its defence. The discussion turned upon the manner in which this money was to be spent. The Army was in favour of a static defence of fifteen-inch guns, capable, in its opinion, of holding at bay any Japanese naval attack. The Air Force was firmly of the opinion that air forces provided a much more flexible method of achieving security, holding that torpedo bombers were a major threat to enemy war vessels; could be used as bombers in land operations and, if Singapore was not threatened, could be sent to reinforce other parts of the Empire that might be under attack. Churchill's interest, as Chancellor of the Exchequer, was to see that the money he had provided was put to the best use, and with his feelings of sympathy for the proper application of air power he may have been disappointed when the Cabinet verdict went in favour of the Army's proposals. His disappointment must have been heightened in 1942 when Singapore fell largely on account of a lack of air resources. The fifteen-inch guns played no part in the defence of the island since they could only fire out to sea, and the attack came overland, something that might have been thought of even in 1925.

Churchill was also concerned in the crippling "Ten-year Rule" which was laid down by the Cabinet in 1919. This rule required that the Service departments should frame their Estimates on the assumption that the British Empire would not be engaged in a major war for ten years. During his period as Chancellor of the Exchequer, in 1928, the ten-year rule was reaffirmed and advanced on a day-to-day basis, provision being made for annual reconsideration. Under this rule any long-term programme of re-equipment and expansion put forward by a Service department, such as was envisaged by the R.A.F. in 1922, could always be cut down by the Treasury. Thus the projected force of fifty-two squadrons approved in 1923 was only partially complete in 1934. But Churchill became a private citizen in 1929, a full ten years before the outbreak of war. From his political wilderness, as the danger grew, he cried out in vain against the follies of successive pacific or lethargic Governments.

In spite of his exile he contrived to maintain touch with the heart of affairs. His journeys abroad and his friends at home enabled him to keep his finger on the pulse of national and international life. There are amusing stories about his contacts at this time, but from them all emerge his intense energy, his amazing grasp of world politics and his far-sighted judgment. He was very active in the sphere of aeronautics. Through the medium of the Hendon Air Display, the various record-breaking flights from England to Australia and else-where, and the development of the Schneider Trophy racing aircraft his interest and influence were felt.

At last, in 1939, he found himself once again in a position of authority. As First Lord of the Admiralty in Chamberlain's war-time Government he could resume his share of moulding and developing the air services. But at first the vast problem of the protection of our sea communications occupied all his powers. The U-boat, the mine, the low-flying bomber and the surface raider were all taking toll of our merchant shipping. Gradually he found time for questions more closely related to the air. Always ready to listen to the ideas of inventors, he selected a few projects for development. Those that affected the Royal Air Force most were certain gliding weapons, aerial mine-fields as a defence against night bombers, and rockets as an easily produced form of anti-aircraft weapon. The then Professor Lindemann —now Lord Cherwell—was instructed to watch these developments, with orders to apply the utmost pressure to the Service department concerned and to make regular progress reports. Few of these schemes came into effective use, with the exception of the rocket, which, though it was not a very good anti-aircraft weapon at this date, was extensively employed when carried in aircraft against land and sea targets—a complete reversal of intention.

On the operational side he supported very strongly the Admiralty claim that part of the bomber force should always be available to strike at the German Fleet when it put out to sea, and that a big effort should also be made to drop mines in German coastal waters and harbours. This alternative proved in the end to be much the more effective form of employment for the bomber force. High-level bombing of a moving target, even with the best of bombsights, was an unrewarding task, and very unpopular with the air-crews. During the winter of 1939–40 merchant-ship losses due to the operations of German bombers and mine-layers became so serious that Churchill used his utmost endeavours to promote the success of newer forms of radar, so that both by day and by night our fighters could intercept and destroy the enemy. Equipment was still in the design stage, but one remarkable feat of improvisation that went a long way to protect our shipping was the establishment by a band of high-level scientists working as labourers of a low-level radar chain all along our east coast in a matter of weeks. From this improvised equipment the successful ground-to-air Interception Unit, which did so much to bring German night bombers to account, was subsequently developed.

It was at this time that my work brought me increasingly into contact with Churchill. As there was no operational command open to me then I had been put in charge of the development of Radar and Radio-Countermeasures, as well as other unusual types of weapons such as gliding bombs and torpedoes. In these developments Churchill, as I have said, took a profound interest, and perhaps three times a week his scientific adviser, Professor Lindemann, was in my office discussing the progress being made by the R.A.F. and the scientists. From time to time I was sent over to the Admiralty to make a statement and once or twice to advise against some project which did not meet with the approval of the Air Council. Later in the spring of 1940 I was given an additional task at the Admiralty as adviser on combined operations. In carrying out my duties I met Churchill very frequently and one sunny spring morning stands out in my memory. The First Sea Lord, Sir Dudley Pound, had summoned me to the Admiralty and, as I joined him, down the passage came Churchill, resplendent in a silk robe (it would be impertinence to refer to it as a dressing-gown) and smoking the inevitable cigar. There was always something heartening in his aspect—unusual certainly, but so cheerful and confident that he cleared away the feelings of depression which affected most of us after reading the over night reports of sinkings and disasters.

It was about this time that I had a head-on collision with him over the planning of the Norwegian campaign. He appreciated to the full the need to seize an airfield in Norway and he intended to capture Trondjheim and its resources, naval and air, by a *coup-de-main*. The Chiefs of Staff, however, did not agree with his scheme and I was one of the planners detailed to produce an alternative, which was finally accepted as offering a prospect of success. Unfortunately, after a preliminary landing against light opposition the second phase of the operation was altered in response to an urgent appeal from outside, with very unhappy results. Rather naturally, I and my colleagues received the brunt of Churchill's displeasure.

It was not, however, until he became Prime Minister that Churchill exercised a really profound influence over the fate of the air services. One of his first acts was to separate the production side of the Air Ministry from the operational. He formed the Ministry of Aircraft Production and put Lord Beaverbrook in charge. At this time an orderly—perhaps rather pedestrian—plan of production was in force, giving considerable priority to the building of the heavy four-engined bombers that were to be the war-winning weapon of the R.A.F. There were, however, a number of shortages, particularly on the radio and radar side, from which the Service was suffering, and the new Minister set about the task of putting matters right with his usual daemonic energy.

Meanwhile events in Europe were moving to a climax. Holland, Belgium and France had been invaded and Churchill constantly flew across the Channel to consult with his French colleagues. His biggest problem at this time was to decide whether to accept or deny the French argument that the only way to restore the military situation was to bring every British fighter aircraft over to France and drive the German Air Force out of the sky and destroy the panzers on the ground. Fortunately for civilization, he listened to the advice of Lord Dowding, who said in effect:

"The French radar chain has been overrun; we have already lost the equivalent of some ten fighter squadrons in France without really influencing the battle; we shall lose the rest if we try to operate them without any early warning system and from unequipped airfields."

After the evacuation from Dunkirk, during which the R.A.F. suffered further important losses, Churchill was faced with the grave threat of an impending invasion by an immensely powerful enemy, against whom the Fleet was hampered by the dangers of dive-bombers, submarines and mines, with an Army that had lost most of its heavy equipment and an Air Force that was reduced in numbers if not in efficiency. So far as the air forces were concerned his first step was to instruct Lord Beaverbrook that fighter aircraft were to have absolute priority. He was convinced that, following his usual plan, the enemy would attempt to achieve air superiority before launching his seaborne invasion. If the Luftwaffe could be held or defeated there was every chance of escaping the horrors of land invasion. Lord Beaverbrook took his instructions very literally. The orderly plan of production conceived by the Air Ministry was, to all intents and purposes, scrapped—and the efforts of the aircraft industry were, in the main, devoted to fighter production. Thus our bomber offensive received a set-back from which it did not recover for some time—but the delay was fully justified. Hardly by any other method could the Hurricanes and Spitfires with their necessary equipment have been produced in time. It was not only the aircraft industry that was thus called into play, but literally thousands of garages and workshops were mobilized as a reserve repair organization. They dealt with minor damage to spare parts and engine overhauls.

Before the war broke out Churchill had been made an honorary Air Commodore in the R.A.F., and as the battle for command of the skies of Britain grew in intensity it became noticeable that he was to be seen in the corridors of the Air Ministry in his uniform. The Service took pride in this indication that the Prime Minister was identifying himself more closely with its activities. He was most welcome too when on his frequent visits to No. 11 Group Headquarters he took a lively interest in the movements of the Luftwaffe and the counter-moves of the R.A.F. As September 1940 drew to its close and the day battle in the air was won, so the night attack on London and our large cities increased in intensity. But though the Prime Minister was profoundly moved by the destruction and loss of life, yet it is clear that he never relinquished the idea of the counter-attack as the best method of defence. He was active in promoting a number of protective measures, but his real interest was in the development of the bomber force and in the perfection of its technique. At this time (1940) the night attack on German industry and military objectives was the sole method by which Britain could bring any real pressure upon the enemy; and from the

Prime Minister's personal point of view, only the minimum effort should be put into defence. Everything that detracted from bomber production and bomber armament was examined microscopically and unless absolutely vital was ruthlessly cut.

In following this policy the Prime Minister faced a singular dilemma. As Chairman of the Anti-U-boat Committee his desire would be, apart from building more destroyers, sloops, frigates and escort carriers, to strengthen the air forces engaged in tracking down and destroying enemy submarines. But the type of aircraft most suitable for this latter purpose was also, in the main, very useful to Bomber Command. The special equipment that could detect submarines at night or in bad weather was also needed by Bomber Command as a blind bombsight. Thus there was an acute conflict of priorities between Bomber and Coastal Commands, and having regard to the Prime Minister's predilection in favour of offensive measures, it was a foregone conclusion that Coastal Command would be second on the list. Very reluctantly, and by slow degrees, Coastal Command was furnished with a proportion of the aircraft it required. But until British aircraft production reached its height and supplies of all sorts from America began to flood into Britain, this conflict of interest continued. Scientists who had been working with the utmost industry to fit Coastal aircraft with a satisfactory submarine detector, only to have it given to Bomber Command as a radio bombsight, took a very gloomy view of the heavy shipping losses which they felt might have been avoided if the equipment had been put to its original purpose. Since the Battle of the Atlantic was won it is clear that Churchill's judgment on the respective needs of the two Commands was correct. But at times "it was a close-run thing", as when 800,000 tons of shipping were lost in a month.

Another of Churchill's preoccupations which had a big influence on air operations was the constant threat to our sea power that was offered by the presence of large enemy naval units in Brest, the Baltic ports, and on the Norwegian coast. A considerable effort was made each day by the Photo Reconnaissance Squadrons to establish the whereabouts of these units, so much so that one squadron produced as its Christmas card a picture of a lonely Spitfire flying over a grim Norwegian fiord, with the caption "Never have so many flown so far for so little".

F*

In the end, of course, this threat was removed by combined air and naval action. *Gneisenau* was wrecked by a mine or mines laid from the air, *Tirpitz* was sunk by Bomber Command, and *Scharnhorst* destroyed off the North Cape by the Royal Navy. But before this happened the R.A.F. and the Fleet Air Arm had suffered heavily, and there had been a diversion of air effort from other targets which represented a serious loss to the offensive against the German homeland.

A major part of Churchill's war policy was the provision of every possible material aid to Russia, and one means of achieving this end was the convoy system between the U.S.A., Britain and North Russia. Air support of these convoys was the responsibility of Coastal Command, but not until a balanced force of reconnaissance, torpedo bomber and anti-submarine aircraft had been established in the Murmansk-Archangel area did this support become effective. The Russians were most reluctant to allow any intrusion into their territory, and it was a major diplomatic success for Churchill's Government when they finally agreed to accept our aircraft within their boundaries. From then onwards the convoys suffered little loss.

Churchill also concerned himself with the development of special types of bombs, such as those that breached the Mohne Dam and sank *Tirpitz*. He was deeply interested too in special air operations directed towards the planting of spies and equipping resistance movements in the occupied countries. His conception of "eccentric" warfare as opposed to the frontal attack alone had obsessed him since the days when he had planned to force the Dardanelles during the early part of the Kaiser War. Aircraft offered opportunities of turning an enemy's flank or disrupting his communications which were most attractive. Thus a large number of sorties were made almost daily from our east-coast airfields with these ends in view, and under the Prime Minister's direct inspiration.

Though the conditions of the 1939-45 war restricted Churchill's flying activities he covered a vast distance. He crossed the Atlantic by sea to meet President Roosevelt and settle the terms of the Atlantic Charter. On three further occasions he travelled to Washington for conferences of supreme importance. Once he visited Quebec, where the outlines of the Far East campaign were decided. His trip to Moscow involved an enormous mileage—U.K., Gibraltar, Cairo, El Alamein,

Teheran and then North-west to Moscow was the route followed, almost entirely by air. From the U.K. he flew to Casablanca and then to Cairo, Adana, Cyprus, Tripoli and Algiers. Again he flew to Cairo and Teheran, after which, on his return journey, he fell ill and had to rest at Carthage and Marrakesh. After D-Day he insisted on visiting the beach-heads and then did an air tour of the liberated areas. During this tour he flew as a passenger in a captured German aircraft—a Fiesler-Storch. Later he flew to the Italian front and toured the South of France Invasion Coast by sea.

For the second Quebec conference he travelled by sea, but to Moscow for the second time he went by air. Greece was visited by air at the end of 1944 and Paris and Belgium in January 1945. In March he flew to Belgium, Holland and the Rhine, and finally in July to Bordeaux and Potsdam in a R.A.F. Skymaster. For a man of his age, to carry out these long and exhausting trips is proof of his amazing vitality and personal courage. Thus, in a period of some thirty-five years, Sir Winston Churchill has, by his personal example, his wisdom, and his vision, profoundly influenced the development and operation of the air services in a manner for which the British nation and the world at large must be deeply grateful.

CHURCHILL THE JOURNALIST

Colin Coote

Colin Coote is Managing Editor of the Daily Telegraph, *a newspaper to which Churchill contributed many articles between the two great wars and which also serialized his history of the Second World War.*

THE difficulty in writing about Sir Winston Churchill as a journalist is that he is not a journalist. It is true, as he himself tells, that he decided to abandon a military career for journalism and politics. It is true that he has been a war correspondent; that he has written great numbers of brilliant articles; that he even spent a less brilliant ten days as something like Editor of the *British Gazette*. But politics have been his primary concern and interest. Journalism to him has been a parergon—or by-product—like painting, though always more of a handmaiden to politics than painting could ever be. In short, he is a free-lance—the word has a suggestion of the audacious and the chevaleresque most appropriate to his writing. It means, of course, one who has no regular attachment to any paper, but supplies articles on demand or on approval. Churchill is certainly the King of the free-lances, but he is not a professional.

In former days the "free-lance" had his sphere, and a very important one, in journalism. He filled quite a large portion of the then unlimited space. Today, only the cream of the free-lances can survive. If a free-lance is a specialist he can, from time to time, get into print on his speciality. But those who can still get into print on anything at any time are extremely rare. Sir Winston Churchill is, of course, one of these select survivals. He could at any time make a *living* as a free-lance. But he will *live* as a statesman and as a historian.

He has himself expressed a preference for being at the making and not at the receiving end of news; and his preference has been very fully accorded to him. But the jobs of being at the receiving end, of sifting out the damned stuff, of making it fit, of deciding what to give and where to give it, of keeping his head during the last bad quarter of an hour on the "stone"—all the dull, merciless, exasperating work that goes into the appearance of a newspaper on our breakfast tables—this he has been spared. I do not suppose that in his whole life one word he has written has ever been blue-pencilled except by himself and by Lord Cromer, who, I believe, revised the early chapters of *The River War*. A proconsul is an unusual sub-editor. I do not suppose that Churchill has ever written against time. We professionals, of course, can be heartily grateful that he did not make journalism his career, for otherwise one of us would not hold the job he does.

Among the foibles of human nature are certain ingrained ideas. Everybody thought they could poke a fire, when there were fires to poke. Everybody thinks they can write. On this latter point, nearly everybody is wrong; but Sir Winston Churchill is right. He can write, whether shortly or at length; and he knows apparently by instinct certain refinements of the art which most journalists have painfully to acquire. Not perhaps altogether by instinct. He himself acknowledges a debt to the late G. W. Steevens, whom he met on the way home from the Omdurman campaign—and Steevens was a Balliol man. A cross between the *Daily Mail* and Gibbon proved fertile, and produced thus early copy which even a modern sub-editor would cut with regret. But it would be unjust to say that either the style or the ideas were borrowed. What really gave his writing its own particular hall-mark was its zest. "Twenty to twenty-five—those are the years!" he wrote much later. They were then, much more than now, the years of spring, of punch, of sublime confidence that life was and would be a ripe piece of fun.

Churchill's literary career began with an engagement in 1895 to write reports for the *Daily Graphic* when he went on a visit to the Spanish authorities engaged in combating a revolt in Cuba. During the trip he came under fire for the first time; but as his period in the field was only three days his output was not voluminous. His first real "assignment" was with the Malakand Field Force in 1897, where he was what we should call the "accredited war correspondent" first of a local Allahabad newspaper and then of the London *Daily Telegraph*.

What I personally find so remarkable about Churchill's writing is that he does not write. He dictates, and revises the results. This spacious method few, if any, professional journalists could employ. I wish they could, for it is singularly successful. Personally the *mot juste* never trips off my tongue; and the most I can hope is that it sometimes leaks from my pen. But it bubbles out of Churchill, sometimes with the roar of a

Niagara, sometimes with the agreeable tinkle of a Highland burn. This facility does not, however, lead to carelessness. Any editor whose paper has had the good fortune to print Churchill's work knows that it is polished and re-polished until anticipation of delivery is replaced by apprehension of non-delivery. But it arrives in time; for Sir Winston has an admirable sense of the virtue of punctuality.

War correspondents have suffered many vicissitudes since they were invented. From august figures, as immortalized by Kipling in *The Light That Failed*, they sank to intolerable nuisances when the military discovered the disadvantages of publicity; and have now, I think, risen to tolerated and often respected camp-followers. But when Churchill started, they were fighting as well as writing men—not unnaturally, since Churchill himself was a subaltern of the 4th Hussars on leave. The experience taught him that the pen was mightier than the sword in at least one respect—it brought in more cash, particularly when supported by an enormous vocabulary and the *Dictionary of Quotations*. I do not say for a moment that he has ever echoed Dr. Johnson's snort that "nobody but a fool ever wrote anything except for money". On the contrary, he has always intrinsically enjoyed writing ever since he found he could do it. But Mr. Micawber's arithmetic is also sound; and it is an attraction to writing if the pen brings in those balancing pence which make the difference between happiness and misery.

This does not mean that any publication can, or ever could, get an article from Churchill for pence. He is no blackleg; and no hack. During the period when he was writing more articles than at any other, that is to say while he was out of office in the 'thirties, he was in the free-lance's paradise. For not only could he get the rate for a quality job, but also he could choose his topic. Nobody writing for his living can be indifferent to the rate, but it was notorious that Churchill was even more insistent about the topic. Indeed, when he was concentrating on some topic, such as German rearmament, he would not write on any other. Both the fact and the fee were barked down the 'phone to inquisitive editors, only some of whom had the sense to boggle at neither.

The interesting thing about his first book (for he was one of the first to create the journalist's habit of tailoring his articles into a volume) is that it contains examples of every style of journalism from what is known as "fine writing" (i.e. more adjectives than facts) to "factual reporting" (i.e. more facts than adjectives). He was compared to Napier; and what could be fairer than that—except possibly King-lake?

After all, even Ruskin argued that the high emotions evoked by war had produced the greatest art; and it must not be forgotten that Churchill not only shared in the experiences about which he wrote but also has a highly emotional side to his temperament. Any journalist worth his salt will go through any trouble or danger to get a good story for his paper, and in this respect I feel bound to modify my remark that Churchill is not a journalist. For nothing could be more wholly in the traditions of the profession than his exclamation during the battle of the armoured train at Estcourt, when he was again serving as a war correspondent. "Keep cool, men! This will be interesting for my paper!" This paper was the *Morning Post*, which had the good sense to commission him both for the Omdurman campaign and for the Boer War.

After he won office in 1906 there were fifteen years of almost unbroken literary silence—partly, of course, because during some of them it was far more important to get the Fleet ready than to keep Fleet Street sweet. But during those years Churchill kept his hand in by writing a tremendous lot of speeches and a tremendous lot of memoranda about his own, and others', jobs. They will be found in the contemporary Press, which then had ample room for verbatim reports, or in *Hansard*, or in that really immense literary triumph recounting the background, course, and aftermath of the First World War published under the title of *The World Crisis*. If the reader studies them, he will see how remarkably Churchill avoids the pitfalls which wait the journalist–politician in both his incarnations.

I can best illustrate the inhibitions of the journalist turned politician by recording the confession of a friend of mine, belonging to that category, that he was quite incapable of making a speech longer than a leading article. Churchill found no difficulty in exceeding such a length. The traps awaiting the politician turned journalist are different. There can be few editors to whom large numbers of undelivered speeches are not submitted in the form of articles. My colleagues will therefore understand me when I say that a good speech seldom makes a good article. The *bon mot* which evokes roars from an audience is often stale, flat, and unprofitable in print. A speech can have a rotundity which, in an article, appears an insincerity. Sparkling impromptus become *non sequiturs*. Churchill's writing did not suffer from his speeches, any more than his speeches suffered from his writing— possibly because he wrote his speeches and spoke his writings.

I now approach his solitary experience of editorship. When the organizers of the General Strike attempted to close down the Press (and did succeed in reducing newspapers to a broadsheet), the *British Gazette* was born from the machines of the *Morning Post*, and Churchill was its wet nurse.

This incursion into professional journalism[1] is, of course, no test of Churchill's journalistic qualities. It occurred when Constitutional Government was fighting for its life, and the atmosphere was not conducive to that balance and objectivity for which the better organs of the British Press are distinguished. War-time communiqués are not usually remarkable for their literary or ethical qualities—at least they were not until Churchill himself made them so by insisting, during the Second World War, that the people should be told the truth, however black. Moreover, you cannot improvise a great newspaper any more than you can breed a racehorse out of a mule. There must be some pride of ancestry and hope of posterity. The *British Gazette* had neither.

During the period when he was out of office, from 1929 to 1939, Churchill wrote a great deal for the papers, though he was by no means unoccupied politically and historically. Indeed the versatility and volume of his output are extraordinary. It may well be asked, for example, how between 1945 and 1951 he could lead the Opposition, make a series of tremendous speeches abroad (such as those at Fulton and Zürich), and produce about a million words of his account of the Second World War. The answer lies in Churchill's method of life and of work. Another point in which he approximates to the professional journalist is that he keeps queer hours. The journalist has to copy the habit of working late, though he cannot copy the tropical habit of the siesta in which Churchill indulges and which enables him to compress

[1] EDITOR'S NOTE: Dealt with more fully in the next chapter, "Churchill the Editor" by Beric Holt, a member of the *British Gazette* staff.

the best part of two working days into twenty-four hours. The habit has classical authority. Herodotus records how a Pharaoh was told by his soothsayers that he had only seven years to live. He replied, "That be d——d for a yarn," or words to that effect, and crammed fourteen years into seven by making nights into days—without abandoning the days.

Churchill also has a number of expert amanuenses, who collect and collate material. If, however, they hope to see anything they write in the form in which they wrote it, they are doomed to disappointment. The text which appears is invariably and wholly Churchill's own.

I know of one case where someone was asked to "devil" for an article on the Philippine Islands and produced an essay in the style of Carlyle, of which that master would have been proud. But Churchill was not proud of it and hardly a comma survived.

The system favours an exceptionally large output. Neither siesta nor satellites would, however, avail to make the output good were there not behind them a prodigious memory and a mental activity like a dynamo. "He has," said the late President Roosevelt, "a hundred ideas a day, of which at least four are good." Moreover, he does not forget what he has read; and since he has now read a lot he is a walking reference library—a fact which saves an incredible amount of time.

It is the easiest thing in the world—any competent journalist can do it—to imitate anybody's style. It is much more difficult to evolve a style of one's own. I think Churchill has done so, in spite of the tendency of commentators to trace all his gems to Gibbon or Macaulay. He conforms to his own dictum that the structure of the English sentence is a noble thing. So, indeed, it is, particularly when, to adapt Bryce, much writing is neither noble, nor English, nor a sentence. The essence of prose, as of verse, is rhythm; and the theory is, at least, interesting that the rhythm should vary with the theme. It can roll, or it can ring. It can fascinate, or it can stab. Take two sentences from Churchill:

"The morning had been golden, the noontide was bronze, and the evening lead; but all were solid and each was polished till it shone after its fashion."

That is from an essay on Lord Curzon. Not only does it summarize the man's whole career and character in its sentiments, but the swing of it reflects the man—proconsular, meticulous, bombastic, pitiful, frustrated.

"Three times is a lot." This is the end of the account of the Battle of Jutland—of pages and pages of judicial, objective exposition of a complicated naval engagement leading up to a summary of the three occasions upon which Jellicoe missed a chance of destroying the German Fleet. The verdict is then given in those five words, monosyllabic, schoolboyish, and shattering.

There are certain tricks or features in his style which make it pretty easy to detect Churchilliana. For example, he has his favourite adjectives; "squalid, sombre, austere, unflinching" are some of them. He also has the trick of hitting off a character in a string of adjectives —generally four of them—like brush-strokes in a picture, "lively, sparkling, insurgent, compulsive" hits off the late Joseph Chamberlain; "furious, luxurious, privileged, acquisitive" General Maregin; "austere, severe, accomplished, tireless" sums up Field Marshal Montgomery; "inexorable, irresistible, benignant" describes the onward roll of Anglo-American relations.

Indeed, even if Sir Winston Churchill does not rank as a professional journalist, he is equipped with all the qualifications to be one. A journalist must have as many tones in his writing as a cathedral organ. Let me list some of them. There is the "vox humana", vulgarly known as "sob-stuff". If it is badly played it is sickly and sickening. It must, so to say, come from the heart, not from the stomach; but when it does come from the right organ, it pierces the soul. Take this passage:

> "Death came very easily to her. She had lived such an innocent and loving life of service to others, and held such a simple faith, that she had no fears at all and did not seem to mind very much."

The reference is to his childhood's nurse, Mrs. Everest.

Then there is invective—Demosthenes' *Philippics*, Cicero's *In Verrem*, Zola's *"J'accuse"*, and Churchill, shall I say?, on the 1936 Government: "They are decided only to be undecided, resolved to be irresolute, adamant for drift, all-powerful for impotence."

To be able to distinguish between sentiment and sentimentality, and between invective and vulgar abuse, is not the whole armoury of the journalist—nor of Churchill. There is also, for example, humour, which covers a multitude of forms and of sins. Churchill's humour often verges on invective, as when he writes that Marlborough and Eugene rated the "absence" of the Margrave of Baden from a battle-field as "well worth 15,000 men". Sometimes, it takes the form of a sudden vulgarism, such as "Some chicken! Some neck!" when commenting on the French view in 1940 that England would have "her neck wrung like a chicken". It is never—at least in public—broad. It takes the form rather of the sudden quip than the sustained jest. The remarkable thing about it is that it nearly always comes off. I say this is remarkable because, in my experience, nothing is so hazardous as the "light touch". It may be as light as Ariel or as heavy as Caliban. Probably the most humorous thing that was ever said about humour was Bergson's definition of it as caused by "repetition, inversion, or the reciprocal interference of series". Quite so, no doubt.

Whatever else the journalist can do without, he cannot do without background; and background is a compound of experience and technical accomplishments. I do not mean by the latter such things as shorthand or typewriting—if they were indispensable, Sir Winston would be low on the list. I mean such accomplishments as knowledge of languages and of literature. Churchill's knowledge of languages is far greater than you would suspect from his habit of anglicizing all foreign words. His memory makes good any gaps in his knowledge of literature. As for the greater partner in background—experience— there are few who more fully fulfil the prescription of Homer of "seeing many cities of men and knowing their minds".

He would not, however, have made a very good interviewer. A descriptive reporter, yes; because description depends on the impact of a scene upon one's own personality; whereas an interviewer has to get the impact of events on the personality of someone else, no matter what the impact upon his own. Just try the process of outlining to Churchill a view with which he does not agree. You will find restive movements developing into mutterings, mutterings developing into thunderclaps, and thunderclaps finally being followed by a torrential rain of argument in which your poor little view is utterly swamped.

He can never resist snatching at any idea which may be floating about, squashing it if he thinks it a mosquito, and causing it to flutter iridescentally if he thinks it a butterfly.

Conviction is, however, not a handicap either in politics or in writing. Any politician and any writer who attempts to polish all the facets of truth simultaneously is a bore. Churchill's advice to the young was to be true and also fierce; and it is good advice to the journalist. He has certainly followed it himself, and if it has led him into valleys, it has also led him to the summit of many peaks. When Admiral Lord Fisher was seventy-four, Churchill wrote of him: "As in a great castle, which has long contended with time, the mighty central mass of the donjon towered up intact and seemingly everlasting." This is not a bad description of himself, on the threshold of his eightieth year. The "mighty central mass" towers up intact; and though nothing in human affairs is everlasting its inhabitant has contributed two things which will be remembered as long as our race is remembered. He has added a noble scroll to British history; and he has added some noble pages to the glorious productions of the English tongue.

CHURCHILL THE EDITOR

Beric Holt

For eight days and nights, during the General Strike of 1926, Winston Churchill was the Editor of a newspaper for the first and only time in his life. That paper was the official Government daily publication the British Gazette, *produced in the office of the* Morning Post, *which, like all other national newspapers, was closed down by the strike. One of Churchill's assistants during those days of crisis and confusion unique in the history of this country was Beric Holt, at that time a member of the* Morning Post *staff. He contributes this chapter on a brief but lively phase in Sir Winston Churchill's life.*

IN the early hours of Tuesday, May 4, 1926, a small procession of men filed up the narrow back stairs of the *Morning Post* building just off the Strand in London.

A few hours earlier the General Strike had begun.

At the head of this procession of Ministers and Departmental officials was the Chancellor of the Exchequer, Winston Churchill. Ten minutes later he was an Editor for the first time in his life—Editor of the newly born *British Gazette*. The new Editor's first task was to sign a Treasury Minute which brought his paper into being.

England was in the throes of her most serious upheaval since the Civil War. The men behind the strike counted it a major achievement that they had succeeded in stopping the Press.

The majority of newspaper workers did not want to strike. But they were afraid to disobey their Unions' orders. This, I know, was particularly true of the printers, who worked to the last minute and even tried to persuade their Union bosses to leave them alone.

Both the Government and the newspapers were keenly alive to the dangers of a stifled Press. Radio sets were not owned by everyone. Rumour, started maliciously or not, magnified as it went from pub to pub and street to street. In no time it was thought the country would be in the grip of what at a later date became known as "fear and despondency".

Not for the last time England in need found the man to lead her—Churchill. All that afternoon the newspaper proprietors had tried to find an acceptable formula for running one paper with their joint resources. As might have been expected, widely divergent political affiliations scotched this idea and they all went home again.

One man was not satisfied. H. A. Gwynne, Editor of the *Morning Post*, dictated a letter. It offered the site, staff and full facilities of the paper to the Government to run themselves.

187

The Prime Minister, Stanley Baldwin, accused of many sins of omission and commission in after years, did the right thing then. He sent for Churchill. England has taken his tip ever since. When in doubt send for Churchill. It was just what the Chancellor loved—a fight against odds. He seemed to be everywhere at once on that night. No staff has ever seen so much of its editor as we of the *British Gazette*.

In an incredibly short time he had found just what he had to work with—the entire editorial staff, and, in those first hours, the whole of the machine-room and composing-room staffs with only one or two exceptions.

Then the first set-back came. The Unions forbade the men to work for the Government paper. I shall never forget the scene as Churchill stood with Gwynne and watched these men—most of whom had given a lifetime's service to the paper—file slowly away into the dawn. It was a moment of high emotion as the two editors, the old and the new, made it plain to the strikers that they understood.

Many of the men were in tears as they left.

Churchill wasted no time. He rang Lord Beaverbrook. In half an hour a taxi brought Sydney Long, night superintendent of the *Daily Express*. He sat down at a linotype machine and single-handed produced the first edition of the *British Gazette*.

It was two pages, front and back, with the inside pages blank.

Churchill stood by the rotary printing machine as the handful of men who had defied their Union and bewildered reporters in dungarees tended the roaring machines. He was handed the first copy.

Already this dynamic editor had organized his distribution. He had asked the Automobile Association for volunteers. They raced to the office in cars of every vintage and that first morning just threw bundles of papers at every newsagent's shop they saw.

During that day the new Editor started to bring order into the chaos. Nothing was forgotten. He brought a submarine crew up from Devonport to help with the machines, he brought London University students who were studying printing to try their hands at the lino-types, he appointed Admiral Hall chief of personnel and security officer.

Outside a huge crowd stood night and day. Hotheads tried to start trouble. Churchill sent for police reinforcements who were billeted in the office. One or two isolated attacks were made on men leaving the building. He sent for the Army. Irish Guards soon joined the policemen in the canteen.

On that second night he went down to the machine-room to find all the presses at work. On the floor stood large enamel jugs.

"What have they got in those?" Churchill asked. "Beer, sir," I replied. (I knew, I had been down before.) "Have they got enough?" he said. The overseer answered, "Oh yes, sir, plenty."

"Nonsense," said the Editor, "nonsense. There is no such thing. Send for some more." A pound note changed hands. It was a remark classed by all who heard it as worthy of inclusion in the imposing list of great Churchillian sayings.

That night the circulation rose from 232,000 to 507,000.

Another hundred thousand copies were added next night. Then Churchill conceived the idea of co-opting other newspapers. Most had at least a skeleton staff. So to every paper in London copies of the *British Gazette* went by car, with a request to "please copy". The *Daily Mirror* brought out a photostat edition, the *Daily Mail* and *Daily Express* ran small, single-sheet printed editions.

With the News Editor of the *Morning Post*, Robert Gray, it was my job to deliver these copies. As we left the building the crowd broke through the police and somebody took a swipe at the News Editor. I managed to catch him across the wrist with a tyre lever.

On our return I was sent for. I told my story to Churchill. He rang a bell. "Police," he said. The superintendent in charge came in. "Tell him," I was ordered. I told my story and from then on mounted and foot police cleared the whole island site before distribution began.

I was to see Editor Churchill again that night. My next job was taking papers off the machine. Suddenly there was a horrible shattering jar. Power was turned off.

An oil can was found in the works. Sabotage?

No one will ever know, but no chances were taken.

Churchill issued immediate orders to Admiral Hall to tighten up on security. No one was to enter the machine-room unless they carried a special pass issued by the Treasury. This mauve pass was issued only after careful screening, which in the end meant that practically only the old editorial staff received one. Students (ever a suspect race) were barred. Churchill was also issued with a pass and was meticulous in presenting it every time he went downstairs.

The next step was to repair the ravaged machine before the next night's run. The chances of the Hoe Company or any other printing-machine makers being able to work were remote. Churchill thought quickly. "Could a Royal Naval Dockyard do the job?" he asked.

He was assured that they could. Next morning I was put in charge of the impressive convoy which took the road to Chatham Dockyard. Into an Army lorry filled with an armed guard policemen lifted the broken machine part. Ahead went a police car full of the toughest-looking uniformed constables Bow Street could provide. In a following car I rode in state with an Australian reporter named Bradstreet, with a policeman in the front seat and two more facing us. Then came another police car to bring up the rear.

Chatham, warned by 'phone, did the repair job in a few hours and the convoy set off for London. About half-way we pulled up at a little pub in a Kent village. To the villagers this armed invasion was terrific. To them the strike was a far-away thing, nothing to do with them. Their lives went on as usual, the farms were farmed as they ever were, the horses were shod, the carrier went about his carrying.

Churchill, who seemed to be fighting the strike as well as running the *British Gazette*, heard of this story and made much capital in that night's Government manifesto of the fact that the strike was anything but complete.

To revert to the mauve passes. They provided many amusing incidents, but none more so than the classic occasion when the entire Cabinet were issued with them and trooped down to watch the wheels go round.

All, that is, except Lord Birkenhead. Tom Greig, in civil life Chief Librarian of the *Morning Post*, was the guard of the door. He was a large and muscular Scot with the accent of London. To him an order was an order.

At an advanced hour he was confronted by the Earl of Birkenhead, then Secretary of State for India, in full evening dress. His Lordship had dined well. "Your pass, sir" said Tom. Lord Birkenhead looked at him with the look which many a poor devil in the dock had learned to fear.

"You surely don't think I am going to undress at this time of night to find the damn thing," he said. "You know who I am, surely?"

"Perfectly," replied Tom, "but I have my orders." By now two specials had ranged themselves beside the keeper of the door. "Tell Churchill," said Lord Birkenhead.

One of the specials went down. Churchill the Editor was vastly amused and told his colleagues. Soon the whole machine-room was laughing and wondering what happened next.

Churchill felt the moment too good to lose. He dragged it out. Eventually Admiral Hall and Admiral Kelly, late of M.I.5, were instructed to escort the Secretary for India downstairs and not to leave his side.

The Editor made no comment but greeted the Earl under escort with a wave of his cigar.

Inevitably the editorship brought Churchill into conflict with the Opposition in the House of Commons. He managed to find time to go down every day if only for an hour. The main Socialist brick hurled at him was, of course, the partiality of the paper he edited.

The first time it was hurled he replied, "The State cannot be impartial as between itself and that section of its subjects with whom it is contending."

Back benchers opposite would not accept the implication that the State was one and the same as the Baldwin Government and said so. They maintained that the masses on strike were the State as being in the majority. This quibble did not hold the Chancellor up for long.

He threw the brick back—never to return—with the classic phrase, "I decline utterly to be impartial as between the Fire Brigade and the fire."

He knew from their silence and from reports he was receiving all over the country that the strike was breaking up. He went back to the Editor's chair at the *British Gazette* office and wrote: "Every man who does his duty by the country and returns to work will be protected by the State from loss of Trade Union benefits or pension. His Majesty's Government will take whatever steps are necessary in Parliament or otherwise for this purpose." This was signed by the Prime Minister and appeared in heavy type on the front page of the *British Gazette*. On that night the machine-room reached its all-high record of 2,209,000.

On the following day the strike was called off, having lasted seven days and twelve hours. That night Churchill was an Editor for the last time and as his final paper was finished he sat back in his chair and relaxed for the first time. His space was full with official pronouncements, with a history of the brief life of his paper, with messages from political leaders calling for toleration and so forth.

He went as he had come—by the back stairs with no fuss, almost unnoticed except for the staff on the doors.

Later that night he suddenly appeared at the old Empire Theatre, Leicester Square. The show was *Lady Be Good*, the stars Fred and Adele Astaire.

Churchill arrived some time after the start of the show. He was soon spotted in the stalls. Somebody shouted "We want Winston." People stood up, necks were craned, fingers pointed. Adele Astaire broke off in the middle of a number.

She walked to the front of the stage and said: "There he is. Three cheers for Winston Churchill." They were given with a will. Adele nodded to the conductor and shouted, "God save the King."

The packed theatre rose in silence until the roll of drums gave them their cue. Rarely has the National Anthem been sung with such sincerity and depth of feeling.

Let me quote the *Morning Post* of the following day, which carried on where the *British Gazette* left off: "It was an eloquent testimony to the delight of the London public at the unconditional withdrawal of the General Strike."

And, may I add, to the man who had so brilliantly led England out of the wilderness.

No one was more conscious of the shortcomings of his *British Gazette* as a newspaper than Churchill. No one was more fully alive to its stabilizing influence on a nerve-racked nation. Instead of Sidney Street battles there were football matches between strikers and police.

Some time after the General Strike there was an occasion when tempers were rising in the House of Commons during a speech by

Churchill and he suddenly paused, looked fiercely at the Socialist benches and said, "I warn you . . ." The silence was complete. "I warn you if ever there is another General Strike . . ." The members on both sides sat tense and angry, waiting and wondering what the bombshell would be, then the whole House exploded into laughter as Churchill concluded, "We will let loose on you another *British Gazette!*"

CHURCHILL AS AN ALLY IN WAR

President Dwight D. Eisenhower

President Dwight D. Eisenhower, as Commander of the Allied Forces that invaded French North Africa in 1943 and afterwards as Supreme Commander of the Allied Forces in Europe, worked in intimate association with Churchill from 1942 until the final defeat of Germany. These two great men established a friendship and harmony of purpose as allies seldom equalled in the annals of war. They fought for nothing less than complete and overwhelming victory and each gave everything he possessed to ensure the realization of that aim. That they held divergent views regarding the broad strategy of the campaign in Europe is well known. Eisenhower was solidly for the direct assault across the English Channel; Churchill agreed to this, provided it was carried out at the proper time, but urged the advantages of a complementary campaign through the "soft under-belly" of Europe. But these differences were settled without any weakening of the two leaders' personal friendship and mutual respect. As Eisenhower has said in his Crusade in Europe, *from which this chapter is extracted, once an operation was launched Churchill supported it to the hilt and provided British help in an even greater degree than promised. A lighter side of Eisenhower's reminiscences of Churchill as an ally in war are his stories of the Prime Minister's determination to be at the scene of action in person and the Supreme Commander's efforts to prevent him from exposing himself to unnecessary dangers.*

D URING the war Churchill maintained such close contact with all operations as to make him a virtual member of the British Chiefs of Staff; I cannot remember any major discussion with them in which he did not participate.

An inspirational leader, he seemed to typify Britain's courage and perseverance in adversity and its conservatism in success. He was a man of extraordinarily strong convictions and a master in argument and debate. Completely devoted to winning the war and discharging his responsibility as Prime Minister of Great Britain, he was difficult indeed to combat when conviction compelled disagreement with his views. In most cases problems were solved on a basis of almost instant agreement, but intermittently important issues arose where this was far from true. He could become intensely oratorical, even in discussion with a single person, but at the same time his intensity of purpose made his delivery seem natural and appropriate. He used humour and pathos with equal facility, and drew on everything from the Greek classics to Donald Duck for quotation, *cliché*, and forceful slang to support his position.

I admired and liked him. He knew this perfectly well and never hesitated to use that knowledge in his effort to swing me to his own line of thought in any argument. Yet in spite of his strength of purpose, in those instances where we found our convictions in direct opposition he never once lost his friendly attitude towards me when I persisted in my own course, nor did he fail to respect with meticulous care the position I occupied as the senior American officer and, later, the Allied Commander in Europe. He was a keen student of the war's developments and of military history, and discussion with him, even on purely professional grounds, was never profitless. If he accepted a decision unwillingly he would return again and again to the attack in an effort to have his own way, up to the very moment of execution.

But once action was started he had a faculty for forgetting everything in his desire to get ahead, and invariably tried to provide British support in a greater degree than promised. Some of the questions in which I found myself, at various periods of the war, opposed to the Prime Minister were among the most critical I faced, but so long as I was acting within the limits of my combined directive he had no authority to intervene except by persuasion or by complete destruction of the Allied concept. Nevertheless, in countless ways he could have made my task a harder one had he been anything less than big, and I shall always owe him an immeasurable debt of gratitude for his unfailing courtesy and zealous support, regardless of his dislike of some important decisions. He was a great war leader and he is a great man.

Our planning and organizational work sometimes involved differences in national conceptions that struck at the very foundation of our basic plan. These points were discussed in an atmosphere of cordiality and objectivity, but they were none the less serious. Whenever I found myself opposed to the views of the Prime Minister, he was, of course, supported by his War Cabinet and technical advisers. That differences should occur was inescapable and natural. Varying situations in national geography bring with them differences in military doctrine, and special war experiences bring with them strong differences in projected strategy.

. . . . .

The Allied invasion of Africa was a most peculiar venture of armed forces into the field of international politics; we were invading a neutral country to create a friend. The Prime Minister gave his personal attention to assuring that the operation should bear the appearance, so far as was humanly possible, of an exclusively American force. He even seriously considered, at one time, requiring all British units that had to participate in the initial landing to wear the uniform of the American Army.

While the 1943 summer and fall fighting was in full swing we received word that the President and the Prime Minister and their staffs were preparing to hold another joint meeting, this time near Cairo.

The Prime Minister preceded the President into our area and I met Churchill at Malta, where we had a lengthy conference. The Prime Minister was accompanied by his military staff and I had an opportunity to spend the day going over a number of subjects of interest to current and future operations.

Churchill, as always, was entertaining and interesting. I have never met anyone else so capable at keeping a dinner gathering on its toes. His comments on events and personalities were pointed and pungent, often most amusing. He looked forward with great enthusiasm to his own meeting with the President, from whom, he said, he always drew inspiration for tackling the problems of war and of the later peace. He dwelt at length on one of his favourite subjects—the importance of assailing Germany through the "soft under-belly", of keeping up the tempo of our Italian attack and extending its scope to include much of the northern shore of the Mediterranean. He seemed always to see great and decisive possibilities in the Mediterranean, while the project of invasion across the English Channel left him cold. How often I heard him say, in speaking of "Overlord" [the code name for the invasion of Europe across the English Channel] prospects, "We must take care that the tides do not run red with the blood of American and British youth, or the beaches be choked with their bodies."

I could not escape a feeling that Churchill's views were unconsciously coloured by two considerations that lay outside the scope of the immediate military problem. I had nothing tangible to justify such a feeling—I know, though, that I was not alone in wondering occasionally whether these considerations had some weight with him. The first of them was his concern as a political leader for the future of the Balkans. For this concern I had great sympathy, but as a soldier I was particularly careful to exclude such considerations from my own recommendations. The other was an inner compulsion to vindicate his strategical concepts of World War I, in which he had been the principal exponent of the Gallipoli campaign. Many professionals agreed that the Gallipoli affair had failed because of bungling in execution rather than through mistaken calculations of its possibilities. It sometimes seemed that the Prime Minister was determined in the second war to gain public acceptance of this point of view.

However, I never at any time heard Churchill urge or suggest complete abandonment of the "Overlord" plan. His conviction, so far as I could interpret it, was that at some time in the indefinite future the Allies would have to cross the Channel. But he seemed to believe that our attack should be pushed elsewhere until the day came when the enemy would be forced to withdraw most of his troops from North-west Europe, at which time the Allies could go in easily and safely.

· · · · · ·

Study indicated the desirability of seizing the island of Pantelleria, lying roughly between Sicily and the north-eastern coast of Tunisia. This island was popularly known as the "Gibraltar of the Central Mediterranean" and was assumed by many to be unassailable. In the actual outcome the capture of Pantelleria was so easy that few people had any inkling of the doubts and fears that had to be overcome in launching the operation.

The Prime Minister, who was then visiting with me in Africa, was very anxious to go along on this operation. I evaded direct reply but would never have agreed to his going, on the grounds that it involved needless risk for a man of his importance. But I had a difficult time indeed explaining to him afterwards that Admiral Cunningham and I had always intended to participate. Two years later he reminded me that I had been very unfair to him on that occasion, especially as he had a personal financial stake in the enterprise.

A small wager between us had grown out of his estimate that there were no more than 3,000 Italians on the island. He offered to pay me five centimes each for all we captured in excess of that number. We took 11,000, and though I had naturally forgotten the joking wager, he paid up promptly, figuring out the exchange himself and remarking that at that rate (a twentieth of a cent each) he'd buy all the prisoners we could get.

· · · · · ·

During the period of preparation [for D-Day] my personal contacts with the Prime Minister were frequent and profitable. He took a lively interest in every important detail, and was able to lend us

CHURCHILL AS AN ALLY IN WAR

Churchill and General Dwight D. Eisenhower inspect glider
and paratroops of the U.S. Army in England before the invasion
of Europe in 1944

an effective hand when some of our requirements demanded extra effort on the part of overloaded British civil agencies.

Visits to Chequers always had business as their main purpose. But the countryside was so pleasant and peaceful that an occasional hour spent in strolling through the fields and woods was real recreation. Chequers was at one time occupied by Cromwell; its setting, architecture, and furniture were all historically interesting.

The Prime Minister would usually ask his guests to arrive during the late afternoon. Dinner would be followed by a short movie and then, at about 10.30 p.m., business conferences would begin. These sometimes lasted until three the next morning. Nearly always present were Mr. Eden and one or more of the British Chiefs of Staff. Every type of problem was discussed and often definite decisions reached. Operational messages arrived every few hours from the London headquarters, and Churchill always participated with the British chiefs in the formulation and dispatch of instructions, even those that were strictly military, sometimes only tactical in character.

Churchill rarely failed to inject into most conferences some element of emotion. One day a British general happened to refer to soldiers, in the technical language of the British staff officer, as "bodies". The Prime Minister interrupted with an impassioned speech of condemnation—he said it was inhuman to talk of soldiers in such cold-blooded fashion, and that it sounded as if they were merely freight—or worse—corpses! I must confess I always felt the same way about the expression, but on that occasion my sympathies were with the staff officer, who to his own obvious embarrassment had innocently drawn on himself the displeasure of the Prime Minister.

There was a guest book in Chequers. Each guest was expected to sign it every time he entered the house. Once, on a trip to the southern coast, I dropped in at Chequers to see Churchill for ten minutes, after which I dashed for the door to continue the journey. Just as I gained the seat of my car I became aware that the family butler, in all his dignity, was standing by to speak to me. He said, "Sir, you have forgotten the book," and his solemn tone meant to me that he found it difficult to forgive my oversight. I corrected the omission and sped on my way.

In spite of all his preoccupations, Churchill constantly evidenced an intensely human side. When London had to endure the "Little

G*

Blitz" of February 1944, he took frequent occasion to urge me to occupy one of the specially built underground shelters in London. He even went to the extent of having an extra apartment, complete with kitchen, living-room, bedroom, and secret telephone, fixed up for me. I never used or even saw the place, yet he never ceased to show great concern for my safety, although paying absolutely no attention to his own. His single apparent desire during an air raid was to visit his daughter Mary, then serving in an anti-aircraft battery protecting London.

In all our conferences Churchill clearly and concretely explained his attitude toward and his hopes for "Overlord". He gradually became more optimistic than he had earlier been, but he still refused to let his expectations completely conquer his doubts. More than once he said, "General, if by the coming winter you have established yourself with your thirty-six Allied divisions firmly on the Continent and have the Cherbourg and Brittany peninsulas in your grasp, I will proclaim this operation to the world as one of the most successful of the war." And then he would add, "And if, in addition to this, you have secured the port of Le Havre and freed beautiful Paris from the hands of the enemy, I will assert the victory to be the greatest of modern times."

Always I would reply: "Prime Minister, I assure you that the coming winter will see the Allied forces on the borders of Germany itself. You are counting only on our presently available thirty-six divisions. We are going to bring ten additional from the Mediterranean, and through the ports we capture we shall soon begin to rush in an additional forty from the United States."

He doubted that we could get the elbow-room to do all this in the summer and fall of 1944 and often observed, "All that is for later; my statement still holds." In reply to my insistence that the picture I had painted him was not too rosy, even if the German continued to fight to the bitter end, he would smile and say: "My dear General, it is always fine for a leader to be optimistic. I applaud your enthusiasm, but liberate Paris by Christmas and none of us can ask for more."

On May 15, 1944, a conference was held at St. Paul's School. At this final meeting every principal member of the British Chiefs of Staff and the War Cabinet attended, as did also the King of England and Allied generals by the score. Field Marshal Smuts came with his old friend, Churchill. During the war I attended no other conference so packed with rank as this one.

This meeting gave us the opportunity to hear a word from both the King and the Prime Minister. The latter made one of his typical fighting speeches, in the course of which he used an expression which struck many of us, particularly the Americans, with peculiar force. He said, "Gentlemen, I am hardening towards this enterprise," meaning to us that, although he had long doubted its feasibility and had previously advocated its further postponement in favour of operations elsewhere, he had finally, at this late date, come to believe with the rest of us that this was the true course of action in order to achieve the victory.[1]

A number of people appealed to me for permission to go aboard the supporting naval ships in order to witness the attack. Among those who were refused permission was the Prime Minister. His request was undoubtedly inspired as much by his natural instincts as a warrior as by his impatience at the prospect of sitting quietly back in London to await reports. I argued, however, that the chance of his becoming an accidental casualty was too important from the standpoint of the whole war effort and I refused his request. He replied, with complete accuracy, that while I was in sole command of the operation by virtue of authority delegated to me by both Governments, such authority did not include administrative control over the British organization. He said: "Since this is true it is not part of your responsibility, my dear General, to determine the exact composition of any ship's company in His Majesty's Fleet. This being true," he rather slyly continued, "by shipping myself as a *bona-fide* member of the ship's complement it would be beyond your authority to prevent my going."

All of this I had ruefully to concede, but I forcefully pointed out that he was adding to my personal burdens in this thwarting of my instructions. Even, however, while I was acknowledging defeat in the matter, aid came from an unexpected source. I later heard that the King had learned of the Prime Minister's intention and, while not presuming to interfere with the decision reached by Churchill, he sent

[1] EDITOR'S NOTE: Sir Winston Churchill has given his own explanation of the phrase, He used these words "in the sense of wishing to strike if humanly possible, even if the limiting conditions we laid down are not exactly fulfilled". (*Closing the Ring*, p. 543.)

word that if the Prime Minister felt it necessary to go on the expedition he, the King, felt it to be equally his duty and privilege to participate at the head of his troops. This instantly placed a different light on the matter and I heard no more of it. Nevertheless my sympathies were entirely with the Prime Minister.

When the Allied armies finally completed their envelopment of the German forces west of the Seine the eventual defeat of the Germans in Western Europe was a certainty. The question of time alone remained.

Our new situation brought up one of the longest-sustained arguments that I had with Prime Minister Churchill throughout the period of the war. This argument, beginning almost coincidentally with the break-through in late July, lasted throughout the first ten days of August. One session lasted several hours. The discussions involved the wisdom of going ahead with "Anvil", by then renamed "Dragoon", the code name for the operation that was to bring in General Devers' forces through the south of France.

One of the early reasons for planning this attack was to achieve an additional port of entry through which the reinforcing divisions already prepared in America could pour rapidly into the European invasion. The Prime Minister held that we were now assured of early use of the Brittany ports and that the troops then in the Mediterranean could be brought in via Brittany, or even might better be used in the prosecution of the Italian campaign with the eventual purpose of invading the Balkans via the head of the Adriatic.

To any such change I was opposed, and since the United States Chiefs of Staff, following their usual practice, declined to interfere with the conclusions of the commander in the field, I instantly became the individual against whom the Prime Minister directed all his argument.

In sustaining his argument, the Prime Minister pictured a bloody prospect for the forces attacking from the south. He felt sure they would be involved for many weeks in attempts to reduce the coastal defences and feared they could not advance as far northward as Lyon in less than three months. He thought we would suffer great losses and insisted that the battlefield in that region would become merely another Anzio. It is possible the Prime Minister did not credit the authenticity of our Intelligence reports, but we were confident that few German forces other than largely immobile divisions remained in the south. Consequently we were sure that the German defensive shell would be quickly pierced and that Devers' troops would pour northward at a rapid pace.

Although I never heard him say so, I felt that the Prime Minister's real concern was possibly of a political rather than a military nature. He may have thought that a post-war situation which would see the Western Allies posted in great strength in the Balkans would be far more effective in producing a stable post-hostilities world than if the Russian armies should be the ones to occupy that region. I told him that if this were his reason for advocating the campaign into the Balkans[1] he should go instantly to the President and lay the facts, as well as his own conclusions, on the table. I well understood that strategy can be affected by political considerations, and if the President and the Prime Minister should decide that it was worth while to prolong the war, thereby increasing its cost in men and money, in order to secure the political objectives they deemed necessary, then I would instantly and loyally adjust my plans accordingly. But I did insist that as long as he argued the matter on military grounds alone I could not concede validity to his arguments.

I felt that in this particular field I alone had to be the judge of my own responsibilities and decisions. I refused to consider the change so long as it was urged upon military considerations. He did not admit that political factors were influencing him, but I am quite certain that no experienced soldier would question the wisdom, strictly from the military viewpoint, of adhering to the plan for attacking southern France.

As usual the Prime Minister pursued the argument up to the very moment of execution. As usual, also, the second that he saw he could not gain his own way, he threw everything he had into support of the operation. He flew to the Mediterranean to witness the attack, and I heard that he was actually on a destroyer to observe the supporting bombardment when the attack went in.

In this long and serious argument the Prime Minister was supported

[1] EDITOR'S NOTE: Churchill in his book *Closing the Ring* (pp. 226 and 304) denies that he contemplated a campaign in the Balkans.

by certain members of his staff. On the other hand, British officers assigned to my own headquarters stood firmly by me throughout.

·   ·   ·   ·   ·

The Rhine was a formidable military obstacle, particularly so in its northern stretches. The assault, on the night of March 23–24, 1945, was preceded by a violent artillery bombardment. Our preparations for the crossing north of the Ruhr had been so deliberately and thoroughly made that the enemy knew what was coming. We anticipated strong resistance. In particular we thought that the enemy would have a great number of guns trained on the river and would attempt to stop our troops at the water's edge with gunfire. This kind of resistance, however, was not encountered.

During the morning I met the Prime Minister. Churchill always seemed to find it possible to be near the scene of action when any particularly important operation was to be launched. On that morning he was delighted, as indeed were all of us. He exclaimed over and over: "My dear General, the German is whipped. We've got him. He is all through."

After I left, the Prime Minister persuaded the local commander to take him across the Rhine in an LCM. He undoubtedly derived an intense satisfaction from putting his foot on the eastern bank of Germany's traditional barrier. Possibly he felt the act was symbolic of the final defeat of an enemy who had forced Britain's back to the wall five years before. However, had I been present he would never have been permitted to cross the Rhine that day.

When Churchill's political party was defeated in the British summer elections of 1945 and he ceased to be Prime Minister he decided to go on a short vacation. He had withstood well the wear and tear of his great responsibilities throughout the war years, but now, with official responsibilities ended, Churchill wanted and needed a short rest. I was honoured and pleased that he asked me to put him up; his suggestion implied that he felt for me some little fraction of the great respect, affection and admiration I had developed for him.

CHURCHILL THE HATED ENEMY

Some characteristic extracts from the speeches of
Adolf Hitler

For years before the war, Adolf Hitler recognized Winston Churchill as his arch-enemy. Even when Churchill was isolated and rejected by the House of Commons during the 1930's, Hitler seemed to know instinctively that if Britian did go to war the people of the country would turn to Churchill for leadership, as the following extracts from his public speeches show. "I cannot prevent the possibility of this gentleman entering the Government in a couple of years," he declared in 1938, and, in the same year, he spoke of the consequences "if Churchill came to power in Great Britain instead of Chamberlain". In 1940, 1941 and 1942 Hitler hurled insults and abuse at Churchill on every possible occasion. "Lunatic", "gabbler", "drunkard", "madman", "unscrupulous politician", "criminal", "bloodthirsty amateur strategist", "war-monger", "hypocritical fellow", "lazybones" were some of the epithets he employed in his attacks. But as the fortunes of war turned against him Hitler made fewer and fewer references to Churchill and in his later speeches seldom mentioned him by name. During Hitler's years of triumph nothing angered him more than Churchill's stubborn refusal to recognize that Germany's tremendous victories were anything more than mere temporary successes that would count for little in the long run, and he denounced the Prime Minister as a "mad drunkard" for treating his peace offers as signs of weakness. In this book, which presents Churchill from so many points of view, these extracts from Hitler's speeches show how he appeared to the dictator who regarded him as his hated enemy.

IF Churchill says, "I don't hate the Germans; they are only a danger to us!" I can only reply, "That is the same here." If there is any man in the world who is authorized to speak for Germany, then I am that man and no one else. After all, Churchill may have 14,000, 20,000 or 30,000 votes behind him—I am not so well informed about that—but I have 40,000,000 votes behind me. The German regime is entirely a matter for the German people, and I will never allow any such foreign schoolmasters or governesses to interfere with it. If these English solicitors of world democracy argue that in one year we have destroyed two democracies, I can only ask—Goodness gracious, after all, what is democracy? Who defines it? Has the Almighty perhaps handed the key to democracy to such people as Churchill? I am only the advocate of Germany. I am not like Churchill, and heaven knows what oppositionalists, who style themselves advocates of the world. If Churchill says, "How is it that the Head of a State can cross swords with a British parliamentarian?" I must say, "Churchill, feel yourself honoured. You may gauge from this how highly esteemed British parliamentarians are in Germany that even the Head of the State does not hesitate to cross swords with one." (November 8, 1938.)

The Governments of the Democratic countries are compelled to maintain freedom, even if it leads to war-mongering. Churchill said he was of the opinion that the German regime ought to be destroyed with the co-operation of forces within Germany, who would probably place themselves thankfully at his disposal. If Churchill communicated less with emigrant circles, that is with traitors maintained and paid by foreign countries, and more with Germans, he would then realize the folly and stupidity of his remarks.

I can assure this gentleman, who appears to live on the moon, that such forces opposed to the regime do not exist in Germany. There is only one force—the National Socialist movement and its leadership and armed forces. I naturally cannot prevent the possibility of this gentleman entering the Government in a couple of years, but I can assure you that I will prevent him from destroying Germany. As long as people talk about disarmament and leave the war-mongers to carry on, I assume that their desire is to steal our weapons and to bring about again our fate of 1918. I can tell Churchill that it happened only once and that it will not happen again! (November 6, 1938.)

＊　＊　＊

We are today a people of power and strength such as Germany has never known before. However, experience must strengthen our resolution to be careful and never omit anything that should be done to protect the Reich. We have, on the other side, statesmen who, we believe, also want peace. But they rule countries whose inner situation makes it possible for them to be replaced by others who do not want peace—and these others exist. If Churchill came to power in Great Britain instead of Chamberlain we know it would be the aim to unleash immediately a world war against Germany. He makes no secret of it. (October 9, 1938.)

＊　＊　＊

1940

I feel a deep disgust for this type of unscrupulous politician who wrecks whole nations and states. It almost causes me pain to think that I should have been selected by fate to deal the final blow to the structure which these men have already set tottering. Churchill has said that he will fight on. Six weeks ago he started off in the field in which he thought he could inflict most harm upon us—that is to say in the air. Of course he said they would attack only military objectives, but in point of fact they have bombed schools and the homes of civilians. So far I have hardly answered that, but they should not think in London that this is the only answer we can give. Awful vengeance can be brought on them. Not, of course, on Churchill, who will run away to Canada, but on the people themselves. I shall speak a great prophecy. A great Empire will be destroyed, an Empire which I had never intended to destroy. But now I realize that the continuation of this war means the destruction of one or the other of the adversaries. Churchill thinks it is going to be Germany. But I think it is going to be Britain. This hour I feel compelled to make one more appeal to reason, even in England. It is possible that Churchill will once again brush aside this statement of mine by saying that it is merely born of fear and doubt of victory. In that case I shall have relieved my conscience of things to come. (July 19, 1940.)

.   .   .

Churchill in the past has won quite a number of so-called victories which in the end always proved to be defeats. Churchill is the same man who discovered in unrestricted aerial warfare the great secret of British victory. For three and a half months this criminal has been ordering German cities to be bombed by night, incendiary leaves to be scattered over German farms and—as especially the inhabitants of Berlin know—has been assigning hospitals as special targets. For three and a half months I watched this inhuman cruelty, which, from the military point of view, was not more than a nuisance. Since the middle of September it was nothing but human feelings which had for so long held us back from replying to the Churchill crimes.[1] Now, however, this war will be waged to the end—namely until the responsible criminals have been eliminated. (December 31, 1940.)

.   .   .

1941

Churchill is determined to continue air warfare. We also are resolved to continue and are preparing to drop 100 bombs for each British bomb until Britain gets rid of this criminal and his methods.

[1] EDITOR'S NOTE: In fact the heavy bombing of London began on September 7, 1940.

Churchill is the most bloodthirsty of amateur strategists that history has ever known. He is as bad a politician as a soldier and as bad a soldier as a politician. Like a madman, Churchill has always been running all over Europe to look for a country to become a battlefield. His May Day speech was symptomatic of a paralytic disease, or the ravings of a drunkard. (May 4, 1941.)

. . . . . .

It was not possible to come to an understanding with this enemy. The English are lunatics, blindfolded people, who, for ten years past, have known nothing else than the slogan, "We want to make war with Germany!" That was Churchill's aim during the last ten years. He wanted the war and now he has got it. All offers were repelled by the war-monger Churchill. He took all my offers as weakness. History will ascertain which has achieved more—Churchill's speeches or my actions. If I were the British Prime Minister I would talk all the time because nothing is happening there. That is the difference between us. (October 3, 1941.)

. . . . . .

I decided to hold out my hand to England and to point out that a continuation of the war could only be senseless for England. That mad drunkard who has now for years directed England immediately saw in this a new sign of my weakness. Once again I was described as a man who no longer dared to continue the struggle. (November 9, 1941.)

. . . . . .

In 1940, when the whole Western Front collapsed, Churchill still saw in the continuation of the war the possibility of business advantage. This was not due to his hope of a possible victory for the British forces, but entirely to his knowledge of American help and, above all, the agreements he had made with Soviet Russia. When Churchill in July and August of 1940 rejected my peace offers, the decisive point for Churchill was not the promised American war deliveries, but the assurances of the Soviet entry into the war. (December 31, 1941.)

. . . . . .

1942

If we look at our enemies we see this gabbler, this drunkard Churchill. What has he done all his life? This hypocritical fellow! This lazybones of the first rank! Of Churchill the future will speak only as the destroyer of an Empire which he—and not we—destroyed. Churchill has said that I want war—and a small clique with him. Behind this clique of drunkards stand the jews who pay them. (January 31, 1942.)

.   .   .   .   .

Since National Socialism took power into its hands there has not been a phase in its development which Churchill has not characterized "encouraging". He was encouraged when Britain declared war on us. He found it encouraging that other nations should allow themselves to be led to the slaughter by British egotism. He is as encouraged by the talks of a handful of Allied generals as by the fireside chatter of the sick man of the White House. Cripps' flight from India was no less encouraging than his flight to Moscow. MacArthur's escape from the Philippines was also an encouraging factor. In the same way it is encouraging when some twenty or thirty Englishmen with blackened faces, rubber-soled shoes and floating kit-bags succeed in landing somewhere on the coast we occupy, only to make off again when German patrols appear. When an *émigré* Government—a collection of nonentities—makes a declaration against Germany it is just as encouraging as when Churchill announces the destruction of German U-boats, or some new invention, or a new offensive, or a second front. Nothing can be done about it. Every people has its own form of encouragement. Britain can win nothing in this war. She will lose, and she will then, perhaps, for once in her history, realize that the fate of nations and states should not be entrusted either to cynical drunkards or to the sick in spirit. (April 26, 1942.)

.   .   .   .   .

If Churchill says he leaves it to us, in our fear, to speculate where the second front will come, I reply, "Churchill, you have never made me afraid." But you are right. We must speculate where the second front will come. Had I in front of me a serious opponent I could figure out where the second front would come. But with these military idiots one never knows where they will attack. The maddest enterprise may be launched and—this is the only disagreeable thing—one never knows what next when faced with such lunatics and drunkards. Of course, we must prepare everywhere. Let me assure Churchill that, wherever he may choose for his next attack, he may consider himself lucky if he remains on land for nine hours. Apart from the second front, our enemies have another means to carry on the war—bombing the civilian population. The man who invented the bombing war now declares that the bombing war will increase in violence in the future. In May 1940 Churchill sent the first bombers against the German civilian population. I warned him then, and I continued to warn him for four months, but in vain. Then we struck back. When we did so they began weeping and whining. There was talk of barbarity and disgusting inhumanity. A man who, apart from the principal war-monger, Roosevelt, is the main culprit, pretended to be innocent. And today they are again carrying on this bombing war. (September 30, 1942.)

CHURCHILL AND THE CENSORSHIP

Rear-Admiral G. P. Thomson
C.B., C.B.E.

For five years during the War, Rear-Admiral G. P. Thomson was Chief Press Censor. In that post he was a buffer between the newspapers of the world and the Government and he achieved the remarkable distinction of finishing up on friendly terms with both sides. There were days when he had to calm hundreds of impatient newspapermen who demanded advance copies of some major speech about to be delivered by the Prime Minister. Churchill made a practice of polishing and correcting his oration to the last possible minute before delivery and it sometimes happened that millions of copies of London papers would be circulated the following morning without a report of the speech made after their early editions had come off the presses. That was but one of Admiral Thomson's minor headaches. A more serious one was Churchill's habit of letting out in the course of a speech some news that had previously been on the "stop" list. So the Censor's recollections of Churchill in the War contribute an interesting sidelight on the Prime Minister's character and activities.

"WHEN *are* we going to get Winston's speech?" That was a question I was often asked in the Press room at the Ministry of Information, during the war. In that room representatives of the world's Press assembled to receive official news bulletins or to submit copy for censorship. Not only news bulletins, but the scripts of broadcasts and public speeches were also handed out there (before they were delivered) for publication and editorial comment. Churchill's speeches were not subject to censorship. In his capacity of Prime Minister and Minister of Defence he, better than anyone, knew when an item of war news could safely be published.

I was often asked the question about an expected speech by Churchill because the Prime Minister had a habit of dotting the "i"s and crossing the "t"s of his speeches almost up to the last moment before allowing the scripts to be sent to the Ministry of Information. This often made it difficult for the newspapers which were anxious to publish them, with comments, in their country editions printed in London early in the evening.

Churchill's habit of revising his speeches up to the last possible minute sprang many surprises on the censorship. On several occasions he revealed an item of information which, until he spoke, had been covered by a strict "stop". I, or my deputy, had then to send a directive to editors cancelling the ban. And not only to editors but to all the censors in the Ministry, in the provinces and in the outlying cable offices. For it was essential for the proper functioning of the censorship that a censorship "stop" should not be in force if the particular item to which it referred had been released elsewhere.

I well remember for example that the use of magnetic mines by the Germans had to be kept secret, as we did not want them to know what success they were having with this type of mine or that we had recovered one and discovered how it worked—and hence, how to counter it. But in June 1940 Churchill evidently had information that our knowledge was no longer any secret to them and announced that the enemy had sowed magnetic mines "in the channels and seas". Then, towards the end of 1941, he revealed that the attack "is now waged continuously by the acoustic mine as well as the magnetic mine in many dangerous combinations".

I at once consulted the Admiralty and was able to inform the Press that they could state the acoustic mine operated by the closing of a trembler circuit and was activated by the sound vibrations set up by a ship's engines; but, I added, no details of our counter-measures could be given.

It was Churchill, too, who in 1940 announced the torpedoing of the British battleship *Barham*—which had been concealed for some months because we had reason to believe that the U-boat did not know the result of her shot. But by then he was also able to announce at the same time that she would soon be ready for active service again. It will be remembered that she was afterwards sunk as the result of another submarine attack. In the same speech Churchill disclosed that since the battleship *Royal Oak* had been sunk, we had not had the use of Scapa Flow—our best strategic base, as it saved the Fleet a great deal of steaming.

Official announcements by Churchill and other Ministers in Parliament presented another problem. Although daylight air raids on London practically ceased after September 1940, it was always feared that the Houses of Parliament might at any moment be the objective of a concentrated attack by German bombers, which could have resulted in the killing of a number of Cabinet Ministers and Members of Parliament. German aircraft did, in fact, twice bomb the House of Commons—in 1940 and 1941—the second time destroying the debating chamber. An incendiary bomb also landed on the House of Lords. But all these incidents occurred during night raids when Parliament was not sitting. With the object, if possible, of rising before dark, Parliament began its sittings during the war at 11.30 a.m., instead of at the pre-war time of 2.45 p.m. and from the autumn of 1940 onwards precautions were taken to conceal from the enemy on which days and at what times Parliament was going to sit, and where.

The Prime Minister often made announcements after Question

Time, which began previously at 2.45 p.m. To give the impression that Parliament sat at its normal peace hours, the evening newspapers were forbidden to report parliamentary Questions until 2.45 p.m. and no statement made by a Minister could be reported until 3.15 p.m. Debates could not be published at all until the next morning.

These restrictions led to complaints from the British Press and the correspondents of the overseas newspapers. For the Prime Minister sometimes announced, in reply to questions, or just after Question Time about twelve o'clock, important news which it seemed essential that the world should know immediately. Until the permitted time, such statements had to be published in this country and telegraphed overseas as: "It was authoritatively stated today that . . ." or, "It was learned in London that . . ." It did not take long however to realize that this was not serving the best interests of the country, since news—particularly news about the war—lost much of its value if it did not come from the lips of Churchill or a Member of the War Cabinet.

I was therefore given authority to allow news to be attributed to the Prime Minister or any other Minister, if I considered it sufficiently important, but I was still not permitted to pass the fact that the announcement had been made in Parliament. One notable example of the latitude given me was in December 1941, when the evening newspaper lunch editions and the 1 p.m. B.B.C. news were allowed to report that the sinking of H.M.S. *Prince of Wales* and H.M.S. *Repulse* by the Japs had been announced by Churchill. Incidentally questions and debates in Parliament provided the only two occasions I can remember when the Prime Minister himself was censored. Twice he accidentally referred to bomb damage to the House of Commons—a rigid censorship "stop"; but the Speaker asked parliamentary journalists not to quote these references, and they were taken out of *Hansard*.

Churchill unfortunately never had the time available to come over to the Ministry of Information and talk to the Press about the war. It is probably not generally realized how much trust was placed in editors during the war years. To enable them to have the correct background to comment on war events—particularly on news broadcast by Germany or by neutral countries giving the German version of events, which of course could be, and was, freely published in this country—Press conferences were held from time to time at the Ministry. Ministers, Admirals, Generals, Air Marshals and others in authority came over to talk to editors and other Press representatives and give them a true account of the events for their own information and sometimes also an appreciation of the war situation in all theatres.

The monthly conferences for the editors of provincial journals held by Brendan Bracken, the Minister of Information, were particularly popular, because the Press knew that he had been the Prime Minister's Parliamentary Private Secretary and was also his close friend. They regarded information or comment from Bracken as coming "straight from the horse's mouth". Much of the information given was not for publication but there were always "tit-bits" which could be published provided the material had been submitted to censorship. To assist editors in avoiding waste of time by submitting items which would not pass the censor, an appropriate censorship adviser was always present at these conferences. I personally attended Bracken's meetings. The adviser's duty was to read out at the end of the conference all the items mentioned by the speaker which were censorship "stops".

I well remember how annoyed Churchill was as the result of one of these conferences. It was held by one of our foremost Generals to give editors an appreciation of the North African campaign in 1940–41. The sequel was another proof of the Prime Minister's complete grasp of the military situation in every theatre of war. The speaker had referred to the likelihood of our attacking Benghazi, adding that the coastal road would not be used. This information was included among the list of "stops" read out by the military adviser to the censorship at the end of the conference.

Unfortunately the editor of a national newspaper who had an important engagement could not stay until the end and was thus unaware of the "stop". He submitted his article that evening before publication, and it was of course referred to the censorship military adviser on duty. Unfortunately, however, the military adviser did not exercise his usual care—possibly because he knew one of his colleagues had attended the conference the same morning—and allowed this important item of news to pass. Churchill, who somehow found time to read the first editions of the newspapers which appeared soon after midnight, was aghast. What happened to the military adviser is irrelevant to this story, but the Prime Minister was not content with the censorship inquest. He saw the General next day and asked him how he could possibly have given information of that kind at a Press conference. "These gentlemen of the Press," said Churchill, "were listening carefully to every word you said—all eagerly anxious for a tiny morsel of cheese which they could publish. And you go and give them a whole ruddy Stilton."

Although the Prime Minister constantly visited areas under heavy air bombardment, we had to include him, for the country's sake, among the very few Very Important Personages whose movements had censorship protection. The Press were forbidden to publish that the King and Queen and Princesses, Queen Mary, the Prime Minister and the heads of Allied States were in a particular place until fifteen minutes after they had left it. Mention of their future movements was always banned. The censors, for example, would not pass the statement, "The Prime Minister will visit Portsmouth on Tuesday." Similarly a confidential letter was sent to all editors in 1940: "Please do not mention where the Prime Minister's grandchild was born." It would have been obvious to the Germans that he was likely to be paying visits to that place.

It was often thought that Churchill and other Ministers flying to the Middle East or other foreign destinations had heavy fighter escort. In fact, over most of the route they had none—secrecy was their defence. Hence it was usually forbidden to say whether Churchill travelled by sea or air. And in 1943 the censors had to "stop" anything about the kind of 'plane he used, including the fact that he no longer flew in the Liberator in which his earlier journeys had been made. I well remember also when Inspector Walter Thompson, Churchill's bodyguard, had an accident with a revolver in 1943 and was taken to hospital with leg wounds. The Press were asked not to refer to the mishap. This was on the—to me unintelligible—ground that the nature of the Inspector's duties made it very undesirable to give publicity to the accident. The ban on publicity about the mishap was removed two days later, but I had to ask editors not to refer to the Inspector's duties. I never quite saw the reason for this, as the fact that he was Churchill's bodyguard had been published previously.

I do not believe there was any secret which I found more difficult to guard than the date and place of a "Big Three" conference. Not only did the whole world want to have this information in advance, but nothing was allowed to be published about it until the conference was over. All sorts of pieces of alleged information about it were broadcast from enemy and neutral radio stations—often originating from enemy agents in the hope of confirmation or denial leaking out from London. To make matters more difficult it was generally known in Fleet Street some days before Churchill left the country that he was going somewhere overseas to confer with President Roosevelt or with the President and Stalin. Indeed it would be announced in Parliament that it was his intention to do so, but not even an approximate date was given.

There was, of course, no security reason why the Press should not publish news that the Prime Minister was expected to leave England shortly to confer with President Roosevelt—and this was great news value to the public—so long as there was no mention of the date and place of his departure or of his destination. Nor could we prevent correspondents reporting that he *might* be going to the United States, to Canada or to North Africa. The Germans could not possibly take any action on information of that kind. But I had to be very careful about reports from parliamentary correspondents round about the time he was leaving the country. For if Churchill was not present in Parliament, the report would at once be telegraphed: "It was noted that Mr. Eden answered questions on behalf of the Prime Minister today." It was necessary to examine these messages very closely. If one of them contained a hint which afterwards proved to be correct, this was regarded as a brilliant scoop.

The Press sometimes submitted stories about these conferences which were very amusing and produced some cutting comments by Churchill. They did not usually reach the censorship until long after a conference was over and were probably picked up at a private dinner party.

One of these stories told of President Roosevelt after a heavy day of conferences remembering at bedtime something he particularly wanted to say to Churchill. So he had himself taken to the Prime Minister's bedroom, knocked at the door and opened it. He found Churchill almost in a state of nature, just putting on his pyjamas.

"Oh, I am so sorry. I'll wait until the morning." "Not at all," replied Churchill, "come in, do. England has nothing to hide." On another occasion when a "Big Three" session had just finished and they were leaning back in their chairs, Marshal Stalin leant over to the Prime Minister and said, through his interpreter, "You know, you've said many unkind things about me in your time." Churchill replied: "Ah, yes, quite true. But you weren't on our side then." The Marshal appreciated the point.

If it is asked how the Press got hold of some of the stories of that sort, the answer is, of course, that the newspapers seem to manage to get hold of anything that is not locked up in a steel safe. As for Churchill himself, he did not like that kind of publicity, and I would not have been popular if I had submitted some of those personal stories to him for his approval. In any event he was too busy to bother reading stories—real or imaginary—about himself. And I was not anxious to add to his burdens.

CHURCHILL AS A GUEST

Mrs. Roosevelt

During the most critical years of the War Churchill paid several visits to the United States to confer with President Franklin D. Roosevelt. The first of these was in December 1941, when he spent Christmas at the White House in Washington, and he was a guest of the Roosevelts again some six months later. He also visited the President and Mrs. Roosevelt at their Hyde Park home in 1943. Mrs. Roosevelt therefore writes of Churchill from the personal point of view of a hostess and tells of the effects of his visit on life in the White House. She relates how the President's daily routine was disorganized by the Prime Minister's practice of taking a long nap in the afternoon and then working far into the night. "Even after Franklin retired, if important dispatches or messages came in, he was awakened no matter what the hour," she writes. "It always took him several days to catch up on sleep after Churchill left." But she tells, too, of the real friendship and affection between the two leaders and their mutual confidence in each other's integrity and ability which played such a vital part in the winning of the war.

AS soon as Prime Minister Winston Churchill heard of the Pearl Harbour attack he made up his mind to come to the United States. His trip was a "top secret" and none of us knew until shortly before he arrived that he was coming. A few days before his visit my husband sent for Miss Thompson, my secretary, asked her whom I had invited to stay in the house over Christmas and asked also to see the list of people invited to dinner. In all the years that we had been in the White House he had never paid much attention to such details, and this was the first time he had made such a request to Miss Thompson; he counted on my remembering to ask people. On this occasion he gave no explanation and no hint that anything unusual was going to happen, so Miss Thompson and I could only conclude that he felt a sudden curiosity.

When we learned that Churchill was coming on December 22, everyone scurried around to get ready. The Monroe Room on the second floor had to be turned into a map room and an office for the British delegation, and we shifted beds around to make room for all our Christmas guests. When I knew definitely how many of the British were going to be staying in the house on Christmas Day, I hurriedly sent someone to buy gifts for them to put around our Christmas tree. Last-minute shopping in Washington was not easy—by the 23rd the shops were pretty well sold out, and I felt we did a very inadequate job.

My husband on that memorable day of December 22, 1941, saw the Russian Ambassador, the Chinese Ambassador and the Dutch Minister, besides filling innumerable other engagements. He left shortly before six in the evening to meet the British Prime Minister, and they all arrived at the White House at six-thirty. We had quite a houseful, but it represented only a very small quota of those who came over with Churchill. We met for the first time the Prime Minister's aide, Commander P. C. Thompson, and his secretary, John Martin, both of whom stayed in the house and were later to become real friends of ours. Two Scotland Yard men and a valet also stayed in the house.

I had been asked by Franklin to have tea ready in the West Hall for our British guests, but I found on their arrival that they preferred more stimulating refreshments. We were seventeen at dinner that night, including the British Ambassador, Lady Halifax, Lord Beaverbrook, Secretary and Mrs. Hull, Under-Secretary of State and Mrs. Welles, and Harry Hopkins. At ten o'clock the gentlemen left us to consult together, while the ladies made conversation until after midnight, when their husbands returned a bit shamefaced to take them home. I had come back to Washington that morning on the night train from New York City and had spent a good part of the day at the office of Civilian Defence. I had gone to the Salvation Army Christmas party, to a Catholic Charities Christmas party, and the Alley Christmas-tree programmes, so I had added a good deal to the already heavy official programme of the day. I still remember that as time wore on that evening I suddenly caught myself falling asleep as I sat trying to talk to my guests.

On this visit of Churchill's, as on all his subsequent visits, my husband worked long hours every day. The Prime Minister took a long nap every afternoon, so was refreshed for hard work in the evening and far into the night. While he was sleeping, Franklin had to catch up on all his regular work. Even after Franklin finally retired, if important dispatches or messages came in he was wakened no matter what the hour, and nearly every meal he was called on the telephone for some urgent matter. It always took him several days to catch up on sleep after Churchill left.

On Christmas Day we went to the Foundry Methodist Church for an interfaith service, accompanied by all our house guests. In the afternoon the military staffs met with their chiefs, but we had our Christmas tree at four-thirty and all the Norwegian royal family joined us, augmenting the number of children. Christmas dinner that night was the biggest Christmas dinner we ever had—sixty people sat down at the table—and after dinner there was a movie and Christmas carols by visiting carollers, but the men again worked until well after one o'clock in the morning.

A number of people have accused me at various times of having no sense of propriety, because frequently I had what they called "unimportant" people to meet important ones. The truth is that the "unimportant" people usually had been asked long beforehand, or had standing invitations, and when the important people came I still wanted my friends and managed somehow to get them into the White House, in spite of overcrowding and the evident disapproval of some members of the White House staff. Then, too, throughout the war years the comings and goings of official people were shrouded in mystery, and it never was as simple as it now sounds to make arrangements for them. They arrived and they left suddenly and none of us were warned beforehand. This fact often accounted for my having conflicting engagements and for the presence of people whom I might not have invited had I known in advance what was going to happen.

I recall that during this first visit of the British Prime Minister I had invited Mr. and Mrs. Louis Adamic, Monroe Robinson, my cousin, and several others to dinner on January 13. Of course, when I invited Mr. and Mrs. Adamic I had no idea that Churchill would be there. At the last minute I included a distant cousin of Franklin's and a young British girl, both of whom were working at the British Embassy, because I thought they would be interested in meeting the Prime Minister. After dinner I took Mr. and Mrs. Adamic, Monroe Robinson and Miss Thompson to a concert, and the evening seemed to me of casual interest.

No one was more surprised than I when Mr. Adamic wrote a whole book, *Dinner at the White House*, based on this one dinner. He seemed to think every smallest detail of the evening had some particular significance or meaning behind it. It was the supreme example of how much can be made of very little. In the book Mr. Adamic repeated a story which was most derogatory to the British Prime Minister; in fact the whole book was anti-British and anti-Churchill. Churchill hotly resented it and sued Mr. Adamic in Great Britain, where the libel laws are somewhat different from ours.[1]

---

[1] Settlement of this libel action was announced in the King's Bench Division of the High Court of Justice on January 15, 1947, when counsel for Mr. Louis Adamic and the publishers of the book formally withdrew the statements that Churchill had complained about, apologised for them and agreed to "the payment of a very substantial sum by way of damages".

Of course, Mr. Adamic to the contrary, the whole evening had been a completely casual affair. That was one of the things which I found it very difficult to learn—in fact I never did learn it in all the time we were in the White House. At the end of twelve years I was still doing what I thought were casual things without ever realizing how momentous apparently they seemed to other people.

On January 1 we took the Prime Minister and quite a party to Christ Church in Alexandria, Virginia, for the New Year's Day service. This is the church that George Washington attended, and Churchill was much interested in seeing it. I remember quietly passing some money to my husband for the collection because I knew he rarely carried any. As I did this, I wondered whether the Prime Minister had the same habit, but felt sure that if he had his aide would be prepared.

Throughout Churchill's visit there were many consultations, and representatives of all the different branches of the Government were called in—not only the Secretary and Under-Secretary of State, Mr. Hull and Mr. Welles, but the military authorities, Admiral Emory Land, who was responsible for the development of our shipping facilities, and the leaders of Congress, who spent much time with the President. For Great Britain there was Lord Beaverbrook, who played an important part in public relations, Sir Arthur Salter and many others.

In these first talks which my husband and the Prime Minister had, they faced the fact that there was a long-drawn-out war ahead during which there would be many setbacks, and that both of them, as leaders of their nations, would have to be prepared to bolster the morale of their people. To explain to one's country that there must be a long period while the military forces are being trained and armed, during which production will be one of the most important factors, and that meanwhile people must be patient and hope at best "to hold the line" is no easy or popular thing to do.

I always had great admiration for the way in which Churchill did this. In some ways he was more blunt with the people of Great Britain than my husband ever was with us. The British people were closer to the danger and I suppose for that very reason could better understand the blunt approach.

Churchill was with us again from the 21st to the 25th of June 1942. The friendship and affection between my husband and the Prime Minister grew with every visit, and was something quite apart from the official intercourse. It was evident that Great Britain and the United States would have to co-operate in any case, but the war could be carried on to better advantage with the two nations closely united through the personal friendship of Churchill and my husband. The two men had many interests in common in addition to the paramount issue of the war. They were men who loved the sea and the navy. They both knew a great deal of history and they had somewhat similar tastes in literature. It always gave my husband great joy when Churchill quoted aptly from Lear's "Nonsense Rhymes", which were among Franklin's favourites. Both of them had read much biography. My husband did not have the same interest in art, but both of them loved the out-of-doors and could enjoy themselves either in the country or in the city. Their companionship grew, I think, with their respect for each other's ability. They did not agree on all things; I heard my husband make remarks which were sometimes inspired by annoyance and occasionally by a realistic facing of facts.

I remember very well his irritation at Churchill's determination that we should attack through Greece and the Balkans.[1] Franklin said that would mean the loss of many men, though strategically it might be a help to Great Britain and might get us to Berlin before the Russians. However, he did not think that was important and he was not going to risk so many men.

But I also remember the day Tobruk fell. Churchill was with us when the news came, and though he was stricken, his immediate reaction was to say, "Now what do we do?" To neither of those men was there such a thing as not being able to meet a new situation. I never heard either of them say that ultimately we would not win the war. This attitude was contagious, and no one around either of them would have dared to say, "I'm afraid."

Franklin knew and understood Churchill's background. He seemed to agree when I said on one occasion that I thought the time that would be the hardest for Churchill would be after the war. The world that

[1] EDITOR'S NOTE: Churchill in his book *Closing the Ring* (pp. 226 and 304) denies that he contemplated a campaign in the Balkans.

had existed before the war had been a pleasant world so far as he was concerned; therefore his tendency would be to want to go back to it, even though in his mind he might realize that there was no way in which one could go back to a pre-war world. Churchill had acknowledged to me in casual conversation that he knew the world could never be the same. He once even said that all he wanted to do was to stay in office until he had seen the men come home from the war and until they had places in which to live.

I shall never cease to be grateful to Churchill for his leadership during the war; his speeches were a tonic to us here in the United States as well as to his own people. The real affection which he had for my husband, and which was reciprocated, he has apparently never lost. It was a fortunate friendship. The war would have been harder to win without it, and the two men might not have gone through it so well if they had not had that personal pleasure in meeting and confidence in each other's integrity and ability.

SECRETARY TO CHURCHILL

Mary T. G. Thompson

Mrs. Thompson was Personal Private Secretary to Churchill through some of the darkest days of the War. As Miss Shearburn, she joined him in 1939 when he was out of office and engaged mainly on his literary works, and she stayed with him when he became First Lord of the Admiralty and, later, Prime Minister. She married his personal bodyguard, Detective-Inspector W. Thompson.

This chapter is an intimate study of Churchill from the secretary's point of view, his idiosyncrasies, his private likes and dislikes, his methods of work, his untiring energy and his personal charm for those in close association with him.

H*

WORKING as the Prime Minister's secretary—Personal Private Secretary, as my colleague and I were called—meant long hours, intense concentration, patience, a good memory and above-average speeds in both shorthand and typing. When taking dictation from him it was necessary at all times to keep a mental note of the number of words which had been dictated—not an easy matter at first—as at any moment he would simply say, "How many?", and expect an immediate answer. I worked for him both before and during the war. When I first went to him all his work—correspondence, the book he was writing (*A History of the English-Speaking Peoples*) and sundry articles and speeches—had to be taken down in shorthand and then transcribed. A good deal of this was done at night, the sessions seldom starting before ten o'clock and usually going on until 2 a.m. and after. My colleague and I took half-hour spells of shorthand and transcribed our notes between periods of dictation. This system required both of us to be on duty every night and it was a relief to us when he decided to dictate everything on to a noiseless typewriter. It was also a considerable help to him as there was no waiting and at the end of each page—and before if he felt like it—he could say, "Gimme!" and see at once what he had said. In pre-war days most pages were then corrected and a fair copy made when the session came to an end. During the war, however, for the sake of speed an enormous amount of official correspondence, directives, etc., went straight out to their destinations as originally typed. This meant that the duplicates had to be typed at the same time, and I had to evolve a technique of slipping carbon sheets between pages whenever he paused to think. This had to be performed not only with dexterity but in silence, as the crackle of paper irritated him excessively.

My career before I became his secretary had been wide and varied and an excellent preparation for my duties with him. I had been a shorthand typist with Morris Motors, secretary to a cinema manager, residential secretary to the owner of a prep. school for boys who intended to enter the Navy, and I had also had several posts in ordinary commercial offices. Being ready to re-start work after an operation, I registered with several secretarial agencies, including Mrs. Hoster's in the City of London. From her, one day in April 1939, came particulars of the post which was going to mean so much to me. I was a little apprehensive about applying for it, feeling that working for such an eminent man—and a politician at that!—would be beyond me. However, I applied and received a letter from Mrs. Hill, at that time his Personal Private Secretary, who wrote from Morpeth Mansions in Westminster and asked me to telephone for an appointment. I subsequently presented myself at the flat and was interviewed by Mrs. Hill, who did not give me any tests but was more interested in knowing whether I was engaged to be married. She explained that when he became used to his staff he did not like changes. I was able to assure her that I was not contemplating matrimony and little thought that the job I was taking on would lead to my meeting and marriage to the Prime Minister's bodyguard, Detective-Inspector Thompson. Having apparently decided that, from her point of view, I would suit, Mrs. Hill said that he would like to have a word with me. I must admit that I was far from ease at the prospect, but my capacity for at least always *appearing* calm stood me in good stead. I was shown into the dining-room and he walked forward and shook hands—giving me also what I felt to be a most penetrating look. He did not smile as he asked me one or two questions, not about my previous work, but my family and where I had been at school. I remember his saying, "I see you are a soldier's daughter," to which he referred again some months later. I had been working very late with him, and as I was leaving his study to go to bed he stopped me and said, "You're not tired, are you, Miss Shearburn?" I was, of course, very tired, but nothing would have induced me to admit it and I simply replied, "No, thank you." He smiled and said: "No, you are a soldier's daughter. Good night, Miss Shearburn." It was an instance of his knack of saying just the right word to encourage one to make every possible effort to keep pace with his demands.

My first interview with him lasted only a few minutes, at the end of which he smiled and said, "I'd like you to come down to Chartwell as soon as possible and stay for a month—to see how we get on together." I went there the following day. The month passed and I found myself intensely interested in the work and beginning to feel a profound admiration for my new employer. Nothing was said after four weeks as to whether I was to stay or go, and one night, after a late session, I reminded him that I was only on trial and asked him to let me know whether I was to remain. He looked quite taken aback—as if the thought had gone completely out of his mind—then, to my great pleasure, he bowed slightly and said gravely, "I am satisfied—if you are." It was one of those moments which he endows with his own especial charm.

Idiosyncrasies which in more ordinary men are petty and annoying seem in a man of his stature to become acceptable and not a little amusing. He cannot tolerate paper clips of any sort and he simply abominates pins. Any documents which came in by post were always subjected to searching examination, the offending pins, etc., removed and replaced by green tags, of which we always had an assortment of sizes and lengths. A paper punch was used to make holes for these tags and during my very first evening with him he astounded me by looking up from the pages of a letter I had just handed him for signature and saying the one word, "Klop." He was obviously asking me to give him something but I had not the remotest idea what it was. Seeing my bewilderment, he explained that he meant "a paper punch". "When I say 'Klop', Miss Shearburn, *that* is what I want." He was obviously amused but I came to know that, although he was always ready to explain anything once, he did not like being asked for the same explanation a second time.

During the war, practically the only time he did not have his dictation taken straight on to a typewriter was when travelling by car. For train journeys we always took a typewriter—packed in a specially made box—and a certain amount of practice was needed to type in a fast-moving train, particularly when one knew that nine times out of ten there was no second chance and no opportunity to make a fair copy. Speeches, however, were the exception and were always subjected to correction and retyping. When the Prime Minister is going to make a speech he gives immense care and thought to every phrase, every word—to ensure that misinterpretation is impossible. When dictating a speech he will walk up and down the room deep in thought, murmuring and muttering to himself, while the uninitiated strains her ears to catch the almost inaudible words. When he is satisfied that he has found the right words he will raise his voice and, at times, almost declaim his choice. He is such a great master of English that more than once I have found it difficult to keep my voice steady when asked to read back a particularly moving passage. At all times it was interesting and stimulating to work for such a man, and it gave me a feeling of immense pride and satisfaction to be an integral part of "Top Secret" matters in war-time, to help to prepare speeches the whole world would hear, and directives having vital and urgent bearing on operations of supreme importance.

By the time war broke out, my colleague and I had come to an arrangement whereby she did the "early work" and I did the "late". That is to say she was on duty at 8 a.m. each day and I started at 10 a.m. After lunch I would take a few hours off and return in the late afternoon or evening, prepared to go on until the Prime Minister was finished. Doing most of the late work meant that I usually took the preliminary dictation of many of his war-time speeches. These were frequently started at 10.30 p.m., or even later, and we worked until his inspiration gave out, or until even his great stamina demanded rest. I well remember one occasion, during the winter of 1940, when we had been hard at work for some hours on a speech for the House of Commons the following day. At 3 a.m. the last words were dictated and, with a small sigh, he said: "There! That's all. Don't bother with a fair copy of that tonight, Miss Shearburn—I shan't want it until eight o'clock." As there were about thirty pages of typescript, the remark had its amusing side, but such is his personality that without the slightest resentment I prepared to go ahead, there and then, with the copying, knowing perfectly well that to retype it would take most of what remained of the night. It was finished before eight and that was all that mattered. He had what he wanted, and I had the personal satisfaction of knowing that I had done my share.

As a rule, letters and directives were typed with two copies—the top one being passed to him and the flimsies to the permanent Treasury secretaries for distribution. "Top Secret" matters, however, entailed giving the Prime Minister the top copy and the flimsies, and even, sometimes, the sheets of carbon, though my normal instructions were to burn these on leaving his room.

The preparation of a speech was, as a rule, a fairly lengthy business. First there was the rough draft on which he made corrections and alterations. This was followed by an unlimited number of re-types, the final "speech-form" very often only being completed within a matter of minutes before the speech was due to be delivered. Typing in what we knew as "speech-form" was quite an art. It was done on octavo sheets for all except broadcast speeches, when quarto was used. The result had the appearance of rather eccentric blank verse. A "verse" represented a sentence, and this was sub-divided into phrases—sometimes even words—on separate lines, so that, as he read it, he could tell at a glance where emphasis was required, where pauses were indicated and where he could draw breath, etc. Many times I have listened over the radio to a speech being made and seldom did he deviate by so much as a word from the script. When he did, I made the necessary alterations on a copy with which I was checking him, so that we had an absolutely accurate record of what he said. When he spoke in the House of Commons he would usually himself insert any alterations which he made, and the copy so altered would go into the record files.

He always uses stylo-style pens and we had a number of these available. Normally there were two in use, one for black ink and one for red, but during his term as First Lord of the Admiralty the number was increased by the addition of a green one—"Must have port and starboard," he said. For any correspondence which he did by hand and for signing letters, etc., he used the black one, but the red and green appeared gaily—and sometimes fearfully!—in the form of comments on Departmental documents, corrections, etc.

When we went away I carried an attaché-case containing a supply of notepaper and envelopes in a variety of sizes and shapes, copying paper and carbons. The famous "Klop" had to go in duplicate—so that when a session of dictation was about to commence, I had one by my side and placed another by him. There had also to be an assortment of the essential green tags, a copy of Vacher's *Parliamentary Companion*, scrap-paper, shorthand notebooks, pens, pencils, rulers, rubbers, scissors, paste, rubber bands and, last but not least, a black band in case he should decide to sleep in the car. This latter was a strip of black satin about two inches wide, with elastic at the back, which he could slip over his head and cover his eyes, thus precluding the possibility of light preventing his obtaining those few vital minutes of sleep which contributed so largely to his ability to work the hours he did.

In time I learnt never to be surprised at any duties which came my way, but I was certainly startled in my early days with him at some of the things which had to be taken in one's stride. One job I particularly disliked. Before the war he was doing a series of articles for the *Daily Telegraph*. These appeared simultaneously in a Paris newspaper, and if the typescript was not ready for the night mail it had to be dictated over the telephone to the French newspaper office. The article in question was about 2,000 words in length and as the typist who took it down in Paris was French—and the line was none too good—I found my first experience of this a little unnerving.

When we moved into No. 10 Downing Street, in May 1940, I had a bedroom on the top floor, but I did not sleep there for very long. When the Blitz started in September we used to go over to the "Annexe", a strong, modern building nearby, as soon as things became noisy, and as I did the late work, I slept over there, while my possessions remained in my bedroom at No. 10. The night came when the bombs on the back of the Treasury did quite a lot of damage to No. 10 itself. My bedroom ceiling cascaded down and lay at an angle across my bed. I had been in the "Annexe" at the time and the Prime Minister's remark on seeing the damage in my bedroom was characteristic: "You would have been all right, Miss Shearburn. The bed is still there."

During my war-time duty I made a number of trips with him and, as his secretary, I was the first woman to travel in a naval ship in the Second World War, when in January 1940—while he was First Lord of the Admiralty—I went with him to France in the destroyer *Codrington*, a trip on which we had some fun shooting up floating mines and dropping a couple of depth charges. When we reached Paris the remainder of the party went on to the British Army zone and I was left at the Hotel Crillon. The following day I had a telephone call from Inspector Thompson, who told me that the First Lord wanted me to join them as he had some work for me. The military authorities in Paris were firm in maintaining that a civilian—and a woman at that!—could not be allowed in the Army zone. Travel restrictions, they explained, were extremely strict. They were sorry but nothing could be done. I said that I knew the First Lord and I knew that when he said I was to join him he meant that I *was* to join him—come what may. They finally gave way and I left the Paris H.Q. the proud possessor of a White Permit, granting me permission to enter "the zone of the British Army in France", and a *"sauf-conduit"* to travel to Arras and return to Paris within four days.

I had one more journey to France with him before the country was overrun. His staff knew that he was going to make the trip but we had been told that the secretary would only be needed on the train to Dover and would then return. Being an optimist I packed an overnight case and took it with me. I was rewarded. As we neared Dover he said: "I have a great deal more work to do, Miss Shearburn, and you will have to come over with me. What will you do about clothes and so on?" I explained that I had brought a case with me, as in war-time one never knew! Despite my efforts to look suitably impassive, he knew how delighted I was and he just grinned at me, expressed no surprise and said no more.

I have, perhaps, given the impression that the Prime Minister was a hard task-master. In some ways, I suppose, he was, but it is only because his own standards are so high and his general knowledge so comprehensive that he demands such high standards of others. To me he was certainly considerate, but it was perfectly understandable that, with his mind occupied with matters of vital importance to the war effort, he could hardly be patient with delays or interruptions which disturbed the flow of his thoughts. Even the pause while a fresh piece of paper was put in my typewriter could be disturbing when he was in the middle of some important dictation. So, as his secretary, I had to keep that in mind and be ever on the alert so that no word was lost. Constantly living at the top of one's form was stimulating in the extreme. No job afterwards could be anything but tame.

GUARDING CHURCHILL

Ex Detective-Inspector W. H. Thompson
B.E.M.

The author of this chapter had for years to bear responsibility for Churchill's personal safety. He was his private bodyguard from early 1921 until, with intervals, he retired in 1945.

Mr. Thompson's duties, however, became wider than that of a protector. As he tells in his story of Churchill from the point of view of his "shadow", his work ranged from helping to clean the artist's palette to joining his charge in wallowing in the mud and slime of an ornamental lake.

His close association with Churchill, both in peace and war, enables him to produce this intimate portrait of the great statesman.

Mr. Thompson is the author of Guard from the Yard, I Was Churchill's Shadow *and* Sixty Minutes with Winston Churchill.

FEBRUARY of the year 1921 was memorable for me. I was instructed during that month to take over the task of guarding Winston Churchill, then Secretary of State for the Colonies. I was far from pleased about this duty. I was at that time under the impression that Churchill was bad tempered and difficult to get along with. How wrong I was! My long years with him taught me what a lovable character he really is. My service, although arduous, turned out to be a wonderful friendship. When I started I had little idea of the many jobs that would fall to me as protector of Churchill. Now I feel that without them my long hours of duty would have become very tedious. To be continually followed about everywhere must become irritating at times, but the "Old Man", or "Father" as many of us affectionately called him, took it all in his stride and I became almost part of the family. My service carried me through thirty different countries and as we travelled Churchill used to relate their histories to me.

My first month with him took me to Egypt and Palestine, where, after his dealing with official matters, we journeyed across the desert on camels, a trip which gave me an early experience of Churchill's determination—and his sense of humour in difficulties. His saddle suddenly slipped round and he fell in the sand. As he sat there a number of gaily dressed Bedouins who had been following our party dashed up on their horses, each offering his animal to Churchill. He rose and replied courteously but firmly, "I started on a camel and I will finish on a camel."

I have spent many hours watching Churchill paint in various parts of the world. He rarely left me alone long before calling and asking for a dab of vermilion or cobalt or some other colour to be squeezed on to his palette. Then, when he had finished for the day, I used to help him to pack up. First, the cleaning of the palette (without cleaning off all the paint), and secondly, the avoiding of any of the dabs of paint dropping on to his picture, which lay at the back of his painting-box. He was busy painting near the Pyramids in 1921 when several British Tommies came up and watched him. One of them commented: "Love-a-duck, Guv'nor, you don't 'alf use some paint one way and another. Lucky for you you ain't a 'ouse painter with me old foreman; you wouldn't 'alf cop it." Churchill turned and smiled and only then did the Tommies recognize him, one saying: "God! It's Winston!" But they were not embarrassed for long, as he started to explain to them at considerable length exactly how the daubs of paint created the picture.

At the various elections which Churchill fought during my service with him, whether he won or lost, he never appeared to turn a hair, except on the occasion of his defeat at Dundee. At that time he had only just recovered from an operation and was far from fit to fight a strenuous election. I had practically to lift him in and out of the hotel where he stayed. When he learned of his defeat he said: "I have tried my best to help the people of Dundee to keep their industries going. I doubt whether their new Member will be able to do as much."

At a later date we were passing the House of Commons while he was driving his small two-seater car. He eased up, looked into Palace Yard, and after a few moments he turned to me and said, "Fancy, Thompson, after a quarter of a century as an M.P., I now have no right as a Member to enter the House of Commons." He then drove on and did not speak again for some time. He was deep in thought.

The Prime Minister's personality is so powerful that even his most minor call or request compels immediate attention whatever the hour or however tired one may be. When at Chartwell Manor, his relaxation took the form of building rockeries, waterfalls and even the formation of several lakes. In doing this work he often continued right through the day, working as hard as anyone else. He and I used to go out together in the morning, wearing clean overalls, and go into the bed of the existing lake, which was being cleaned. Black mud and slime were everywhere. Both of us would set to work, sometimes slipping over in the mud and looking like wet chimney-sweeps when we finished at night. But how happy he seemed to be with this form of relaxation!

My duties with him in peace time often involved working days of sixteen hours or more, but, although tired myself, it always gave me much satisfaction to know that he too had been at work practically all the time I had been on duty. He undoubtedly expects much from his subordinates, but he, in turn, gives every minute to his work.

War-time service with the Prime Minister was entirely different from my experiences during the years of peace. I had retired a few years earlier, and it was with pleasure in August 1939 that I received a telegram telling me to meet him at Croydon Aerodrome, and, then, after proceeding to Chartwell, to be told that I was to guard him again. The easy ways of peace were soon shattered by the long arduous hours and difficulties of war.

I had always admired his fearlessness, but I did feel that during the war he carried it a little too far. Time after time he would remain at Downing Street till well after the Alert had sounded and bombs were dropping. He would then come out and the two of us, with steel helmets on, would walk round St. James's Park before going into the Downing Street Annexe, which was an exceedingly strong building. One night we had been inside the building only a short time when a 1,000 lb. bomb dropped on to the pavement at the end of King Charles Street, which we had walked over just previously. Later Churchill discovered that the roof of the Annexe was flat, so he walked on it on many occasions to watch the bombing of London. If he saw a fire within reasonable distance he would sometimes say, "We will go over there," and off we would go.

When the Annexe, which had been specially reinforced and made into a powerful shelter, was ready for occupation, it housed the Cabinet, the Chiefs of Staff and many others, so that the work of the Government could go on. We all felt relieved that the Prime Minister was at least in a reasonably safe building, until we learnt that he had decided that his own office and domestic rooms should be above the shelter. There he carried on right through the war, only going downstairs occasionally to sleep. He used Chequers during the week-ends when he was able to get away from London, but he missed the relaxation he had previously had at his home at Chartwell.

I was sometimes surprised at the various forms of relaxation he favoured. He wore his well-known "Rompers" or "Siren Suits" on many occasions at Chequers and over them he would wear a multi-coloured dressing-gown. At times, so dressed, he would walk alone in the Great Hall, beating time to the various tunes played on records on the automatic radiogram. I would often stand for some minutes and watch him with amusement. Suddenly he would become aware of my presence, look up and smile one of those charming, boyish smiles so familiar to those who know him well. At other times he would relax by watching films, *Lady Hamilton* being one of his favourites. I can also remember occasions when at the end of the film, apparently oblivious to his guests, he would go to a small bagatelle table and play for some time, absolutely in earnest, as though the game was of the utmost importance. He would mark down his scores carefully and then, as suddenly as he had started to play, he would stop and begin an animated conversation with his visitors.

I recall the day he became Prime Minister in 1940. After visiting King George VI he said to me, "You know why I have been to Buckingham Palace, Thompson?" "Yes, sir," I replied, and I congratulated him on his appointment. He looked pleased but was obviously tense and strained. So I went on: "I am very pleased that at last you have become Prime Minister, sir, but I only wish that the position had come your way in better times, for you have taken on an enormous task." He replied grimly: "God alone knows how great it is. All I hope is that it is not too late. We can only do our best." It seemed to me that tears came into his eyes as he turned away, muttering something to himself. Then, I thought, he appeared to set his jaw and, with a look of determination, mastered all his emotion, and began to climb the stairs. His determination to win through never left him. At the time of Dunkirk we were at the British Embassy in Paris and he was receiving news from time to time of the thousands of troops who were getting back to England. Every time he saw me his face lit up as he told me of the latest figures. His most anxious period of the war, it seemed to me, was at the time of the loss of Singapore. He appeared then to be most despondent and deep in thought. When asked by friends what had happened he would look up with sorrow in his face and reply: "I really do not know. I cannot understand what has happened."

But even though Churchill had to face these reverses and anxious

SECRETARY AND BODYGUARD

Churchill visits a shipyard during the early days of the War accompanied by two of the contributors to this book. Mrs. Thompson, then Miss Shearburn, Churchill's Personal Private Secretary, is in the centre of the picture, and walking in front of her, on Churchill's left, is Detective-Inspector W. Thompson, his bodyguard

times, his sense of humour often rose above them. To me it was most noticeable how happy and boyish he became when he first journeyed to meet President Roosevelt on what has become known as the Atlantic Charter meeting. He was all eagerness to be off, and although the car was ordered for a certain time he was actually at the door of Chequers waiting for it long before the time arranged. His buoyancy continued on the train, where he did some leg-pulling with Lord Cherwell. This mood prevailed also on board the *Prince of Wales*, where Churchill really relaxed and enjoyed films, etc., until the morning of his meeting with the President. He then seemed deep in thought. After the preliminaries of handing a letter from the King to the President had been concluded and Churchill had returned to his cabin, I noticed on his dressing-table a red leather bookmark. On it was inscribed, "Ask and it shall be given you, seek and ye shall find." I drew his attention to it and suggested that it might be a good omen for the Conference about to take place. He appeared pleased at the idea and replied, "I hope it will be; I have much to ask."

The visit to Washington in December 1941 further cemented the friendship between the President and the Prime Minister. There is no doubt that they differed in many ways but they still remained friends and respected each other's ideas. Prior to leaving for England, Churchill paid a short visit to Palm Beach, where he enjoyed the sunshine and sea bathing. Such relaxation did not stop him from carrying on his work between times, often to the early hours of the morning. On our last day there I was waiting for him to go in to bathe when an American Security officer shouted that a fifteen-foot shark had just passed within a few yards of the shore. Churchill came out of the villa and I told him about it. I added, however, that it was a sand shark and harmless. "I am not so sure about that," said the Prime Minister, "I must see his identity card before I trust myself to him." And then he dived straight into the water!

Churchill is irritated by whistling and was much disturbed by it during the war. On one occasion he asked his secretary to open the window and tell people who were whistling as they walked on the Horse Guards Parade to stop. She naturally told him that he could hardly interfere with the public in that manner, but he tried it himself one day. We were walking down King Charles Street, on the way to

No. 10 Downing Street, when a newspaper boy came towards us whistling as loud as he could. When the Prime Minister got close to him he turned to the boy and said very abruptly, "Stop that whistling!" The boy looked at him for a moment and then replied, "Why should I?" Churchill then said firmly: "Because I don't like it. It's a horrible noise!" The boy strolled past us, gave a side glance at Mr. Churchill and said, "You can shut your ears, can't you?" This reply seemed to amuse the Prime Minister as much as it surprised him, for as he entered the Foreign Office Yard he chuckled to himself and kept repeating, "You can shut your ears, can't you?"

Guarding the Prime Minister during the many conferences he attended during the war was a most exciting task. We were surrounded on all occasions by many strangers belonging to the various delegations. It was necessary to make myself fully acquainted with one and all immediately. Even so I had to be constantly on the alert for the slightest error and the possibility of even One Person getting through.

I have often been asked whether any serious attempt has ever been made on Churchill's life. The answer is No. It must be borne in mind, however, that the methods of guarding important people give the possible assassin much to think about before he makes any attempt. He realizes, for instance, that those around are armed and capable of quick action. Guarding does not entail a fear of constant danger; rather does it involve the possibility of sudden and unexpected danger. I can think of only three occasions when it looked as though we might be in for some real trouble, but fortunately nothing happened.

Following the assassination of Sir Henry Wilson by Sinn Feiners in London in 1922 the guarding of Churchill was intensified and he received full protection throughout the whole twenty-four hours of the day. One of my duties at that time was to arrange for his car, an armoured Rolls-Royce, to travel by different routes to Whitehall to avoid possible ambush. One morning we were driving through Hyde Park, travelling parallel to Bayswater Road, when I noticed two men, who looked suspicious to me, waiting by the side of the road. One of them gave a signal to someone ahead of us while our car was travelling slowly owing to the traffic in front. I saw that Churchill had also noticed the incident and had evidently read into it the same significance that I had. He calmly suggested that the car should be stopped. "If they want trouble they can have it," he murmured with a smile, and I knew that he had his own Colt automatic ready. But it was not part of my duty to allow him to become involved in any affray. My job was to avoid trouble and prevent anything happening. I leant over to the chauffeur and snapped, "Step on it; drive like the Devil." He immediately responded without question, swung the car into the middle of the road and sped on to Whitehall without incident.

At a later date, when Churchill was travelling on the cross-Channel steamer from Dover to Dieppe, I spotted a group of men with Sinn Fein badges near his cabin. I saw to it that Churchill remained in his cabin while I contacted a colleague on shore. At Dieppe he was first off the boat and we lunched at a local hotel. Later we drove some miles into the country and I observed that we were being followed. However, our pursuers were shaken off by my boarding the train to Paris while Churchill went in another direction. The strangers followed me on to the train but I had no difficulty in losing them in Paris and later returning to Churchill at Dieppe.

In 1931, when he made a lecture tour of the United States, I had been warned before leaving England that certain members of an Indian society in America had been threatening that he would not leave the country alive. I was therefore well on the alert for trouble, but nothing occurred until after a lecture in Chicago. Here Churchill was talking to a group of people in the foyer when an Indian passed quickly through the swing doors and hurried towards him. I drew my revolver and went forward. As soon as the Indian saw me he turned and dashed out into the street and into the arms of a detective. As I followed I noticed another Indian further down the street jump into a car and drive off. The man who had been seized was not armed and was allowed to go. But that was the sort of incident with which we could never take any chances.

Probably the most dangerous trip Churchill made during the war was the visit to Athens during Christmas 1944. Hidden snipers made several attempts on members of the British delegation and on one occasion there was firing as the Prime Minister stepped from his car. But this time even Churchill was taking no chances. He slept on board the *Ajax* and when ashore travelled about in an armoured car. Whether the three-quarters of a ton of dynamite which was discovered in a sewer close to the hotel where the British delegation were to have stayed was meant for us was problematical.

Churchill is likely to move at any time on the spur of the moment and do the most unexpected things. At the Casablanca Conference, he had walked down to the sea, and after returning by a circuitous route by car he eventually came to a mass of barbed wire which prevented our passing through to the road leading to our villa. A short distance away stood the U.S.A. sentries guarding the incoming open road. As the barbed wire obstructing us meant a long trek back, Churchill, without more ado, said, "We can climb over that," and eventually made his way right through the wire. As the remainder of the party reached him we were suddenly challenged by the sentries, who were covering us with Sten guns. Fortunately the officer in charge recognized the Prime Minister, but was none too pleased at our forcible entry and said so in no uncertain terms. Churchill apologized and the matter closed.

I have never felt more uncomfortable during my service with Churchill than at the Moscow Conference. From the moment I arrived till our return to Teheran I was most anxious. It seemed that any and every move we made was closely watched. On the Saturday, when Churchill and I went to the Kremlin alone, I waited a while and was then called and told to go downstairs to the car. Churchill was not to be seen and I tried to make the officials understand that I must stay and wait for him. Shrugging of shoulders and waving of hands told me nothing. I refused to go to the car and waited at the doorway. After some time I decided to walk in the roadway in the Kremlin grounds, keeping the doorway in sight. I was surprised to find myself being followed by two members of the Ogpu; I did not like this and I returned to the doorway, where I finally learnt that the Prime Minister was remaining with Stalin for dinner and that I was to go and obtain my own meal.

The Teheran Conference appeared to be the most dangerous threat to the lives of the three principals. We had been in the British Legation (now British Embassy) for a matter of only a few hours when the Prime Minister sent for me to tell me that there had been threats against President Roosevelt, Marshal Stalin and himself, and that enemy agents were in Teheran to make attempts at assassination. I immediately got down to the job in real earnest and, after surveying the surrounding buildings, had searches made of those overlooking the grounds of the Legation. Fortunately, President Roosevelt became the guest of Marshal Stalin at the Soviet Embassy and by closing the road between the British Legation and the Soviet Embassy, Churchill was able to pass from the side entrance and cross the road to the Russians in comparative safety.

The years I spent in guarding Churchill were happy years. As I have already explained, I entered his service with some apprehension. But with time my affection grew and he commanded my absolute and complete loyalty.

I have at times considered him unfair in his attitude with me, but never unfair for long. If he criticized and subsequently found the criticism to be unfounded, he apologized.

Churchill does not seek cheap popularity. As I saw and knew him his outstanding characteristics are his fearlessness, honesty, patriotism and his sense of destiny.

CHURCHILL
AND THE EX-SERVICEMEN

Sir Ian Fraser, M.P.

*Lieutenant-Colonel Sir Ian Fraser, who was blinded in the
First World War, is National President of the British Legion and
Chairman of the Executive Council of St. Dunstan's for men and
women blinded on war service. He entered Parliament in 1924 and
is now M.P. for Morecambe and Lonsdale.*

SIR WINSTON CHURCHILL has the knack of always looking happy when he is keeping public engagements; he seems to have acquired naturally an art which some public men have to cultivate carefully. But nobody watching the Prime Minister can doubt that when he is at a gathering of old soldiers he is genuinely at home and glad to be there. He has a quick, kind, impulsive way with him which makes you think that his meeting with you, however casual, really matters to him.

Churchill has a fellow feeling very highly developed and he always seems to have time for a passing word with the most unlikely people. It is quite extraordinary what detail seems to be stored in his mind and how his memory will produce the apt word at the right time.

When we are going to vote in a Division Lobby at the House of Commons I always find my way by process of feeling and hearing and remembering the familiar route and I may proceed along the journey of a hundred paces entirely by myself. On the other hand, I may fall in with a friend and joining up we will walk through the Lobby together. On many occasions it will be Churchill, with all his pre-occupations, who, coming up behind me, will say: "Hallo, Ian, this is Winston. I will be your guide as well as your leader."

This friendliness is always apparent at Service and ex-Service reunions. It is obvious that it is no mere sense of duty that takes him there.

Churchill's post-war speeches at the Alamein gatherings have been short, and delivered in the main without those full notes which he uses for all his parliamentary and platform speeches. None the less, he has never been under the illusion that an ex-Service audience is content with a few platitudes and a few jokes about "the good old days". He has always spoken to the men about current world problems, and dealt with the principles underlying Britain's defence and foreign policy.

Not that Churchill is ponderous and heavy on these occasions. He knows his audience expects some humour. In 1951 he went to the Alamein gathering on the eve of the General Election; in 1952 he was there as Prime Minister. "Last time I was here I was out of a job," he observed, "but as you may know I found one shortly afterwards."

In 1941 the British Legion's National Executive Council appointed Churchill a Life Member, and he is President of the Westerham Branch. His practical interest in its work for the well-being of ex-Service men was shown five years later. He was presented with Kippington Court, near Sevenoaks, Kent, in 1946, and decided to donate it to the Legion. Renamed Churchill Court, it has been in use ever since as a convalescent and rest home. He opened it for use in October 1946.

My own most vivid memory of Churchill is of the evening in January 1947 when he came to a St. Dunstan's dance at Seymour Hall in London. He was deeply moved by the tumultuous reception he got from a hall crowded with blinded men from the two wars who stood to cheer him for minutes on end.

That evening marked the completion of my first twenty-five years as Chairman of St. Dunstan's. Its members at home and overseas had raised a fund to make a presentation to Lady Fraser and myself. Churchill had come along to hand over part of the presentation—a suitably engraved walking-stick.

Churchill recalled his long interest in the work of St. Dunstan's, which goes back to the years just after World War I when he was a personal friend of Sir Arthur Pearson. Then I found it intensely moving as he spoke of my own career as illustrating "how vital, happy lives can be lived in spite of what seems to be an overwhelming calamity". He seemed to sense the tension in the air as he developed this theme. So he was quick to add a joke as he handed over the stick, calling it "a symbol of gratitude to him and a crutch to aid him, not only in finding his way about, but in disposing of anybody who stands between him and the high purpose he serves".

During the last war, when he had so many other—and some people would say so much more important—matters to attend to, Churchill devoted a great deal of time to the question of what medals should be awarded to those who were taking part in the various battles and campaigns. It was characteristic of the man that he should have appreciated the importance of the issues involved, and that he should have decided to investigate them himself rather than delegate responsibility to a subordinate. I would add in passing that King George VI shared his Prime Minister's close interest in these matters, and was frequently consulted by him before statements on the subject were made in Parliament or White Papers were issued.

King George VI was indeed very interested in medals, medal ribbons and other military details and had an encyclopaedic knowledge of them. Sitting next to me at the Festival of Remembrance at the Albert Hall on one occasion, he said: "I am glad you have got your medals on. I always wear mine and I like the ex-Servicemen to wear theirs. It shows they're proud of the service they rendered."

"We must never forget that these medals are the poor man's escutcheon," Churchill observed in one of his war-time statements on the matter in the House of Commons.

There you have the clue both as to why he went so carefully into the number of medals to be issued and the qualifications for them. You also have in that short and simple sentence a revealing glimpse of Sir Winston's whole attitude to the ex-Serviceman. To him what matters most is that the individual should take pride in having served his country, and that the public should honour those who have served. Too many medals too easily won or too widely distributed would lessen that pride, and lessen public esteem. Therefore, strict limits must be imposed.

In these, as in other matters, Churchill kept a sure touch with what the men in the Forces were thinking and feeling. That was partly because in his war-time visits to the troops at home and abroad he used to seize every opportunity of mixing with men of all ranks, but in the main it was because he has always at heart been a soldier and has never lost the instincts of the ordinary fighting man.

I remember how during an all-night session in the war years he came down to the House of Commons an hour or two before the end of the debate and apologized for coming thus early as it had been expected that he would wind up. "I have come now," he said, and his voice was relaxed and tired so that it was not easy to hear exactly what he said. "But it has been arranged," he went on, and as the thought

entered his mind his voice changed and became sonorous and clear—
"It has been arranged that I spend the night with the men in the trenches
and on the defences of our coast-line." I remember I had a lump in
my throat as I thought of this giant leaving the cares of his office to
spend the night with the troops, a job which you might have thought
could have been done by a junior. But Churchill was right, for not only
did he bring encouragement to those on the job, but also to the nation
at large, who saw photographs of him or read about him in the newspapers the next day.

To address a gathering of soldiers or ex-Servicemen is a high test
for any politician. The pitfalls are many and deep. To the man at the
front or the man who has been at the front, patriotism and glory are
sentiments to feel privately, but at all costs to hide, or at the worst to
keep silent about. A speaker who drags such deep and intimate sentiments out into the open can easily evoke the kind of revulsion that
Kipling records in *Stalky & Co*. But there can have been few of the
thousands of the Eighth Army who were not both moved and delighted
when Churchill addressed them in Tripoli in February 1943. Let me
give just one extract to show the temper and quality of that speech.
"After the war when a man is asked what he did, it will be quite
sufficient for him to say 'I marched and fought with the Desert
Army.' And when history is written your feats will gleam and glow,
and will be a source of song and story long after we who are gathered
here have passed away."

But before the old soldier fades away there will come a period
when he likes to reflect upon the past. It is my experience that the older
you get the more you tend to swap stories about the services you
rendered or the experiences you had in various parts of the world as a
soldier, sailor or airman. Shortly after the war you are fed up with all
these thoughts and leave them alone, but some years later you become
retrospective and you like telling tales and are even willing to listen to
them from others about campaigns and battles and dug-outs and
trenches and ships and aeroplanes and officers. The older you get, the
less survivors there are of your experience, so that your imagination can
have full play without fear of informed criticism. This human trait may
account for the fact that the British Legion reached its peak of membership some ten years after the First World War and that at this moment,

some eight years after the end of the second, the numbers are increasing, especially amongst the younger men.

Of course, Churchill knew what the first hope and prayer of all the men in the Forces was—to get home. "Their hearts' desire is that after their duty has been done and the job is finished they shall come back home," he said to a Conservative Conference in London in March 1945. This complex business of getting the men home, turning Servicemen into civilians, was perhaps of all post-war problems the one he faced with most concern.

Churchill had unhappy memories of what had happened after the 1918 Armistice. Far too little consideration had been given by the Lloyd George Administration to the details of its demobilization plans. These were drawn up primarily with an eye to the industrial and commercial needs of the transition period, and Churchill subsequently complained that the authorities had not accorded proper weight to the feelings of the troops in such matters. If they had done so they would never have sanctioned the release of "key men" on such a scale. "Key men", by the very fact of their indispensability to industry, had usually been the last to be called up, and many of them had not been enrolled until the war and manpower crisis of March 1918. Yet they began to get back into mufti—some of them by influence and personal pull—while men who had been through the bloody battles at Ypres and the Somme, years before, stayed on in France and Germany.

Churchill was not in the least surprised that this affront to the troops' sense of fair play led to a breakdown of discipline, and in some places to actual mutinies.

It fell to him to put things right. When Lloyd George reconstructed his Government after the Election, he made Churchill Secretary of State for War and Air—instead of sending him back to the Admiralty as he expected. Tackling the demobilization muddle was the first job that faced him when he went to the War Office in January 1919. With characteristic speed he drew up a new plan under which length of service was the main guide to priority in release, and he got the Generals to agree to it and embody it in new Army orders. Then he hurried over to Paris, took the Prime Minister away from the Peace Conference to discuss and approve the plans, and then went back to London to see them put into immediate operation. The Churchill plan

struck the troops as fair; the mutinies ceased. Soon demobilization was
proceeding smoothly and soldiers were returning to civil life in a
steady and accelerating stream.

But like a good many other people, Churchill in 1919 was making
the mental resolve "Never again". When he became Prime Minister in
1940, and appointed Ernest Bevin as his Minister of Labour, he soon
took up with him the question of demobilization plans, distant though
the prospects were of their being put into operation. This time, he
was determined there must be an orderly plan worked out in detail and
not a hasty, last-minute improvisation. So the "age plus length of
service" formula was drawn up, and the troops were told just what
would happen.

This war-time plan had, of course, been based on the assumption
that it would take a year or more to beat the Japanese after the war in
Europe had been brought to an end. Use of the atom bomb falsified
that assumption; but the Labour Government adhered to the letter of
the Coalition's demobilization scheme. It was on this issue that
Churchill based his first attack on the new Government. He demanded
reconsideration of the scheme now that it was keeping thousands of
men in the Forces doing nothing merely because there was insufficient
shipping to bring home from the Far East others who had a prior
claim to release. The new Government, with its overwhelming
majority, was not much disposed to listen; but by concentrating
parliamentary and public attention on the matter Churchill undoubtedly helped to speed up releases.

Another complaint Churchill had in 1945 about the Labour
Government was on the form in which Parliament should express its
gratitude to the victorious Forces. Traditionally, military commanders
have been voted substantial sums of public money at the end of a
war. In 1945 this tradition was broken for the first time. No grants
at all were made. Churchill, protesting at this—and at the less understandable omission of even the names of the commanders from the
parliamentary resolution of thanks to the Forces—encountered a rough
reception. He was shouted down with cries of "Tommy Atkins".

The ex-Premier glared and growled at his interrupters. "There is
no set of His Majesty's subjects," he declared, "who would be more
gratified than the Army to know that this House had at any rate given

its thanks to the distinguished commanders who have led them to victory."

I have no doubt at all that Churchill there spoke for the great mass of Servicemen and ex-Servicemen. Whether a majority would have gone all the way with him in regretting the dropping of these grants of £100,000 and more is a different question. It is interesting, none the less, to reflect that while in 1945 special payments in the military field ceased, they continued for the scientist and the inventor. I am surprised that the implications of this have not as yet formed the theme of a Churchillian speech.

When the war-time National Government broke up in May 1945, and the General Election came, Churchill was determined on two things. There must be no auction between parties trying to outbid one another in promises to the ex-Serviceman. He had been active during the war in promoting increases and improvements in the pensions schemes, but in May 1945 he flatly declined to promise any increase on the eve of the Election. "I trust there will be no popularity-hunting at the public expense in this or kindred subjects," he told the House of Commons.

Equally firm was his conviction that it would be unfair to the returning soldiers if the politicians made radical changes in our social life and system before they were back and had settled down in civil life. At a Conservative Conference just before VE-Day he ridiculed the Left-Wing view that the ex-Servicemen would want to find a brave new world all ready for them when they disembarked at Liverpool, in the Clyde, at Southampton or at Tilbury Docks. That, he said, was not what the fighting men were looking forward to. They wanted to come back to a home and a job. They did not regard themselves as a slum-bred, serf population: they loved their country. When they were home and settled down, when their country was again a going concern, then would be the time for them to settle what form and shape our society should assume.

Churchill seldom forgets an old friend or servant. Once he wrote to me commending an old soldier who had served him well. "He drove for me," said Churchill, "and if you can help him I shall be glad. Perhaps you could get someone at the British Legion to look into his case and give it a fair wind." I did.

CHURCHILL
IN INTERNATIONAL AFFAIRS

Lord Altrincham

Lord Altrincham, formerly Sir Edward Grigg, is Editor of the
National Review. *He was Military Secretary to the Prince of*
Wales (now the Duke of Windsor) during his tours of Canada,
Australia and New Zealand and was Private Secretary to David
Lloyd George during his Premiership. He was Member of Parlia-
ment for Oldham 1922–25 and for Altrincham from 1933 to 1945.
In the National Government during the War he was Parliamentary
Secretary to the Ministry of Information 1939–40, Financial
Secretary to the War Office 1940, Joint Parliamentary Under-
Secretary of State for War 1940–42, and Minister Resident in the
Middle East 1944–45. Lord Altrincham has written several books
on international affairs including The Greatest Experiment in
History, Britain Looks at Germany *and* British Foreign Policy.

A N astonishing paradox confronts anyone who reflects on Sir Winston Churchill's unequalled record of service to his own country, Europe and the English-speaking world. He has influenced the relations of Britain and America and also the history of Europe more profoundly than any statesman for at least a century; he enjoys a wider respect in all the continents than any of his predecessors in Downing Street; he has held almost all the great Cabinet posts; but—and here is the paradox—he has never been Secretary of State for Foreign Affairs. It must therefore be understood that this brief appreciation cannot rightly be confined to "foreign policy" in the narrower sense which occupies the Foreign Offices of all Powers from week to week; it must take a more spacious view and survey nothing less than world history over a period of fifty years.

The first and foremost duty of any statesman who deals with international relations in any age is to guard the life and strength and well-being of the nation, or community of nations, which he serves. For British statesmen in this century that has been a terribly exacting task; for they have had to deal with formidable changes in the balance of political and economic power—changes which must in any event have reduced Britain's international stature as other Powers caught her up, but which were accelerated and intensified beyond all prediction by the strain and stress of two World Wars. Out of the last fifty years Britain has in fact spent at least twenty-five either in the shadow of threatened war, or in actual and total war, or in wrestling with the aftermath of war. The cost of this ordeal in life, wealth and all the material aspects of power has been so terrible that it might well have left her mortally crippled had she been, in the years of actual crisis, less wisely and bravely led. For a democratic nation hers has been an unparalleled ordeal. All other nations of Europe have undergone it, but they all for the time being collapsed under the strain,

Britain, happily for her, was an island. That gave her a certain time for self-collection; but it gave her no security other than her own unaided courage could maintain. She owed her survival to two things which she has never lacked—innate character and leadership.

Given her innate strength of character, the measure of the greatness of her leaders can therefore best be read in the measure of the foresight, nerve and judgment which they showed in guarding or striving to guard her most vital interests against the threat or in the crucible of war; and it is by that measure that the outstanding value of Sir Winston Churchill's services in the international field can best be appraised. The tragedy is that his genius in this field was largely frustrated by faults either in himself or others for twenty-nine years after his appointment as First Lord of the Admiralty in 1911, and that he was prevented in 1945 from reaping for his country the full benefit of what his leadership had achieved. By that year, nevertheless, he was by general acknowledgment the greatest man of the whole free world and he has since then, whether in or out of office, done more than any other man except the late Marshal Stalin to shape the course of international affairs.

In order to do full justice to this achievement it is necessary further to remember how profoundly the conditions of this century have differed from those of the Victorian age, in which Britain had had to wage no wars but highly localized ones such as the Crimean War and various frontier affairs. From 1815 to 1914 no British Government had been confronted by any serious threat to the supremacy which sea-power and a tremendous lead in commerce had given us after the Napoleonic Wars. In these circumstances our leaders in both Parties had come to regard the Navy and Army as little more than a glorified amphibious Police maintained to protect our trade upon the seven seas, to show the flag in distant places (especially in places where British interests might be threatened), and generally to safeguard the Pax Britannica on our frontiers and on the sea-ways and sea-boards of the world. Until the last year of the nineteenth century this easily sustained peace system seemed destined to flourish indefinitely, and its long continuance almost atrophied the combined political and strategic sense which never slept in men like Nelson, Wellington and the Pitts. Our population in their time was, of course, less than a fourth of what it had become by 1914. They had therefore to husband man-power by every possible means and to foster our insular resistance to the continental enemy by building up alliances and to some considerable extent financing them, while using our own sea-power to blockade his ports and to harry him by sea-borne attacks upon his flanks or rear. The two main principles of this war strategy were diversion and careful economy of the flexible but limited power which we possessed; and they were to prove as vital to our survival in the twentieth century as in any previous one.

When Napoleon had at last been defeated by these means, the ancient challenge to our insular security from a predominant European Power seemed to have been dismissed for ever, despite an occasional flurry caused by our secular suspicion of France. We reclined upon our laurels for the rest of the century without interruption to the vast development of our national business or any sense of menace to our established status as the only World Power existing in that age. As Imperial Rome relied for her security upon frontier legions to which she gave but little thought, so Imperial Britain relied upon the Navy and a minute Army to keep the Empire safe; the idea of mortal peril, and with it the study of war *à outrance*, war for very life, went into complete eclipse.

But when the youthful Churchill matriculated into politics, events had already rung the knell of this long Victorian truce. The South African War, largely engineered by persistent German intrigue, had shattered the idea that our nineteenth-century Army would be equal to our twentieth-century needs; and almost simultaneously the steady enlargement of the German Army and Germany's declared intention of making her strength in battleships equal to ours showed that Britain was once more confronted by the challenge of a dominant continental Power. Our reply to this was threefold: first, a rapid expansion of the Navy, with the new Dreadnought battleships and the battle-cruisers to reinforce our battle strength; secondly, the creation of the Territorial Army and a new Expeditionary Force; and, thirdly, the negotiation of the Entente Cordiale with France, later extended by the inclusion of Russia into the Triple Entente, and by an alliance with Japan.

These wise and timely measures were rightly designed primarily as a guarantee of peace; our leaders at the time had given little thought to the further question: how best to exploit them if, despite our efforts to avert it, war nevertheless broke out. Germany's attack on France and Russia in the first week of August 1914 accordingly found this country unprepared in mind for such an emergency as well as plunged into fierce domestic controversy, on the brink indeed of civil war. I am drawing on very vivid memories of the chief personalities of both Parties at that time when I say that on the actual outbreak of war, forced upon a divided and most reluctant Cabinet by Germany's unconscionable breach of treaty faith, only three of our outstanding statesmen or military chiefs fully appreciated what in fact had happened and—still more important—what lay in store. They were Lord Roberts, a veteran of eighty-two years; Lord Kitchener, a mature but still vigorous soldier of sixty-four; and Winston Churchill, a Cabinet Minister of forty—and only the last had at that moment his hand on the levers of State.

He had already played a considerable part in building up the Fleet, and he mobilized it now without Cabinet sanction before the declaration of war. Unfortunately this triumph of foresight could not be put to its most effective use in the military sphere. A Council of War was convened at No. 10 Downing Street on the afternoon of August 5, as the German armies streamed through Belgium into France. Lord Roberts, who had foretold this turning movement, advised, when called to the Council with Lord Kitchener, that our Expeditionary Force should land at Antwerp and, with the Belgian Army, attack the Germans' lengthening right flank and rear. This was the classic British strategy of diversion applied with Roberts's infallible instinct to a situation which he had foreseen. Unhappily our traditional strategy had been forgotten by the Services and the statesmen in the long nineteenth-century peace, and no thought had in consequence been given to such diversionary use of the Expeditionary Force. Churchill reported that, thanks to his initiative in anticipating the mobilization of the Fleet, the Admiralty would waive the condition on which it had hitherto insisted that two Regular Divisions should be kept in England at the outset of war. All seven Divisions could therefore be moved at once, but only to French ports west of the Straits of Dover, because the naval dispositions as planned in advance made it impossible to guarantee a large movement of transports east of the Straits. In addition, the French Grand Quartier Général had been led to expect the Expeditionary Force as an immediate reinforcement on the left of the French front. So the British Army joined the French Army in the famous retreat; and though both turned with powerful effect upon the Marne, we were from that moment doomed to the long deadlock in France which engulfed so much of the cream of British youth. "Victory," wrote Churchill years later in his history of the war, "was to be bought so dear as to be almost indistinguishable from defeat."

It was no fault of his that the pre-war Army plan had thus been made inflexible for the first decisive phase of hostilities, and he recognized very quickly that the minds of the commanders in the field, such as French and Haig, were closed to other alternatives. They believed, despite the headlong initial retreat, that the German Army would be driven back by frontal attack with such little manœuvre as battle movements might make possible in the centre or on the flanks. They insisted therefore that every officer and man should be thrown into the *mêlée* at once, convinced that, if this were done, the war would be over by Christmas. Officers in England and India who had not gone to France at once lamented that they would never get to the front. But Churchill, like Lord Kitchener, saw differently, and made one last gallant effort with his naval resources to preserve Antwerp with its invaluable port facilities and its strong surrounding forts and inundations as a hinge for manœuvre on the left of the rapidly stabilizing front; but his forces were inadequate, and they came too late.

I dwell upon this, the first example of Churchill's impact on British international policy, because it is the key to the splendid leadership he gave this country and the Commonwealth from the moment he became Prime Minister in the Second World War—a leadership which not only saved the freedom and genius of Europe's most civilized peoples from eclipse, but also carried Britain triumphant with no more than a third of her former sacrifice of life through a Second World War half as long again as the First, and even more perilous. Not one, in fact, of the great Englishmen who have possessed the priceless combination of political and military sense—not Marlborough or Chatham or Nelson or any other—has surpassed Churchill in the distinctive genius for statesmanship in peace and war on which the greatness of this little island has been built, namely an infallible instinct for the balance of power indispensable to its security, alertness to any threatened disturbance of that balance however far ahead, and imaginative resource, when the balance has been disturbed, in righting it by the most effective and economical use of our always inadequate strength. It is due, I repeat, to this, the dominant element in his genius, that Western Europe is not at this moment a dependency of either Nazi Germany or Soviet Russia, and Britain still the lynch-pin of security for both Western Europe and the English-speaking world. It is therefore worth marking, from his own writings, on what lines that genius works.

The secret is to be found in an enlightening passage of a chapter entitled "The Deadlock in the West" at the beginning of Part II of his book *The World Crisis 1911–1918*, in which he emphasizes the vital importance of manœuvre in war. Manœuvre, he explains, may take many forms—"in time, in diplomacy, in mechanics, in psychology". Military and political thought must in fact be combined in order to find "easier ways, other than sheer slaughter, of achieving the main purpose" —the same principle (one may add) applying to peace-time policy with the sovereign difference that provident statesmen may then avoid not only slaughter but all open appeal to force. "The distinction between politics and strategy," Churchill concludes, "diminishes as the point of view is raised. At the summit true politics and strategy are one." It is on that summit that his mind has dwelt continuously; from it derive his range, resource, and imaginative grasp, and therewith his prodigious influence and achievement in international affairs during the thirteen years of violent struggle and fundamental change which have passed since he first became Prime Minister.

The most signal example of that gift in World War I—for which, ironically enough, he was deprived of office and power—was his project of forcing the Dardanelles. The political arguments for that undertaking were as weighty as the military ones. If successful— as it very nearly was—it would have eliminated Turkey from the war, with consequences of great value throughout the Middle East; it would have prevented Bulgaria from entering the war on Germany's side; it would have permitted the reinforcement of Russia with all the equipment of which her splendid manpower stood in need; and, with Germany held between two extensive embattled fronts, east and west, which she could not afford to weaken, it would have opened her most vulnerable flank in Austria to a deadly thrust with the great port of Constantinople as its base. Churchill's was the mind which first perceived all this when tortured by the threatened cost of frontal offensives against an entrenched German line in France which by Christmas 1914 had no flanks. It was the classic political and military solution to a problem of that kind; and it would have succeeded had the naval and military operations been better combined and the Suvla Bay landing driven home.

"Everyone save the wilfully purblind," wrote Captain Liddell Hart twenty-three years later, "now realizes that, in the words of the German official account, 'Churchill's bold idea was not a fine-spun fantasy of the brain', and that the real sufferers from delusions were the commanders on the Western Front. . . . We too now know, as the Germans did in the War, how feasible was the Dardanelles project, and how vital its effect would have been."[1]

We know too the cost of the blindness—a needlessly protracted war and millions of lives!

It was not Churchill who carried us through that World War, but it is a fact that the history of Europe would have been entirely different had his ideas as to the Dardanelles and more than one other subject at that time prevailed. Our national life has thus been permanently deprived of a twenty-years' swath in the best of its ripened or ripening manhood because we had lost our traditional wisdom in placing and husbanding our strength. The cost is reckoned in a tragic passage of Churchill's book *The Aftermath*, which shows what that old wisdom might have saved us in 1914–18 and what, reincarnate in him, it was worth to his country and the free world in 1939–45. In this passage he summarizes the comparative figures of British and German casualties on the British sector of the Western Front from February 1915 to October 1918—that is, from the moment when the armies were immobilized by opposing systems of trench defence covered by many square miles of barbed wire and disposed in many longitudinal miles of depth to the final break-up. The British figures are those published

[1] *Through the Fog of War*, by Liddell Hart, 1938, p. 288.

by the War Office; the German figures were obtained from the Federal Archives in Berlin. This is how, in appalling contrast, they work out:

> "The total number of British Officer casualties was 115,741, and of German Officer casualties 47,256. The total number of British Other Ranks casualties was 2,325,932 and of German Other Ranks casualties 1,633,140. The casualties among British Officers compared to German were therefore about 5 to 2, and of British Other Ranks compared to German Other Ranks about 3 to 2."

What more awful condemnation of the strategy of 1914-18, which Churchill strove to correct! What more eloquent tribute to the strategy of 1939-45, which, as we shall see, Churchill managed to pursue despite many difficulties with President Roosevelt and despite Premier Stalin's unrelenting demand for a premature Second Front!

Before, however, I proceed with this theme into World War II, I must pause to interpolate, with chronological correctitude, a necessarily telescoped reference to another of Churchill's contributions to international history—his strong and consistent support of Zionism. He had—so far as I know—nothing to do with the Balfour Declaration of 1917, out of which the State of Israel was born; but he was responsible as Colonial Secretary for the Middle Eastern settlement, which, in the winter of 1920-21, established the British Mandate in Palestine and at the same time the Kingdom of Iraq (then including Syria) and the Emirate of Transjordan, in both of which (like a new Kingmaker Warwick) he seated Hashemite princes upon newly created thrones. It would be impossible to abridge the story that resulted, both before and after World War II, without dogmatizing on "might-have-beens" which are still in violent dispute. But in view of subsequent Arab wrath against him, it is right to quote what Lawrence of Arabia, no enemy of the Arab peoples, said of the settlement which he then devised and imposed:—

> "Winston Churchill was entrusted by our harassed Cabinet with the settlement of the Middle East. In a few weeks at his Conference in Cairo he made straight all the tangle, finding solutions fulfilling (I think) our promises in letter and spirit (where humanly possible) without sacrificing any interest of our Empire or any interest of

the peoples concerned. So we were quit of war-time Eastern adventure, with clean hands, but three years too late to earn the gratitude which peoples, if not States, can pay."

This quotation, which is taken from *The Seven Pillars of Wisdom*, ends with a touch of cynicism which suggests that Lawrence had little genuine confidence in the concordat which Churchill hoped he had made between Arabs and Jews. Despite, however, all that has gone wrong in Palestine between that year and this, I say with confidence, as the member of Churchill's Government who was resident in the Middle East in 1944 and 1945, that the Arab-Zionist issue in Palestine would have been peacefully settled, with the indispensable support of the United States, if Churchill had not been ousted by Attlee in 1945 at a moment when all was at stake. The rest of the story is Ernest Bevin's, who did not understand either Jews or Arabs and failed to prevent President Truman from playing American domestic politics, crude and unashamed, with a Middle Eastern question of vital moment to the freedom of the West. The N.A.T.O. nations are still paying for that; but Churchill has no responsibility for the state of suppressed war between Israel and her neighbours which the Kremlin is now busily exploiting. Nor has he yet said his last word upon that issue. All is at present on a razor's edge—and that is that. But while the issue remains uncertain, Churchill's mind and method in dealing with it have been so distinctive that they throw much light upon other aspects of his record and so demand a passing note.

Sir Winston Churchill has a vivid sense of history which is sometimes more romantic than correct, and also a strategic instinct which—as I have already said repeatedly—is never at fault. Both made him a Zionist. The home-coming of the Dispersion to Palestine, the seat of David and Solomon, is a restoration from which no historian—be he Old-Testament Christian or liberal hater of imperialisms—can easily dissent. As for the strategic side, Churchill was right in judging from the first that an infusion of Jewish capacity might do much to refertilize the many empty and long-neglected lands in what was once justly called the Fertile Crescent. The fact that Palestine doubled its population under the Mandate and that Arabs constituted a good half of that increase proves the justice of his belief. If only Jews and Arabs had been able to co-operate, both Syria and Jordan as well as Palestine would now be highly prosperous, contented and reasonably stable States. This was Churchill's aim, based on the desire to bring a new non-alien element of strength and stability into the critical strategic area which stretches from the Nile to the Persian Gulf; and it was not unreasonable to hope for its success, since the Jews belong ethnically to the Arabs' own Semitic race.

The danger lay in a clash of Arab and Jewish nationalism, only to be prevented (as I myself believed) by working for a Palestinian State of double nationality, in which Jewish capacity would undoubtedly have taken the lead but of which the Arabs of Palestine would have been equal members with a security now lost. Many Zionist leaders of high standing agreed that the Jewish Home in Palestine could best be developed on these lines—such men, for instance, as the late Dr. Magnes, who was head of the Jewish University on Mount Scopus, now in Arab territory and derelict. But others like Israel's late President, Dr. Weizmann, a scientist of outstanding talent and a leader strong in personality and faith, moved steadily towards the conversion of the Jewish Home into a Jewish National State; and this became the purpose of the Jewish Agency in Palestine, though it involved some infringement of the Mandate and the wholesale alienation of Arabs not only in Palestine itself but throughout the Middle East.

I myself shared in 1945 the conviction of Dr. Magnes that, despite the fanaticism of the modern Jewish *sicarii* (who murdered Lord Moyne, my predecessor as Middle Eastern Minister), it would still be possible, with firm American support, to bring Jews and Arabs together in a bi-national Palestinian State and thus to prevent the bitter strife which has divided the Holy Land and Jerusalem itself between two hostile Governments. Churchill has assuredly not been responsible for any part of that tragedy; but it is, I think, a fact that since 1945 he has underrated the psychological reaction of the Arab world to Israel's national mystique and that, but for this, he might have done much with his enormous influence to modify the one-sidedness and incomprehension which have distorted the Middle Eastern policy of the United States. Arab pride is now most deeply wounded, and much suffering has been caused by the expatriation or flight of two-thirds of the Palestinian Arabs from their ancestral homes. All this need not have happened, and there will be no security against Communist imperialism in Egypt or the Arabian Peninsula until it is repaired.

The story is worth attention here, not only because Churchill's Zionism has been a constant element in his approach to international affairs, but also because it illustrates a strong tendency on his part to overlook the ingrained particularities of ancient peoples in the sweep and broad good sense of his international ideals. There was some of this, as we shall see, in his handling of his magnificent campaign for European unity. For deep-seated suspicions and fears, which will yield but slowly to healing statesmanship, are not peculiar to the Arabs; they also divide the French and the Germans despite all argument that their not-so-ancient feud should be buried with Hitler, whose diabolical soul, despite his *Götterdämmerung* obsequies, is still alive in Germany, and, like John Brown's, marching on.

Having dealt at some length with Churchill's Zionism, I must be brief with the only other excursions which he made into international politics during his second term of Cabinet office in the Lloyd George Ministry of 1918–22. One of these was his zeal while at the War Office for supporting Kolchak, Denikin and the other White Russian forces against the new Soviet régime. There was never any real hope for leaders representing little but their own memories and those of *émigrés* who had abandoned their fatherland in opposition to a revolution that pretended to give greater freedom and a better status to the long-suffering Russian peasantry. In the pursuit of that adventure Churchill's heart was stronger than his head. Justly foreseeing how dangerous to peace and order in Europe the Soviet Revolution might be, he would have been better advised not to exacerbate by foreign interference a hatred and suspicion of the ancient Powers of Europe which were already sinister and deeply imbedded in the Soviet mind. But he made magnificent amends for that error—and, most characteristically, without admitting or expressing the least regret for it—by the broadcast which he delivered almost without preparation on the very day when Hitler broke his 1939 agreement and flung his armies into the vast West Russian plain.

His other incursion of that period into the international sphere was his prematurely published message to the Dominions as Colonial

Secretary on the need for holding the Turks at Chanak. Here he showed his usual impeccable judgment on the broad political and strategic value of resisting the Kemalite armies and supporting the Greek. The alternative was surrender to a minor Power which we had quite recently defeated, thereby liberating the whole Arabian Peninsula from the mortifying though mild and cynical grip of Ottoman rule. But it was also an affair of honour. The Greek Government had said to us that they could hold the Turkish counter-attack—as undoubtedly they could, having good divisions on the Chatalja Lines—if we would allow them to occupy the key to Thrace—that is, Constantinople and the Bosphorus. Constantinople had, however, been declared a neutral zone by the Allied Powers. We had accordingly, as in honour bound, refused the Greeks' request—adding, however, that this veto would be enforced with equal stringency on their Turkish enemy.

Churchill's foresight was vindicated by the sequel, but unfortunately Lloyd George's Ministry, already tottering, fell. Bonar Law's Government, which succeeded it, ignored our promise to the Greeks (alas for Lord Curzon, who continued as Foreign Secretary into the Bonar Law régime!) and allowed the Turks to cross the Bosphorus and occupy Constantinople. The result of this appalling breach of faith, which was completely unwitting so far as public knowledge was concerned, was absolute humiliation before Kemal Ataturk in the eyes of Europe and the whole Middle Eastern world, signed and sealed by Lord Curzon himself in the Treaty of Lausanne.

Churchill's period of office as Chancellor of the Exchequer from 1924 to 1929 does not concern me here; nor shall I dwell upon the ten long years of frustration during which, from 1929 to 1939, he was excluded from power, because he himself has summarized it once and for all in the first volume of his history *The Second World War*. I cannot, however, refrain from a word of comment on the irony of what occurred. Churchill resigned from the Conservative Shadow Cabinet in 1930 because he was deeply at variance with his leader on the Indian question. He was consequently left out of the National Government formed in 1931 under Mr. Ramsay MacDonald, who was certainly not drawn to the excluded genius by the title of Boneless Wonder which that genius about then conferred on him. The constitution to be bestowed on India was of great importance but not a matter of life and death like the growing menace of Hitler, who achieved supreme power in 1933. It is ironical indeed that during the next six terribly critical years Churchill's influence was reduced so gravely by alienation from his Party on that lesser issue and later also by his warm-hearted championship of King Edward the Eighth in the Abdication crisis, which estranged him still further from the House of Commons and from ordinary, steady-going, conscientious feeling throughout the Commonwealth.

Neville Chamberlain, very rightly, brought him into the Cabinet in 1939, immediately after the outbreak of war, and thus began his finest hour—a long and arduous hour. But for the first nine months there is little to relate except frustration so far as he is concerned. Our Expeditionary Force was once more committed without plan to the left of the French line, where no defences had been made; and during the winter it was decided that in case of a German attack on Belgium it should advance to a line east of Brussels, while all the French divisions that could be spared from the rest of the line were placed on the northern coast under General Giraud for a rapid counter-offensive against the German right. Furthermore, the Grand Quartier Général under Gamelin held firmly to Pétain's opinion that no German attack of serious weight could be pushed through the Ardennes. The British right was therefore left endangered, and the whole front without the mass of manœuvre which should have been held in reserve. All this was decided at an Allied Council in Paris attended by Chamberlain and Lord Halifax with the C.I.G.S., General Ironside, as their military brain. Churchill, at the Admiralty, was not consulted. No wonder that he was dumbfounded by the awful predicament confronting him as Prime Minister when the French front crumbled in the following May.

One suggestion which he pressed with vigour during those nine months was delayed until it was too late to be useful. This was the mining of Norwegian territorial waters. His anxiety as to Norway was prophetic, and he bears no blame for the tardiness and futility of the efforts to save Norway which we ultimately made.

That we should have repeated the major initial follies of 1914 hardly bears thinking on today, and I have recalled it here for one purpose only—to emphasize the debt we owe to Churchill, not merely for the clarion tones in which he heartened us for our long and at first most lonely ordeal, but also for the fact that he so directed the rest of our immense war effort as to make the ultimate victory possible without losses even more crippling than those of World War I, as would assuredly have been the case had our long-drawn effort not been guided and controlled by him.

I would love to illustrate this in detail, but the story need only be streamlined, since it may be read in his own words, told without hindsight by reference to contemporary papers and records—suggestion, consultation, argument, decision as documented at the time. The major rulings were, first, the early concentration of strength in Egypt, though Britain was still threatened with invasion when in the autumn of 1940 an armoured force was sent from her very naked shores. Next in the great series comes the broadcast making common cause with Russia, delivered on the evening of the day when Hitler launched his attack. There follows, immediately after Pearl Harbour in that same year, the agreement arrived at in Washington that the United States should make the defeat of Germany in Europe her primary objective—a decision, let me add, much assisted by Hitler's declaration of war on the United States only a few hours after Japan's. There then unfolds the whole splendid project for clearing North Africa, opening the Mediterranean, and exposing Hitler's long southern flank from the Black Sea and Dodecanese to the Pyrenees. In pursuit of this grand objective British and American divisions sent from Britain or direct from the United States landed in French North Africa. These, as we know, took the German and Italian forces retreating westward before Alexander and Montgomery in the rear and ended by destroying them. The campaign sweeps on to the invasion of Italy, which brought her from Germany's side to ours and held more than twenty divisions on the North Italian front while the German forces were being driven out of France. Last—and most important of all—I must cite the Western Allies' firm refusal to launch an invasion of France until the landing could be made and pressed in sufficient force to preclude all danger of committing irreplaceable life to a protracted battle of attrition such as had wasted the strength and quality of Britain in World War I.

This magnificent deployment, stage by stage, was something far more than a military and strategic achievement; it was first and foremost a triumph of statesmanship, because all depended upon the cohesion of a great Alliance of three Powers with entirely dissimilar points of view which subjected their collaboration to perpetual stress and brought it near breaking-point at more than one turn. Many shared the glory of that triumph—throughout, indeed, it was a woven tissue of brilliant individual strands; but I say with complete assurance that the master-mind which conceived the shape and sequence of the complex design was Churchill's, working always, I must repeat, at that commanding altitude where "policy and strategy are one". Without his over-all leadership, indeed, the awful lack of foresight and plan which marked the first nine months of the war so disastrously might easily have continued to the end—a very different end, assuredly, from that which we attained.

On this subject the figures for our permanent loss of young life in the two wars speak for themselves. Between 1939 and 1945 for all the Armed Forces on all fronts from Normandy to South-East Asia British dead numbered less than half those of 1914–18. World War I, moreover, lasted four and a quarter years only; World War II lasted six.

Not that no mistakes were made. For many the responsibility lies with President Roosevelt rather than Churchill—for instance, the costly failure (costly in the main to us) to clear the whole Mediterranean after the Tunis victory, push the conquest of Italy with greater speed and force, and bring Turkey's fifty or more divisions into the war. But Churchill bears (and accepts) his share of responsibility for one most grave political error, namely the insistence on "unconditional surrender" almost casually agreed in 1943 at the Casablanca Conference. It was also on his initiative, taken almost overnight, that in July 1940 we offered complete political union to France. This was, in fact, no more than a despairing gesture to keep the French Government in the war; but it illustrates two weaknesses in Churchill's make-up which have more than once marred his judgment and achievement in the political sphere. One of these is a tendency to impulsive and emotional decisions in which his political instinct has shown itself much less sound and thorough than his strategic: another instance of this (not relevant here) was his hasty plunge into a General Election in

1945. The other weakness is a certain lack of constitutional sense. This has been manifested ever since his salad days in an attitude towards the House of Lords strikingly at variance with his devotion to national tradition in other forms; and it has greatly marred the effect of the call for unity in Europe which he launched from Zurich in 1946. As right in essence as his even more historic address at Fulton in the same year, this appeal was not, in a psychological sense, attuned to the ears of France, and it was marred by a wilful and, I think, mistaken vagueness on the constitutional side which roused unwarrantable hopes of British readiness to abandon both Crown and Commonwealth in order to become a province in a federal European State, whose constitutional apex, whether to be Monarch or President, no one has yet had the courage even to discuss. A clear proposal for closely interlocked alliances and co-operation on the Commonwealth plan would have been not only more practicable but also in accord with our deeply ingrained monarchical tradition and with our family sense as one of many nations united round the Throne. It would also have prevented any revival of the *Perfide Albion* cry which has militated seriously to reduce our harmonizing and balancing influence in European affairs.

No man is faultless; and Churchill's faults are of the same kind as his genius: vivid, combative, intuitive and warm. But they are fortunately not comparable to his genius in scope or scale, and they have not detracted seriously from his achievement or precluded him, even when out of office here, from exercising an almost unprecedented leadership of international thought and action in the post-war world.

Of that the most salient example is the speech delivered at Fulton, Missouri, in March 1946, for it illustrates better than any other his instinct for fundamental realities in world affairs and for the political and strategic balance necessary, in a world divided as this world now is, to the preservation of peace. In it he called attention to the Iron Curtain—he coined that phrase—which had fallen across Europe, not only cutting off the Western Allies from their great Eastern partner in the war but dividing Germany into two. He observed that the twin dangers of War and Tyranny once again menaced the homes of the people throughout the West, and argued that the Western peoples must unite to avert those dangers, since neither appeasement nor passive indifference would stay the Russian autocracy, which admired nothing so much as strength. The United States, he pointed out, already had a Permanent Defence Agreement with Canada. But since the great Republic "stands at the pinnacle of world power", it had, in his opinion, "an awe-inspiring accountability for the future" which could not be effectively met unless it brought the whole English-speaking world, beside an United Europe, into a single organized system of defence.

There is no question that from that memorable utterance has sprung the organization of the North Atlantic peoples, which, with the atomic bomb, now constitutes the main shield and buckler of freedom and is gradually being extended, through Greece and Turkey, to the Middle East. It is astonishing that it should have been possible for an Englishman, speaking in the presence of the President in a mid-Western State, to deliver, with ultimate acceptance, an argument and appeal thus weaning the American democracy from doctrines to which it had hitherto held through all its history in time of peace. No Englishman but Churchill could have done it, because he is equally compounded of American and English blood and understands the American people as intuitively as he understands the British. By contrast, he does not thus understand peoples of fundamentally different race. The Fulton speech has since quite rightly been christened "The Sinews of Peace".

In this immortal service, the bringing together without constitutional bonds of the two great divisions of the English-speaking world, he has with good reason regarded himself as a man of destiny. Full awareness of his peculiar fitness for it seems to have dawned upon him first on his visit to Washington for the Christmastide of 1941, when he was invited to address the Congress of the United States. This is what he wrote about that most historic day long afterwards in the third volume of his history of World War II:

"It was with heart-stirrings that I fulfilled the invitation to address the Congress of the United States. The occasion was important for what I was sure was the all-conquering alliance of the English-speaking peoples. I had never addressed a foreign Parliament before. Yet to me, who could trace unbroken male descent on my mother's side through five generations from a lieutenant who served in George Washington's army, it was possible to feel a blood-right to speak to the representatives of the great Republic in our common cause. It certainly was odd that it should all work out this way; and once again I had the feeling, for mentioning which I may be pardoned, of being used, however unworthy, in some appointed plan."

He ended his speech to the Congress by avowing his "hope and faith, sure and inviolate, that in the days to come the British and American peoples will for their own safety and for the good of all walk together side by side in majesty, in justice, and in peace".

Again and again since that time, first in the pursuit of victory and then in the guardianship of peace, he has given true and faithful counsel to that end; and he will surely go down to history as the greatest architect in these uncertain times of the only combination of faith and power which can save the far-descended freedom and glory of the Western world.

CHURCHILL AND THE EMPIRE

Sir Evelyn Wrench

Sir Evelyn Wrench, founder of the Overseas League and of the English-Speaking Union, has lectured and written extensively on Empire subjects. During the First World War he was Deputy Controller of the British Empire and U.S.A. sections of the Ministry of Information. He was Editor of the Spectator *1925–32 and is still its Chairman.*

A WORLD in which Winston Churchill was not playing an important part on the stage of Empire affairs seems very remote. It was while I was at Eton that I first became familiar with his name and was told by some of my elders that he would go far. As a true Etonian I was convinced that all Empire-builders or Pro-Consuls came from my *alma mater* and there was pity in my heart because he had to start upon his career with the drawback of being an Harrovian! One of my school fellows was young John Leslie (later to become known as "Shane"), whose mother was Lady Randolph Churchill's sister. When I came to live in London at the end of 1900, Shane's mother was very kind to a young man of eighteen and it was through her that I first met Churchill.

An early entry about him occurs in my diary on October 29, 1905: "While having tea at the Bath Club Winston Churchill walked in and he was very friendly and we chatted for about 20 minutes, and then we were joined by Major Jack Seely, M.P., and they took me off for a delightful Turkish bath at Princes Club. Very amusing."

Churchill fully realized the importance of the Press and probably thought it was just as well to be on friendly terms with a young man in the Harmsworth organization. The aspect of Imperial affairs we discussed on that particular occasion was probably about South Africa and the campaign against Chinese labour then being carried on, about which I was much concerned. In those days I was a warm supporter of Lord Milner. In that very month Churchill had declared that if the Liberals were returned to power the importation of Chinese labour would cease and all the Chinese coolies would be repatriated in three years.

I had always been interested in Empire affairs and Cecil Rhodes was one of my deities. I had joined the staff of Lord Northcliffe in July 1904 and a few months later I became editor of the *Overseas Daily*

Mail, which circulated throughout the Empire and among British communities in foreign lands.

On Election night, January 13, 1906, my diary records an evening I shall always remember: "Dined at Berkeley Square with the Chief (Lord Northcliffe). . . . I worked the telephone and read out the results as they came in. The Liberals gained seventeen seats and the Labour Party four. Balfour was defeated by 2,000 in his own constituency— Winston Churchill won by 1,200. There is indeed a wave of Liberalism sweeping the country, and I should think we may expect five or six years of Liberal rule." (For ten years the Liberals were in power, till Lloyd George formed his Coalition Government in 1916.)

Consternation filled my being. I had kept in touch with South African problems and I knew what the Unionists and Progressives out there, the followers of Milner, would feel about the termination of the recruitment of Chinese for the mines in the Rand. Nearly two years before that Churchill and Seely had voted against the Conservative Government and one of them had emphasized the serious danger of the Chinese labourers "becoming goods and chattels, or, in other words, slaves".

Seven years later, when I was in South Africa, I realized how great a part Churchill had played in creating friendly relations with the Boers. When Sir Henry Campbell-Bannerman was returned to power, he offered Churchill the post of Financial Secretary to the Treasury, with a salary of £500 per annum more than that of an Under-Secretary of State, but Winston had other views. He asked "C. B." to let him go to the Colonial Office, for he knew that South African affairs must play a dominant part in the programme of the new Ministry. In view of the fact that the Secretary of State, Lord Elgin, was in the upper House, the exposition of the South African policy of His Majesty's Government in the Commons rested on the broad shoulders of Lord Randolph's son.

When I was in South Africa in 1913, crusading for the cause of Imperial unity, I had several long talks with Botha at Pretoria, and he opened his heart to me. At our final interview Botha put his hand on my shoulder, and after telling me how he sympathized with the cause of promoting friendship between the nations in the British Empire— we did not use the term Commonwealth then—he spoke with feeling of his gratitude to the Government of Campbell-Bannerman and his immediate colleagues, Winston Churchill among them. They had trusted him and his fellow countrymen and had given them self-government as soon as they were returned to power. As long as Great Britain treated South Africa in this way, he and his friends would be ready to take up arms in the defence of the Empire. I little thought on that sunny October day in 1913 that within ten months that pledge would be so faithfully redeemed. Botha and Smuts stood by Great Britain in August 1914 and subdued the Beyers Rebellion and sent much-needed rifles to England in her hour of need. Churchill is certainly fully entitled to take pride in his share in forging links of friendship with the Boers in the critical years before the First World War.

To return to Churchill's term at the Colonial Office. Early in 1906 I decided to spend the summer in Canada. My diary of June 25 contains this entry: "Went round to see Winston Churchill at the House of Commons. He was very friendly and talked to me for over half an hour." He arranged for Lord Elgin to give me a letter to Lord Grey, the Governor-General, and wrote a letter in his own hand to Sir Wilfrid Laurier.

Another entry in my diary occurs on November 1, 1906: "At 1.0 I walked round to Winston Churchill's rooms at 12 Bolton Street. There were five of us at lunch, Marsh, his secretary, W. Mackenzie King (Churchill's first meeting with the young Canadian, then Deputy-Minister of Labour in Laurier's Government, and later Prime Minister of Canada for so many years), John Burns, President of the Local Government Board, and myself. John Burns expressed himself lukewarm as to my desire to increase the flow of emigrants from the mother country to the vast empty spaces of the Empire. "Why," he asked, "do you wish to establish under the British flag replicas of Tooting around the seven seas?" Churchill smiled benignly; evidently he was not shocked by my views, for he asked me to come and see him for a quiet talk another day; he could understand my youthful enthusiasm. He was himself not yet thirty-two!

Despite the Liberal Government's preoccupation with social reform at home, Empire affairs and especially the future of South Africa were very much to the fore. I do not know the exact moment that Churchill

K

was made aware of the meetings of the members of Lord Milner's Kindergarten in the Transvaal, who were hatching, with the help of far-sighted Afrikanders, the plan for the creation of a Union of South Africa. Its fulfilment is surely one of the most dramatic event in Empire history in the twentieth century. May 31, 1910, was the official date of the creation of the Union—but by then Churchill was more immediately concerned with home affairs.

During 1912–13 I made a tour of the Empire, lasting seventeen months, but only in South Africa, as already recorded, did I find much interest taken in Churchill. His adherence to Free Trade principles did not make him popular in protectionist circles in Canada, Australia and New Zealand. While Ulstermen, very numerous in Ontario and else-where, did not then approve of Asquith's Home Rule policy, they would have been even more disturbed had they known that as First Lord of the Admiralty in the days of tension in March 1914 Churchill would order a cruiser squadron to Scottish waters, opposite to North East Ulster, in readiness to land a force of Royal Marines in case of trouble. After the assassination of Archduke Franz Ferdinand in Sarajevo on June 28, 1914, however, Irish squabbles were forgotten in the common peril.

When I became private secretary to Lord Rothermere, first Air Minister, in 1917, and later when I was in control of the Empire Section of the Ministry of Information, under Lord Beaverbrook (1918), I met Churchill on various occasions, and after a period "in the wilderness", as Minister of Munitions he had many Empire contacts. When it was known later that he had been largely responsible for the development of the Tank, his reputation soared again.

Churchill also took a deep interest in flying and was one of the first to realize the implications of the development of aviation as a means of drawing closer the sister nations in the far-flung British Empire. I had attended most of the lunches given in honour of pioneers of flight from the welcome to Blériot, the conqueror of the Channel in 1909, to London's welcome to Colonel Lindbergh in 1927. I never remember a more dramatic occasion than when Churchill delivered a speech of welcome at the lunch to Captain J. Alcock and Lieutenant W. Brown when they made the first *direct* Atlantic flight. They left St. Johns, Newfoundland, at 5.13 p.m., British Summer Time, Saturday June 14,

1919, and landed in Western Ireland at 9.40 a.m. on Sunday, June 15—a coast-to-coast flight of 1,880 miles of 15 hours and 57 minutes. Churchill can rarely have performed an historic task with greater enjoyment than when he presented the *Daily Mail* cheque for £10,000 to Captain Alcock. He enjoyed Lord Northcliffe's message that it was a happy augury that the two airmen had departed from the Dominion of Newfoundland (as it then was) and had arrived in "the future equally happy and prosperous Dominion of Ireland"—a prophecy which has, alas, not been realized.

Certainly Churchill can look back with satisfaction on Irish peace-making, and if Eire under Mr. de Valera elected to withdraw from the Commonwealth he is nowise to blame. When Churchill became Secretary of State for the Colonies fifteen years after his memorable term as Under-Secretary in the Campbell-Bannerman Government, he played a prominent part in the making of peace with Southern Ireland. It was Michael Collins who said, "Tell Winston we could never have done anything without him." And as far as I am aware Arthur Griffith, the founder of Sinn Fein, held similar views. I had taken a hand in Irish peacemaking fifteen months earlier, and had a little imagination been displayed in high places, peace might, in my view, have been made the previous year. In the summer of 1920 I had arranged, with the help of my father, who as an official in the Irish Government had to remain in the background, a meeting between Arthur Griffith and one of his closest colleagues representing Sinn Fein, and Mr. Andrew Jameson and Sir Harry Greer on behalf of the Southern Unionists. At the time Griffith, an honest and likable man, was suffering from strain, as was natural. We had a private discussion in one of the committee rooms of the Royal Dublin Society at Balls-bridge. I was convinced of Griffith's sincerity and I left the meeting with my rough notes, on the back of an envelope, as to the terms Griffith would be prepared to accept on behalf of Sinn Fein. They were Dominion status; the King to be King of Ireland, as the Emperor Franz-Josef had been King of Hungary; Ireland to have control of her own finances and customs; Ireland to control her own forces but there was to be common defence policy with Great Britain and she and Great Britain were to agree on a joint foreign policy. Finally the Province of Ulster was to be entitled to remain outside the Irish

Dominion until such time as she elected to join of her own free will. I have always thought that had I gone to Churchill on that occasion, peace might have been made. As matters turned out, my friend Philip Kerr (Lord Lothian), whom I sought the day after the meeting, was absent from Downing Street and I could make no headway with Sir William Sutherland. He said the Government would never let Ireland off her share of the national debt. Such is the unwisdom of those in high places that fifteen months later the British Government did this very thing and agreed to much less favourable terms from the standpoint of Empire unity.

On many occasions T. E. Lawrence spoke appreciatively to me of the part Churchill had played in bringing peace to the Middle East. Lawrence, in the immediate post-war years, was very critical of the Government's policy in Western Asia. He was enthusiastic about what he called "Brown Dominions"—it was the first time I had heard the phrase and it arrested my attention. Churchill, as was to be his custom in the Second World War, went in 1920 to the Middle East to study on the spot the conditions for himself. The outcome of his conference was the appointment of an Arab king, Feisal, to rule over the Iraqis. At that time it was not easy for a politician to gain "T. E.'s" praise, but in *The Seven Pillars of Wisdom* he wrote enthusiastically of Churchill's successful achievements at the Cairo Conference.

Churchill's Indian policy in the between-war years has often puzzled me. The man who could show deep sympathy with the Boers in 1906; who took a prominent part in Irish peacemaking; who won the encomium of T. E. Lawrence; who had served as a young subaltern on the North-West Frontier and had read avidly about India, for a time joined hands with the die-hards. When Lord Irwin (now Lord Halifax) advocated what was in effect Dominion status for India, Churchill became alarmed; even more so when the Viceroy released Gandhi to enable him to attend the Round Table Conference. The thought that Great Britain, after subduing the sub-continent "from barbarism, tyranny and intestine war", would, under Dominion status, permit the Brahmins to seize power disturbed Churchill. After the withdrawal of the British raj, who, he asked, would look after the interests of the minorities, the eighty or so millions of Muslims, and sixty millions of Untouchables; who would guarantee the rights of the

Indian Princes? As far as the Muslims were concerned Churchill could not foresee the growing power of the Muslim League under Jinnah. Churchill did not regard Dominion status as practicable in 1931 and he said: "I am against this surrender to Gandhi. I am against these conversations and agreements between Lord Irwin and Mr. Gandhi." Had he but realized the fact, the granting of Dominion status in 1931 would have prevented long years of struggle with the Congress Party. When I was in India in January 1942, Mr. Rajagopalachari, destined to be the first Governor-General of the Indian Republic, told me that Mahatma Gandhi and he would, up to 1931, have been prepared to accept Dominion status; Gandhi, when I visited him at Sevagram Ashram in 1941 and 1942, confirmed this statement.

In spite of his split with Baldwin at the time of the Round Table Conference, ten years later Churchill, when he was Prime Minister, made in 1942 a very magnanimous offer to India. I was present in New Delhi when Sir Stafford Cripps made known the British Government's momentous proposals. The new feature of the offer was that the Indian Government was to have the right to withdraw from the Commonwealth should it so desire. After the departure of the mission many leading Indians admitted to me that the refusal of the offer was a blunder.

Some of Churchill's most intimate associations with the peoples of the Empire were during his first five years as Prime Minister. I was in London during the first year of the war but left England on a lecture tour at the time of the Battle of Britain and visited many parts of the Empire, finally taking a position under the Government of India for over two years. It was a very moving experience for the travelling Englishman during those early war years to listen to Churchill's broadcasts. It is hardly an exaggeration to say that in those anxious months we *lived* for Churchill's periodical surveys of the war. I first witnessed the hold he had on a Canadian audience in the main lobby of the University Club at Montreal. Just before the lunch hour a vast assembly of members listened spellbound to his familiar voice telling them of the possibilities of a Nazi invasion of England. Wherever I went in Australia, New Zealand, Singapore or India, I listened to that voice, which, however dark the prospects of the war, inspired confidence by the indomitable spirit behind the sombre words. Even in the leading hotels of Java large V-signs were affixed to the walls and the portrait of Churchill hung alongside that of Queen Wilhelmina.

When I drove through the Khyber Pass, on the way to Afghanistan, I watched with pride the Union Jack from the fort of Shagai—we were back in the pages of Kipling, and I thought of the young Churchill who had done his first soldiering in these inhospitable regions. At Kabul in 1943 one of the few British residents told me of the difficult times they had been through in 1940, when many Afghans were convinced that the Axis was winning. My friend had to go for money to a German-controlled bank. The clerks were elated over the news of each fresh Nazi triumph. One day the chief cashier was more than usually insolent. That evening my friend listened to one of Churchill's speeches and it gave him new courage and he added, "Next time I visited the bank, I gave as good as I got!"

After the war, during the difficult years of austerity and disillusionment, Churchill once again, as in 1915, and in the decade before the Second World War, found himself out of office, but before the accession of the Queen he was again First Minister to the Crown. He assuredly is glad to have been the adviser of Queen Elizabeth II at the beginning of what we hope will be a second "Elizabethan era", with a fruition of things of the mind and spirit throughout the Empire.

No one has a deeper conviction than Sir Winston Churchill that our Empire of free peoples is one of the chief buttresses of human freedom, order, and good government and has a supreme part to play in the future. To work for peace and prosperity in the closest alliance with the freedom-loving nations of the world, and to help the great territories under our flag in Africa and elsewhere to take their share, as free partners, in the task of preserving our world status, is the vision which he constantly holds before us.

CHURCHILL AND RUSSIA

Lieut.-General Sir Giffard Martel
K.C.B., K.B.E., D.S.O., M.C.

Few men could write on Sir Winston Churchill's relations with Soviet Russia and its late leader, Marshal Stalin, with the knowledge and authority possessed by General Martel. The Prime Minister appointed him Head of the British Military Mission to Moscow in 1943 and he was present at the meeting of Churchill and Stalin at Teheran. For many years General Martel has made a close study of Anglo-Russian relations. His book, The Russian Outlook, *was published in 1947 and the whole problem is brought up to date in his recent book* East v. West. *He has also contributed many articles to the Press on the menace of Soviet aggression. His military appointments include the post of Deputy Director of Mechanization, War Office, 1936–39, Commander of the 50th Division 1939–40 and Commander of the Royal Armoured Corps 1941–42.*

THE first contacts between Churchill and Russia occurred during the concluding stages of the First World War. The Germans had been assisting the Revolutionary Party in Russia in every possible way and before the end of the war the Bolsheviks had succeeded in undermining the morale of the Russian soldiers. This caused the final collapse on the Russian front. In Russia the Bolsheviks had a precarious hold on the capital and the central provinces. In the outer provinces there were a number of anti-Bolshevik movements led among others by General Wrangel, Admiral Denikin and Admiral Koltchak.

The Allies had pledged themselves to support these movements with munitions and some British and Allied troops were fighting on Russian soil. Churchill hated Bolshevism in those days just as much as he does today and these actions had his full support.

After the Armistice however these commitments became a source of anxiety. With the defeat of Germany there was a strong feeling against taking on new engagements with Russia. An urgent decision was needed from the Allied statesmen at Versailles as to the policy which was to be followed. There is little doubt that Churchill with his great foresight saw the possibility and the opportunity of crushing the Communist revolution at this early stage. No great or lengthy extension of our war activities might have been needed to put the anti-communists back in power. What a great change this might have made to the future peace in the world!

Churchill pressed for a decision on this matter. After long delays it was decided to carry out the pledge to help Admiral Koltchak and his associates with arms and money but to withdraw the other Allied troops.

In the meantime our forces had been fighting side by side with White Russian troops. In our country we do not lightly abandon our friends who have fought with us. There was however no indecision on the part of Churchill when the policy had been settled. An evacuation of troops in war is never easy and he had to raise and send out new forces to cover these operations. This raised considerable criticism in our country but it was an essential step and as a result our forces were withdrawn very successfully.

In the period between the two World Wars Churchill does not appear to have had much contact with Russia. With the arrival of the Second World War, however, one of the most difficult problems was the policy which we should adopt as regards that country. Russia made a non-aggression pact with Germany but it is doubtful if either side had much trust in the other. The matter was decided by Germany when she broke her treaty and launched a great attack against Russia on June 22, 1941. For twenty years Churchill had consistently denounced the Communist Party. He was now head of the Government. Would he be prepared to sink political differences with the Soviet? Would he denounce this act of aggression in the same way as he had denounced Nazi aggression against Poland and France?

Churchill made the answer quite clear. In his stirring broadcast on the evening of that day he referred to Hitler as that monster of wickedness. He made it clear that we would give Russia full support and that we would fight to the end against Nazidom. At the same time the necessary steps were taken to complete a formal alliance with the Russian Government. This was one of the most important decisions in the Second World War.

Good relations were then established between our country and Russia. This was fully endorsed by the peoples of both countries and antagonisms that had prevailed since the Bolshevik revolution were gradually diminishing. In May 1942 their Foreign Secretary, M. Molotov, came to England with a Russian delegation for final formalities. They were the guests of the Prime Minister at Chequers. The agreement was to last for twenty years and was to cover the future period of peace as well as mutual assistance during the war. One wonders whether Stalin and Molotov were genuine at that time. It now seems very unlikely.

This cordial feeling between the two countries raised a very strong desire in the British Empire that we should give greater military assistance to Russia. She was holding some 200 German divisions on the Eastern Front and there was a strong demand that we should open a second front on the West without delay. Demonstrations were held in Trafalgar Square and the words "Open a second front now" were chalked on walls and on the tarmac in many places in the country. There is no doubt that Churchill, with his usual courage, was doing all he could to support the Russians in this way. In fact he must have gone very near to promising to open a second front, for a Foreign Office communiqué stated that agreement had been reached between the two countries on this matter. At that time the organization of our Chiefs of Staff at Washington and London was well established and they had been making a detailed examination of the possibilities of opening a second front in the summer or autumn of 1942. We can be sure that Churchill pressed them very hard but he agreed with their decision that no attempt should be made to do so with the existing state of Allied strength and preparation.

This decision was naturally received with great displeasure in Russia and Churchill decided that he should pay a visit to his ally, Marshal Stalin, at Moscow. He travelled by air from Egypt on August 12, 1942, with the Chief of the Imperial General Staff and other Service officers and Sir Alexander Cadogan. There was the usual Kremlin party in Moscow but in spite of the lavish hospitality little progress was being made in the discussions. The Russians made no attempt to hide their disappointment that the opening of a second front would not take place for some time. On the last day, however, Stalin invited Churchill to supper and discussions continued until 3 a.m. on the following morning. By his outstanding personality our Prime Minister was able to make much headway in breaking down the Soviet mistrust. The natural disappointment of the Russians could not be removed but their suspicions were abated. This was a great achievement. Although no second front could be opened in 1942, Churchill was able to inform the Russians of the plans that we were making with America for landing in North Africa. This would draw off considerable German forces and thus relieve some of the pressure on Russia. It must also be remembered that the Allies were sending large quantities of munitions to Russia and we carried out all the work of safeguarding these convoys from attack by sea or air. This was a considerable responsibility and Churchill arranged for Lord Beaverbrook to use his boundless energy in pressing forward with this work at full speed.

On his return from Russia Churchill gave an account of his visit. He explained that he had found it difficult to make the Russians understand the very great difference between moving divisions from one part of the front to another, compared with moving divisions to land on enemy soil, which was entailed if a new front was to be opened in the West. He explained this by saying that we and the Americans were sea animals whereas the Russians were land animals. He went on to make a very striking statement about Stalin which read as follows:

> "It is very fortunate for Russia in her agony to have this great rugged war chief at her head. He is a man of massive outstanding personality, suited to the sombre and stormy times in which his life has been cast; a man of inexhaustible courage and will-power and a man direct and even blunt in speech, which, having been brought up in the House of Commons, I do not mind at all, especially when I have something to say of my own. Above all, he is a man with that saving sense of humour, which is of high importance to all men and all nations, but particularly to great men and great nations. Stalin also left upon me the impression of a deep, cool wisdom and a complete absence of illusions of any kind. I believe I made him feel that we were good and faithful comrades in this war—but that, after all, is a matter which deeds, not words, will prove."

On October 23, 1942, the Battle of Alamein was launched and on November 8 the Anglo-American forces landed in North Africa. The great success of these operations needs no mention here.

In January 1943 a conference was held at Casablanca, where President Roosevelt and Churchill and their Chiefs of Staff met for a full discussion. It was a great regret to them that Marshal Stalin felt that he was unable to leave the Kremlin and join the conference. Churchill referred to this matter of his own recurrent absences from his country on November 11, 1942. He pointed out that Hitler could summon his subordinates to Berlin without difficulty, but for the Allies consultation was far more difficult. Roosevelt had so far found it impossible to leave the States and Stalin could not leave Russia. It was therefore left to himself to make long journeys in each direction accompanied by his military authorities. This liaison between the Allied nations was some of the finest work carried out by Churchill during the war.

My own contact with Churchill dated back to 1916 when I was at Tank Corps headquarters in France and I met him several times during the First World War. In the Second World War we started with one weak armoured division in Egypt and practically nothing at home. It was obvious that we would have to raise and train at least a dozen armoured divisions at the earliest possible moment. For this purpose I was put in command of the Royal Armoured Corps in December 1940. I was given a fairly free hand to carry out this task. I think it was probably Churchill's decision that I should undertake this task of raising the armoured forces. We succeeded in forming these divisions and allotting them to their tasks in the various theatres of war. The organization and tactics which we evolved stood the test of the whole war. The Ministry of Supply produced splendid cruiser tanks for our mobile operations that were second to none, but they failed to produce the heavy tanks for which we had constantly pressed. We suffered severely from the lack of these tanks in the static warfare on the Normandy landings.

In October 1942 I went to India to put their armoured forces on the same organization and training. I returned home in January 1943 and on my way back I met Churchill at Cairo and had a short discussion with him.

When Germany attacked Russia in 1941 we sent a British Military Mission to Moscow to keep touch with them and to render any possible assistance. The Russians would not, however, co-operate with our mission. The Communists have always wished to clothe their activities in secrecy. As a result our mission was of little value. In February 1942 the Germans were still pressing the Russians very hard and were working their way through the Caucasus. If they had succeeded they might well have reached and captured our Persian oil fields and in consequence they might have won the war. The situation was very serious and Churchill made the proposal that we should send an Anglo-American air force to land on Russian soil and operate against the Germans who were advancing in that direction. Friendly discussions took place with the Russians, but it soon became apparent that they had no intention of allowing such a large force to be established on their soil. The reason for this was that the Russian people would have seen the far higher standard of living of the Western Forces. They preferred to accept the considerable risk of a German advance through the Caucasus rather than that of allowing their people to see the true position.

Although the situation was very serious our Mission in Moscow could not send us any information. In fact our Chiefs of Staff hardly knew if the Russian Army still existed. This was the alarming state of affairs early in 1943. It was in no way the fault of our Mission, but at this stage Churchill stepped in and said that someone must be found to go out as head of the Mission who would be able to break the ice and establish proper liaison with the Russians. It so happened that I had been invited by the Russians to go and see their manœuvres in 1936 and to discuss tank warfare. I had gone out with General Wavell and we had a very happy party with Generals Voroshilov and Budyonny. I was therefore sent out to be head of the Military Mission in the hope that my previous acquaintance with them would enable me to establish proper liaison.

I was naturally not very pleased at being sent out to a Mission which had been such a dismal failure, but I saw Churchill's point of view. I then began to ask for advice as to how to deal with these difficult people. My written instructions were that I should do nothing which might annoy the Russians and that I should continue with the appeasement policy that we had adopted all along. Having seen the resultant failure I was not very happy about this advice. Presently I was given some quite different advice by Foreign Office officials who were not very near the top. They explained to me that if I arrived in Russia as a normal Englishman with a smile on my face the Russians would form the view that they need not bother very much about me. If, however, I arrived as a tough man and objected to everything that they did in no uncertain terms, then the Russians would say: "Ah, we must do something about this. We understand that language. We have people like that in our own country." It was, of course, quite easy to give this advice but it was quite another matter to carry it out. It might easily mean that I would have to be offensive to the first Russian marshal whom I met, and in point of fact that is what happened.

I arrived at Moscow on April 5, 1943. Churchill had given me a special letter of introduction to Marshal Stalin, which I handed to him and which had a marked effect. In a short time I found that the tough policy worked splendidly. I was soon discussing the main military problems with the Russians. After a few very useful discussions they informed me that they intended to launch an offensive against the Germans in the summer of 1943. This would have been fatal and I told them so very bluntly. They were annoyed at this and their Chief of Staff closed the meeting, and I had to return to my headquarters. I thought about my written instructions! They rang me up a little later, however, and said they would like to discuss the matter further. I told them that they had much better do so. We met again and arranged to have a series of meetings in which everything was discussed. They then decided to remain temporarily on the defensive, which was undoubtedly right.

For six months I had these good relations with the Russians. They gave me two of their latest tanks, which I sent home via Archangel. The Chiefs of Staff expressed their pleasure at this valuable liaison. Of course there were difficulties over such matters as soldiers or sailors who misbehaved themselves occasionally on Russian soil, but these were not very serious. Incidentally Churchill in an Appendix to Volume V of his book refers to my "ill success" in Russia at this period. I think he must have had some other period in his mind when he wrote this. The C.I.G.S. certainly did not hold this view.

In October 1943 a conference was held with the Russians at Moscow in order to pave the way for settling our future plans. Anthony Eden and Cordell Hull from U.S.A. and Molotov attended the conference. Arrangements were now made for a full conference to be held at Teheran. Before this conference could take place, however, it came to light that there was considerable divergence of views between the British and American staffs on the main policy. A conference was therefore laid on at Cairo in the last week of November 1943. There were other points to discuss but the main matter was to reach agreement between ourselves and the U.S.A. before meeting

Stalin at Teheran. I went by air from Moscow to Cairo to attend this conference.

At an early stage in the Second World War Churchill had made it clear that he hoped that we would be able to disperse the German defence by advancing against her from the Mediterranean. He referred to this as attacking the "soft under-belly". In principle this was right and there would have been many advantages in advancing on these lines against Germany. By the end of November 1943, however, the Germans were constructing a number of launching sites in Northern France and the Low Countries for their V weapons. If their programme had been completed they would have been able to carry out a widespread destruction of London and the ports with these weapons. There were therefore very strong reasons for attacking across the Channel on to the Normandy beaches so that these V-weapon installations could be put out of action by the advance of our troops. Indeed it eventually came to light that we were only just in time with our advance in Normandy to do so. If we had made our main advance from the south, or delayed our attack in Normandy, London would have been very severely bombarded and our country might have been paralysed.

The general agreement at the Cairo conference was that we must concentrate on the Anglo-American assault on Normandy (known as Overlord), though Churchill quite rightly stressed the importance of supporting this attack from the Mediterranean in several ways. An attack in the South of France was one method. Other proposals that he made were that we should endeavour to bring Turkey into the war and also that we might support Yugo-Slavia.

After the conference at Cairo we all moved to Teheran for the main conference with Marshal Stalin. We numbered about twenty and we sat at a round table. The main Sessions were on November 28, 29 and 30. I was seated immediately behind the Prime Minister. The talks have been given in considerable detail in Vol. V of Churchill's *Second World War*. There was, however, a certain humorous and interesting side to these discussions which does not come out in this book and which I will now record.

It so happened that I arrived a little early in the hall on the first day, and I found Marshal Stalin alone there for a few moments. By that time we knew each other well and I had a few words with him. I saw that

CHURCHILL AND RUSSIA
Churchill and Stalin in the Conference Room in
the Livadia Palace, Yalta, February 1945

he was not in a good mood. It was, of course, quite clear to him that the U.S.A. and ourselves had met at Cairo to reach agreement and he no doubt had in mind that we had come together to Teheran to impose these views on Russia.

When the plenary session opened Churchill asked that President Roosevelt should start the talking. From what the latter said it was clear that he doubted whether Churchill was whole-hearted about Overlord and that he was perhaps putting undue stress on the operations which he had suggested should be carried out in the Mediterranean in support of Overlord.

Churchill replied that he could not agree to abandon the operations which he had proposed in the Mediterranean, even though Overlord was the operation of primary importance.

I was watching Marshal Stalin carefully. Far from his having to meet two naughty boys who had hatched a plot to put across him, he now saw that there was considerable difference between their views. He was, of course, delighted at this and he gave us one of his broadest smiles. The conference then continued to discuss these vast military problems but without making any great headway.

Before the second plenary session on November 29 Churchill presented a large and very fine Sword of Honour which was a gift from His Majesty to commemorate the glorious defence of Stalingrad. Marshal Stalin received the sword and it was a very impressive ceremony.

The discussion at this second session continued on much the same lines but towards the end a suggestion was made by Churchill. He proposed that there should be a meeting of the General Staffs of the three nations to hammer out the details of the matters that had been discussed. This did not suit Marshal Stalin at all. He feared that his General Staff representatives might be led up the garden path. He therefore replied at once: "Meeting of the three General Staffs? What for? I am not going to send anybody." Churchill pressed the point and asked Marshal Stalin again. He replied, "Oh, all right then, I will send Marshal Voroshilov." The latter was a leader from the old revolutionary days and Stalin no doubt felt that he would say very little and would not commit him in any way. In his book Churchill has referred to this meeting of the General Staffs as the Military Committee. At the conclusion of this session, and in response to a direct question from Marshal Stalin, Churchill gave the assurance that the British staff believed fully in Overlord.

The staff had of course been considering all these problems between the sessions and they now began to come to agreement on the main issues. At the start of the third session on November 30 Churchill proposed to Marshal Stalin that General Sir Alan Brooke should read out the summary of the agreement which the combined General Staffs had reached. This was done and Churchill then asked Marshal Stalin whether this met with his approval. With hardly any pause at all Marshal Stalin replied that he agreed. All the main issues as regards Overlord and who should be in supreme command had been discussed and also all the additional issues as regards further operations from the Mediterranean, and the vital matter of the distribution of landing craft. It was a wonderful achievement for the staffs of three nations to reach agreement in this way in so short a time.

Discussion then turned on to "cover" plans to deceive the enemy. Marshal Stalin spoke at some length on the ways in which they had mystified the enemy on past occasions. There was then a pause and Churchill saw the opportunity for a peroration at which he is a past master. He said that we had reached agreement between the three nations and now we must push forward with our plans for launching the second front with the maximum strength and intensity and with the mystification of the enemy. At this stage Marshal Stalin evidently thought that Churchill had had rather too good an innings and he interrupted to say the mystification of the enemy was all right so long as there was no mystery about the second front! Everyone rocked with laughter and I fear it upset the flow of Churchill's argument.

This conference was one of the greatest successes of the war. Though we knew that it might not last for long it produced a splendid spirit between the three countries, and it was undoubtedly Churchill who led the way throughout. This final day of the conference on November 30 was Churchill's birthday and a very memorable dinner was held in the British Embassy that night at which all the main personalities were present.

After Teheran, Churchill and Roosevelt and their staffs returned to Cairo and settled a considerable number of affairs which had arisen from the Teheran meeting. The operations in the Mediterranean continued on the lines that had been agreed. All the necessary preparations were made and eventually the great assault was delivered on the Normandy beaches. There was little contact between Churchill and Stalin during this period.

By this time I had spent nearly a year in Russia. As the crisis in that country was passed I had asked whether I might be allowed to come back and command troops again. I received my orders in February 1945 and returned to England. Within a few days of my arrival I was wounded in an air raid and lost an eye. I was bound to be on the sick list for some time and Churchill wrote to the C.I.G.S. to remind him to keep an appointment for me. It was like him to think of a detail of this nature when he was immersed in so many great problems and difficulties.

Marshal Stalin was most profuse in the admiration which he expressed for the success of the operations in Normandy. While this was happening, the Russians played their part to the full on the Eastern Front. It then became clear that another great conference would be needed to make the Allied plans for concluding the victory and to consider certain post-war problems. The latter included the military occupation of Germany, the settlement of the frontiers for Poland and the future government of the liberated States. The questions affecting the new world organization for security would also have to be discussed. Arrangements were therefore made to hold a meeting at Yalta in the Crimea in February 1945. The Big Three were to be present with their staffs and the Russians did everything to promote the cordiality of the Allied delegations. A palace was put at the disposal of each delegation. The long agenda was carried through and a large measure of agreement was reached. It seemed as if Yalta would go down to history as the finest feat that had ever been achieved for establishing world peace.

On looking back now with our present knowledge it is clear that these views were sadly exaggerated. Most of the great conferences at which Churchill played such an influential part during the war can easily stand up to post-war examination, but that is not the case with Yalta. The agreement that was reached over Poland was making the best of a bad job and anyway was later ignored by the Russians. As regards the Russians, Churchill stated that as a result of his contacts with Marshal Stalin he believed that they "wished to live in honourable friendship and equality with the Western democracies".

As regards the new League of Nations, the Russians had in mind that this would be based on the Big Three powers, but the views of Churchill and Roosevelt prevailed that the authority of the smaller nations should not be unduly depressed. The weak position of U.N.O. under this plan is now apparent and there is a strong and wide support for the idea that the smaller nations will have to group themselves to the bigger nations before we can reach an effective world organization for this purpose.

Summing up the position it seems clear that the Yalta conference has led to many disappointments in spite of the acclamation which it received at the time. It was the beginning of placing Russia in an unduly favourable position in Europe. She had already started to set up communist autocracies in the countries which she had overrun in spite of her pledge to allow them to have free or democratic rule.

When victory came there was strong admiration in our country for the brave deeds that had been performed by the Russians. There was a keen desire to maintain the alliance that had been formed during the war. During my period as head of our Mission in Russia I had made close contact with most of the leaders in the Kremlin and I reported several times that they were insincere. They were secretly determined to absorb each country which they overran in East Europe and to set up a communist autocracy in every case. This process was to be continued till they had subjugated the world.

Churchill was probably one of the first to realize the danger into which we were drifting. In the spring of 1946 he made his famous Fulton speech in America which exposed the true position. This speech made a great sensation. It was a long way ahead of public opinion but it was undoubtedly right. Previous to this he had sent a telegram to Marshal Stalin as follows:

"There is not much comfort in looking on to a future where you and the countries you dominate, plus the Communist parties in many other States, are all drawn up on one side, and those who rally to the English-speaking nations and their associates or

Dominions are on the other. It is quite obvious that their quarrel would tear the world to pieces and that all of us leading men on either side who had anything to do with that would be shamed before history. Even embarking on a long period of suspicions, of abuse and counter-abuse of opposing policies, would be a disaster hampering the great developments of world prosperity for the masses which are attainable only through our trinity."

This telegram was not made known to the public till a much later date. There does not appear to have been any response from Marshal Stalin.

From this time onwards affairs grew worse between the Soviet and the Western nations, and we have now reached the present position in which collaboration has ceased between them.

CHURCHILL AND FRANCE

___

Paul Reynaud

M. Paul Reynaud was Prime Minister of France in 1940 and it was to him that Churchill addressed his offer of union between Britain and France and common citizenship for the peoples of the two countries. In this important chapter M. Reynaud throws new light on that historic offer and on Churchill's relations with France and his affection and admiration for her people.

OF all men now living Sir Winston Churchill is incontestably the most generally popular in France.

To the French he typifies resistance, tenacity in the face of odds, and victory. After France's defeat and Pétain's armistice in June 1940, he stood alone, braving the storm, until the day mighty America joined indomitable England. In sublime language he heartened the British engaged in the fight and the French wanting to continue it, as well as those who, remaining in France, declined to submit even though they had not been imprisoned, as Georges Mandel and I were, for refusing to capitulate.

Before the war Churchill and I were drawn together because both of us strove hard in our own countries to awaken our rulers and people to the danger threatening their liberty from Nazism. We were both dubbed "war-mongers" by those who allowed themselves to be taken in by Nazi propaganda and who returned from Berlin only too ready, willingly or unwillingly, to believe all that Hitler, Goebbels, Goering and company had said to them. My task in France was the harder of the two because the terrible loss of life my country had suffered in the First World War—probably exceeding all the losses suffered by our British friends in all the battles fought in the course of their long history—had temporarily brought about a decline in French morale. The headlines appearing, on the day of Munich, in the royalist newspaper *L'Action Française*—a patriotic paper during the First World War—show to what a pitch feeling against war had risen in France. They consisted of a verse of the *Internationale* adapted as follows:

> *"S'ils s'obstinent, les cannibales*
> *A faire de nous des héros,*
> *Il faut que nos premières balles*
> *Soient pour Mandel, Blum et Reynaud."*[1]

[1] A rough translation of this would read:
"If they insist, the cannibals,   Then our first bullets must be fired
On making heroes of us,   At Mandel, Blum and Reynaud."

On the eve of Munich, the Czecho-Slovak radio declared that the Benes Government had yielded to Hitler's demands because France and England had advised it to do so, France, moreover, having let it be understood that if Czecho-Slovakia did not follow her advice, she would consider herself quit of all responsibility towards her. Mandel, Champetier de Ribes and I immediately handed in our resignations to Daladier, the Prime Minister, for I had been given a promise by a former Council of Ministers that this argument would never be employed. Churchill came to Paris to urge us to withdraw these resignations, pointing out to us the consequences of our going if graver events, easily foreseeable, should occur. As a matter of fact, we did do so, Daladier having declared that the announcements made by the Czech radio were inaccurate, and having produced a telegram from our Minister in Prague to this effect.

This common effort made by Churchill and myself to induce our countries to arm marked the beginning of our friendship, which grew when we were, as he put it, companions in distress during the war. Throughout the five years all but four months I spent in prison, thanks to Hitler's hatred of me, I never for one moment doubted Churchill's unshakable determination.

.   .   .   .   .

In writing of "Churchill and France", it is interesting to recall his views on French political life. This is how, in his book *Great Contemporaries*, he speaks of the dual nature of the French as personified by Foch and Clemenceau. After evoking memories of the burning intensity of Clemenceau, he writes:

"There was another mood and another France. It was the France of Foch—ancient, aristocratic; the France whose grace and culture, whose etiquette and ceremonial has bestowed its gifts around the world. There was the France of Chivalry, the France of Versailles, and, above all, the France of Joan of Arc. It was this secondary and submerged national personality that Foch recalled. In the combination of these two men during the last year of War, the French people found in their service all the glories and the vital essences of Gaul. These two men embodied respectively their ancient and their modern history. Between the twain there flowed the blood-river of the Revolution. Between them towered the barriers which Christianity raises against Agnosticism. But when they gazed upon the inscription on the golden statue of Joan of Arc, 'La pitié qu'elle avait pour le royaume de France', and saw gleaming the Maid's uplifted sword, their two hearts beat as one. The French have a dual nature in a degree not possessed by any other great people. There is nothing like this duality in Great Britain or the United States, or even in Germany. It is an unending struggle which goes on continually, not only in every successive Parliament, but in every street and village of France, and in the bosom of almost every Frenchman. Only when France is in mortal peril does the struggle have a truce. The comradeship of Foch and Clemenceau illustrates as in a cameo the history of France."

In the same chapter, after describing scenes in the French Chamber at the end of the last century in a way that Maurice Barrés himself would have thought melodramatic, since he goes so far as to declare that they conjured up visions of the Chicago underworld, Churchill adds:

"But here they were presented upon the limelit stage of the most famous of the nations before an audience of all the world. The actors were men of the highest ability, men of learning and eloquence, men of repute and power; men who proclaimed the noblest sentiments, who lived in the public eye; men who directed armies, diplomacy and finance. It was a terrible society, grimly polished, loaded with explosives, trellised with live electric wires. Through the centre of it, turning to make a front now here, now there, and beating down opponents with his mace, Clemenceau long strode, reckless, aggressive and triumphant."

Such were the feelings of mingled admiration and terror which French political life of that day inspired in this great English gentleman.

It was, unquestionably, the heroism of the French during the First World War, their indomitable and bloody resistance at Verdun, where a platoon commander uttered the famous cry, "Up, you dead!", which were the determining factors in Churchill's affection and admiration for France.

.   .   .   .   .

As to the period of the war during which Churchill and I were the heads of our respective Governments, I shall refer chiefly to our personal contacts, and this imposes on me, I fear, the necessity of speaking as much about myself as about him. And I must explain, when they are of historic interest, certain matters where, judging from his *Memoirs*, Churchill has not accurately recorded them. That is quite understandable.

First let me deal with the purely military plan, on which, although we had differences of opinion, they did not give rise to any ill-feeling between us.

Before the War, Churchill used to pay visits from time to time to military chiefs in France, such as General Georges and General Giraud, who had become his friends. These chiefs, who were also friends of mine, were unfortunately wedded to a convention which was wreaking havoc in our Army. They upheld the theory of Marshal Pétain and General Weygand, according to which a break made by an attacking force in a continuous front must constitute a calamity for the attacker. They asserted, in fact, that attacking troops who have pierced the enemy front are soon encircled, with the result that they form a hernia which the enemy can strangulate. The bigger the hernia, the greater is the catastrophe for the attacker. This idea dated from the 1914–18 War, when armies advanced at the pace of the infantry, and it had, as a matter of fact, been proved erroneous at the end of that War when tanks came into use. But this last lesson had been forgotten.

In vain did I draw a picture, from the rostrum of the Chamber on March 15, 1935, of what would take place if France were invaded by Panzer divisions coming through Belgium. In vain did I bring in a Bill to create the corps of armoured divisions demanded by General de Gaulle. Our military chiefs were looking backwards, and the Government and Parliament followed suit.

I have often regretted since the War that I did not take up this vital matter more strongly with Churchill. I might perhaps have succeeded in convincing the man who conceived the idea of the tanks during the First World War. I said to him then, and he notes my remark in his *Memoirs*: "England does not want compulsory military service. All right. But in that case why don't you have a mechanized army? If you had six armoured divisions at your disposal, you could put up a good show of military power on the Continent."

The financial and industrial strength of Great Britain would have rendered this possible. Mr. Hore-Belisha, the Minister for War, with whom I was on friendly terms and to whom I made the same suggestion, objected on the ground of the system of overseas reliefs in the British Army. He did not convince me, but neither did I convince him. And the influence of the French military chiefs on their British colleagues was exercised in a retrograde direction, in spite of Captain Liddell Hart's warnings.

It was because I had been unable to convince Churchill that the French military chiefs' doctrine of warfare was out of date, that I was at variance with him about the consequences of the piercing of our front by the German Panzer divisions in May 1940. These divisions, under a cover of Stukas, made their way at high speed through the rear areas of our armies. Our artillery, who were still firing at a point seven kilometres away, saw them suddenly appear at their gun muzzles. They were followed by motorized divisions, and these again by lightly equipped divisions; then came the mass of the ordinary divisions. It was in this way that the scythe-like attack on Dunkirk was delivered, an encircling movement which would have resulted in the capture of all the Allied Forces in Belgium, if Hitler had not approved Rundstedt's decision to halt his Panzers, thus enabling a part of the British and French Armies to embark at Dunkirk, thanks largely to the devotion and heroism of the British manning the small boats of all kinds which came to their aid.

The disagreement concerning the new strategy between Churchill and myself was revealed on May 15, 1940, when I telephoned to inform him of the disaster. He disputed the scope of it, asked my permission to telephone to General Georges and telegraphed that afternoon to President Roosevelt, "I think myself the battle on land has only just begun, and I should like to see the masses engage."

The following day, May 16, I informed my entourage that the Government might have to withdraw to North Africa and continue the War from there, after offering resistance on the Seine and the Loire. My diplomatic principal private secretary, M. de Margerie, talked freely in the afternoon to Churchill, who had arrived in Paris that day. When, on May 31, Churchill came back to Paris for a meeting of the Supreme Council, he told M. de Margerie, "When you spoke to me a fortnight ago, I wondered whether you hadn't suddenly gone mad, but I realize fully now the extreme gravity of the situation." Several days later he told General Georges that this plan had seemed to him to show signs of defeatism. I must add that, with his customary magnanimity, Churchill had not breathed a word of this criticism to me during our conversations. I regret this, for I would have then done my best to enlighten him about the situation, which was due to a lamentable failure on the part of the military chiefs of both our countries to appreciate the revolution brought about by the internal combustion engine in modern warfare.

The discussion about the evacuation of the Allied troops from Dunkirk, which took place in the Supreme War Council held in Paris on May 31, 1940, was very pathetic.

Once more I was brought to realize the affection in which Churchill held my country. After emphasizing the disproportion, up to the moment, between the number of British evacuated, 165,000, and that of the French, 15,000, I urged that the evacuation operations should be prolonged to enable more French soldiers to get away. Addressing myself to Churchill I asked if he wished an order to be issued that French troops should form the rearguard and cover the final embarkation. Deeply moved, Churchill declared that he had no wish to see further sacrifices imposed on the French troops, and I obtained the extension asked for, with the result that the number of French soldiers evacuated was raised to 110,000.

.   .   .   .   .

In speaking of what took place at Tours and Bordeaux, I am afraid I have to mention my own part in the proceedings, as new documents have thrown light on those historic hours.

During the martyrdom of the weeks following the breaking of the

Allied front, there was never any change in the solidarity and close friendship between Churchill and myself. This shows that Churchill with great nobility and understanding realized what must be the state of mind of the head of the French Government when the French armies were on the point of being wiped out and when the people of France were fleeing to the South with such of their belongings as they could carry with them. I endeavoured to obtain the maximum help from our ally and appealed to him constantly for all possible assistance from the Royal Air Force. I begged for it quite shamelessly, picturing the situation at its worst, warning him that I should be overthrown and that Pétain, Weygand, Chautemps and their followers would demand an armistice if they could claim that France's ally had not done his utmost for her in this life-and-death struggle. At the Supreme Council at Tours I went so far as to beg Churchill himself to support my final appeal to Roosevelt not to abandon France if I were overthrown by those who were advocating an armistice. In the report of this meeting, published by M. de Margerie, in 1952, in the form in which he had drawn it up immediately afterwards, it is stated twice over that in this eventuality there would have to be a Government of which I was not a member, consequently not my Government. But the British secretary at the Council in his report, cited in part by Churchill, appears to have thought that an armistice could be concluded either by my Government *or* by another, and this in spite of the fact that, after emphasizing Franco-British solidarity and my faith in final victory, my last sentence attributed to me by this report is, "If I lost this faith, I should at the same time lose all desire to go on living."

The truth is that, on that day, in my mortal anguish, which I did my utmost to conceal, I adopted towards Churchill the same attitude he was adopting that same day towards Roosevelt, on whom he was bringing similar pressure to bear and supporting, as he promised, my call for aid from the United States. On returning home from Tours, he telegraphed to the President:

"Although the present Government and I personally would never fail to send the Fleet across the Atlantic if resistance was beaten down here, a point may be reached in the struggle where the present ministers no longer have control of affairs and when very easy terms could be obtained for the British island by their becoming a vassal state of Hitler's Empire. A pro-German Government would certainly be called into being to make peace and might present to a shattered or a starving nation an almost irresistible case for entire submission to the Nazi will."

It will be seen that he went even further than I did.

When Churchill left Tours, I went to Cange, where the Council of Ministers held a meeting. My first words were reported indignantly by General Weygand in his written deposition at the preliminary investigation of the Riom Trial as follows:

"M. Paul Reynaud announced that a meeting of the Supreme Council had just taken place with Churchill and Lord Halifax. At this Council M. Paul Reynaud declared it was the intention of the French Government to continue the fight. There was complete agreement between the French and British Governments on this point. This declaration gave rise to two protests. . . ."

In the afternoon of June 16, 1940—the last day my Government was in power—I received a telephone call from General de Gaulle, whom I had sent to London to ask for ships needed to take some of our troops to North Africa to carry on the war there. He informed me of Churchill's grandiose plan to create a *Franco-British Union*. This was a most sensational move. I visualized the possibility of compelling the Council of Ministers—due to meet at five o'clock—to continue the war. And this shows how excited I was at this news.

Since the publication of my last book *Au Cœur de la Mêlée*, I have received information about the listeners-in to the telephone employed by General Weygand to report my conversations to him. The document revealing this, which is to be found in the records of Pétain's trial, proves that up to the very last moment I strove to keep France in the War, though certain advocates of the Armistice have insinuated the contrary, hoping thus to associate me with them in their culpable weakness.

The following are parts of the conversations overheard and recorded in the Palais Gallien, Bordeaux, between June 15 and 17:

16th June 1940 *at* 12.30 p.m.

General de Gaulle, in London, to M. Paul Reynaud.

de Gaulle: I have just seen Churchill. There is something stupendous in preparation affecting the entity of the two countries. Churchill proposes the establishment of a single Franco-British Government, with you, perhaps, *M. le President*, as head of a Franco-British War Cabinet.

Paul Reynaud: It is the only possible solution for the future. But it must be done on a large scale and very quickly, above all very quickly. It is a question of minutes.[1] I give you half an hour. It would be splendid.

16th June 1940 *at* 4 p.m.

General de Gaulle, in London, to Paul Reynaud.

de Gaulle: There is going to be a sensational declaration.

Reynaud: Yes, but after 5 o'clock (17.h) it will be too late.[1]

de Gaulle: I will do my best to bring it to you at once by plane.

Reynaud: Yes, but that will be too late. The situation has seriously deteriorated within the last few minutes. Unforeseen events have occurred.

16th June 1940 *at* 4.40 p.m.

President of the Republic to the Prime Minister.

President Lebrun: Can I see you before 5 o'clock?

Paul Reynaud: Yes certainly. I am making a note of the conversation I have just had with London. This goes far beyond what I led you to expect. It is extremely important.

At five o'clock the Council of Ministers met. Weygand, who had learnt from the listening-in posts of the British Government's proposal, had been campaigning among the supporters of the armistice against it. So I had hardly finished reading it out to the Council, and giving reasons why it should be accepted enthusiastically by France, when they broke out into denunciations of it, declaring that they would never agree to France's becoming a British Dominion (*sic*)—a wilful misinterpretation on their part of the spirit of the letter proposing the Union. Personally, I preferred to collaborate with my allies rather than with my enemies, as I wrote later from prison to Marshal Pétain.

[1]Because of the meeting of the Council of Ministers due at 5 p.m.

L

To my extreme surprise, not one voice was raised in support of me in the Council, even among those who till then had backed me most strongly in my desire to continue the War; neither Mandel—contrary to what was reported to Churchill—nor anyone else. It is needless to say that my isolation at such a crucial moment made a deep impression on M. Lebrun, and was instrumental in his refusing, after the meeting, to allow me to create a Government of resistants to keep France in the War. Thus, this proposal made by Churchill and intended to strengthen my position, as it should have done, had instead the effect of weakening it.

I note, by the way, that Churchill, who was not at Bordeaux and received only a second-hand account of what happened there, gives the impression in his *Memoirs* that I abandoned the struggle owing to exhaustion, and that this made me advise M. Lebrun, after the meeting of the Council of Ministers, to turn to Marshal Pétain. The evidence obtained by the Commission of Enquiry of the National Assembly, of which Churchill had known nothing when writing his *Memoirs*, cleared up the whole of this matter. Consequently, as Herriot said in his deposition at Pétain's trial, when the President of the Republic requested me, in the presence of the Presidents of the two Chambers, to execute Chautemps' proposal to ask the enemy for his terms, I declared that *I would not go back on my word*. M. Lebrun, moreover, told the Commission of Enquiry that when I entered his study, and before discussion with the Presidents of the Chambers, I was hoping he would charge me with the creation of a government of resistants; and that in answer to his request for the execution of Chautemps' proposal, I said, "If you wish to pursue this policy, you must apply to Marshal Pétain."

It is obvious that Churchill had been misinformed on this point, for he writes in his *Memoirs*, "This action must be judged precipitate."

Moreover, Edouard Herriot, in an article giving an account of all this, which was published on July 13, 1946, in *la Democratie Meriodionale*, wrote this about me:

> "I can bear witness that never at any time did he, any more than we ourselves, propose that Pétain should succeed him. He was at daggers drawn with the Marshal and with General Weygand.

That same day he had asked us to come and support him in the Council of Ministers."

This is the reason why Hitler, who was fully informed of all that had happened at Bordeaux, insisted that I should be imprisoned and then handed over. Four years later, he ordered Vichy to have me brought back to France, together with Mandel, to be murdered by the Vichy militia. I have no idea why Vichy agreed only as regards Mandel, who was assassinated on July 7, 1944, in the Forest of Fontainebleau.

This is an historical fact of interest not only to myself.

During the time that Georges Mandel and I were imprisoned in the sinister fortress of Portalet in the Pyrenees, one of my associates was visited in September 1942, in his villa on the Riviera, by a South American diplomat whose story was that he had been sent by the Churchill Government to find out whether Georges Mandel and I were disposed to attempt an escape. To prove that he was not an impostor, he asked my friend to say a few words that he would like the B.B.C. to repeat three days later. This was done. I agreed to the suggestion but stipulated that I would not abandon Mandel, who was incapable of making the descent by a slippery rope down the seventy metres of sheer rock from our cells to the torrent below.

I had thought out another way of escape for Mandel when, following the Allied landing in North Africa, the Germans invaded the southern zone of France. They reached Portalet the same day at nine o'clock in the morning, and several days later Mandel and I were in solitary confinement in the Camp at Oranienburg. In our cells we had the satisfaction of thinking that Churchill had not forgotten us.

.   .   .   .   .   .

After Pétain's armistice, Churchill rendered France a great service when he told General de Gaulle in London in July 1940, "I regard you as the Leader of the Free French"; for this enabled de Gaulle to gather round him his countrymen who wished to continue the fight.

Centres to welcome and recruit them were set up for the French who reached London and Churchill secured for them means of remaining in touch with France. Secret 'planes enabled them to accomplish missions on the Continent and bring Frenchmen to London. He placed the B.B.C. at their disposal and so, daily, hope was poured into the hearts of their fellow-countrymen still in their own occupied land.

Churchill recognized de Gaulle first of all as Leader of the Free French, then as President of the French National Committee, and finally as President of the Liberation Committee established in Algiers.

He promoted the rallying of Madagascar, freed by the British, and promised that it should be put under the jurisdiction of *La-France Libre*.

A great deal has been said about the personal differences between Churchill and de Gaulle. One day in September 1942, Mr. Anthony Eden, then as always a true friend of France, went to see de Gaulle and, taking a paper from his pocket, said to him, "I have been charged by the War Cabinet to give you this message: 'We have ten times more trouble with the Committee of the Free French than with all the other Allies put together.'"

"I have always maintained that France was a very great country," replied de Gaulle.

The Syrian Affair embittered relations between Churchill and de Gaulle. It provoked the dispatch of an ultimatum from Churchill to de Gaulle after M. Helleu, the latter's representative, had ordered the arrest of the Opposition leaders. Churchill threatened to have them freed by British troops.

But Churchill never ceased to think of the sufferings of the French people. All those who heard his broadcast to the French on October 21, 1940, retain an unforgettable memory of the deep emotion they felt when listening to it.

"Frenchmen! For more than thirty years, in peace and war, I have marched with you, and I am marching still along the same road. . . . We are waiting for the long-promised invasion. So are the fishes. . . . Remember we shall never stop, never weary, and never give in, and that our whole people and Empire have vowed themselves to the task of cleansing Europe from the Nazi pestilence and saving the world from the new Dark Ages. . . . Good night, then, sleep to gather strength for the morning. For the morning will come. . . ."

What words could better stimulate the spirit of resistance in the French!

.   .   .   .   .

At the end of the War, and after, Churchill showed once again, in deeds as well as in words, his love for France.

At Yalta, President Roosevelt proposed an occupation zone in Germany for French forces. Churchill agreed and it was understood that the zone should be formed by allocating parts from the British and U.S. zones provisionally determined at Quebec the previous summer. At the next meeting Churchill went further, pointing out with emphasis that the presence of French forces in a zone in Germany was not in itself enough. *A strong France* was vital for the future defence of Western Europe as a whole.

Such was Churchill's attitude towards France. And this magnanimous attitude has contributed to the greatness of England. Churchill has strengthened still further the bonds which unite our two democracies.

The French are so profoundly conscious of this solidarity that at this time, the summer of 1953, there are many among us who are opposed to the European Defence Community just because England is not a party to it.

If I may be permitted to express a wish, it is that "the greatest living Englishman" should utilize the immense prestige he enjoys in his own country to make her understand that the past is the past, however glorious it may be. It is to the interest of both our peoples that we should step out boldly on the road to the future.

CHURCHILL THE ORATOR

_____

Lord Justice Birkett

The Rt. Hon. Sir Norman Birkett, one of Britain's most distinguished lawyers, has been a Lord Justice of Appeal since 1950. He was President of the Cambridge Union 1910, and Member of Parliament for East Nottingham 1923–24 and 1929–31. He was called to the Bar in 1913 and established an international reputation by the brilliance of his advocacy particularly as Counsel for the Defence in many noted murder trials.

GREAT versatility in men is always a little under suspicion. "Let the cobbler stick to his last" has always seemed to contain the accumulated wisdom of the ages. To be supremely good in one particular field of human endeavour is the most that the highly gifted individual can normally expect or achieve. But Sir Winston Churchill is a law unto himself in this as in so many other matters. He seems scarcely to be bound by the limitations that enclose the lives of ordinary men. He stands out from his contemporaries as a great and resplendent figure with none to rival him in his many-sidedness.

In the fullness of time the historians of the future with critical eyes will analyse and dissect all the events of his long life, and all the qualities that went to the making of his great achievements. They will have abundant material. Before them will lie the massive volumes in which he has recorded the history of two great wars when he was at the centre of those great and terrible events. They will also have the many volumes of speeches collected by discriminating hands, and presented in a form that was not available to many of the great orators and statesmen of earlier ages. Strangely enough, the reputation of some of our very greatest orators does not rest on the text of the speeches they made, but on the reports of those who heard them and who wrote about them and whose writings have been preserved. The immense fame of Lord Chatham lives on to this day, but at the time when his most famous speeches were delivered there was no reporting of speeches as we know it, and the spell of the orator is preserved for us in the recollections of those who saw and heard him. Horace Walpole, for example, was present at the opening of Parliament in 1755 and heard Chatham deliver his tremendous speech. He retained the memory of that great and memorable occasion all his life and recorded at the time:

"You will ask, what could be beyond this? Nothing but what was beyond whatever was, and that was PITT. His eloquence like a torrent long obstructed burst forth with more commanding impetuosity. . . . There was more humour, wit, vivacity, fine language, more boldness—in short, more astonishing perfections than even you who are used to him can conceive."

The future historian will lack nothing of this kind when writing of Sir Winston Churchill. Not only will he have the text of the speeches, but he will have a thousand descriptions of the orator in action—the voice, the eye, the gestures, the passion and the fire, the humour, the grace, and "all those brave sublunary things that made his raptures clear"—and he will be able to give to the future generations a pretty clear picture of the man we have been privileged to see. The historians will speak of him as one of the greatest of parliamentarians, as Morley spoke of Gladstone, and Rosebery of Chatham; they will speak of him as the statesman to whom the whole world looked for guidance when the very skies seemed about to fall; they will recount his mastery of the written and the spoken word; they will discuss every element in his many-sidedness; and the great figure who has dominated our age will take his destined place in the long and noble line of those who, in serving their day and generation, have been clothed with a kind of immortality.

But it is fairly safe to say that his enduring fame in the world at large and in the eyes of posterity will rest in large measure on the great events of a few years; and all the years that had gone before will be regarded as the years of preparation. He was blessed with length of days, and he came to the supreme achievement of his life schooled and disciplined by long experience of great affairs, familiar with the handling and control of national problems, full of practical wisdom, and with a part to play that he alone could most magnificently fulfil. The "tooth of time and razure of oblivion" work their inexorable will, and men who bestrode the earth in their day are frequently forgotten as the long years pass by. But Sir Winston Churchill, it may be confidently said, will never be forgotten. He will be remembered beyond all other things as the man who rallied the forces of freedom all over the world when it was confronted by a "monstrous tyranny

never surpassed in the dark, lamentable catalogue of human crime".
And apart from all else—the courage, the tenacity, the vision, the
indomitable purpose, the power of decision, the force of personal
example—can it be doubted that he will ever be remembered by the
quality of his oratory? So long as the English language lasts, so long
will many of his inspired speeches endure, and the speeches he made
in the years 1940 to 1945 will rank as the greatest of their kind. Many
of those speeches were examples of superb narrative, of the power to
marshal complicated facts into the most lucid exposition, of the gift
of expounding policy, and permeated throughout with the spirit of
unbreakable resolve. Many of the great passages have already gone
into the common speech, and they will be upon the lips of generations
yet to come, generations that never saw or heard him, but who will
yet fall under the spell. For great oratory is most often the expression
of the deepest feelings of the ordinary man or woman, and the orator
with the gift of language appropriate to the occasion can clothe
that expression in a form that will never die. That Churchill was
inspired in the highest sense by the great events of the war years seems
to permit of no doubt; again, as in so many periods of history, the
crisis had produced the man. It was Clarendon who said of Cromwell:

". . . yet as he grew into place and authority, his parts seemed to
be raised, as if he had concealed faculties, till he had occasion to use
them. . . ."

There is a famous and much-quoted passage in Gladstone's *Homeric
Studies* that seems to have some application to Churchill:

"The work of the orator from its very inception is inextricably
mixed up with practice. It is cast in the mould offered to him by the
minds of his hearers. It is an influence principally received from his
audience (so to speak) in vapour, which he pours back upon them
in a flood. The sympathy and concurrence of his time, is, with his
own mind, joint parent of the work. He cannot follow nor frame
ideals; his choice is to be what the age will have him, what it
requires in order to be moved by him; or else not to be at all."

Gladstone is acknowledged to be one of the most consummate orators that this country has ever known. He had a commanding presence, a noble voice, the gift of choice and elegant words, and a complete knowledge of the subjects on which he spoke. He had trained himself most assiduously in the art of public speaking. The precepts of Quintilian and the maxims of Cicero had been studied and absorbed by him, yet with all this he could write:

> "I wish you knew the state of total impotence to which I should be reduced if there were no echo to the accents of my own voice."

And it would seem to be true of Churchill that he reached the greatest heights when he knew with the orator's true instinct that he had "the sympathy and concurrence of his time". Two familiar illustrations may perhaps be given. In a speech which he made in the House of Commons in 1940 he was reviewing the first year of the war, and surveying what he called "the dark, wide field". In the midst of a long detailed account of the country's defences this passage appears:

> "The gratitude of every home in our island, in our Empire, and indeed throughout the world, except in the abodes of the guilty, goes out to the British airmen who, undaunted by odds, unwearied in their constant challenge and mortal danger, are turning the tide of the world war by their prowess and their devotion. *Never in the field of human conflict was so much owed by so many to so few.*"

That last sentence, so exquisite in its form and the simplicity of its expression, voiced the feelings of millions of hearts, so that it has not merely gone into the common speech, but it is but sober truth to say that it ranks with the reputed saying of Pericles "of famous men the whole earth is the tomb", and will be quoted as one of the great sentences of mankind.

Again, after the miracle of Dunkirk, when the nation had feared a disaster of the most grievous kind, Churchill made another speech to the House of Commons when he said:

". . . we shall not flag or fail. We shall go on to the end; we shall
fight in France, we shall fight on the seas and oceans, we shall fight
with growing confidence and growing strength in the air, we
shall defend our island, whatever the cost may be; we shall fight
on the beaches, we shall fight on the landing grounds, we shall
fight in the fields and in the streets, we shall fight in the hills; we
shall never surrender. . . ."

That, too, was the noble and inspiring expression of the indomitable
spirit of the people of Britain, when the prospect was of the darkest
and gloomiest kind. It would appear therefore that oratory is made up
of many elements about which something must be said as it applies to
Churchill. There is the orator himself with his understanding heart and
mind; his power of expression, his readiness and resource; his courage;
the occasion which calls forth the oratory with all its dramatic
possibilities; the theme of the orator, whether noble and lofty or tragic
and pitiful; the form and the beauty of the expression of these things;
and it becomes quite clear that the thing said can never be separated
from the moment of its saying, and certainly any attempt to recapture
the fire and the glow of past moments is foredoomed to failure if the
thing said is considered alone.

For the written word, however beautiful it may be, can never
convey the orator's true power. The most powerful imagination cannot
recapture the particular tones in which the words were said, the
instinctive gestures, the native fire and glow, or the mysterious element
that came from the exact circumstances of the particular occasion.
When Sheridan made his great speech at the trial of Warren Hastings,
Charles James Fox, Edmund Burke and the younger Pitt, all of them
great masters of English speech, acclaimed the speech of Sheridan as
something utterly phenomenal, Pitt saying that "it surpassed all the
eloquence of ancient and modern times". The speech itself can be
read with interest and admiration, but nobody now can recapture
the wonder and the glory of that memorable occasion which called
forth the rapturous language of some of the greatest orators of their
time. In one of his famous essays Hazlitt embroiders the same theme
when he says:

"The thunder and lightning mixture of the orator turns out a mere dark-coloured suit in the person of the pure writer. . . . What we read is the same; what we see and hear is different—the self-same words but not to the self-same tune. The orator's vehemence and gesture, the loudness of the voice, the speaking eye, the conscious attitude, the inexplicable dumb show and noise—all those brave sublunary things that made his raptures clear—are no longer there, and without these he is nothing."

Many of Churchill's famous speeches were made in the House of Commons and heard only by the members of that House; many were broadcast to the world over the air when millions listened to him as man was never listened to before. The generations who never saw him, and never heard him, and who will read these speeches, will never be able to supply the essential things that belong to oratory, but nevertheless will have a splendid consolation in the magnificence of the written word. For Churchill was the born orator and the born writer, a combination as rare as it is remarkable.

But, it may be asked, what were the qualities that gave Sir Winston his supreme power as an orator? It is sometimes said that oratory depends upon the quality of the orator himself, the occasion on which he speaks, the subject matter of the oration, and the form in which the speech is cast. Enough has perhaps already been said about the importance of the occasion when considering the speeches of Churchill. But what about the man himself? When Lord Rosebery, himself a master of the written and the spoken word, came to analyse the oratory of Chatham he concluded a brilliant exposition with the words:

"It is not merely the thing that is said, but the man who says it that counts, the character which breathes through the sentences."

This just observation applies with especial force to Churchill. Those who heard him and saw him were "under the wand of the magician", as the younger Pitt said of Fox, but they had before them at all times the quality and character of the man himself. They knew him to be a man in whom the love of country burned with a mighty flame, and it burst forth in all his famous exhortations.

"Let us therefore brace ourselves to our duties, and so bear ourselves that, if the British Empire and its Commonwealth last for a thousand years, men will still say, 'This was their finest hour.'"

This trumpet-call to duty, to sacrifice, to "blood, toil, tears and sweat", made its overwhelming appeal because of the source from whence it came. This note of noble patriotism was nothing new. It had characterized many speeches that he had made over the years, and men remembered some of the great occasions. There is one speech that seems to have been overlooked by the compilers of the volumes of his speeches which deserves to rank with the greatest of all his utterances. It was made in April of 1925 at the unveiling of the Royal Naval Division Memorial and bears his characteristic impress when speaking of "our island" and the men who died to protect it.

"Here under the shadow of the Admiralty building, where, eleven years ago, the Royal Naval Division was called into martial life, this monument now records their fame and preserves their memory. Their memory is thus linked for ever with the Royal Navy, whose child they were, of whose traditions they were so proud, and whose long annals, rich with romantic and splendid feats of arms, contains no brighter page than theirs. But if the place is well chosen, so also is the day. This is April 25th, and ten years ago the astonishing exploit of landing on the Gallipoli Peninsula was in full battle. And we here, who have so many memories in common, almost seem to hear the long reverberations of the distant cannonade, and certainly we feel again in our souls the awful hopes and awful fears of those tragic hours. . . .

We are often tempted to ask ourselves what have we gained by the enormous sacrifices made by those to whom this memorial is erected. But this was never the issue with those who marched away. No question of advantage presented itself to their minds. They only saw the light shining on the clear path of duty. They only saw their duty to resist oppression, to protect the weak, to vindicate the profound but unwritten law of nations, to testify to truth and justice and mercy among men. They never asked the question, 'What shall we gain?' They asked only the question,

'Where lies the right?' It was thus that they marched away for ever, and yet from their uncalculating exaltation and devotion, detached from all consideration of material gain, we may be sure that good will come to their countrymen and to this island they guarded in its reputation and safety so faithfully and so well."

There indeed was the character of the man inspired by the greatness and the solemnity of the occasion.

Nobody reading these words can fail to notice that the speech has the power to thrill and to move when read, just as it had power to move and impress when it was first delivered. What then is the secret? Wherein lies the spell? It is made up of a great number of things in combination, but this at least may be said. Whilst opinions have often been expressed about the character of the highest oratory, many of those best qualified to judge have insisted that simplicity of speech, linked with the expression of the deepest feelings of mankind, has always possessed the power to stir men's hearts in all ages of the world. The two names that come to the mind instinctively are those of Abraham Lincoln and John Bright.

In the speech which he delivered at the dedication of the cemetery at Gettysburg, Lincoln used ten sentences and spoke for five minutes, after Everett, the orator of the day, had spoken for nearly two hours. The speech of Everett is now forgotten, but the speech of Lincoln is still repeated as one of the great utterances of the world. Contrary to popular belief, Lincoln had prepared the speech down to the very smallest word. He had revised it and pruned it, and delivered it with the notes of the speech in his hand. Lincoln was one of the supreme orators who can divine the significance of the occasion, and the dedication of that hallowed plot to the memory of those who had died filled him with the deepest emotion. Much of the power and the beauty of the speech cannot be separated from the solemnity of the occasion; but Everett was conscious of that too. What then makes the speech of Lincoln live on, whilst the speech of Everett has long since been forgotten? The answer must be: because of the extreme simplicity of the diction. It is nearly a century ago that it was spoken, but it still remains one of the very greatest examples of what has been called "the unrivalled efficacy of plain speech".

CHURCHILL THE ORATOR

Prime Minister Churchill addresses the United States Congress at Washington in December 1941. Behind him are William P. Cole and U.S. Vice-President Henry Wallace, and lower left is Senator Alben W. Barkley

When John Bright spoke in the House of Commons almost a hundred years ago, too, and used the famous words—

"the angel of death has been abroad throughout the land; you may almost hear the beating of his wings"

—he displayed the same authentic quality of simple speech. When he returned thanks to his constituents at Birmingham on his re-election, he said:

"There is a passage in the Old Testament which has often struck me as being one of great beauty. Many of you will recollect that the prophet, in journeying to and fro, was very hospitably entertained by what is termed in the Bible a Shunammite woman. In return for her hospitality, he wished to make her some amends, and he called her to him and asked her what there was he should do for her. 'Shall I speak for thee to the King,' he said, 'or to the captain of the host?' Now it has always appeared to me that the Shunammite woman returned a natural answer. She replied, in declining the prophet's offer, 'I dwell among mine own people.' "

The beauty and simplicity of the language has never failed to make a sure appeal since the day the words were first uttered. And many of the greatest effects achieved by Churchill have the same quality of great simplicity. When he concluded a great speech at the Free Trade Hall, Manchester, in January of 1940, he used these words:

"Come then: let us to the task, to the battle, to the toil—each to our part, each to our station. Fill the armies, rule the air, pour out the munitions, strangle the U-boats, sweep the mines, plough the land, build the ships, guard the streets, succour the wounded, uplift the downcast, and honour the brave."

But do not let it be supposed that ALL great oratory must needs have this element of simplicity. Those who heard Gladstone have said that one of the charms of listening to him was to see him escape from the bewildering mass of parentheses with which his speeches were filled;

and the great speeches of Erskine in the courts of law, which thrilled every listener, so that a man like Crabb Robinson could say in his diary that "the effect he produced was beyond any power to describe", are very far from being simple.

But whether the speech be simple or ornate, the great orator must have a profound sense of the value of words, and an instinctive sense of the value of words in their right order, so that the words and their rhythm can make their quite magical appeal. The late George Sampson in his essay on "Truth and Beauty" has spoken of that age-old miracle, the mysterious power of words arranged in a certain order.

> "You take a few words," he said, "you put them together, and in a way not explicable, they flash into life, and you have not a sentence but a song, a revelation, a new creation, a joy for ever."

Words are the raw material of all speeches, and they have a life of their own. They have colour, and sound, and meaning, and a quality that comes from association in their use by the great masters of the language, or what C. E. Montague called "the glamorous prestige of high adventures in great company". Sir Winston Churchill possesses this supreme gift. He chooses the right word not only for its sound but with an instinctive knowledge of its decorative and emotional meaning. Listen to, and read again, a few examples.

> ". . . the fact that the British Empire stands invincible . . . will kindle again the spark of hope in the breasts of hundreds of millions of down-trodden or despairing men and women throughout Europe, and far beyond its bounds, and that from these sparks there will presently come *cleansing* and *devouring* flame."

> ". . . The British Empire and the United States will have to be somewhat mixed up together in some of their affairs for mutual and general advantage. For my own part, looking out upon the future, I do not view the process with any misgivings. I could not stop it if I wished; no one can stop it. Like the Mississippi, it just keeps rolling along. Let it roll. Let it roll on full flood, *inexorable, irresistible, benignant*, to broader lands and better days."

"Death and Sorrow will be the companions of our journey; hardship our garment; constancy and valour our only shield. We must be united, we must be undaunted, we must be inflexible. Our qualities and deeds must burn and glow through the gloom of Europe until they become the veritable beacon of its salvation."

"We shall not fail or falter; we shall not weaken or tire. Neither the sudden shock of battle, nor the long-drawn trials of vigilance and exertion will wear us down. Give us the tools, and we will finish the job."

"I have never promised anything but blood, tears, toil, and sweat. Now, however, we have a new experience. We have victory—a remarkable and definite victory. The *bright gleam* has caught the helmets of our soldiers, and warmed and cheered all our hearts."

Nobody reading passages such as these can fail to notice the choice of the words, and the unfailing rhythm of the sentences; and much of Churchill's power to hold men's minds and to enthrall their hearts lies in the fact that he is the possessor of the magical gift of which George Sampson spoke—to put the right words in the right order, at the right time, and in the right place. How much this is due to patient and prolonged labour, and how much to sheer native genius, it is impossible to say. But in the *De Oratore* Cicero said:

"Writing is said to be the best and most excellent modeller and teacher of oratory; and not without reason; for if what is meditated and considered easily surpasses sudden and extemporary speech, a constant and diligent habit of writing will surely be of more effect than meditation and consideration itself . . . and all the thoughts and words, which are the most expressive of their kind, must of necessity come under and submit to the keenness of our judgment in writing; and a fair collocation of the word is effected by writing, in a certain rhythm and measure, not poetical, but oratorical. Such are the qualities which bring applause and admiration to good orators; nor will any man ever attain them, unless after long and great practice in writing."

It has already been observed that the combination of the supreme writer and the supreme orator is exceedingly rare. Sometimes the qualities that make for excellence in literature are the very qualities that are defects in oratory. Burke has left to posterity many great speeches that are read with admiration to this very day; yet when they were delivered they were failures. When he made his great speech on conciliation with America, Erskine, who heard it, said that it drove everybody away, including people who, when they came to read it, read it over and over again, and could hardly think of anything else.

Churchill's speeches carried immediate conviction to his hearers by his superb oratorical power, but the form and content of those speeches will make their appeal to readers in far distant generations when read in quietude, even when the voice and physical presence of the orator are no longer there. For it would seem that the qualities which made Churchill a great writer and a great orator are in essence the same, so far as the complete mastery of the language is concerned. When Augustine Birrell in his essay on Pope asked the question, What is it that constitutes a great writer? he answered it in the words of Cardinal Newman, and the answer would appear to apply with equal force to Churchill as an orator. Newman said:

"I do not claim for a great author, as such, any great depth of thought, or breadth of view, or philosophy, or sagacity, or knowledge of human nature, or experience of human life—though these additional gifts he may have, and the more he has of them the greater he is—but I ascribe to him as his characteristic gift, in a large sense, the faculty of expression. He is master to the two-fold 'logos', the thought and the word, distinct but inseparable from each other. . . . He always has the right word for the right idea, and never a word too much. If he is brief, it is because few words suffice; if he is lavish of them, still each word has its mark, and aids, not embarrasses, the vigorous march of the elocution. He expresses what all feel, but all cannot say, and his sayings pass into proverbs among his people, and his phrases become household words and idioms of their daily speech, which is tessellated with the rich fragments of his language, as we see in foreign land the marbles of Roman grandeur worked into the walls and pavements of modern palaces."

What the future of oratory in general will be it is impossible to forecast. The English word "orator" seems to have fallen on evil days. It is rarely used without a slightly derisory accent as when men say with curious emphasis, "I am no orator as Brutus is." The orators of ancient times felt themselves to be engaged on a task of the highest worth and value. They were "shaping works for all the future" and "offering themselves to be examined by all-testing Envy and Time", as one of the ancient writers said when defending and praising the scrupulous care taken by Demosthenes. Today, the care and attention given to the art of public speaking has sensibly declined. It is not to be expected of course that men and women in these modern days should bestow upon the art of public speaking the infinite pains that were taken in the ancient world. The growth of the power of the written word since the introduction of printing, the special conversational technique of broadcasting, the immense growth in the numbers of those who do speak in councils and committees and meetings of all kinds, and many changes of a similar kind, have all tended to lessen the interest in the more polished or more ornate kinds of speaking; and men and women in this busy age have little time to strive for perfection in the form of what they say.

Sir Winston Churchill is in many respects a survivor from the golden age of oratory. No doubt it could be said of him as was said of the great orator of ancient times, "he adopts no thought, no word at random, but takes much care of both the arrangement of his ideas and the graciousness of his language". But however this may be, he is certainly in the great tradition. English oratory is adorned with many famous names. Chatham, Burke, Sheridan, the younger Pitt, Fox, Canning, Brougham, Erskine, Bright, Disraeli, Gladstone, and a score of others need fear no comparison with orators of other days.

And into that great company Sir Winston Churchill enters as of right. From his lips have come some of the sublimest utterances in the language. For more than fifty years he has expressed himself on great

national and international matters, and the volumes of his speeches are
a history in themselves of these tremendous years. Many of his speeches
will live as examples of human speech at its highest and best, and they
will be woven into the fabric of our own history and the history of the
world. For many of these speeches made history before our very eyes.
They changed the shape of events. They proclaimed the greatness of
our past and the nature of our great traditions. They shed a clear light
upon the path of duty, and they implanted in ordinary men and
women the resolve to make the day of danger their finest hour. They
appealed to the noblest and deepest feelings of mankind when discouragement and despair besieged their hearts, and brought triumph
out of the jaws of defeat; and many of those speeches will remain a
great possession for all time of the country whose interests they preserved and maintained.

They will also remain as an undying memorial to the man who
made them and became the greatest figure of his age.

CHURCHILL THE BIOGRAPHER AND HISTORIAN

Malcolm Muggeridge

Malcolm Muggeridge is Editor of Punch *and was formerly Deputy Editor of the* Daily Telegraph. *His appointments in journalism have included posts as Moscow Correspondent of the* Manchester Guardian, *Assistant Editor of the* Calcutta Statesman *and Washington Correspondent of the* Daily Telegraph. *He has also been a lecturer at the Egyptian University, Cairo.*

In recent years he has written much literary criticism and in this chapter reviews Mr. Churchill's biographical and historical works.

IN Churchill's novel, *Savrola*, it is observed of the hero (who bears a decided resemblance to his creator) that he has in his library the works of Gibbon, Macaulay, Plato, Darwin and Thackeray. The first two—Gibbon and Macaulay—might have been taken for granted. Their stamp is upon all Sir Winston Churchill's writings. This is especially true of his biographical and historical works, even though Macaulay's judgments, particularly of Marlborough, came in for severe censure. Incidentally, *Savrola* is a too little appreciated book of Churchilliana. Many of the views it expresses are those which have governed, and continue to govern, its author's conduct of his own life —for instance:

> " 'Would you rise in the world?' said Savrola. 'You must work while others amuse themselves. Are you desirous of a reputation for courage? You must risk your life. Would you be strong morally or physically? You must resist temptations. All this is paying in advance; that is prospective finance. Observe the other side of the picture, the bad things are paid for afterwards!' "

Savrola, a sort of revolutionary aristocrat, beloved of the people and concerned for their liberties, goes into voluntary, if still poignant, exile. Sir Winston, too, has known such periods of exile, though not in the literal sense of having to leave his native land. For him, to be out of office, not at the centre of things, constitutes a kind of exile, which he has filled by plying his pen. His immense vitality has found an outlet, and at the same time his finances have been replenished, by the exercise of the profusion of letters during the periods of his exclusion from office, especially in the 'thirties, when it looked as though his political career was prematurely ended—as, indeed, might well have been the case but for the 1939–45 war, and the crisis caused by the German break through Belgium and the Netherlands into France. What he has produced in these lulls exceeds in quantity and distinction the total lifetime production of many a professional writer.

Of his purely biographical works, the most impressive is unquestionably his life of his father, Lord Randolph Churchill, first published in 1906, and at once acclaimed for its literary excellence and filial piety. Philip Guedalla's judgment of it stands. "*Lord Randolph Churchill*," he has written, "is, perhaps, the author's most completely satisfactory book. His heart was in the subject, his prose was still unimpaired by platform eloquence, and it remains as one of the best political biographies in English." Though its length is considerable—a solid Victorian two-decker—and though many of the political controversies, and even some of the principal actors, like Stafford Northcote, are now largely forgotten, its interest is sustained. The character of Lord Randolph emerges in clear lineaments—a brilliant, moody, incalculable man, whose brief, meteoric political career made its clear mark on history.

From the point of view of this generation, however, the biography's fascination lies in its bearing rather on the son who wrote it than on the father who provided its subject. Churchill's veneration for his father, and burning sense of his shabby treatment by his fellow Conservatives, has deeply influenced his own manner of thought and parliamentary strategy. The party of Tory Democracy which Lord Randolph attempted, without success, to found went marching on in the person of his son, leading him for a time into the Liberal ranks, and giving a Radical tinge to all his thinking and policies in the years of his Conservative leadership. In a sense, indeed, the son may be said to have fulfilled the father's purposes. His *Lord Randolph Churchill* is a blueprint for his own life, even down to such details as his style of oratory and of invective, and to the ill-disguised contempt with which he regards some of his fellow Conservatives.

Yet when all this is said, it remains a very fine biography indeed, displaying, in the manner of Morley (who went carefully over the proofs), a thorough historical grasp of the course of the events, such as the Irish question, with which Lord Randolph was concerned, and of the play of political forces within and outside the Conservative Party. What it does not even seek to do is to convey the intimate, personal characters of Lord Randolph and his associates. W. H. Smith, in Sir Winston's eyes, is no more than a "stout-hearted bookseller"; Joseph Chamberlain appears in the conventional role of the Birmingham demagogue; Salisbury's politics are sagaciously and cogently expounded, but not the mainsprings of interior motive and purpose which, since Freud, have played so large a part in our reading of human personality and conduct. As a biographer and historian, in fact, Churchill has remained obstinately Victorian and pre-Lytton Strachey. He is content to survey the upper portions of the iceberg which is human personality, and to leave the four-fifths under the water largely unexplored. In Lord Randolph's case, of course, there were obvious reasons of taste and duty in such a procedure, but it may be doubted whether Sir Winston would even now feel constrained, or even see any necessity, to fill in the large blank spaces in his portraiture. In the case of his *Marlborough*, where there was no necessity for reticence to a great extent, the same preoccupation with the public, to the exclusion of the private, man can be noted. Likewise with his brief biographical studies of his contemporaries,[1] with many of whom, such as F. E. Smith, Balfour and Asquith, he was on terms of great intimacy. There are the achievements, the eloquences, the triumphs and the failures, but one looks in vain for the man.

This lack of, as it were, a biographical dimension is implicit in Sir Winston's whole approach to the study of men and of history. Like all great leaders he is for ever and irretrievably a participant rather than an onlooker. The past only excites him to the extent that it relates to the present, and those who lived through and shaped past events are only interesting in so far as he might have been of their company. For him, history is politics and politics are history. He has made history, but, by the same token, history has made him. Gibbon's style he may echo, but Gibbon's aloofness, his utter detachment, as he sat quietly in Lausanne, from the turbulent events he was engaged in describing, would have been unattainable to Churchill, even had he wished or striven to attain it—which he never has.

Thus his passion to justify Marlborough, to defend him against charges of corruption and double-dealing, is so intense and immediate,

---

[1] *Great Contemporaries*, of which one critic remarked, not without reason, "Mr. Churchill gleams back at us from twenty-five looking glasses, formidable, affectionate and lovable."

that the reader comes to think of Marlborough as a contemporary. In the same way, with all the wonderful flow of the narrative, and the admirable descriptions of persons and events, *The World Crisis* and *The Second World War* belong irretrievably to the present, and as it recedes tend to fade like old newspapers. They are photographs rather than paintings; they are oratory rather than literature; they are, in the highest and greatest sense, journalism rather than history.

H. G. Wells used often to remark that this is an age of journalism. If so, Churchill is one of the greatest practitioners. He uses words with the same daring and abandon as he does colours when he is painting. He daubs them on boldly, recklessly. Yet, as one reads, it is the voice one hears—that voice so unforgettable, so often imitated, and so unique, which those who lived through the dark days of 1940 will never forget. Since his early works—*Lord Randolph Churchill*, *The River War*, *My Early Life*, *The Malakand Field Force*—he has, literally, dictated his writings, often after a turbulent or strenuous day. His later books, that is to say, record the spoken rather than the written word. This tends at times to give his style what Philip Guedalla called "the fatal lullaby of a majestic style". He has also, again to quote Guedalla, developed a faculty for "organizing large works". His *Marlborough*, *The World Crisis*, and still more *The Second World War*, must be considered as, in a sense, the productions of a committee rather than of an individual author.

There is nothing derogatory in this. The idea that learning consists of information, to be absorbed by individual minds and kept ever ready for public delivery, is a modern and very foolish illusion. As Johnson had his team working on the Dictionary, or Pope his working on the *Iliad*, so Churchill has had his digging out and assembling material for his *Marlborough*, and his two large treatises on World Wars I and II. The material was duly presented, but it was Churchill who, as it were, "processed" it; spoke it forth in his unmistakable manner, and then, after it had again been checked, gave it the finishing characteristic touches. It may be doubted whether history and biography have ever before been produced in such a manner, or are ever likely to be so produced again. The combination of talents in Sir Winston Churchill of artist and statesman, of orator and writer, is most rare, if not unique. For the most part, men of action, like Napoleon on St. Helena, have nothing to say when they look back on their colourful lives, or, like Bismarck and Frederick the Great, trace only banalities when they take up their pens. Whatever judgment history may pass on the troubled times through which Churchill has lived, it cannot but recognize in him an outstanding exception to the rule that artistic gifts are incompatible with effectiveness in the world of action. The dynamism in word and deed which makes him a great leader infuses his writing, and vice versa.

As biographer, then, Churchill must be considered as both too human and too alive to portray, in other than a highly individual style, either his friends or his enemies. He is ready to make every sort of allowance in judging personal conduct, and is a strong exponent of *de mortuis nil nisi bonum*, whether in the case of someone inherently unsympathetic like Sir Stafford Cripps, or inherently sympathetic like F. E. Smith. Posterity will look in vain, in his short or full-length portraits, for the cold, aloof judgments, the relentless exposure of inadequacies in character or in conduct. In dealing with his subjects he uses rather the old-fashioned general practitioner's bedside manner than the surgeon's knife and deadly accuracy in dissection; still less the psychologist's searching questions. Already it is apparent that his Asquith is too kindly, his Lloyd George too adulatory, his Marlborough too forensic and partisan. And if his Balfour takes on here and there a hint of unkindness, this is doubtless because Balfour, in his view, was less than kind, or even loyal, to Lord Randolph. He also, humanly, has sensed an unfairness in Balfour's effortless success, and in the easy circumstances which relieved him of all material anxiety.

Posterity, however, would be most ill-advised to neglect Churchill's portraits. They may be what journalists call "angled"; the light, admittedly, passes through a most powerful prism, which serves both to stain its radiance and deflect its direction. Even so, there is a richness in their texture, a glow about them, even though only reflected from their creator's own zest for living, which belongs, if not necessarily to them personally, at any rate to the age in which they lived. Sir Winston Churchill is no Aubrey, certainly, revivifying his contemporaries in terms of anecdote and personality; but the warm ferment of their lives, the crowd scenes, are conveyed in a most lively and vigorous manner. Princess Marthe Bibesco, in her reminiscences of Proust, compares him to someone looking into human society like a naturalist studying an aquarium. Churchill is in the aquarium himself, swimming about lustily, and, at the same time, eagerly observing the other fishes.

It is natural that his most memorable observations as a biographer should relate to political rather than personal dramas. Parnell's adventure with Mr. O'Shea, for instance, is considered, in relation to its political consequences, as a somewhat ludicrous aberration. Nor are occasional essays in philosophizing particularly convincing. They represent no more than the workaday conclusions of an industrious and outstandingly successful worker in the political vineyard. Where Sir Winston Churchill's biographical talent finds its most effective exercise is in the delineation of what is so justly called in *Macbeth* "vaulting ambition". This, of all others, is the passion which, for obvious reasons, he handles with most assurance and verisimilitude. What could be better, for instance, than his account of George Nathaniel Curzon waiting, in May 1923, at Montacute House in Somerset for the summons to succeed Mr. Bonar Law as Prime Minister and Leader of the Conservative Party?

"The moment then at which his life aimed, had come. . . . All Monday Lord Curzon waited for the summons that was sure to come. At last it arrived. Towards evening a telegram from Lord Stamfordham was delivered, calling the Secretary of State to London. The journey to town on Tuesday was filled with the making of plans. There was no doubt in Curzon's mind—nor indeed should there have been—as to the meaning of the summons."

Churchill then goes on to describe how Balfour was summoned to Buckingham Palace to give advice, and how, though ailing, he went because "he felt he had a duty to perform".

"Arrived at the Palace, he expressed with conviction the view that in these days a Prime Minister must be in the House of Commons. He confined himself strictly to this point. He was careful to use no other argument. It was enough. When late that night Balfour returned to his sick-bed at Sheringham after his fatiguing journey, he was asked by some of his most cherished friends who were staying with him, 'And will dear George be chosen?' 'No,' he replied placidly, 'dear George will not.' "

Very much the same general judgment must be made on Churchill the historian as on Churchill the biographer. *The Second World War* will necessarily remain a work of reference and a classic, if only for the minutes and other special documents (included as appendices) which were written, or dictated, when he was Prime Minister, in the heat of conducting the 1939-45 war. These, more than any other of his writings, show the wide range, as well as the minuteness, of his interests, the unrelenting vigour which animates his thought and judgments. They are historic more than historical, glow with the making, rather than the writing, of history. The narrative itself, as has been said, despite the majesty of its presentation, is, in a sense, too alive to be entirely satisfactory as a record. It is what the French call an *actualité*. It careers along like an impassioned oration rather than a reasoned argument. If its claim to be history may be challenged, historians, we may be sure, will always use it and be beholden to it. Even more than *The World Crisis*, it will remain an imperishable monument to one who, in an age of littleness, has shown himself to be a great Englishman, a great European, and a great man.

CHURCHILL
THE CONVERSATIONALIST

Collin Brooks

*Collin Brooks, author, poet, economist, broadcaster, was Editor
of the* Sunday Dispatch *1936–38, and Editor of* Truth *1940–53.
He has known Sir Winston Churchill for many years, and has
talked with him both in and out of Britain. In this chapter, on
Churchill as a conversationalist among his intimates, Collin
Brooks draws on his memories of many meetings with the Prime
Minister.*

M

SHY men and tongue-tied men are apt to think that the rest of mankind is divided into two categories—men who talk much and men who talk well. There is a third category—that of men who talk both much *and* well. Of that category the supreme example in our time is, to me, Sir Winston Churchill.

His renown as a talker is not helped, but harmed, by the specimens of his quick, sometimes malicious, wit which fly round the clubs and penetrate into the gossip features of newspapers. People who have not had the good fortune to be near him in all his moods, and during the exercise of all his versatile talents, seem to conceive him as an incredibly busy man who, in moments of relaxation, throws off a shower of good things, but, for the rest, is immersed in the writing of State documents, memoranda, instructions, or in the preparation of speeches and broadcasts—all in the intervals of conducting the business of Government, writing books, painting pictures, laying bricks or brooding over oriental fish or butterflies.

His renown as a talker has, also, perhaps been a little harmed—great as it is—by the way in which the great statesman of the 1940s and the elder statesman of the 1950s tends to overshadow in men's memories the ebullient politician of the early 1900s and the loquacious subaltern of the 1890s, who was over-apt to argue the point with bigger fry.

I find that, with his enormous fame and prestige, his almost—perhaps quite—unrivalled personal memory of a span of political history from Salisbury to himself, his listeners now tend to become more silent, more deferential, less provocative than were those of a score to fifty years ago. When it comes to words, fellow fencers of his own calibre are few, and are little inclined to offer themselves as targets for the gleaming blade of wit, or that Johnsonian broad-sword of satire or contradiction, which he wields so superbly and, at the moment, with such little apparent mercy.

The truth of the matter is that it is impossible to write of Sir Winston Churchill as conversationalist, for he is ten different kinds of conversationalist. I find it difficult to convey the conversational quality of any one of those ten, because, when he talks, it is not only the words, and their management, or their spontaneous aptitude, which grip the listener; it is the whole personality.

As in his speeches and broadcasts, so in his table talk—that slight, never quite conquered, difficulty with the letter "s", far from marring the uttered sentences, gives them a special kind of emphasis, a tang uncommunicable in the printed word.

In his public utterances he gives the impression of a mode of speech which is poised, carefully weighed, slow in pace and heavy in emphasis. In his private talk I found that the sentences seemed to flow much more quickly, but without any loss of that same poise and deliberation. The casual epigrams—the wisecracks that are really wise—flash out. Some quick verdicts on men and measures positively dart out, sometimes with venom. But the general flow of talk is even, unhurried, but not slow—interrupted every now and again by a pause which may be made to obtain a wanted effect or may be a genuine staying of speech until the right, the just, the telling word is found.

Long before the crowning year of 1940, he was in argument always assertive. If he were not at table, his intensity would cause him to pace the room, stopping every now and again to face or stand over his interlocutor while he made some especially vital point. He seemed to move on little, twinkling feet. At times, when the lust for pure argument had waned, and he was busy expounding the factual basis on which his argument was founded, the pace would become slower. To some people, his vehemence seemed to exhaust them of vitality even while they listened, though his own vitality seemed to surge and mount the more absorbed he became in the dialectical battle.

As an argumentative talker, he was to me always scrupulously fair. His vehemence did not prohibit him from listening. Indeed, he positively invited retort, reasoned contradiction or disagreement. Having listened, having received the retort, he would seize upon it with avidity. The reasoning would be carefully examined; if found fallacious it would be torn to rags, if hopelessly false it would be dismissed with some stinging and contemptuous observation, delivered, strangely enough, with no discourtesy—the opinion derided rather than the man who uttered it. It was only when the fool and his folly had taken themselves elsewhere that the true derision would find utterance.

But such contemptuous flashes contained but the malice of the moment. The irritation of half an hour would be summed up in a sentence, and forgotten. One of the most characteristic Churchillian utterances, and one of the most frequent, is not even original: it is the repetition of an ancient proverb. One can hear the voice uttering it—"with me, bygones are bygones."

To many of those about him, the most fascinating talk in which he indulges, when everyone is well content to let it be a monologue, is when some odd remark starts a reminiscent vein. I have known him, in a shaded villa room in the South of France, leaning on the table edge, his nimble hands paring a piece of fruit, begin suddenly to recall some incident or episode in his long career—of how he first came under fire when he was twenty-one, of his boyish delight in the proximity of danger, of his glee that he was actually "seeing the real thing".

That baptism of fire was in Cuba, so it may not have been very much of "the real thing", but, as he spoke, his son was on the eve of departure for a European battle front, and the father grew almost lyrical in praise of the effect upon character which follow the hazards and discomforts of war.

If anyone thinks this was the "war-monger" talking—it was before the Second World War—let him dismiss the thought, for, at the same table, if not actually that very day, I heard Churchill analyse and dissect the folly and sordidness of modern war, ending with a phrase afterwards to be echoed in cold print—"modern war is no gentleman's business: to hell with it!"

Of his interest in the art and science of war there is, of course, no doubt. It fascinates him, and it needs but little, in table-talk, to put him into an expository vein, didactic but not dogmatic. Between Churchill talking of some illuminating campaign of the past and the usual Colonel Blimp, scattering the table-cloth with pepper-pots and fish forks to illustrate battle movements, is a world of difference. Churchill brings to *his* expositions that remarkable memory of his from which detail never escapes. He is as graphic and vivid describing the raids of Jeb Stuart in the American Civil War as when he is recounting his own experiences in the Sudan or in South Africa; long before the great life of Marlborough was written, perhaps even planned, that ancestor of his was frequently in his conversation.

This interest in war stems from the conviction that at certain times war becomes a necessity. One day at table someone incautiously remarked that nothing was worse than war. Churchill, with the full organ of his voice, replied, "Dishonour is worse than war—slavery is worse than war!" It was not a rebuke; it was the enunciation of what he knew to be a profound truth.

The fact is that he hates anything which lowers the dignity of the human being, as modern war does, as serfdom and tyranny do, but he knows which is the worse.

As with warfare, so with politics. He seems as interested in the political clashes of the past as in those of the present. To most of us, it would seem that the world he knew when he was first in Office in the Liberal Government of 1906 is hardly recognizable as the world in which we now live, the world which he has done so much to protect and shape; to him, as he reveals himself in reminiscence, his contemporary colleagues of half a century ago seem as vivid and alive as the men now actually about him. Oddly enough, those whom, in his stormy middle-years, he was most inclined to remember and discuss were not his fellow fire-eaters, but the quiet, more scholarly men who showed him kindness and tolerance even when they most disapproved of his vehemence and exaggeration—Asquith himself, Haldane and John Morley. Although he has a reputation, which has not lessened with the years, for quick, abrupt action, he has a quite palpable respect for men whose outward characteristic has been caution and patience, for men of *thought*. The reason is not hard to find; he is, for all his surface impetuosity, himself a man of thought and caution. "I discovered that Asquith liked memoranda; what gave me my standing with him were my carefully reasoned Cabinet papers—of which, need I say, I was not sparing."

Although his quarrel with the Tories in the last days of the Balfour Government made many estrangements, they did not lessen his appreciation of the leaders from whom he parted. His assessments of them, years afterwards, were not only shrewd but kindly. He has said, revealingly, that of Balfour it was difficult to appreciate the effect on his career of the fact that he had never any personal financial anxiety.

He seems to have been impressed in Joseph Chamberlain by that statesman's capacity for sustained contempt, and even hatred, as displayed once when the youthful Winston, boating on the Thames, pointed out to Chamberlain the figure of Labouchere asleep in a deck-chair on his lawn. Churchill confessed that he was excited by the sight of that already almost legendary figure, but Chamberlain just gave a glance and spat out the phrase, 'Ah, a bundle of old rags,' and dismissed him.

One hesitates to quote the Churchillian opinions and *obiter dicta* from memory, but that anecdote confirms one's impressions that he found political relations and enmities far more bitter in his youth and early years than he has found them even in our own strongly divided days. As the biographer of his father, he recalls almost at first hand the days when friendships and families were split on such issues as Irish Home Rule. With him "bygones" may be "bygones", but he cannot quite forget that, when he first changed his Party on Army reform and Free Trade, it was the habit of some of his old friends and associates to refer to him as "the Blenheim Rat", though, characteristically, he pleads in their extenuation, "I did not exactly, either by my movement or my manner, invite any great continuing affection".

In his public utterances he has paid many notable tributes to the parliamentary institutions of our Democracy, but it is in private talk that the deeps of his devotion to Parliament are unveiled. During the years when parliaments had either toppled or were toppling in Europe —Russia, Italy, Germany, Hungary—he and I were motoring in France in the company of an unusually gifted young Conservative who, after a decade in the House of Commons, had abruptly abandoned a parliamentary career. Churchill was eager for his return. For perhaps half an hour, he delivered himself of a eulogy on the House of Commons equal to anything that Dr. Johnson might have said on such an occasion. I do not pretend to remember his exact words, but I have never forgotten their purport.

"We know all the trite things said of parliamentary life, and some of them are true. But where, in these days, in what forum, what arena, can a man so test, develop and apply his gifts and his qualities? There is scope for everything—industry, gallantry, inventiveness. It is alike the instrument of the reformer and the conserver, for him who would enlarge our liberties and him who would strengthen our discipline. Its mode of oratory, we know, has changed, but the House still has a place for those who cultivate the rhetorical graces, as it has a place for those content to give a silent but well-weighed judgment on great issues. You may say that the life of a Back-bencher—and even of some Front-benchers—I am not immune—is one of thwartation, but it is not really so. Anyone who has anything constructive to offer to his country should endeavour to make his way into the House of Commons, for it is there that the ultimate seat of power is to be found."

That, or something like it, was said without affectation, but with great conviction. It was followed by a reservation.

"Our weakness today is not in the decline of Parliament itself, but in the diminished interest which the Press gives to it. It is, indeed, heart-breaking for any man to go down day after day in these turbulent times to deliver speeches which, by their content, if not by their form, are of great importance, and to realize that they are heard by but a few hundreds of his fellow Members, and read by but a scattering of people who habitually read Hansard."

This, be it marked, was before the days of paper rationing.

Those who imagine that Sir Winston Churchill has the Gladstonian fault of addressing private auditors as if they were a public meeting are gravely in error, though he is capable, on occasion, of doing so. It is equally an error to suppose that his private talk is in the mode of his major written works. There must, obviously, be a similarity, and, now and again, those Macaulay-like periods do roll out. There do happen those purple patches—of a very royal purple. But the best idea of his table-talk to be had from the written word will be found in his lighter volumes. The two volumes My Early Life and Thoughts and Adventures, and many of his magazine articles, including the most famous one on Painting, do give very much the flow and tone of his normal conversation. Oddly enough, one of them gives a description of David Lloyd George as a talker which would almost—but not quite—serve as a description of Churchill himself.

> "Extraordinary as have been his successes in public, it is in conclaves of eight or nine, or four or five, or in personal discussion man to man, that his persuasive arts reach their fullest excellence. At his best he could almost talk a bird out of a tree."

So far, the comparison is exact.

> "An intense comprehension of the more amiable weaknesses of human nature; a sure gift of getting on the right side of a man from the beginning of a talk; a complete avoidance of anything in the nature of chop-logic reasoning; a deft touch in dealing with realities; the sudden presenting of positions hitherto unexpected, but apparently conciliatory and attractive—all these are modes and methods in which he is a natural adept."

There a difference emerges—it is not "a sure gift of getting on the right side of a man" which distinguishes Sir Winston in talk; it is a fixed determination to get on the right side of the question, and then to drive home to a man his folly in being on any other.

That is not the only difference. Churchill says of his old colleague:

> "He never in the days when I knew him best thought of giving *himself* satisfaction by what he said. He had no partiality for fine phrases. He thought only and constantly of the effect produced upon other persons."

But Churchill has a partiality for fine phrases; he loves to give himself satisfaction. He is the best connoisseur of his own best things. This is not egotism. The appreciation is quite detached. He would utter the phrase, coin the fine thing, were his immediate listener too muddy-minded to appreciate it. This he would do for the sake of the phrase itself. It is almost as if he had a "Harvey" or a "McConnachie" on whom he relies to enjoy with him any touch of wit or turn of English which those to whom he talks may not fully savour.

M*

It was said of Dr. Johnson that when, in argument, his pistol missed fire, he would use the butt end; it is rarely, if ever, that the Churchillian pistol misses fire, but at times, even after all six chambers have been gloriously discharged, he is still apt to use the butt end.

I remember once, in the late 1930s, when the League of Nations was failing dismally, and Churchill was intent upon the creation of a kind of Commonwealth of the smaller European nations, venturing, greatly daring, to contest the efficacy of any such new institution. He had given every reason for that efficacy. When I said, "But supposing you create it, and supposing a strong Note goes to Hitler, and the Germans completely ignore it, as they have ignored the Eden Note— what do we do then?" he paced the room for a moment, and then came back to me.

I expected a further exposition of the new diplomacy. What I received was a pair of blazing eyes, a kind of grim chuckle, and the words: "What do we do then? What do we do then! Fight the beggars." It was, indeed, what we eventually had to do.

Many of his quick descriptions of persons have become classic— as when, having parted with a tall, lugubrious colleague, whose temperament and antics had been particularly awkward, he remarked as the door closed, "Thank God, we have seen the last of that Wuthering Height!" It is probably only *ben trovato* that, after a serious argument, almost a quarrel, with a great transport chief, he remarked to his Private Secretary, "Never let me see that—that—that canting bus-driver again."

The sting is taken from his gibes at others by his tremendous relish in recalling gibes about himself. He tells with glee of how, when he was Member for Dundee, and much in the public eye, his great opponent, and bosom friend, F. E. Smith, set a big public meeting in a roar by saying in the middle of his speech, "I see from the *Dundee Advertiser*—I mean the newspaper, not the politician——"

Allied to his affection for a genial story against himself, told to do honour to the wit of another, is his habit of often taking himself lightly, even when something possibly serious is involved. He doesn't exactly laugh at himself, but he is amused by himself. Soon after he was called into the Chamberlain Government as First Lord, I called at Admiralty House for a talk with him. I was seeing a book through the Press, and it had to do with rearmament. There was a reason why I wished to consult him, for some of the things the book recalled had happened when he was Chamberlain's critic. He left matters entirely to my discretion, but he said, in a sentence that changed swiftly from the impressive to the humorous, "I stand by every speech I made against the present Government—I stand by them ALL—but I don't particularly want them 'hotted up'."

In similar mood he ruefully remarked after the Tory defeat of 1945, "Some people tell me it is a blessing in disguise—all I can say is that it is a very good disguise."

But, as I have said, it is idle to try to recapture any Churchillian talk in the printed word: the emphasis and the mannerisms mean so much. What in print might seem acid, in talk seemed only pleasant raillery, as when during the war, after a very satisfying luncheon in unexpected circumstances, he congratulated the host, and added, good-humouredly, but inconsequentially, "It is perhaps as well that I was not accompanied by my colleague, the Minister of Aircraft Production (Sir Stafford Cripps), for there is a man who habitually takes his meal off a handful of peas, and, when he gets a handful of beans, counts that his Christmas feast!"

It was not only radio listeners who were amused by his stalwart insistence on giving foreign names an English pronunciation. One evening, his great friend the late Lord Mottistone chaffed him about this. Said Churchill very deliberately: "Jack, when you cross Europe you land at Marsai, spend a night in Lee-on and another in Par-ee, and, crossing by Callay, eventually reach Londres. I land at Mar-sales, spend a night in Lions, and another in Par*i*s, and come home to LONDON!"

He startled a friend of mine one day by saying something which sounded like, "I have had a letter this morning from er-beansh." It emerged that the mysterious word "er-beansh" was a wilful Church-illianism for Herr Benes.

It was always a lesson in concentrated hatred to hear him say "these Nar-zees", even when he was talking at his least oratorical.

During the war—when one-course meals were the rule—he was boyishly delighted by the sight of a noble salmon sent by some friend. Recalling, no doubt, the boy Bailey, at Mrs. Todgers', he said: "That is indeed a magnificent fish: I must 'have some of him'." Then came the characteristic second thought: "No! No! I will have meat. Carnivores will win this war!"

He is frankly fond of the good things of the table, though as the talk flows on he seems hardly aware of what he is eating and drinking, until some word or two of approval shows him to have been very well aware of what has passed his palate.

His defence of smoking is classic—that, too, has passed from the spoken to the printed word. "Some people say that I have smoked too much: I don't know. If I had not smoked so much, I might have been bad tempered at the wrong time."

It was matched by his recent remark, "All I can say is, that I have taken more out of alcohol than alcohol has taken out of me."

In his various circles there have been many notable three-bottle men, and he is himself an enjoyer of good liquor, but he once said reflectively, "We all despise a man who 'gets drunk'."

Despite so many epigrammatic flashes, so many excursions into humorous reminiscence, the chief memory that remains of most of his table-talk and personal conversation is of that flow of comment and exposition that I have tried to describe earlier. Whether at his most intense or at his most light-hearted, it is his zest for the serious discussion of permanent values that gives his talk its charm—serious discussion lightened, it is true, by all manner of verbal gymnastics and mental pyrotechnics, and often rounded off by a sudden colloquialism that from most other people would be an anticlimax.

Never was a talker so variously gifted, so ardently listened-to, so little of a prig; never was a man so wedded to precision and verbal nicety so little of a pedant.

It perhaps sums him up to say that, as a talker, and an inspirer of talk, Sir Winston Churchill would have been equally welcomed by Falstaff in Eastcheap, Ben Jonson at the Mermaid, or Burke and Johnson at the Mitre—that is, in any coterie where the talk is masculine, the wit and humour spontaneous, the erudition unparaded, and where gusto is the prime quality.

CHURCHILL AND THE TRADE UNIONS

─────

The Rt. Hon. George Isaacs, M.P.

George Isaacs is outstanding among the leaders of Britain's Trade Union Movement. He was Secretary of the National Society of Operative Printers and Assistants for forty years from 1909 to 1949, a President of the Printing and Kindred Trades Federation, Chairman of the Trades Union Congress General Council 1945, and President of the World Trade Union Conference in London in 1945. He first entered Parliament in 1923 as Labour Member for Gravesend and now represents Southwark. He was Minister of Labour and National Service in the Labour Government from 1945 to 1951 and Minister of Pensions 1951. In this chapter, which deals with a number of controversial questions, Mr. Isaacs has given references and authorities for his statements.

IN the year 1900 Winston Churchill began his parliamentary career, and the British Trade Union Movement, through the Labour Representation Committee, made its effective entry into parliamentary politics. In the next dozen years the accidents of political office brought Churchill into contact with the trade unions on several occasions, and in this period he first earned a reputation which has caused him to be regarded with suspicion or hostility by trade unionists for most of his long political career. The following pages may show that this attitude is not altogether fair, but it is clear to a trade unionist that Churchill, for all his political talent and experience, has never properly understood the significance or the methods of the Movement which entered party politics in the year of his own initiation.

It is well known that in his early years Churchill was very conscious of the political heritage of his father, Lord Randolph Churchill, apostle of "Tory Democracy" and leading spirit of "the Fourth Party". This heritage he apparently found compatible with Radical Liberalism after 1905. So far as trade unionism was concerned he would presumably argue that the Tory Democrat, like the Radicals, recognized the industrial working class as a powerful and legitimate political force entitled to its own forms of association and to a more secure place in the fabric of society.

As President of the Board of Trade, Churchill was brought into contact with organized labour through the representations made to him on a variety of matters by the Parliamentary Committee of the T.U.C.—as the General Council was then called. This contact was maintained when he became Home Secretary and, despite other and unhappier relations with trade unionism, the influence of his father's beliefs and of his own Radicalism at this period led him to tell the T.U.C. Parliamentary Committee in an interview of 1911:[1]

[1] T.U.C. Parliamentary Committee, 8th Quarterly Report, March 1911.

". . . when I take up the long list of resolutions passed by the Trades Union Congress to be submitted to the Home Secretary, I cannot but feel and be powerfully impressed with the enormous value of the work which the Trade Union body are doing in studying from year to year, in so much minute and patient detail and practical knowledge, such a vast variety of necessary and almost non-party questions. These subjects are all deserving of close attention; some are ripe, and others are ripening, for action. It is of the greatest use to a public department like the Home Office that the official study of these questions, which is maintained within these walls from year to year, should be supplemented by the constant experience that you gentlemen, in touch as you are with every trade and every class of worker in the country, are alone able to bring to bear upon the problems."

The South Wales Coal Strike of 1910-11 first brought Churchill into discredit with organized labour for his use of the Metropolitan Police and troops to maintain order in the valleys. There was a tradition of violence in the conduct of strikes in South Wales, and an element of the population ready to take advantage of the chance of disorder. Churchill himself declared:[1]

"The rioters did not represent the mining population of South Wales.

"They are a well educated, peaceable, intelligent and law-abiding class of men and have often, I may express this personal opinion here, been very hardly tried in more ways than one."

The mine owners and managers on their side were both alarmist and provocative, and their attitude added greatly to the bitterness of the dispute. Once rioting had started the local police were in a difficult situation, not made any easier by the demands of mine managers who appear to have regarded them as their employees. Reinforcements were brought in from as far as Bristol, but the Chief Constable of Glamorgan thought it necessary to call in troops. An application was made direct to the military authorities, but Churchill, as Home Secretary, collaborating with the Secretary for War, refused to authorize

[1] *Parliamentary Debates*, Vol. 21, Col. 239, February 7, 1911.

the immediate movement of troops into the area. Instead he sent a strong force of Metropolitan Police by special train and held the troops in reserve. He attempted to start negotiations with the miners and mine owners, but met with resentful hostility on the side of the owners, while the men were by then in no mood to negotiate.

The riots culminated in the battle at Glamorgan Colliery, and the attacks on shops and houses in Tonypandy, on November 8. As a result of these events the Home Secretary authorized the movement of troops into the area the following day, but the crisis was then over. Conflict on a lesser scale continued and the attitude of the owners and mine managers led to sharp exchanges between them, the Home Secretary, and the officers of the Army and Metropolitan Police.[1] General Macready had to be authorized to prevent the import of blacklegs if this would worsen the situation, and Churchill had to insist that the police and military were not brought in as strike breakers nor were they the personal retainers of the coal owners. Troops were held ready to deal with further riots on November 21, but were not brought into action. They were, however, kept in the area until the following July.

Churchill came under strong criticism from both Left and Right for his part in this affair. The Conservative Opposition complained that he did not allow the military to be used effectively, while Labour M.P.s and some of the more militant trade unionists denounced the use of police and troops. His defence was vigorous, and in particular he insisted that the immediate use of troops would have inflamed the strikers. Looking back at it now it is difficult to see what else a resolute Home Secretary could have done, given the situation in which such bitter industrial relations were allowed to develop. On later occasions it could be said that Churchill was too ready to use troops, but on this occasion his influence appears to have been a moderating one. Certainly he showed little sympathy with the coal owners and their agents, although determined to enforce civil order.

His general attitude on the use of troops was declared by him on one or two occasions in this period of industrial unrest. In August 1911, he said in Parliament:[2]

---

[1] *Colliery Strike Disturbances in South Wales*, 1911, Cmd. 5568, 1911.
[2] *Parliamentary Debates*, Vol. 29, Col. 1884, August 15, 1911.

"There can be no question of the military forces of the Crown intervening in a labour dispute in the proper sense of the words. That, so far as it can be done, is the function of the Board of Trade. It is only when a trade dispute is accompanied by riot, intimidation or other violations of the law, or when a serious interruption is caused or likely to be caused to the supply of necessary commodities, that the military can be called in to support the police; and then their duty is to maintain the law, not to interfere in the matter in dispute."

On another occasion he told Parliament that local authorities had a tendency to ask for soldiers instead of relying on the police in labour disputes; that such authorities were often connected with local employers and that they were apt to send for soldiers (who cost them nothing) in cases where the police would have been quite sufficient.

Controversy over this issue flared up again during the London Dock Strike in July 1911. The Port of London Authority refused to negotiate with the unions and at first was supported by the Government. Churchill asked for 25,000 troops to be used if necessary to move essential supplies. Fortunately the Port of London Authority later gave way under Government pressure and a serious conflict was averted. Ben Tillet has said that credit was due to Churchill at this time for his resistance to the wilder demands made in the Press and elsewhere for the forcible suppression of a well-conducted strike.[1] He, with John Burns, was active in sponsoring negotiations and both signed the settlement on August 18.

The autumn of 1911 saw yet another industrial crisis, this time on the railways. A long period of unrest came to a head with unofficial local strikes, and eventually the railway unions threatened a national strike unless the companies agreed to meet them and negotiate. The seriousness of this threat to the transport system when road transport was in its infancy brought the Government into the dispute. Asquith, the Prime Minister, offered a vague promise of a Royal Commission and told the unions that, if necessary, troops would be used to maintain rail traffic—apparently the Royal Engineers were to run the trains.

[1] Tillet, B., *History of the London Transport Workers' Strike*, 1911.

Nevertheless the strike took place and industrial dislocation assumed alarming proportions. On this occasion Churchill acted with less restraint than previously and troops were sent to many rail centres without requests from the local authorities. An ugly situation began to develop and in South Wales two men were shot dead, and others accidentally killed in the course of riots at Llanelly. Churchill[1] justified the display of force at this time and the wide discretionary power given to the military by claiming that a national rail strike was a unique event of the gravest consequences for a country like Britain. It was therefore imperative in the Government's view that steps should be taken to maintain the movement of food and other essentials. At the same time he paid tribute to the railwaymen and to their trade union officials for their conduct of the strike, and cleared them of responsibility for the disorders which took place.

The action of the Home Secretary in this strike was severely criticized by trade union and Labour leaders and was regarded as a new departure both for the Government and for the Home Secretary personally. The criticism previously made against Churchill was greatly reinforced by these events and his reputation with organized labour suffered a severe blow. He might, in time, have lived down his earlier actions, for which there was considerable justification, but the 1911 Rail Strike created an indelible impression upon the minds of trade unionists. The General Strike of 1926 deepened this impression and it was not erased even by Churchill's service in the last war. The later controversy over the *British Gazette* in 1926 was also foreshadowed in this strike of 1911 when Churchill issued bulletins regarded as tendentious by Labour opinion.

A more constructive episode occurred in 1913, when Churchill took part in getting the Trade Union Bill of that year through the House of Commons. This Bill was, of course, the result of the second Taff Vale Judgment which prevented unions from using their funds for political purposes—an act of judicial interpretation which brought to a head guerilla warfare conducted for years by the Courts against organized labour. Churchill had long regarded the attitude of the Courts in this respect as unsatisfactory. In June 1911, when interviewed

[1] *Parliamentary Debates*, Vol. 29, Col. 211 ff., August 22, 1911.

by the Parliamentary Committee of the T.U.C., he expressed strong criticisms of:[1]

"... statements (which) have been made from the bench reflecting on the trade unions in language which is extremely ignorant and wholly out of touch with the general development of modern thought, and which has greatly complicated the administration of justice, and created bitterness and a sense of distrust in the ordinary administration of the law".

In the debates on the Bill he repeated these strictures and declared that where class issues were concerned the Courts did not command confidence among working-class people. It was therefore necessary to find a bulwark between the Courts and the unions, and this the Bill sought to provide.

In his speech on the Trade Union Bill, Churchill made two other declarations of importance to our theme.[2] He said, first:

"I should have no hesitation in saying that it is quite impossible to prevent trade unions from entering the political field. The sphere of industrial and political activity is often indistinguishable, always overlaps and representation in Parliament is absolutely necessary to trade unions even if they confine themselves to the most purely industrial form of action."

He followed this by saying:[3]

"I consider that every workman is well advised to join a trade union. I cannot conceive how any man standing undefended against the powers that be in this world could be so foolish if he can possibly spare the money from the maintenance of his family not to associate himself with an organization to protect the rights and interests of labour."

Whether Churchill appreciated the implications of these statements is a matter for further comment later. There is no reason to believe that

---

[1] T.U.C. Parliamentary Committee, 9th Quarterly Report, June 1911.
[2] *Parliamentary Debates*, Vol. 26, Col. 1015 ff., 1913.
[3] Ibid.

he was insincere, but he may not have been prepared to accept the logic of his own arguments.

After 1911 he left the Home Office and plunged into naval affairs, with which we are not concerned in this chapter. His reputation was not enhanced among the general public by the Dardanelles campaign, and organized labour, at least unofficially, used this as an additional stick with which to beat him in the elections of 1918 and 1923. As Minister of Munitions in 1917 he had, of course, to deal with the growing labour unrest at that time, but at this period Labour criticism concentrated on the Prime Minister and it was Lloyd George, too, who bore the responsibility for the clumsy handling of the 1919 Rail Strike.

Churchill clashed with the Labour Movement again in 1920, over Allied intervention in the Russo-Polish war. He made no secret of his hatred of Bolshevism, not only for itself but for its effect in taking Russia out of the war with serious consequences for her allies. He regarded Poland as a barrier between Russia and Germany behind which the Germans would have a chance to rebuild their nation in co-operation with France and Great Britain.[1] He had to admit that after eighteen months of independence the Poles showed no signs of political wisdom and there is cause to question his belief that the Polish attack on the Ukraine was a desperate measure of self-defence. Nevertheless he was prepared to support Poland against the Red Armies and also, it seems, to support the various White Generals fighting the Red Army in Russia. The Labour Movement on the other hand, although finding co-operation with the Bolsheviks difficult even then, was sympathetic to the Revolution and opposed to Allied intervention. The effects of intervention and blockade upon the lives of Russian workers and peasants shocked a Labour deputation to Russia in the early summer of 1920, and their report[2] was published just as the Poles, with Allied support, launched an attack deep into the Ukraine. The feeling within the ranks of organized labour was therefore favourable to drastic action, and this occurred when London dockers refused to load supplies for Poland into the ship *Jolly George*.

In late July and August the situation became very critical as the

[1] *Evening News*, July 28, 1920.
[2] *British Labour Delegation to Russia, Report*, 1920 (T.U.C. and Labour Party).

impression grew that the Government was preparing to support Poland on an increased scale. The Russian counter-attack forced the Poles back over the "Curzon Line" and to the outskirts of Warsaw. The British Government then delivered an ultimatum to the Russians and prepared for outright war. A Council of Action was set up on August 9 representing the T.U.C., the Labour Party and the Parliamentary Labour Party, to co-ordinate industrial action to defeat any attempt by the Government to wage war on Russia over Poland. On the 13th a special conference, called by the Council of Action, heard its President (Mr. W. Adamson, M.P.) declare:[1]

". . . I do know that the recent activities of our Secretary of War [Churchill] were sinister and dangerous, and we repudiate him and his works."

Later Ernest Bevin said:[2]

"They have been speaking with two voices all through. You have had the protestations of the Prime Minister that he stood for peace. You have had the indication from time to time that at any rate he was endeavouring to arrange with the Allies to open up recognition of Soviet Russia, and various proposals were made. Coincident with these arrangements and declarations you had Winston Churchill not merely writing to the Press, which welcomed his declarations, but appealing to the old enemy—with whom we were never going to speak or trade—to rise to the occasion and defeat Soviet Russia."

And the veteran Robert Smillie added:[3]

"I want to thank our comrade Winston Churchill for uniting the British democracy. We could not do it: the people would not believe us. But Winston and his friends have done it. Now that we have secured unity, God send us sense to remain united."

[1] *Report of Special Conference on Labour and the Russian-Polish War*, p. 4, August 1920.
[2] Ibid., p. 6.
[3] Ibid., p. 22.

These attacks upon Churchill were based largely on his action in writing a provocative article in the London *Evening News*[1] on July 28, in which he not only supported Poland but also urged the Germans—should the Poles collapse—to build a dike against Bolshevism. However, although his hostility to Soviet Russia could not be doubted, it seems probable that suspicion of him in Labour circles exaggerated his "sinister and dangerous" activities. The main responsibility for the attitude of the Government at this period must rest upon the Prime Minister, Lloyd George, whose manœuvres strengthened in the Labour Movement a distrust aroused by his handling of the railway strike a year earlier.

The threat of industrial action made by the Council of Action, combined with the Polish military recovery late in August, caused the Government to abandon its plans for large-scale intervention in Poland. What would have happened if Warsaw had fallen and the Allies had started full-scale operations against Russia (if that were militarily possible) is one of the great question marks in history. The Council of Action would certainly have attempted to organize industrial action, and public opinion, war-weary and hostile to further adventures, might have made this effective. Even the Army could not then be relied upon, as may be inferred from the Government's reluctance to use it in 1919 as it was used in the 1911 Rail Strikes. However, the crisis passed and the effect from the point of view of Churchill's relations with the trade unions was to embitter these still further.

There can be no doubt that the industrial and political power of the trade unions as shown in the strikes or threatened strikes immediately before and after the 1914–18 war made a great impression upon the mind of Churchill. It must be recalled that this growing power was accompanied by a widespread belief in syndicalist ideas later merging with other revolutionary doctrines arising from the Bolshevik success in Russia. It cannot be said that there was ever a deliberate revolutionary movement of any significance, but there was a great deal of phrase-mongering, no doubt in all sincerity, which might well alarm anyone incapable of analysing more deeply the political and economic policies of organized labour. Churchill was

[1] Loc. cit.

certainly impressed by the dangers which the socialist influence within the trade unions seemed to hold for the traditional system of parliamentary government, and if one reads over the speeches of Labour leaders in that period there is some ground for this belief, superficial though such an analysis may be. It was not until 1926 that the trade union leadership seems to have recognized the logic of some of their declared policies, although the earlier collapse of the Triple Alliance should have been a warning that in an industrial conflict with the Government the trade unions might suffer a heavy defeat.

Before dealing with Churchill's next clash with organized labour, it is necessary to review the stages by which the country drifted towards the conflict of 1926. This drift began in 1910–11 and the strikes or threatened strikes already discussed because of Churchill's connection with them were incidents in a greater movement. From the closing years of the nineteenth century the growing concentration of industry and the spread of education made it both more necessary for labour to organize and easier for them to do so. This trend was, of course, aided by war-time conditions and labour shortage and increased Government control of industry (the latter unworkable in a democratic country without the co-operation of organized labour).

At the beginning of the war, so far as most trade unionists and their leaders were concerned, patriotic feelings overwhelmed the earlier beliefs in the international solidarity of labour, and trade unions continued in the main to support the war effort until the end. But this did not prevent the advocates of "direct action" from taking advantage of the strong position of organized labour on occasions when important principles were thought to be at stake. The power of the unions to cripple the war effort was recognized by the Government, and they sought to make strikes illegal by the Munitions of War Act, 1915. The futility of legal prohibitions which did not obtain the willing support of trade unionists was revealed almost immediately, when South Wales miners struck with impunity in July 1915, forcing the Government to concede most of their demands. The general control over industry exercised by the Government brought them directly into disputes throughout the war years, and their control over mines and railways continued to embroil them in disputes until 1921. Only the support of the great majority of trade unionists for the war and their restraint in accepting worsened conditions "for the duration" prevented even more industrial unrest.

It became clear by 1918 that the State was faced with powerful organized groups of its citizens who were ready to challenge its formal authority. How far this had gone was shown when the police came out on strike in 1918; they were driven to it by bad conditions. Their union was never recognized, and the strike was rapidly smashed, but a strike in such a quarter alarmed the Government. They therefore began to prepare for further conflicts and for the reassertion of their effective power in the country.

In the 1919 Rail Strike they appear to have overestimated their strength and had to give way when the railwaymen, aided by all the publicity resources of the Labour Movement, proved able to win over a large section of public opinion to their side.[1] In 1915 the railwaymen, miners and other transport workers had formed the Triple Alliance for mutual support on matters of vital importance. When the miners went on strike in the autumn of 1920 they called for the support of this Alliance, and only the fact that the Government gave way and met the miners' claims to some extent prevented a national transport strike. The Government, however, then passed the Emergency Powers Act, 1920, which gave them wide scope for action should any great strike threaten to dislocate industrial life.

When coalmining was handed back to private ownership in 1921 a dispute arose between the miners, bitter over the Government's failure to implement the Sankey Report, and the owners, determined to cut back wages to meet the slump in the coal trade. A lockout was declared and again the Triple Alliance was invoked, while the Government declared a state of emergency and used its new powers to call up troops and to prepare for drastic action. Because of a failure to agree upon the terms under which negotiations could take place, the Triple Alliance collapsed on "Black Friday", April 15, and the miners went down to defeat two months later. The economic depression undoubtedly weakened the position of the unions in this conflict, but Ernest Bevin, one of the leaders of the Alliance, saw the collapse as an organizational failure due to lack of a common policy.[2]

[1] See: Webb, S. and B., *History of Trade Unionism*, p. 535 passim (T.U.C. Edition).
[2] Williams, F., *Ernest Bevin*, p. 99.

The Triple Alliance was not the only form of organization developed by the trade unions in this period. 1920 saw the establishment of the General Council of the T.U.C. as a body able to speak for organized labour at a national level, and its powers were strengthened in 1924 when it had become clear that it could assist in consolidating trade union organization. It was thus the General Council itself which became involved in the next great industrial conflict with the Government.

This digression has been necessary to set the stage for the re-entry of Churchill, whose part in the events just described is still obscure. As Secretary for War from 1918–21 he must have played a major role in the framing of the Emergency Powers Act and in preparing for the mobilization carried out in the spring of 1921. His bitter hostility to Bolshevism no doubt influenced his attitude towards a Labour Movement which used its industrial power to protect the Russian Revolution. Not only Bolshevism but Socialism in general was seen by him as the major political danger of the times, and the Liberal *débâcle* in the immediate post-war years seems to have convinced him that the Conservative Party was the only effective anti-socialist party. After an electoral defeat in 1923 he returned to the House in 1924 as a Constitutionalist and became Chancellor of the Exchequer in Baldwin's Conservative Government.

Churchill's term as Chancellor of the Exchequer from 1924–29 is remembered mainly for the return to the Gold Standard, at pre-war parity values, in April 1925. Maynard Keynes, almost alone amongst economists, protested[1] against this decision and declared that the miners would be the first, but only the first, sufferers from it. This prophecy turned out to be only too true. In June 1925 the miners were faced with the threat of a lockout if they refused to accept lower wages and longer hours. In this situation they immediately turned to the General Council of the T.U.C., under its new constitution, and asked for assistance and advice.

The General Council called a Special Conference of Trade Union Executives[2] and this pledged support to the miners. Plans were drawn up for an embargo on the movement of coal, with a threat of

[1] See: Keynes, J. M., *The Economic Consequences of Mr. Churchill*, p. 23.
[2] *The Mining Crisis and the National Strike*, 1926. *Official Reports*, T.U.C. 1927.

a general strike in the background. The miners opened negotiations with the Government, claiming that the industry should be subsidized, a claim which at first was rejected but eventually accepted at the eleventh hour. Telegrams instructing the transport unions to begin the embargo on coal movements would have been sent out within a few hours had this decision not been taken. The Government concession, therefore, looked like a victory for the unions. The subsidy was conditional upon a Commission to examine the industry's economic situation and the crisis was in fact only postponed for nine months.

These nine months were used by the Government to perfect their plan for emergency services in the event of a national stoppage. A Proclamation was prepared to declare a state of emergency under the Emergency Powers Act, and local authorities were circularized with details about the organization which would be set up in the event of the Proclamation being issued. The trade union leaders, on their side, having no revolutionary intentions, regarded the issue as an industrial dispute in which the miners had to be supported not only on the merits of their case but also in self-defence against the danger that other workers would suffer next.

Far from creating any revolutionary organization, very little preparation for a renewal of the struggle was undertaken by the General Council at all, even in the vital fields of publicity and communications. It was not until April 27[1] that a special committee was appointed to co-ordinate action in the event of a general strike, i.e. only six days before the strike actually began. Even regarding the strike as an industrial dispute it seems surprising now that further preparations were not undertaken for its organization, and it says much for the latent administrative ability within the Movement that the improvised arrangements ran as well as they did.

A full and authoritative history of the General Strike has never been written. The story is hidden in Cabinet papers, the files of Transport House and the personal papers and memories of the participants. Churchill's part in the strike is still not clear although something can be pieced together from what has since been published. There is no doubt that he was ready to face a show-down on the

[1] *The Mining Crisis and the National Strike*, 1926. *Official Reports*, T.U.C. 1927, p. 138A.

threat of a great national stoppage and probably thought that this clash was inevitable. On the other hand, he does not seem to have been one of the more truculent members of the Cabinet in the early stages, possibly because of his former experience of the unco-operative attitude taken by the mine owners. Neville Chamberlain and Lord Salisbury were regarded as the "die-hard" leaders at this stage. It has been suggested in some quarters that Churchill joined the "Fight it Out" group when the Cabinet had the news that trade unionists on the *Daily Mail* staff had refused to print a provocative article on the impending strike.[1] Whether he was in fact one of the Cabinet Ministers who threatened to resign unless the Government demanded the withdrawal of the strike notices before reopening negotiations is not known to me, but once Baldwin had decided to take this action Churchill appears to have thrown himself into the fight with enthusiasm.[2]

His immediate job was issuing a newspaper to put over the Government's case, supplementing their control of the infant B.B.C. In this respect the General Council's decision to close down the Press is thought by many to have played into the Government's hands. The *British Gazette* issued under Mr. Churchill's control had a larger circulation than the *British Worker*, with which the General Council attempted to counter its appearance. Opening with a violent attack on political action by trade unions, the tone of the *British Gazette* was provocative throughout its short life. The misleading nature of its reports and the extreme bias it exhibited aroused real anger and derision among trade unionists. It certainly did not ease the tension of those critical days and seems to have reflected Churchill in his most irresponsible mood. The failure of the *British Gazette* to print the

[1] It is commonly believed that the men objected to the heading "For King and Country" being given to this article, on the grounds that it brought the King into an industrial dispute. As Secretary of the National Society of Operative Printers and Assistants, however, I was told at the time that their objection was to the use of the word "intended" in a phrase which declared that a General Strike was a revolutionary movement intended to inflict suffering upon the community and thereby to put forcible constraint upon the Government. The action of the men in refusing to print this article was, of course, entirely unauthorized by the Printing Trades Unions or by the General Council.

[2] For these events see (*inter alia*) Williams, op. cit.; T.U.C. Official Report, op. cit.; *New Statesman*, May 22, 1926; Fyfe, H., *Behind the Scenes of the Great Strike*, 1926; Martin, K., *Harold Laski*, 1952; Cole, M., *Growing up into Revolution*, 1949; Young, G. M., *Stanley Baldwin*, 1952; Jones, T., *Lloyd George*, 1952; Sitwell, O., *Laughter in the next Room*. 1949.

appeal made by the Archbishop of Canterbury for moderation and the reopening of negotiations, until forced to do so by parliamentary pressure, was widely condemned by responsible opinion in the country. The general tone of the *Gazette* has long been remembered against Churchill by trade unionists, and was recalled when he made his notorious "Gestapo" speech in 1945.

There was an impression in some Labour circles at the time that many other aspects of the Government's conduct in the strike bore the Churchillian stamp. The attempt to recruit a strike-breaking weapon in the "Organization for Maintenance of Supplies", drawn largely from the middle classes and students, was one such effort. Others were the recruitment of a large number of Special Constables, the establishment of an auxiliary Civil Constabulary Reserve to suppress non-existent disorders, and the rushing about of armoured cars and lorries filled with helmeted troops. All this show of unnecessary force (greeted with derision by the strikers) was attributed to Churchill's military tendencies and sense of showmanship. More serious were rumours[1]—never definitely denied—that he and other Ministers were urging the Government to take advantage of Sir John Simon's dubious legal doctrine that the General Strike was illegal and to arrest General Council members and confiscate union funds. The truth of all this, however, is not yet known and happily the General Strike ended without any serious disorders or repression.

The Government were not content with the defeat of the General Strike and the consequent exposure of the limitations of "direct action". They proceeded to embitter trade unionists still further by the introduction of the Trades Disputes Act, 1927. This Act made sympathetic strikes or strikes designed to coerce the Government illegal. Picketing was restricted, Civil Service unions were forbidden to join the T.U.C., breaches of contract in essential employment were made illegal and "contracting in" to political funds was substituted for "contracting out". The Act was thus intended to cripple not only the industrial power of unions to bring about major stoppages, but also to hamper their political activities. It was bitterly and continuously resented by the Trade Union Movement until it was repealed *en bloc* by the first majority Labour Government in 1945.

[1] Quoted in Fyfe and Sitwell, op. cit.

In the passage of the Bill through the House of Commons in 1927 Churchill was drawn into the debate on one or two occasions. He took the opportunity to declare[1] that in his view the trade unions ought to be free from politics and to have the same relations with all Governments. He made clear his opposition to the close association between the unions and the Labour Party, although he did not explain how he reconciled this view with his earlier belief, quoted above, that it was impossible to prevent trade unions entering the political field and that they must have representation in Parliament. He also repeated the fantastic claim that the General Strike had been a carefully organized attempt to overthrow constitutional Government worked out like a military operation. It is hard to tell whether he really believed this or not. Possibly he was so accustomed to thinking in such terms himself that he assumed others also played at strategy and tactics.

After 1927 Churchill had no further brushes with organized labour during his remaining two years of office.

In 1928 there was a humorous incident, given prominence in the Press. Brick-laying was one of Churchill's hobbies and in a light-hearted moment the local organizer of the Amalgamated Union of Building Trade Workers invited him to join the Union. Churchill, playing up, filled in a membership form and sent this and his entrance fee to the Area office. As he no doubt foresaw, this news reached the Press and was given wide publicity. Some members of the A.U.B.T.W. protested that Churchill was ineligible for membership and the union's Executive Council found on investigation that his membership form was incompletely filled up; there was no proposer or seconder and he did not say how long he had been at the trade. They therefore declared him ineligible for membership and (some real feeling having been roused) exculpated the local organizer from blame. Churchill, never averse to publicity, made a mock protest at being "expelled", but in fact he was never accepted: his cheque for the entrance fee is still in the possession of the organizer concerned.

In 1931 Churchill intervened briefly[2] in the Trade Union (Amendment) Bill, 1931, introduced by the minority Labour Government. Again, but in milder terms, he expressed regret that trade

[1] *Parliamentary Debates*, Vol. 202, Col. 199, February 9, 1927.
[2] Ibid., Vol. 247, Col. 1009, January 28, 1931.

unionism had become so closely linked with party politics. He thought the Bill itself inadequate (as indeed it was, being dependent upon Liberal support) and in a final speech,[1] best known for his description of Ramsay MacDonald as the "Boneless Wonder", he suggested facetiously that MacDonald had asked Lloyd George to "take it upstairs and cut its dirty throat". In fact the Bill never became an Act because the ill-fated Labour Government was defeated on it in Committee.

Throughout the 1930s suspicion of Churchill was one factor in preventing any attempt by the trade unions to make a closer alliance with him in opposition to the foreign policy of the Baldwin and Chamberlain Governments. None the less it gradually became clear that Churchill, from whatever motives, was sincerely and resolutely opposed to continued appeasement of the dictators. When in 1939 he at last took office again at the Admiralty, he was one of the few Ministers in whose ability and resolve to fight the Nazis Labour could have confidence. When, in May 1940, a Coalition Government was proposed to meet the rapidly worsening military situation, Churchill was the obvious choice for a Prime Minister, and he then entered a new phase of his relations with organized labour.

This phase was foreshadowed before he took over the Premiership, when he made contact with Ernest Bevin[2] in organizing the trawler fleet into its minesweeping and fishing components. In him Bevin found at least one Minister willing to treat the trade unionists on an equal footing with the employers. It must be stressed that the readiness of the trade unions to support the Government and to set aside their old quarrels with Churchill was due in large measure to the fact that in Bevin they had a personality who could meet the Prime Minister on level terms. Bevin, as Minister of Labour, was a necessary condition for the partnership which, despite all strains, lasted until the Nazis were defeated.

During this period of war-time collaboration Churchill left labour affairs very largely in the hands of Ernest Bevin. He was satisfied that the necessary mobilization of labour would be obtained once Bevin had outlined his drastic measures for the direction of labour, and

[1] *Parliamentary Debates*, Vol. 247, Col. 1022, January 28, 1931.
[2] Williams, op. cit., p. 216.

accepted the conditions which Bevin insisted were needed to make these a success—the raising of wages for lower-paid workers and a clear understanding about the restoration of trade union practices after the war. The consultative machinery established at this time brought the trade unions into a much closer relationship with the Government and industrial leaders than in the First World War, and far more drastic measures of labour direction were applied with far less industrial unrest. In all these matters Churchill was content to rely upon the energy and prestige of Bevin, and on the whole the arrangement worked smoothly.

The principal disagreement which arose between the unions and Churchill during the war was over the Trades Disputes Act, 1927. Chamberlain, when Prime Minister, was requested by the T.U.C. to amend this Act in February 1939. He finally decided in March 1940 that the subject was too controversial to be raised in wartime and suggested that the support of the trade unions for the war effort would strengthen their position in seeking an amendment of the Act after the war. This reply disappointed the T.U.C. but the military crisis in 1940 and the changes in the Government caused them to refrain from raising the matter again until February 1941.

On this occasion Churchill expressed the view that to amend or repeal the Act would start a controversy which might hamper the war effort. The T.U.C. were all the more disappointed by this reply because in verbal discussions with a deputation from the National Council of Labour Churchill seemed willing to make some gesture towards the trade union point of view. It was thought that there had even been a retrogression, since while Chamberlain had at least said that the trade unions would be in a strong position to make representations after the war, Churchill did not go beyond saying that the matter was one which he would be willing to discuss at that time.

The matter was taken up again in April 1941 and a further deputation saw the Prime Minister. The T.U.C. were ready to accept a limited amendment to the Act, allowing the Civil Service unions to re-affiliate to them, and withdrawing the prohibition on the "closed shop" in public employment. Churchill revealed in his reply that he was hoping that a Coalition Government would continue after the war and might then deal with this matter. He did not entirely close the door on negotiations and was prepared to consult his colleagues again. He later adopted a suggestion by the T.U.C. that the General Council should hold discussions with representatives of the Conservative and Liberal Parties; these, however, did not lead the Conservative Party to modify its view that the matter should be left until after the war. Churchill therefore felt unable to take any further action at that time.

A more serious situation developed in 1943, when the Union of Post Office Workers announced that it would apply for affiliation to the T.U.C., despite the Act. The T.U.C. said that if the U.P.W. were ready to take the risk their affiliation would be accepted.

Churchill then interviewed representatives of the Civil Service unions and spoke in rather lurid terms of the dangers that political affiliations might hold for Civil Servants. He held out the threat of disestablishment for members of Civil Service unions affiliating to the T.U.C., and did not appear to appreciate at first that political affiliation was not involved. When this was pointed out to him he agreed to reconsider the position. However, the U.P.W. agreed to withdraw their application for affiliation, in the interests of national unity. This question was brought to a close when after further approaches from the T.U.C. the Prime Minister said in March 1945 that the overwhelming mass of Conservatives would not support an amendment to the Act. A General Election was then in prospect and the issue therefore went out of Churchill's hands.

The impression left with members of the General Council who took part in the negotiations on this matter was that Churchill himself would not have opposed some modification of the 1927 Act, at least so far as its industrial clauses were concerned. He was, however, a prisoner of the Tory Party, whose M.P.s were strongly opposed to the suggested amendment. There is no doubt that the attitude of the Tory Party on this issue and Churchill's inability to overcome it showed up very clearly the impossibility of any post-war Coalition reaching agreement on this or the other highly controversial issues which were bound to arise as soon as the war ended.

After the General Election of 1945 Churchill, as Leader of the Opposition, was faced with the determination of the Labour Government—and of Ernest Bevin in particular—to repeal the 1927 Trade Disputes Act. He took no part in the debates on the repealing of the

N

Act but limited himself to saying, when the Government announced its intentions, that the trade unions would be unwise to reinstitute the political levy on the old basis; at the same time he said:[1]

> "Personally, I feel that we owe an inestimable debt to the trade unions for all they have done for the country in the long struggle against the foreign foe. . . ."

The Conservative Party voted against the Trade Union Act of 1945 but Churchill himself did not vote on the second or third Readings and he made no further reference of note to this issue during the time of the Labour Government.

Since his return to office in 1951 there have not been any major clashes between Churchill and the Trade Union Movement. The T.U.C. have made it clear that while opposing many of the measures introduced by the present Government, they would also be prepared to consult with them and to work with them wherever necessary in the interests of trade unionists. On two or three occasions the T.U.C. has sought the Prime Minister's intervention in matters of general policy. For example, some alarm was expressed in 1952 over certain developments in Government policy towards Wages Councils, and the Prime Minister received a deputation from the T.U.C. Again, the question of basic trade union rights was raised over the D. C. Thomson dispute, and the Prime Minister was asked to use the influence of the Government to get a satisfactory settlement.

On all these occasions the T.U.C. representatives have received the impression that Churchill was anxious to be on good terms with organized labour and would seek to maintain amicable relations although not willing to give way on policies such as denationalization, which he knows are strongly opposed by the Trade Union Movement. There are, of course, good political reasons why Churchill should avoid trouble with the unions as far as possible. They are now in a strong position in organization and status, and outright trouble with them could have a serious effect both economically and politically. Moreover, Churchill is too experienced a politician not to see the desirability of maintaining friendly relations with the organizations which provide his political opponents in Parliament with most of their

[1] *Parliamentary Debates*, Vol. 413, Col. 94, August 16, 1945.

financial strength. The unions are in a delicate position at the present time, seeking on the one hand to safeguard the interests of their members from day to day, and therefore having to enter into consultation with the Government, while on the other hand they follow political policies opposed to the Government through the Party which they created over fifty years ago. Churchill can be assumed still to hold the view that the Trade Union Movement should not be so closely associated with the Labour Party and it would be naive to expect him to miss any chance of trying gently to insert a wedge between the two wings of the Labour Movement.

It is probable that Churchill's personal reputation among trade unionists was partly responsible for the extent of the outburst which followed the publication of a goodwill message to him from the Chairman of the General Council for 1952–53, Tom O'Brien, M.P., when Churchill visited the United States in January 1953. The message was sent in the name of the Trade Union Movement, but there was an immediate and spontaneous reaction from trade union branches, shop stewards, Trades Councils and many union Executive Committees, dissociating themselves from O'Brien's action. Some criticized the content of his telegram, others his action in speaking for the Movement without authorization, and there were several references from local bodies to Churchill's "anti-trade union record". No doubt a message in similar circumstances to any Conservative Prime Minister would have aroused protests, but there was clearly an element of personal hostility to Churchill among the active rank and file.

At the end of this review of Sir Winston Churchill's relations with the Trade Union Movement a few tentative conclusions may be drawn. It seems clear that his view of the role of trade unions in modern society has not changed fundamentally since his entry into politics. This role appears to be that of a strong and influential body of opinion representing workpeople generally, entitled to freedom of association and to be consulted on a variety of matters which fall within the experience of their members and officials. On their political activities Churchill's views are not entirely clear, but he seems either to have abandoned his earlier belief that trade unions must be represented in Parliament or not to have made up his mind how this representation should work in practice. What has alarmed him in his political career is obviously the Socialist policy which the Labour Party has adopted since the 1900s. But he has sometimes spoken as though the unions should not be connected with any parliamentary Party at all, perhaps on the analogy of United States practice.

This attitude shows up his failure to understand how the Trade Union Movement has been obliged, in a British setting, to adapt its methods to parliamentary institutions and to the economic framework of this country. There have been times when parliamentary institutions seemed unable to meet the social demands of organized labour and when the reins of economic power appeared to be held elsewhere than in Parliament. At such times there has been pressure within the Trade Union Movement for more direct methods to be employed to attain political and economic ends. But although the unions have in the past been led into action which, if carried to a logical conclusion, would have taken the supreme economic and political power out of the hands of Parliament, no one who really understood the nature of British trade unionism would have expected them to abandon parliamentary democracy as long as it showed itself capable of slow but definite modification into an instrument of social democracy. Trade unionists have been accustomed to fight for every gain they have made, and the fight has sometimes been against anti-trade union Governments, but it has never been pressed to the point where a violent social revolution looked possible, whatever Churchill may have thought.

Churchill has also failed to understand the nature of trade union leadership in this country. He was himself born into a family and a social class accustomed to exert personal influence upon the leading public men of the day. His outlook upon political affairs must necessarily be very different from that of a trade union leader, who has to rely upon the strength of a voluntary organization to give him authority. Churchill was trained as an Army officer and found the training and the military life congenial to him. He was thus accustomed to exercise authority backed by strict discipline and has never disguised his taste for sufficient power to follow his own policies within the very wide limits set by constitutional practice. The art of gaining and holding leadership in organizations such as trade unions is quite foreign to him and it is doubtful whether he has ever understood its rules or limitations.

Above all, Sir Winston is an individualist in an aristocratic tradition. The Trade Union Movement has thrown up its own individualistic leaders—Bevin being the greatest example. But such men have always been conscious that their authority was based on their representative capacity; if they failed to remember this their careers collapsed, sometimes suddenly and tragically. For a Churchill, however, purely personal qualities of political judgment are of greater importance—he cannot reasonably be regarded as a "typical" capitalist or even a "typical" aristocrat. His political acumen, greater than his father's, enabled him to survive periods of relative obscurity, whereas it would be difficult for a trade union leader to retain his hold upon the Movement if he was for years in his prime no more than a backbencher even in a relatively safe seat.

Some day a more thorough analysis of Sir Winston Churchill's place in twentieth-century politics will have to be written; it is hoped that this sketch of his relations with the new political force of the twentieth century—the Trade Union Movement—will be of some assistance in making that analysis.

HOW CHURCHILL INFLUENCES AND PERSUADES

The Rt. Hon. Leslie Hore-Belisha

Leslie Hore-Belisha was a small boy when he first met Churchill and he has known him for nearly half a century. They were in Parliament together for more than twenty years and fellow members of the War Cabinet in 1939–40. In this chapter he writes of Sir Winston's tremendous power in argument, his ability to persuade and influence his colleagues in the Cabinet and in private conversation. Mr. Hore-Belisha was M.P. for Devonport from 1923 to 1945. His Ministerial posts have included Parliamentary Secretary to the Board of Trade 1931–32; Financial Secretary to the Treasury 1932–34; Minister of Transport 1934–37; Secretary of State for War 1937–40, and Minister of National Insurance 1945.

WHEN I was a boy of ten, I was sitting in what today would be called the "back parlour" of my uncle's house in Manchester. The year was 1904.

The maid opened the door and showed in a masterful, yet slightly stooping, figure. The pink face was topped by reddish fair hair.

"This way, sir," she said.

So did I first set eyes on Winston Churchill. Although I had never seen him before, I had heard my uncle—a prominent Liberal in the area—talk about him and of the question, Free Trade, on which he had left the Conservative Party. He was then the Conservative Member for Oldham and was being considered for nomination as the Liberal candidate for North-West Manchester.

I looked inquisitively at the man who had been a topic of conversation in my uncle's house for so long. The picture is still bright in my mind today.

He was dressed in a frock coat with silk facings and below his chin was a large winged collar with a black bow tie.

He strode into the room talking with an unmistakable lisp. Then he walked up to me, patted me on the head and said: "What a nice little boy! Would you like to come for a drive in my carriage?"

I never went for the drive and I know now that the pat on the head was not due to any merits I may have possessed. It was just a political pat. None the less, I must have been impressed, as the memory remains.

Later in the same month I was taken to a big political meeting in the Midland Hotel, Manchester. The same man was on the platform. As he spoke, he held the silk-faced lapels of his frock coat. Two words in his speech attracted my attention, "Chocolat Meunier". They have remained in my mind. Strange words to remember all these years. It was not until I started to write this chapter that, searching the annals of the *Manchester Guardian*, I found out why he used them. Here is the context:

"Animated by a laudable desire to stimulate home industries, the German, Austrian, French and Russian Governments decided to give bounties on the growing of sugar beet. Every peasant begins to grow beet in his back garden. There is consequently a gigantic production of beet sugar. And, as competition is excluded, producers who are able to charge what they like in their own market make very great fortunes.

Every foreigner has to pay more for his sugar and, consequently, he buys less, and the consuming power in those countries steadily declines. Over-production on a gigantic scale takes place. Then begins a cut-throat competition between the different great trusts for the inestimable privilege of supplying the English market at a loss. Now look at England on the other side of the picture. In England sugar becomes cheap, it becomes cheap in proportion as it gets higher in the countries where it is actually grown. On the basis of this cheap sugar a whole range of secondary industries has sprung up—jam, biscuits, soda water, sweetmeats, preserved fruits and pickles. We have become the world's confectioners. Chocolat Meunier is already made in London. Confectioners in other countries move their businesses into this great free market where distribution of the good things of the earth is not distorted and twisted by the avarice and the folly of man."

This was the classic case for Free Trade, which at that time was the dividing issue between Liberals and Tories, presented lucidly, vividly and appositely by the new standard-bearer. Needless to say, in the home of Free Trade it made its appeal, and Churchill was in due course elected.

From that Manchester meeting onward I followed everything Churchill did. I watched the papers for his speeches; I scanned the pictures of his latest dress. To my mother's consternation I even went so far as to buy—and wear in private—a large winged collar. Thus the imagination of a small boy was captured.

It was many years before I heard Churchill speak again. It was at a meeting of the Oxford Union when I was an undergraduate. He came over from Blenheim Palace with F. E. Smith (afterwards Earl of Birkenhead) to take part in a debate. I noticed that he had taken trouble to become the master of his case. I was also struck by his self-assurance. Later I heard from one of the dons with whom he had dined earlier that in fact he had been highly apprehensive at the prospect of addressing undergraduates, though no one would have suspected that he had any fears about his speech, his audience or the outcome of the debate. A self-confident manner is often a mask which conceals internal terror, as I myself know well.

Since that early period I have come to know him more closely. We sat in the House of Commons together for many years. He visited me in Whitehall when I was Secretary of State for War and he was in the political wilderness. I was a fellow-member of the War Cabinet with him in the early days of the war and he gave me office in the "Caretaker" Government he formed between the end of the war in Europe and the General Election of 1945. So I have watched him from one angle or another in his years of promise, in his years of Ministerial achievement, in his bitter years of isolation and in his supreme moments as war leader and main architect of victory.

What is the secret of Sir Winston Churchill's remarkable ability to impress, persuade and dominate, in his speeches, in conversation, in committee, in the Cabinet itself?

Firstly, I think, one must recognize that Churchill naturally, and without apparent effort, looks and behaves like somebody important. He is "news" and looks news.

Throughout his political career, whether in Opposition or in Government, he has always been in the forefront. In appearance, in manner, in dress, and above all in speech, he is an individualist.

He gets the last ounce out of the English language—his unique command of which is one of his most persuasive gifts—by his characteristic modulations of voice and by his defiantly Anglo-Saxon pronunciation of foreign words. When he spoke of the "Narzis", for instance, the very lengthening of the vowel carried with it his message of contempt. By these means he can, when he wishes, make not only every phrase but every word significant.

His unusual hats which startled the public fancy in his early years have given place to the cigar, an equally precious gift to the cartoonist. Perhaps such foibles call attention to himself. But what of his V-sign? There we have his knack of evoking a patriotic emotion. It is a gesture of genius.

But all that is spectacular, showing that Churchill, almost alone among British political men, appreciates that an appeal can be addressed to the eye as well as to the ear.

More fundamental is his meticulous study of any subject under discussion. With care and patience he builds up a case. First he reads every document to be found on the subject, and with Churchill to read is to remember. Few men have a greater capacity for assimilating facts. I have never known him to go into a conference with an ill-prepared or half-digested case. He knows when he enters a Cabinet or Committee meeting what he wants done. He has a scheme, a plan, a solution. Not for him the patient hearing while others sort out their views. He takes the initiative with a proposal of his own for others to support or, if they are so inclined, attack. Many eminent statesmen, after listening to all sides of a case and carefully weighing the pros and cons, only then, and in a judicial manner, decide on a course of action. Balfour and Asquith were in this category.

But one would have an entirely wrong impression of Churchill if one visualized him only as a student of briefs and books and a protagonist of theoretical opinions. He is a man, *par excellence*, who believes in seeing for himself, and he has never lost that boyish characteristic of asking "how it works". He enjoined on me in my own Ministerial career not merely to accept advice but: "Always see for yourself. Once you have seen a thing working, you know how it works."

Throughout his life he has followed this "See for yourself" practice. As a young soldier he went off to Cuba because, at that time, it was the only place in the world where there was real fighting. As Home Secretary he startled his political associates by going almost into the firing line in the "Battle of Sidney Street". His top hat glistened among the policemen's helmets. As Prime Minister in war he took every opportunity of visiting the battlefronts, the munition factories, the airfields, the bomb-ruined houses of the people. It was all part of his method of getting to know the facts at first hand. Even the wall he built himself at Chartwell is a reflection of that part of his plan of life.

For the same reason he likes having models made of things that specially interest him. During the early part of the war he had an idea for a machine for tunnelling underground to burrow beneath enemy fortifications. So he had a model made and having studied its possibilities he asked me to go to the Admiralty and see it. His aim was to break the stalemate of position warfare, just as he had hoped to do in the First World War with the tank.

He always has a fresh and original approach to an old problem, often by introducing some new device or gadget. On this plane are his siren suit and his shoes which do up with zip fasteners instead of laces. I remember an occasion when I had lost a most important bunch of keys. Churchill heard about it and told me that he had once had the same misfortune. But, he added, it could never happen again, so far as he was concerned, because he now kept his keys on the ends of a thick, silver, snake-like chain. This chain, he explained, went round his back, threaded through the sides of his braces and the bunches of keys at either end rested safely in his trouser pockets. They could not be lost. After telling me all this he went one better and had a similar chain made for me, which I still have. I have not lost my keys since!

Graphs and maps likewise appeal to his visual imagination and they are often included in his armoury when he is presenting a case.

It was when he was a critic of the Government during the late 1930s that I first learned of his interest in such things. He was advocating the use of the rocket in anti-aircraft warfare and he showed me diagrams to illustrate its ballistic characteristics. On the wall of my room at the War Office was a map of Europe, which impressed him. He liked to stand with his hands on his hips looking at it and discussing the problems of the future. I gave him this map and he hung it in his study at Chartwell.

His quest for knowledge is facilitated by his innumerable contacts in all spheres of our national life. There was never a man with more sources of information. In the course of his career he has become Honorary Bencher of Gray's Inn, Chancellor of Bristol University, Honorary Academician Extraordinary of the Royal Academy, Honorary Fellow of the Royal College of Physicians and Honorary

Fellow of the Royal College of Surgeons, Fellow of the Royal Aeronautical Society, Fellow of the Society of Engineers, Fellow of the Royal Society of Literature, Fellow of the Royal Institute of British Architecture, Fellow of the Royal Geographical Society, Fellow of the Institute of Journalists, Fellow of the Zoological Society, Honorary Member of Lloyd's, and so on; the list seems endless. In addition he is Hon. Colonel of several regiments, Hon. Air Commodore, and an Elder Brother of Trinity House. Far outside the range of Government Departments and Civil Servants do his antennae stretch.

He has a peculiar sensitivity of what is happening in the world and little escapes him. He does not wait until breakfast-time to read the morning newspapers, but often sends for them during the night when they come off the Press. I have a vivid recollection of seeing him frequently in the Smoking Room in the House of Commons absorbed in the early editions of the evening newspapers. Only when he has finished reading them is he prepared to talk.

In his power to influence and persuade Churchill has another great asset—his dogged determination. If he cannot win his way in an argument he will probably propose the adjournment of the meeting to another day, when he will appear again, reinforced with new and weightier evidence, facts and information and renew the attack. He never gives up and he never accepts a negative for an answer. How many Prime Ministers have felt themselves strong enough to call upon the House of Commons formally to reverse a vote deliberately given? Yet Churchill did this in the war on the issue of Equal Pay for Equal Work for male and female schoolteachers during the passage of the Education Bill.

Consider how he has risen superior to electoral defeats. When I was first elected to the House of Commons in 1923 Churchill was not a Member. He had been defeated at Dundee. He stood again at Leicester West and was defeated. He then tried at the Abbey Division of Westminster and again the electors rejected him. Three defeats in a row would have been enough for most men, but Churchill was not discouraged. He presented himself to the people of the Epping Division of Essex, where, although the constituency is now called Woodford, he has remained ever since.

Never does he envisage failure. I recall Dame Margaret Lloyd

George telling me how Churchill had bought a farm. He was quite new then to farming.

"He insisted," Dame Margaret said, "that he was 'going to make it pay whatever it costs'."

The farm would be something of a recreation but it would also be a study and a new interest; something from which he could learn as he always does from his hobbies, whether painting, bricklaying, making an ornamental garden, or, in more recent years, horse racing.

In an analysis of the sources of his power and influence it would be impossible to overestimate his tremendous capacity for work, which is enhanced by his equally tremendous capacity for relaxation. With him this takes the form not of idleness but of a change of occupation. While his brain is at work, I have often noticed he has a singular facility of resting his body. He will, for instance, do much of his reading and writing propped up in bed.

Churchill is a tough opponent. He is conscious of his strength, too, and is not reluctant to let his adversary of the moment realize his confidence. I remember once being engaged in a controversy with him and he had hit me pretty hard. Then in conversation he said, "If you attack me I shall strike back and, remember, while you have a 3.7-inch gun I have a 12-inch gun." This was a reference to the fact that he was Prime Minister, with all the authority of his position, whereas I was a critic. He gave his warning with a twinkle in his eye but I knew that he meant business. I nevertheless went into action, but it was not long before his high explosives and shrapnel were falling all around me.

This reminds me that he conceives argument almost as a military art, as anyone who follows his metaphors will realize. He is always "mustering" and "deploying".

Those who have been close to Churchill know of his intense loyalty to friends, even if he falls out with them politically. While you are a friend you can expect support to the hilt. But you must know that if you cross him Churchill will be an unrelenting opponent. Yet even in the heat of the argument he will often retain a deep regard and even personal affection for the man he is fighting, particularly if the man he is fighting really fights back.

The impetus of Sir Winston Churchill's vitality is within himself, but I have often wondered what it is in the conditions of his life that seems to free him from fret and strain. What is it that enables him during long bouts of activity to come into every round of a struggle apparently refreshed? Is it perhaps the loyalty and devotion with which he is sheltered in his home? The career of politics keeps men away from their wives and families and deprives them of many human enjoyments. That is part of the forfeit exacted from those who live under the servitude which men call power. What a great solace and stimulus it is to a politician to have his base secure! Churchill alone knows how much he owes to his good fortune in this respect. Long may his public service and his domestic happiness continue!

CHURCHILL THE BROADCASTER

Richard Dimbleby, O.B.E.

Richard Dimbleby has received National Awards as the out-standing personality of British radio and television. He was appointed the B.B.C.'s first News Observer in 1936 and the B.B.C.'s first War Correspondent in 1939. He is a regular broadcaster on Royal, State and Governmental occasions.

IT is not enough, when trying to assess the skill of Sir Winston Churchill as a broadcaster, to listen to him. Even the recordings of his great speeches made during the Second World War, and so jealously guarded by the B.B.C., do no more than bring back some of the supercharged atmosphere of those years. They certainly confirm the man's ability as a broadcasting speaker, but they do not explain how or why. At the time they were made, of course, no one wanted to know the reason for the hold that the speaker had over them; it was enough that Churchill was broadcasting, that as Prime Minister he would probably have something important to say, and that, even in the darkest days, there would be comfort and inspiration in his words.

Now that the time comes for a closer examination of Churchill's broadcasting, it is difficult to know how to set about it. The investigator is dealing with one of the great figures of the world. He is what an over-enthusiastic staff officer during the war tried to dub a "V.V.I.P.", a Very Very Important Person, when plain "V.I.P." was the highest category known. When asking questions about a V.I.P. you are apt to meet with evasions and silences; your informant will hesitate, then say "I'm not sure I ought to tell you this," or "Perhaps you'd better not say that." This is the case frequently when the question, and the answer, are of the simplest and most harmless kind. Perhaps it is that those few people who have been near Sir Winston Churchill when he is preparing or delivering a broadcast are naturally anxious not to seem to be breaking any confidence, particularly as broadcasting from one's own home or office can be quite an intimate occasion.

A further difficulty lies in the tendency of people to regard any details of the methods of a Prime Minister as coming within the meaning of that all-embracing word "security". The word has only to be mentioned once in any conversation on war-time topics, however innocent it may be, to bring the talk to a standstill. There is, in fact, no security involved in any revelation of Churchill's ways of broadcasting, nor, in 1953, does it matter if we discuss the various once-secret places from which his greatest broadcasts were made, for undoubtedly in any future national emergency the places chosen would be quite different.

Meeting these obstacles early in my investigations, I decided to divide my subject into four, and to consider the Prime Minister as a broadcaster in the light of the immediate technical background (which has a direct influence on the work of all broadcasters), the dramatic world situation which was the canvas upon which he was working, the factual material which was at his disposal, and his own methods of speech and delivery, by which the greater part of his audience throughout the world has already judged him.

The Outside Broadcasting Department of the B.B.C. is the department charged, as its name suggests, with the handling of all programmes emanating from places other than a studio. The scope of its activities is very wide, for it is responsible not only for the more obvious broadcasts like those of State occasions, commentaries on the Boat Race or the Derby, or descriptions of the Cup Final, but also for relays from theatres and music halls, from cinemas where the organ music is broadcast, and from churches. In fact, the engineers of the O.B. Department, as it is known within the B.B.C., are to be found wherever, on land, sea or in the air, apparatus has to be installed to enable a broadcast to take place. Furthermore, they are in charge of the relaying of broadcasts from certain places—the Albert Hall in London is an example—where the installation is a permanent one. The broadcast, after all, is still "outside".

The engineer in charge of outside sound broadcasts is Mr. R. H. Wood, whose experience of important occasions in the last twenty years must be as great as anyone's. On all major occasions he takes personal charge, and the fact that he is a Member of the Royal Victorian Order may indicate the share that he has had in the success of Royal broadcasts during the years. It is he who has been alone with the Sovereign during those last minutes before three o'clock on

Christmas afternoon, when all over the Commonwealth loyal subjects were gathering at their sets to hear the King's, or the Queen's, words; it is he who has administered the necessary "level", or voice test, given technical approval and retired to his apparatus outside the door to switch on the red starting signal at the right moment. Inasmuch as this is the procedure with all B.B.C. "Grade One" relays, it has applied also to Sir Winston Churchill.

An explanation is necessary of the B.B.C.'s war-time system of handling top-level broadcasts. Obviously secrecy was essential. When the daily journeys of the King were made public only in retrospect, the B.B.C. could not announce that His Majesty would speak from Buckingham Palace on the following Sunday at a certain time, or the King would have been "pinpointed" at once. Similarly, no advance announcement could be made of the place from which the Prime Minister would be speaking; nor, in fact, was much notice given at all of his intention to speak, since the likely places from which he would broadcast were few, and subject to enemy visitation.

So the B.B.C. adopted a code language in which Buckingham Palace, Windsor Castle, Downing Street, the underground Cabinet headquarters at Storey's Gate, Westminster, and the week-end house, Chequers, in the Chilterns, were known as "Place One, Place Two, Place Three", and so on. Mr. Wood was told simply "Place Three, nine-fifteen on Friday", and took action automatically. He would take one other trusted engineer in his own car, with any odd pieces of apparatus not already stored at Place Three on the back seat, but not visible. Together they would make all the arrangements and the B.B.C., having no axe to grind in the matter of the Royal or Prime Ministerial scripts, was content to leave it to the engineers. No programme representative attended, for in security circles "the fewer the better" is a basic maxim.

Of the "places" used by Churchill during the war, his underground nerve centre at Storey's Gate was by far the most interesting. This had been prepared as a Government control point well before the war, and lay deep below pavement level close to the entrance to St. James's Park. The custodian of the place was Mr. Rance, and in military circles it had become the custom when talking of the troops used for the protection of this most important place to refer to them as

"Rance's Guard". R. H. Wood remembers well the austere surroundings in which he and his colleague worked when preparing a relay from Storey's Gate. The room used was generally Churchill's own little study-cum-bedroom, furnished with a table and chair, a wardrobe, and a narrow bed. There was no attempt at decoration, and only the pipes and ducts of heating and ventilation festooned the otherwise bare walls. Early on in the war there was some doubt as to whether such bareness in a small room would give adequate acoustics for broadcasting—the dreaded "bathroom" echo is all too easily obtained in such surroundings and is very distracting—but some rearrangement of the microphone position proved satisfactory. I doubt if any member of the B.B.C. staff could have told, from the sound of the relay, whence it was coming.

Churchill was indeed at the very hub of the war when he spoke from Rance's place. Within a few feet of him, outside the door of his small room, was the emergency Cabinet Room, with its big maps on the wall, and next to it the Map Room itself, wherein the whole course of the war was accurately charted according to the latest information. Thus it was that, at the last moment before a broadcast, the Prime Minister could bring his facts right up to date.

Chequers, in contrast to the cramped quarters below ground in Westminster, was commodious in the extreme, but no less vital in its atmosphere. The B.B.C. engineering party, visiting it for the first of the war-time week-end broadcasts, was surprised at the urgency of the place. They had forgotten, perhaps, that wherever Churchill went, urgency went with him. He did not move to Chequers, for a week-end of "relaxation", without taking with him the staff and machinery to enable him to keep in immediate touch with the war, minute by minute, and his broadcast script would often contain a fact or a figure received a minute or two before the red light came on.

The procedure at Chequers for a broadcast was unchanging. Wood arrived early in the day, met the Post Office engineers responsible for the land lines from the big house to the B.B.C., and carried out tests with them. There was a good deal to do, for, as in the case of all "Grade One" relays, everything was in duplicate. From microphones to transmitters, there was always a spare part ready to come into instant use in the event of a failure. Thus, though the direct landline circuit from Chequers went straight to London, there was a second circuit that passed through several towns and formed something of a geometrical pattern before arriving at the same ultimate destination. Should enemy action interfere with one circuit, the other would take over, since it was in use simultaneously.

In the study where the Prime Minister sat at the microphones, arrangements were simpler. The room had been wired for broadcasting, and it was only necessary for the microphones and signal light to be plugged into sockets fitted in the wainscoting. Similar fixtures exist at No. 10 Downing Street.

I have gone at some length into the background of the Churchill broadcasts in wartime because an appreciation of the atmosphere of urgency and secrecy in which they happened is not out of place in considering the man as a broadcaster. The public reaction to any celebrity is conditioned to some extent by what the French call, with a word almost untranslatable, his "*ambiance*". It is worth while remembering, when judging the Prime Minister's performance at the microphone, that he was given every possible help in broadcasting in an easy and comfortable way. It was just as simple technically for him to address millions of people all over the world as it was to make a telephone call.

. . . .

When writing of background, I must also include the far greater and more significant world background against which Churchill spoke. Public censorship, a necessary evil of war, was starving the people of news and information. With censorship there is always the suspicion that the truth may be concealed, and a false picture given of events for "policy" reasons. Though there was very little justification for such misgivings, the public turned to the Prime Minister as the man who would give them all the facts that he could straight from the shoulder. Furthermore, there was always the hope that he would say more than had been said already, a hope that was sometimes fulfilled. He was, after all, one of the few men in the land who could not be censored.[1]

[1] See also the chapter "Churchill and the Censorship", by Rear-Admiral G. P. Thomson.

For these reasons alone, Churchill had a ready-made, keen, sympathetic audience. He had created enormous national confidence in himself. The great majority of the people—there were, of course, his opponents—trusted him, supported him and were avid for anything he had to say, even if his major promises were of "blood, toil, tears and sweat". Here, they felt, was a man who would say what had to be said, however unpleasant it was, and who would always hold out some hope of better things.

Of course the man himself was deeply conscious of this waiting audience, of the fact that he was speaking with authority, with a full private knowledge of the truth. There has never been a broadcaster, particularly one concerned with public affairs, who did not feel himself buoyed up by the drama or significance of an occasion, and a speech to the hungry public of a nation fighting a life-and-death battle was indeed "an occasion". As a professional commentator myself, I can vouch for the fact that the greater the event, the more one's powers seem to swell to match it. I remember such different occasions as the discovery of the dreadful concentration camp at Belsen, the first mass air raid on Berlin, the lying-in-state of George VI, when the knowledge that people would want to hear what I said brought with it an exaltation that lent power to every moment of the commentary. Though I make a humble personal comparison, I am quite sure that the Prime Minister, armed with facts vital to the life of his people at moments critical to them all, must have known that same breathless feeling. It is the feeling of sharing in history.

It was not only in Britain or the countries of her allies that people hung on Churchill's words. I was told recently by a German broadcasting official who worked at Hamburg during the war that he walked into the offices one night and found normal work at a standstill. Even William Joyce, then in the full foul flood of his radio oratory as "Haw Haw", was away from his desk. Asking what was up, the official was told to be quiet—"Churchill's broadcasting."

There is now to be considered the question of the Prime Minister's material, and material is as important to the success of a broadcast, scripted or impromptu, as the ability of the speaker.

Once again, Churchill had all the advantages. He had at his disposal the whole truth of the war situation, received either from his own map room or through the Chiefs of Staff. In addition, for material of a specialist nature, he could call for immediate memoranda from any of his Ministers. There was no side of the national life upon which he could not be fully documented.

That he made ample use of his resources there is plenty of evidence. His broadcast talks were not dictated as complete scripts but built painstakingly upon the known facts, fitted together like jig-saw puzzles so that everything relevant could have its place. Only when a working script was available did the Prime Minister infuse into it his own personality, his own phraseology and flashes of humour. This, in its turn, required rewriting and polishing, which often continued until the last minute before the broadcast was due. Even if the B.B.C., or the censorship, had wanted an advance copy of the Prime Minister's utterance, they could not have had one until practically the moment that he went on the air.

I have mentioned only the material for the war-time talks by Churchill. To include in this chapter discussion of his broadcasts in the post-war period, whether as Premier or as Leader of the Opposition, would be to enter the realms of Party Political Broadcasts, and it is not by these, surely, that Churchill at the microphone will be best remembered.

I have touched upon the technical background to Churchill's broadcasts, the drama of their setting, and the material of which they were composed. In each case, everything conspired to help the speaker, but future historians, I am sure, when they hear the recordings of his talks, will agree that all this was worthless without the magic of word and phrase, the forceful delivery, the mastery of language that made each of his great war-time broadcasts a pageant in itself.

I was asked once what it was, in a nutshell, that made Churchill so outstanding at the microphone, and I replied, "The fact that he breaks every accepted rule of broadcasting." This is true. He drops his voice where he should raise it, he alters the recognized system of punctuation to suit himself (some of his scripts were virtually un-intelligible to anyone else), he speaks much of the time with anything but clarity. Yet such is his power as an orator, and such his feeling of the public pulse, that during the war years he was sure of a silent and appreciative audience of millions, following every word and phrase with relish.

My friend Lynton Fletcher, who is at the head of Recorded Sound Ltd., one of the foremost sound-recording studios, and is chairman of the Association of Professional Recording Studios, has helped to adumbrate the picture of Churchill at work before the microphone. Fletcher has recorded the Prime Minister several times at his home at Chartwell or at Hyde Park Gate or in his own studio off Piccadilly, and has had much to do with the training and recording of public speakers in London; he has, therefore, a keen appreciation of microphone style. With correct professional reticence, he would not be drawn into a detailed description of Churchill at work, but he did tell me that he had never met anyone who worked so hard on his script beforehand as the Prime Minister. Nor had anyone been more willing to persevere until a recording was exactly right. There was an occasion when a mistake in timing necessitated a repeat recording of a longish speech. Fletcher was asked his opinion of the second version. Being an honest man and essentially a professional in the matter, he replied, with some courage, "Not as good as the first." "Come on, then, we'll do it again," said Churchill. "We must get it right."

Therein lies the key to much of the Prime Minister's success at the microphone—his willingness to attend to every detail. Once he has made up his mind that something is worth doing, nothing is too much trouble for him. Once he has started the business of recording or broadcasting, nothing else is allowed to interfere.

Some time ago, in the course of a lecture on recorded history, I played part of a gramophone record made more than forty years ago. The speaker was Winston Churchill, then President of the Board of Trade, and his subject was the famous People's Budget of before the First World War. There was no need for me to announce the speaker, for the first half-dozen words established his identity. The passage of nearly half a century has made virtually no difference to the voice, except to deepen and thicken it slightly. The same faint sing-song is there and the same lilting cadences, though there is never a cadence where you might expect it, at the end of a sentence. Generally the voice goes up, leaving the listener with the feeling that the sentence has not really ended at all. The most familiar musical phrase that recurs in Churchill's war-time speeches is one that he used, probably unconsciously, as a young man. Translated on the piano, it represents approximately the notes G . . . A (below) . . . C sharp (above).

But these mannerisms, however endearing they may be, are only details. They are the highlights that Churchill uses as he lays his splendid pattern of colours on the canvas. If there is a hard core to his mastery of broadcasting, it lies in his mastery of the English language. His love of words and phrases stands out in his public utterances, and most of all in his broadcasts, when there is no gesture or platform trick to help them. These are words, phrases, sentences that roll through the ether, perfectly made for broadcasting and perfect for history.

The historian will not fail to note that description of Mussolini as "this whipped jackal, frisking at the side of the German tiger—this absurd impostor". Von Ribbentrop was "that prodigious contortionist", and those who dared to ask what it was that Britain and France were fighting for (in the spring of 1940) were "thoughtless dilettanti or purblind worldlings". The actions of Russia in October 1939, as they seemed to the then First Lord of the Admiralty, were "a riddle wrapped in a mystery inside an enigma", but there was no puzzlement about the character of "Herr Hitler and his group of wicked men, whose hands are stained with blood and soiled with corruption". Then there were the neutral States, each one of which "hopes that if he feeds the crocodile enough, the crocodile will eat him last". The crocodile was seen in another form when it turned upon Russia in June 1941. . . . "Now this bloodthirsty guttersnipe must launch his mechanized armies upon new fields of slaughter, pillage and devastation."

These were fighting words, words that made sorely tried men and women chuckle, words which expressed exactly what they themselves would have liked to say. All those associated with Churchill in his broadcasting or recording are agreed that throughout the whole of the war he knew better than anyone exactly what the public was thinking and what the public wanted. If a moment's relief was needed at a time of great tension, he gave it. When the enemy was bombing and machine-gunning merchant vessels and fishing boats at the end of 1939, he said, "I am glad to tell you that the heat of their fury has so far exceeded the accuracy of their aim," but in the summer of 1940 his mood was very different. "London . . . this strong City of Refuge which enshrines the title deeds of human progress." And when Britain stood alone after the fall of France, how magnificent was that sentence, "Faith is given to us, to help and comfort us when we stand in awe before the unfurling scroll of human destiny."

Such oratory, delivered in words so simple and yet so stirring, was itself a mighty weapon of war and the despair of those who tried by every means known to broadcasting to wear us down. This was surely the art of the microphone, or the art of the orator adapted to the microphone, at a level higher than had ever been reached before or has ever been attained since. Whatever have been the fortunes of Sir Winston Churchill in the years since the war, whatever public utterances he may yet have to make, he will always be remembered by the people of Britain for the way in which he spoke to them in their homes when death was very near.

CHURCHILL THE ARTIST

Professor Thomas Bodkin

Professor Bodkin, Director of the National Gallery of Ireland 1927–35, and Barber Professor of Fine Arts and Director of the Barber Institute of the University of Birmingham 1935–53, has an international reputation as an art critic and writer. He has taken part in many B.B.C. broadcasts and television programmes on Art. His books include The Approach to Painting, Hugh Lane and His Pictures *and* My Uncle Frank.

TO appraise Sir Winston Churchill's abilities as an artist-painter, and to assess accurately the value, aesthetic or monetary, of his pictures, is a task which none of his contemporaries can set about hopefully. The critic must be prejudiced, one way or another, by the knowledge that the man who produced these pictures has amply proved himself to be the possessor of genius as a statesman, as a historian and as an orator. He is, very probably, the most remarkable Englishman who has ever lived and likely to remain for ages the most admired of Englishmen in the eyes of other races. If he chooses to spend much of his scanty leisure in painting, surely it must be assumed that he is intelligent enough to know that such time is well spent, and that he would have sufficient power of self-criticism to refrain from preserving with care, and some pride, the results of his efforts should these prove to be of negligible worth.

It is all very well to ask the critic: What would you think of his pictures if you came suddenly upon a large number of them, unsigned and untitled, for the first time in a public exhibition? A competent critic would, beyond all shadow of doubt, reply at least that he would be much impressed by them and would want to see that exhibition again, fortified by some outside knowledge of the painter's personality and career. Good work in any art provokes curiosity about its author. To assert that knowledge of an artist's life is irrelevant to the judgment of his art is an affectation, often indulged, but one which runs counter to experience. The more we know about his antecedents, his environment, his ambitions, his fortunes, his family and his physical and intellectual equipment, the more likely we are to understand whatever he may be trying to say to us in the language of his art, be that a language made of words, of sounds, or of visual images. That is the fundamental reason why we welcome with enthusiasm all new information that may be discovered about the lives and personalities of the great artists of the past, and use it to throw light on their achievements.

Knowing a great deal about Sir Winston Churchill as a man, we expect to find his salient qualities reflected in his painting. We are not disappointed in this expectation. A striking characteristic of his pictures is their quite extraordinary decisiveness. Each is a clear and forcible pronouncement. He does not niggle nor retouch. His paint is laid once and for all with no apparent hesitation or afterthought. It is never fumbled or woolly in texture. Spaces are filled with obvious speed. His colours are bright, clean and well harmonized. His drawing makes factual statements, though these may not always be quite accurate in detail. His knowledge of perspective, for example, is far from being that of a well-trained and practised professional artist. Sometimes the façade of a building, standing at an angle to the horizon, will seem to spread open rather than contract as it recedes from the eye of the beholder. Reflections shown in water will not always chime in correct alignment with the objects reflected. But were he more scientific, it is likely that he would lose some of the spontaneity which is one of his most potent attractions. His inaccuracies are never of substantial importance.

His ability to devise a good composition might well be envied by many a successful modern professional. He does not try to say two or more things at the same time. Each of his pictures is the presentation of a distinct theme: a tower, a village, a church, a lake, a harbour, a range of mountains, a pool, a group of palm trees, an English grove, a Grecian temple. The dominant motive is never obscured by irrelevancies. The spectator's eye is never tempted to wander outside the confines of the frame. This power to design well is one which may be developed by attention to rules and formulae. But in his case there seems to be an inherent natural ability in action, without much planning or preoccupation, which brings about results that wear a delightful air of improvisation.

The range of subjects that appeal to him is also very remarkable; and he is never repetitive. When he brings off a convincing effect he shows no desire to continue in the same strain; and his next picture is apt to be concerned with some quite different problem. He is primarily interested in landscape, but shows no desire to subject natural

CHURCHILL THE ARTIST

Smoking the familiar cigar and wearing his grey, wide-brimmed
hat, Churchill paints in the little town of Camara Delobos in
Madeira, in January 1950

appearances to romantic or dramatic conventions. He does not attempt to deal with storms, night-scenes or, even, lurid sunsets. Light and peace, those qualities which all wise men most value in life, are indubitably those which chiefly distinguish the scenes that he prefers to paint.

"Escapism" is a word that has sometimes been used to describe Sir Winston's attitude to pictorial art. It is an ugly word, often carrying a sense of denigration. Yet the function of art, alike for those who produce it as for those who enjoy it, is primarily to release the human spirit from the undue pressure of mundane affairs, or to shield it from the more sordid aspects of reality. The Greeks and the Florentines, each in their Golden Age, lived amid lovely surroundings and knew nothing of the grim horrors of total war or mass manufacture. Their art was, therefore, principally centred on the human body portrayed in postures carefully calculated to enhance mankind's normal ideals of dignity and power. The vast population of modern Europe and America must, for the most part, live in densely over-crowded cities, dark with smoke and throbbing with ceaseless noise. They long for the quiet of green fields and clean skies; and so the art of the landscape painter is the one which best fulfils their spiritual need. It was a branch of art that only existed precariously and in a subsidiary way a few centuries ago. Now it has outgrown all the others. Landscape predominates in every contemporary exhibition of pictures.

Sir Winston cannot avoid being a man of his period. His long working life has been largely spent under the urgent pressure of public business and in contact with innumerable people. Naturally when he first took seriously to oil painting, after he had passed his fortieth year, it was to landscape that he looked for inspiration.

He himself has told the story of his beginnings in an article entitled "Painting as a Pastime", which appeared in *The Strand Magazine* and was reprinted soon afterwards in his book *Thoughts and Adventures*, published in 1932. That article, amplified, forms a large part of the persuasive lively book, also entitled *Painting as a Pastime*, which came out in 1948 and has been selling steadily ever since. Its call to Everyman to paint for himself, reinforced by good coloured reproductions from sixteen well-selected pictures by its author, must have powerfully stimulated the sale of artists' materials during the past five years: and the number of those whom it has led astray into mis-spent effort must greatly exceed those whom it has led safely into a promised land. Poussin was, in some respects, a more reliable guide to would-be painters when he remarked about pictures, *"Ces ne sont pas des choses q'on puisse faire en siffliant"*.

The germ of the impulse to paint must have lain dormant in Sir Winston's spirit from an early age. This may be deduced from the fact that, as a very young man, acting as a war correspondent in the Boer War, he used to supplement his written dispatches with sketches drawn in the field and sent home to be worked up as illustrations for the *Graphic* by draughtsmen on the headquarters' staff of the paper. However, the crowded and adventurous life which he led for the next fifteen years or so left him no leisure in which to develop his inherent artistic talent. It was not till 1915, in a time of extreme frustration and forced inactivity, that his thoughts turned again to the practice of pictorial art.

At the outbreak of the First World War he held office as First Lord of the Admiralty, and he conceived the strategic scheme of taking the enemy in the rear by a joint naval and military assault through the Dardanelles. It was a bold, imaginative idea which held great promise of success. But the political support which he received for it was faint-hearted, and some of the admirals and generals concerned with the actual operations were not inspired by his own fiery zeal for the plan of campaign. The operations hung fire and in May 1915 he was succeeded at the Admiralty by Mr. Balfour. Sir Winston remained a member of the Cabinet and of the War Council but, having now no executive office, he had less work to occupy his abounding energies. Irked by such unaccustomed inactivity, he picked up, in an idle moment on a Sunday morning in May, a box of water-colours belonging to one of his children and made a few tentative experiments which excited him and suggested at once further possibilities. There and then he sent an order for a full equipment for painting in oils: easel, canvases, paints and brushes in lavish supply and of the best quality.

A few days afterwards he took his stand before a blank canvas and a rural prospect in a momentary and unwonted state of hesitation. Armed with set palette and charged brush, as though with shield and sword, he shrank from striking the first blow, but soon decided to

attack through the sky. The attack was more in the nature of a reconnaissance than an assault. He himself has described how he gingerly
mixed a little blue paint on the palette with a very small brush, and
then with infinite precaution made a mark about as big as a bean upon
the canvas. There was no resistance. As he was preparing to push
cautiously forward, Lady Lavery, the beautiful, audacious wife of the
well-known Royal Academician, arrived unheralded to pay a call and
took over the command. Seizing the tyro's biggest brush, she mixed
a lavish quantity of pigment on his palette and proceeded to lay it on
in bold swift strokes. Her practical demonstration demolished his
unprecedented timidity. From that day forth he has held and
practised the creed that "Audacity is a very great part of the art of
painting".

In the thirty-eight years that have passed since then, he has painted
whenever he has found a chance to do so in the midst of his multifarious
and mountainous responsibilities. During that time he has produced
pictures in a quantity that would be creditable to a painter who had
nothing else to do but paint. There are hundreds of them covering every
wall of his studio in the grounds of Chartwell, literally from floor to
ceiling. Hundreds more are stacked in racks in the house itself. Dozens
adorn the walls of his home. Others, some of the best, hang in good
company, without losing face, in the rooms and corridors of
10 Downing Street. Despite the duties of his high office, but never to
their detriment, he still takes time to paint in his rare moments of
leisure. During his recent short holiday in Jamaica he worked on three
pictures.

Lady Lavery was the first, but by no means the last, instructor from
whom he has taken technical advice. Her husband, Sir John, soon
supplemented her teaching. He depicted Sir Winston, some thirty years
ago, sketching at his easel in the open air. Sir John's effort now hangs
at Chartwell. In his turn he was portrayed by his distinguished pupil at
work in his studio. There is little to choose between the merits of these
portraits. Mr. Paul Maze, who is an old friend of Sir Winston, is
another to whom some praise is almost certainly due for helping to
develop his skill. They have often worked in company. But Mr. Maze
persistently denies all credit as a mentor. Hints and counsel were
accepted by the novice from the late Sir William Orpen and the late Sir

William Nicholson, each, in differing ways, an astonishingly accomplished craftsman. One of Sir Winston's best pictures, which at present hangs on the stairs at Chartwell, shows a rush of his cherished black swans across a lake, and has an evident affinity in style to two charming small pictures by Nicholson at present in Downing Street.

Sir William Orpen many years ago advised Sir Winston to invite the late James Sinton Sleator, who was first his pupil, then his assistant, and eventually the President of the Royal Hibernian Academy, to come to Chartwell and paint in his company so that he might profit from observing dexterity resulting from long practice. When Sleator was painting my own portrait a year or two before he died, he liked to beguile the sittings with anecdotes of that memorable visit. His host's artistry had enormously impressed him. But as a shrewd, humorous Ulsterman he took special delight in telling me how, when the time had come for him to leave, Sir Winston had tried to persuade him to accept a fee for his professional assistance. Sleator, who had felt himself to be a privileged guest, refused and was pressed to reconsider his refusal. He thought to give pleasure by saying that he would greatly prefer the present of a picture. Though Sir Winston so hates to part with his work that he might fairly be described as a collector of it, he graciously granted the request. Sleator, a notoriously casual individual and one wholly indifferent to possessions, forgot to take it away with him. But, though he always loathed writing letters, he sent an apologetic one some days later asking that the gift should be forwarded to him. He received a firm reply to the effect that as he had not bothered to take it with him, he could not have cared much for it, and it had better stay where it was.

It is not easy to see Sir Winston's work in bulk. Few people, and they are almost all close friends, possess examples of it. It has seldom been exhibited until of recent years at the Annual Exhibitions of the Royal Academy. The total number of pictures there shown only amounts to thirty to date. His first exhibited painting was not a landscape but the portrait done in 1915 of Sir John Lavery at work in a studio with a mirror in the background. It was recognized as an excellent likeness when it was shown in the exhibition held by the Royal Society of Portrait Painters in 1919. The only other recorded instance of his submitting his work for exhibition occurred shortly before the late war, when the French painter Charles Montag organized a one-man show for him in Paris at which six of his canvases, described as being by Charles Maurin, were sold.

Sir Winston's modesty about his painting is a surprising trait of his character. When he was first persuaded by Sir Alfred Munnings to send some of it to the Royal Academy in 1947 he insisted that it should be submitted under the pseudonym of "Mr. Winter" for the judgment of the Committee. He told the President that unless he was treated as an outsider and his work put in with the rest to go before the Selecting Committee he did not wish to send. The late Sir Edward Marsh, who had been his close friend and secretary in so many Ministries, and was a connoisseur of proved taste, went to help him to pick out a few of the best pictures for the test, and reported that he found him "very choosey and resolute" and only willing to send forward two.

These were entitled *Winter Sunshine* and *The Loup River, Alpes Maritimes*, and were accepted on their manifest merits. He followed them up, in 1948, with three others: *The Goldfish Pool, at Chartwell*, one of his own favourites; *Blenheim Tapestries*, possibly his best interior; and *The Blue Sitting Room, Trent Park, 1934*, which was sold by auction at "Christies" in 1949 for 1,250 guineas for charity. The popular and artistic success of these exhibits was so great that his election to membership of the Academy was confidently proposed and, in what one of its more literary members has described as "a most unanimously settled affair", he was admitted under the appropriate designation of Royal Academician Extraordinary. This enabled him to send his full quota of six pictures, as of right, to the exhibition of 1951. But in 1952 he was again Prime Minister and limited his contribution to four.

He may think, for all I know, that his reputation as a statesman might suffer from his activities as an artist. In this country a love of music or the visual arts is still too often considered to be evidence of mental instability. Had Gladstone composed symphonies or Disraeli carved statues it is unlikely that either would ever have found himself at the head of one of Queen Victoria's Governments.

Churchill's activities and capabilities as an artist are widely known in the United States. Millions of Americans are well acquainted with his pictures through excellent coloured reproductions. The issue of the

American magazine *Life* for January 7, 1946, contained sixteen of these, several measuring twelve inches by nine.

It is natural to speculate on the monetary value of his pictures, but most difficult to estimate it. Very few of them have ever been sold: beyond the six bought at his exhibition in Paris, the only other market test to which any of them has been submitted, before the sale of the *Blue Room* in 1949, was the sale of *The Cross in Saint Paul's Churchyard*, by auction in a charity fête at Balmoral, to which it was presented at the request of King George V. Sir Winston had painted it while holding office as Chancellor of the Exchequer between the years 1924–29.

The Blue Room was smaller than the generality of his pictures. It measured $19\frac{1}{2}$ by $13\frac{1}{2}$ inches. The size he almost invariably prefers is 25×30 inches. When I was privileged lately to look over the contents of his studio I noticed that he had recently been at work enlarging an early version of one of his compositions to a scale of about $3\frac{1}{2}$ feet by 5. Three other blank canvases of the same dimensions, with a biscuit-coloured priming, stood by ready for use.

This reminded me vividly of a meeting which I had with Sir Winston at the Royal Academy Banquet in 1951. The dinner and the speeches were over and the guests were free to wander at will through the galleries at Burlington House. I was standing with Mr. Dring, before Mr. James Gunn's group of the *Royal Family at Tea in Windsor Great Lodge*, which is now in the National Portrait Gallery, when we were joined by Sir Winston and Mr. Oliver Lyttelton. The four of us then drifted together on a tour of inspection through five or six rooms. For me it was a fascinating experience. Sir Winston examined the pictures closely and was free with his criticisms, which were well informed and generous. It was pleasant to note that his sympathies went out immediately towards anything characteristically British in theme. The curve of a Berkshire Down crowned with beeches, a crowded mop-fair in a provincial city, won his approval, largely because they reflected familiar scenes. After a while we found ourselves in front of one of his own smaller pictures. It was a pleasing thing, but not outstanding. We were all silent: I because I was determined not to risk an appearance of that flattery with which I felt the painter was likely to be only too well acquainted. He was the first to speak, and remarked pointedly, "Well, I think it's pretty good, considering I could only spend seven hours at it." He then went on to tell us that he planned to paint some day on a much grander scale, on canvases eight feet by twelve, where he could fill in big forms with masses of bold colour. I could not refrain from asking, "Won't that give you a lot of strenuous exercise?", to which he retorted: "Exercise? Why?" I reminded him that, working on that scale, he might find it necessary to move constantly back and forwards, in order to get the whole composition within his range of vision so as to preserve a just relation of tonal values while he built up his picture with progressive touches. That seemed to give him pause; and he remarked: "No, that wouldn't do. I always paint sitting down." But he is not a man to be easily deflected from his purpose; and, no doubt, he is now in process of devising a method of painting effectively on the scale towards which his temperament impels him.

When *The Blue Room* in 1949 fetched a bid of 1,250 guineas at the auction, for the benefit of the Young Women's Christian Association, in which it was sold at Lady Churchill's request, the fact was at once established that the collection of pictures at Chartwell represents a great fortune. For the purchaser, Senhor Francisco de Assis Chateaubriand, who bought it for presentation to the Museum of Sao Paulo in his native Brazil, while professing no particular interest in the charity concerned, did declare that he had been prepared, if necessary, to bid up to £13,000.

The picture is one of the very few which are signed. It bears the linked initials W. S. C. Those remaining in their painter's own possession are not merely unsigned for the most part; they are not arranged in either chronological or topographical order, and there is nothing inscribed on them, back or front, to indicate their titles. From either a financial or a scholarly standpoint, these are omissions that call for remedy. In some instances it is likely that no one but Sir Winston himself can say authoritatively where or when a particular picture was painted: he has worked from nature in so many foreign places far apart and different in aspect. Como, Monte Carlo, Hendaye, Cannes, Cap Ferrat, Lugano, Maggiore, Genoa, Athens, Antibes and, above all, Marrakesh have inspired him on occasion.

It would be a cool and confident critic who could attempt to establish a present ratio between the intrinsic and the association values of his work. Truth is the daughter of Time. At the moment all that can be safely conjectured is that the association value preponderates. The painter himself is singularly modest in speaking persistently of his painting as a mere pastime. He goes too far towards suggesting that there is a great gulf fixed between what he calls "the real artist", highly trained, and the man who paints for pleasure, largely by rule of thumb, when he can find time to do so amid more pressing pursuits. There have been masters of the first rank who painted as instinctively as a bird sings and needed little tuition. Corot was one of these.

Sir Winston Churchill himself is another instinctive painter, though one who is always searching for fresh ways and means to produce the desired results. Madame Balsan has described him painting the moat at her country house in France. He decided that the still water did not contribute to the effect he sought. So a boat was moored to the bank in order that an oarsman therein might churn up ripples on its surface. Finally, a photographer was called in to record their pattern for future reference. Photographs have also been used as aids to the drawing and placing of some of the rare figures in Sir Winston's landscapes. The purist may object to this, though Degas is known to have learned much from photographs, and Sickert relied on them with increasing frequency throughout his life, and never hesitated to acknowledge his debt.

Chesterton on hearing someone described as a "Minor Poet" took hot exception to the term, insisting that the significant word was "poet" and that the word "minor" was an uncalled-for disparagement. By analogy Sir Winston as a painter should be described comprehensively as an Artist. No one, least of all himself, wishes to describe him as a Master. In a wise, learned and, unfortunately, half-forgotten book, *The Science of Picture-Making*, the late Sir Charles Holmes postulated that all pictures should possess the qualities of unity, vitality, infinity and repose. All these, in varying degrees, seem to be present in Sir Winston's pictures. Another quality which, to my mind, should characterize a true work of art is inexhaustibility. The melody, the poem, or the picture should exist as a fountain that flows always or a fire that never dies, to which a man may return hopefully whenever he needs refreshment or enlightenment. It is precisely that strange quality which transmutes verses into poems, and paintings into pictures.

Sir Winston's paintings often possess it. As I write, there comes to my mind a tall canvas on which he has shown a long perspective of the golden walls of the city of Marrakesh soaked in tropical sunlight, and sentinelled by a rank of slender, green-crested palm trees. In the lower left-hand corner three erect, dark, motionless figures are standing in a mysterious group. It is one of those many pictures of his which, I think, any wise man would wish to contemplate again and again.

o*

CHURCHILL'S HUMOUR

A. P. Herbert

Sir Alan Herbert, who has been for many years outstanding among Britain's humorous writers, was Independent Member of Parliament for Oxford University from 1935 to 1950.

FROM time to time people rashly ask me to "lecture" on Humour, and I give them a rambling address which seems to please them, but does not, I suspect, leave anyone much the wiser. For Humour, like the right of criticism, belongs to every Briton—and even a foreigner or two.

Towards the end of the first hour of this "lecture" I come to "British Humour", and I say: "Who—would you say?—is the greatest living British humorist?" Those who are still awake give secret votes to Johnny Morton, to P. G. Wodehouse, to Belloc, Nat Gubbins, Noël Coward, Bevan, Wyndham Lewis, Lane-Norcott (and, by the way, they make a long and goodly list): but my own answer is:

"Sir Winston Churchill, who, at any time, in any conditions, in any company, on any subject, with never a fault of taste or tact, can make laughter when he wills. And you can't say fairer than that.

"If he had done nothing else," I add, "he could, and would, have made himself famous in this field alone."

That is all very well before an audience who presumably approve of laughter. But in this weighty work I must go more carefully. For Sir Winston Churchill is (before all the other people he is and has been) a statesman: and it is not everyone who approves of statesmen being funny. It is, indeed, a fairly new and unusual combination. It is difficult to think of any celebrated joke that was made by Burke, by Pitt, by Charles James Fox, by Disraeli or Gladstone in the House of Commons. Lord Chesterfield, Sir Harold Nicolson tells us, said:

"Frequent laughter is the characteristic of folly and ill manners. It is the manner in which the mob express their silly joy in silly things. Laughter is a low and unbecoming thing."

That was about the time of Dr. Johnson. But Sir Harold Nicolson, in the modern *Spectator*, seems to go some way with Lord Chesterfield:

"For years . . . I have upon this page denounced the sense of humour as a flabby attribute, as an escape from difficult reality, as an indulgence, destructive of concentration and will-power, as a practice unworthy of an alert and logical mind. . . . Yet there are moments when I regret that, unlike most of my compatriots, I am devoid of a sense of humour. . . ."

This assertion will much surprise anyone who has enjoyed the honour of Sir Harold's conversation. But he compels us to face the question:

"What is Humour? What is a humorist?"

"Man," said Hazlitt, in the *English Comic Writers*, "is the only animal that laughs and weeps: for he is the only animal that is struck by the difference between what things are and what they ought to be."

"The difference between things as they are and things as they ought to be". That seems to me to cover, broadly, almost every form of laughter. It is another way of saying, perhaps, that the sense of humour is the twin brother of the sense of proportion.

All men, in different degrees, possess, or may possess, this sense, this perception of the difference between perfection and fact. The humorist is merely one who, with a lively phrase, or a sharper lens, is able to exhibit the difference more tellingly than others.

If this theory is sound, no statesman, surely, should be reproached for deploying the sense of humour. That ruler of men who can see, and express most clearly, the difference between things as they are and things as they ought to be, is likely to be among the best. If Hitler had had a sense of proportion, if he could have laughed at himself, as Sir Winston Churchill can, he might be alive today. So let us leave Lord Chesterfield (with some contempt) and turn with relief to our Prime Minister.

First, a few examples and episodes from private life. Many public comedians—the world has observed—are sad or silent dogs off parade; but this cannot be said of Churchill.

Like the rest of us, he has often to express an ordinary thought, to hammer home a common truth. But, unlike the rest of us, he always seems to find new words for it, grave or gay. He never seems to say an ordinary thing. Early in my House of Commons days he was urging me to take more part in general politics instead of concentrating on my own pet subjects, divorce, etc. "Don't spend yourself," he said, "on your soiled doves." "Soiled doves"! Could the business of broken marriages be better, more briefly, described? We have all said, "Like father, like son." Hear how Churchill said it, at a private party, about twenty years ago. There was then a well-known but not very popular Conservative Minister in office. He was considered pompous, and, unjustly, I believe, by scribblers like myself, a prig. I was invited to a luncheon-party at Westminster by General Spears and his wife (the American novelist Mary Borden). On the way in, on the Underground, I read that that Minister's son had made his first public utterance. He had, I thought, a comical Christian name, and seemed to have been reading his father's speeches. The company at lunch were all well-known politicians except Mary Borden and myself, and, at sherry-time, at least, I was rather alarmed and silent. But someone mentioned the Minister, and I thought, "This is my cue for a remark." "Did you see," I said, "that ——'s son, appropriately named Galahad, has said so-and-so?" Churchill, who had been quiet in a corner, suddenly marched across towards me and said: "Yes, I saw that too: and I said to myself, 'Isn't it enough to have this parent volcano continually errupting in our midst? And now we are to have these subsidiary craters spouting forth the same unhealthy fumes . . .!' " There was a lot more that I have forgotten, but these words, that wonderful, shocking, image, especially "the subsidiary craters", have always stuck in my mind. I never wrote them down before.

Some people have wondered whether he prepares such good things in bed or bath and waits till some turn of debate or conversation gives him his cue. It may be so, here and there: but most of them, I swear, come bubbling up, without notice or effort, from an inexhaustible spring. This is almost capable of statistical proof, if anyone cared to attempt it: for so many of the sparkling things have been said in conditions which he could not possibly have foreseen.

He had no notion, for example, that, against all advice, I was going to make a provocative "maiden" speech on the second day of the new Parliament in 1935, set most of the House against me, and distress some good and important friends who wanted me to do well. Alone of all the swells, he sought out and comforted the naughty boy, and even paid me some compliments that I got from no one else. Then he relaxed and, with that delightful sound, half grunt, half chuckle, said: "Call that a maiden speech? It was a brazen hussy of a speech. Never did such a painted lady of a speech parade itself before a modest Parliament!"

I cannot pretend to be an ear-witness of the next tale, though it was a favourite in my time. A certain statesman, they say, had been making, in the Chamber, a worthy but woolly speech about the League of Nations and all that. Someone came to Churchill and said, "What did you think of it, sir?"

"Well," he said, "I thought it was very good. It must have been good: for it contained, so far as I know, all the platitudes known to the human race, with the possible exception of 'Prepare to meet Thy God' and 'Please adjust your dress before leaving'."

A mere procession of witticisms in print may leave a sense of inhumanity, like a lot of men marching past in "comic opera" uniforms. This would be singularly unjust to Churchill, whose fun is firmly founded in humanity, in "human kindness". Cold print can do justice to an epigram of Wilde's, or some acid utterance of Voltaire's. But few sayings of Churchill's can carry all their proper guns without some knowledge of the scene, the circumstances, the unique and vibrant voice, the pause, the chuckle, the mischievous and boyish twinkle of the face, and all the tiny signs that something grander than wit is on parade. I have described elsewhere a truly "humorous" example of Churchill's magnanimity. I think it was in 1947 or 1948. It was in the Smoking Room of the House of Commons, and all things said there are confidential. But this saying was to the credit of all, and can do no harm: so I will risk it. Rather late at night Churchill was leaving the Smoking Room. As he passed a little group of us—all Parties— we said, "Good night, sir!" He stopped and beamed upon us—that wonderful genial beam! There is no face I know that can express so humorously, so grimly, so many emotions. His glance fell on my friend—nay, the friend of most of us—Richard Stokes, the Socialist Member for Ipswich. Dick Stokes never loses his temper (which is a most unfair handicap to those who disagree with him), and says the most frightful things with a smile so youthful and warming that I think of him always as a junior Pickwick. All the war he was attacking Churchill, fearlessly, continuously, about tanks (among other things). I never knew enough about tanks to know whether he was talking sense or not, but certainly he was a formidable enemy to Churchill and his Ministers. Now Churchill came back and put a hand on his shoulder and said: "Of course, I've forgiven you. Indeed, I agree with very much that you are saying about the Germans. Very good." He moved away a few paces and said, as if we might be surprised by what he had said, "Such hatred as I have left in me—and it isn't much—I would rather reserve for the future than the past." He beamed again and moved off a pace or two, but stopped again, and made that inimitable sound I have mentioned, and he said: "H'm. A judicious and thrifty disposal of bile."

Here, once again, is "the little more" that means so much. You or I might have said that we reserved our small store of hatred for the future. But only one man in this world would have thought of adding, "a judicious and thrifty disposal of bile", and left his company both moved and mirthful.

All these, so far, have been private occasions, the faded memories of one who cannot claim to have been "close" to the great man at any time, has only two or three times spent an hour or two at the same table, and now has not had a word with him for many years. But if ever you meet anyone who is working or living near to him you will hear at once of two or three bright sayings which are only a day or two old. The staggering thought is that this unmatched Parnassian spring is bubbling all the time; the sad thought is that there is no Boswell with a ready urn to catch and keep and bottle it. No one man could do it; but one day, surely, a little band of his friends and Ministers and secretaries and servants should be shut up in some tower or dungeon and not let out until they have massed their memories in a golden book. Much trouble has been taken to do the like for Confucius and Marcus Aurelius. They said some things worth saying, no doubt. But, let us confess, they are not much fun.

Now let us pass to the public arena. How shocked, how horrified, Lord Chesterfield would have been if he could have heard the great gales of laughter the Prime Minister has caused in high and solemn debate—not only in peace-time, and not only in the British House of Commons. What does the world remember of a speech he made before the Canadian Senate and House of Commons at Ottawa? A joke—and not a scholarly, well-turned joke, almost a music-hall joke—"Some chicken—some neck!"

Lord Chesterfield and his like forget what a solvent of suspicion and animosity, what an antidote to fear, honest laughter can be (and by honest laughter I do not mean the jeer or the cat-call, but the laugh that springs from human understanding, from the sudden assertion of the sense of proportion). Time and again, in those great war-speeches in the House, full of facts and figures, fine phrases and resolute defiance, when fears were strong and doubters many, Churchill would pop in a little joke, wholly relevant and natural at the moment but having the effect of miraculous timing, which relieved the tension and made the whole House happy. Many will remember the terrible debate on the Vote of Censure, of July 1-2, 1942. It was moved by a Conservative and seconded by Mr. A. Bevan (Labour). Powerful, patriotic men of all Parties were behind it. "The House," said the Motion, "has no confidence in the central direction of the war." What it amounted to, in the minds of many (and some said as much), was "Churchill Must Go". By a horrid chance, too, on the morning the debate began Rommel began his assault on the South Africans, before the gates of Alexandria: and who knew what was happening there? Churchill replied to the debate with a grim and stately speech of about ninety minutes. Half-way through it Hore-Belisha interpolated:

"What about the Churchill tank?"

"At the present moment," said the Prime Minister, "I have not got there."

Later, he did.

"This tank," he said, "the A.22, was ordered off the drawing-board, and large numbers went into production very quickly. As might be expected, it had many defects and teething troubles, and when these became apparent the tank was appropriately rechristened the 'Churchill'." (We laughed a little, sympathetically, at that.) "These defects have now been largely overcome. I am sure that this tank will prove, in the end, a powerful, massive and serviceable weapon of war."

At that, I remember, we laughed as if we had never laughed before. Some have said that the little joke, turned against himself, but yet obliquely an answer to the whole attack, took the sting and strength out of it. That, I think, is going rather far; for, after all, twenty-five Members did support the Vote of Censure in the Lobby. But certainly the world seemed suddenly a better place, Rommel a menace no more, and Churchill the only man.

I credit, too, the humorist's account with a thing he said a little later:

"I have not made any arrogant, confident, boasting predictions at all. On the contrary, I have stuck hard to my blood, toil, tears and sweat, *to which I have added muddle and mismanagement,* and that, to some extent, is what you have got out of it."

Can anyone imagine serious rulers like Hitler and Stalin saying such a thing in a war-oration at a time of danger and disaffection?

Here, though it was in less anxious days, is a reply to a supplementary question which would have given Lord Chesterfield an apoplexy. In 1943 the Prime Minister announced that the church bells would no longer be reserved for use as a warning in case of invasion. Sir Thomas Moore asked:

"Will my right hon. Friend say what alternative arrangements have been made?"

The Prime Minister: "Replacement does not arise. *For myself, I cannot help thinking that anything like a serious invasion would be bound to leak out.*"

Mr. Austen Hopkinson: "How can the news possibly leak out, when it is an offence to spread alarm and despondency?"

The Prime Minister: "Factual statements of that kind, especially if well intentioned, would not fall into that category."

Superb nonsense—but all strictly fitted to the parliamentary formula. And, let all observe, there was no chance to prepare *those* sallies "in the bath". In his late seventies, he is matchless still in the swift and shattering reply to an interruption or "supplementary" question. Like other lords of wit and fun, he can shoot to kill, if he wishes; but he is even more a master of the retort that flattens, but leaves the impudent alive.

I laugh still, years later, when I think of "the horse" affair. It was in the 1945 Parliament. Colonist II, his obscure and inexpensive race-horse, had won several races, and become a popular favourite. Churchill, in the House, was making a tremendous general attack on the Socialist administration. They had squandered all the resources and reserves of the nation and the Empire, so carefully gathered by generations of better men, etc.; nationalization was frittering away what little was left, etc.; they had reduced the value of the pound, flung away our best possessions, etc. (these are not his words, which were better but longer). Some rash fellow on the Labour benches cried, "Why don't you sell your *horse?*" Most Members—most Ministers—would have grinned genially and said that they wanted to keep their horse. Others would have glared haughtily and said something testy about irrelevant interruptions. But the old hunter, without a moment's hesitation, let loose with both barrels, and got a bird with each. My recollection is that first he said, "Well, that at least is a piece of property which has increased its value since it came under my control." (A big laugh—a happy contrast to the "resources" "frittered away" by His Majesty's Ministers!) Most of us would have been content with that; but, when the laughter died, he went on: "As a matter of fact, I was strongly tempted to sell the horse; but I am doing my best *to fight against the profit motive.*" Glorious, general laughter; and not a grain of bitterness anywhere. This kind of thing will never be quoted in any anthology of humour: but it is champion's work.

He got a similar right and left this year on the protests against Her Majesty's title—"Queen Elizabeth II". First a Member rose and asked if the right hon. Gentleman was aware of the strong objections which had been uttered by the Irish Government (or something like that). Churchill, without rising, asked, "*Which* Irish Government?" And that was that. Then another Member asked, "Is the Prime Minister aware that there is a strong feeling in Scotland about the Oath being taken to a Queen Elizabeth II on the ground of historical inaccuracy? In view of his great claim to historical accuracy himself, will he not do something to meet this very strong resentment in Scotland?"

Churchill replied, "I shall be very glad to hear from the Hon. Member if he will put his Question in the pillar-box."

This raised a storm of laughter, for indignant Scotsmen had been blowing up pillar-boxes with the objectionable inscription on them. An elaborate joke, relying, not in vain, on the knowledge and the wits of his audience; but made on the "spur of the moment". How nimble and how sure the old gentleman is!

There sticks in my mind, too, a big laugh he gave the House in the grim year before the war. This is a strange memory: for he was a "back-bencher" then, making, from the corner seat "below the gangway", all those full and careful "defence" speeches, which got small applause, and less laughter, from any quarter. The joke had something to do with the appointment of Sir Thomas Inskip as Minister for the Co-Ordination of Defence; and perhaps the complaint was that there was no defence to co-ordinate, or something of that sort. At all events, at the peak of the argument, he said, "It is as if the cart, as it were, preceded the horse." That does not look very funny, sir, on paper, I know: but then, sir, you were not there. The House was crowded but cold: but, as he said those words, he turned to the right and looked towards the Bar of the House, and made a small gesture with his right arm, as if to say, "Come on, good cart and horse." I was sitting lower down on the same bench: I looked towards the Bar myself, and I can still *see* that cart and horse coming slowly up the empty Floor. Others, I heard that evening, saw them too, and, for a minute or two that cold, divided House were warmed and drawn together in the light of laughter by one who, then, was the warm friend of very few. This, again, will never find a place in any Book of Quotations, or even, probably, in any biography of Churchill. You may well say: "But what a story! A joke of which you can't remember the point! Words which are a mere paraphrase of an ancient saying!" Exactly, sir. It was magic: such an assembly in one person of so many powers, so much art and experience, so much command of nerve and body and man, as in the old days would have earned a charge of wizardry: so I cannot explain it, and shall not try.

"But," may I add, "he has so keen a perception of the difference between things as they are and things as they ought to be, so high an ability to advertise the difference, that I take the proposition with which I began to be proved."

CHURCHILL AND SCIENCE

Professor A. M. Low

Professor Low demonstrated the principle of Television at the Institute of Automobile Engineers in London in 1914. He designed and flew the first guided missile in 1917 while commanding the Royal Flying Corps Experimental Works and designed an electrically controlled rocket in 1917. He is President of the Institute of Patentees.

T HE story goes that Gladstone was once induced to watch a demonstration of one of Michael Faraday's great electrical discoveries. At the end of it the politician asked, "But tell me, Mr. Faraday, what use is it?"

To which Faraday replied, "No doubt, one day you will be able to put a tax on it."

We cannot imagine such a story being told about Sir Winston Churchill. He would never have asked such a question. Rather, having seen the demonstration, his imagination would immediately and vividly have explored the possibilities, foreseeing applications that had not even occurred to its discoverer, grasping the implications in one field of human activity after another, considering in turn the impact on war, politics, society and ethics. Demonstrating to Churchill, the danger that Faraday might have encountered would not have been the negative attitude of the narrow utilitarian, but the optimism of a mind able to foresee all possible, and some impossible, applications, coupled with unlimited confidence in the ability of science to solve any technical problem.

Many would, no doubt, deny that Sir Winston Churchill is a scientist. The description "scientist" is extremely loose, meaning simply one who practises science, or acquires knowledge systematically by observation, experiment and deduction. Academically, Churchill's technical qualifications would be insufficient to secure him the most junior appointment. Prospective employers would probably regard his Fellowship of the Royal Society, given in 1941, with some suspicion. He has not even the humblest of those technical diplomas or degrees that are now essential to set foot on the lowest rung of the scientific ladder. But if we are to deny him the description "scientist" for that reason, we must deny it also to Faraday, to mention only one of many great men who succeeded by practice rather than the memory test of examination.

From the academic point of view, Sir Winston Churchill has what I suspect some regard as an even greater failing—wide interest in and some knowledge of all the sciences, especially in regard to their effect upon human beings. He is, in other words, a "popular scientist", more concerned with the broad sweep of recent research than the publication of a paper in some professional journal to be read by a few thousand and understood by less than a hundred.

His attitude has always been the antithesis of that of the mid-twentieth-century scientist, the specialist who finds out more and more about less and less. In an age of specialists, Churchill is a phenomenon. He may be regarded as a man whose interest in life has always been too great to specialize in any one thing or whose brain and energy is so remarkable that he has been able to specialize in every subject that has interested him. It has been no small advantage to Britain and indeed to the world that during the first half of the twentieth century there has been in positions of authority a man of this kind and that a string of scientific doctorates or fellowships after the name of Winston S. Churchill would have been a poor exchange for the freedom of his mind to range the field of discovery, plucking from it whatever seemed likely to be of benefit at the moment.

But we must go back to the beginning. I began this tribute with a story of Faraday, the man who by his work on magneto electricity virtually gave us electric light. The home of Churchill's father, Lord Randolph Churchill, in Connaught Place, was the first private house in London to have electric light. It is a small matter, but no doubt it had its result on the growing boy who thus early obtained first-hand experience of the comforts that science could bring. Pass on seventy years and we read of Winston Churchill, now Prime Minister, issuing one of those famous, brief commands, that a hot-water system capable of providing a morning bath for both himself and his guests be installed at Chequers, a house that is the very embodiment of traditional England. No man has a greater regard for tradition than Sir Winston Churchill. But not in matters of science.

Churchill's formal education was in the days when "gentlemen" still learned Latin and Greek, and Churchill, like Shakespeare, had little liking for either. But he has given a clue to his early interest in science, which then, generally speaking, was an "outsider" at the great public schools. Writing of his efforts to gain entry into Sandhurst, he has said: "There were five subjects, of which Mathematics, Latin and English were obligatory, and I chose in addition French and Chemistry. In this hand I held only a pair of Kings—English and Chemistry." This was a remarkable pair sixty years ago and it is interesting to speculate how our literature might have been enriched if the youthful Churchill had continued to specialize in this manner, for the tradition of writing science as literature died with the nineteenth century.

Apart from this hint of early inclination, he has recorded that his determination to enter Sandhurst was such that he mastered mathematics up to the "dim chambers lighted by sullen, sulphurous fires reputed to contain a dragon called the Differential Calculus". But he had no taste for mathematics, pure or applied. Where pure mathematics was concerned, he "saw it all—Depth beyond depth was revealed" to him, but his interest took the practical form of persuading the examiners that he was equipped to study military science. When, by a feat of memory, he obtained 2,000 marks out of 2,500, his interest in mathematics diminished. "I am assured," he has written, "they are most helpful in engineering, astronomy and things like that. It is very important to build bridges and canals and to comprehend all the stresses and potentialities of matter, to say nothing of counting all the stars and even universes and measuring how far off they are and foretelling eclipses, the arrival of comets and such like. I am glad there are quite a number of people born with a gift and a liking for all of this." From the point of history what mattered was that the examiners asked a particular question about "Cosines or Tangents in their squared or even cubed condition", the answer to which young Churchill had learned just the week before. Otherwise he would have chosen some other career. The whole course of his life and not a little of the history of Britain and the world might have been different.

Whistler, not so fortunate in a similar examination, used to say that if selenium had been a gas, he would have been a general. Churchill might say that if he had not known what a cosine was he might have become President of the Royal Academy. And that would have been a loss to science, for although this ended Churchill's formal scientific studies, he has never ceased to be a scientist in the more vital sense of observing, experimenting and deducing. Even more important, perhaps, in the positions of power he held, he has given the other kind of technician, who is as familiar with test tubes or the slide rule as he is with his own wife, the encouragement and the means to carry on his work for the benefit of the nation.

For the next few years Churchill was wholly concerned with the science of war, not to mention some of its emotional appeal during the last years when it was the sole preserve of professional soldiers who still fought with weapons little changed for centuries. Churchill, perhaps more than any man, has taken part in the twentieth-century revolution in military science. When he first put on uniform, it was gold lace, pantaloons and pill-box cap. Fifty years later he became familiar to the world in the "siren suit" of his own design. In those fifty years the lance and sabre of the Hussars has changed to the armoured vehicle and Bren gun. War had entered a third dimension—the air—and it is characteristic of Churchill, the soldier-scientist, that although he was introduced to war when it was an affair of much smoke and comparatively little fire power, he at once became master of the destiny of vast forces when a single explosion could kill more men than died by explosive in the whole Boer War. Always, in fact, one step in front, rather than five steps behind, the scientists.

Lieutenant Churchill did not remain in the Army long enough to become a Colonel, but there was never the slightest danger of his becoming what is called a "dug-out colonel", a man preparing to fight the next war with the weapons of the war before last. His appreciation of technical progress, coupled with his powerful but controlled imagination, has, if anything, led him to demand weapons for the war after next, and his energy and administrative ability has sometimes resulted in his getting them most successfully!

He went to the Admiralty in 1911 when the "super-Dreadnought" was the queen of the seas and key to naval supremacy. As a scientist he observed, experimented, made deductions. Two new weapons were then engaging science—the submarine and the aeroplane. Only a decade before even the brilliant H. G. Wells had forecast that the "blind fumblings" of the submarine would never result in any more than the torpedoing of a hulk in a harbour and had suggested that he might be thought optimistic in forecasting that by 1940 an aeroplane would actually have risen and alighted safely! Churchill fought to start the Royal Naval Air Service. He saw the possibilities of launching aircraft from the decks of battleships and of torpedoing ships from the air at a time when naval experts, who had talked about submarines as "Fisher's toys", believed that aircraft were no business of the Navy and not likely to be of much use to anyone.

Churchill actually took part in the naval aircraft experiments. The amount he contributed to the solution of technical problems was probably small, but in getting results his encouragement was worth the work of a battalion of "back-room boys". Britain became the first country to have an aeroplane carrying a machine-gun and the first to launch a torpedo from the air.

Curiously, it was through his interest in the young naval air service that Churchill became the "father" of the tank, the weapon that was to be decisive in World War I and was to play such an important part in all future warfare. The R.N.A.S. early established itself on the continent. The base had to be protected against roving armoured cars. Trenches were dug and other obstacles erected. The fertile brain of Churchill naturally considered means by which armoured vehicles might surmount these obstacles. And thus when the battle fronts settled into static, fortress warfare, Churchill urged that the deadlock should be broken with the aid of caterpillar vehicles capable of crossing trenches or crushing them in. He also, incidentally, suggested the smoke screen laid down by an armoured vehicle. The exact part that Churchill played in the development of the tank has been disputed. He certainly did not "invent" the tank. He was not, perhaps, even the first to conceive the general idea. But it is absolutely certain that without Churchill the tank might not have been born at all, certainly not in 1915. It is characteristic of British methods that the tank, the decisive land weapon, should have been developed with the aid of funds supplied by the Navy and as a result of the enthusiasm of a young man for flying!

It is yet another example of the advantages of the active mind of wide interests in science, as distinct from the specialist who may touch on an invention or discovery of first importance but, because it is not in his special limited sphere, does nothing more. Science needs both kinds of men, and the brilliant "all-rounder" is more rare than the highly qualified specialist. He is born and not trained in his art by "unending weighings and measurings".

From the scientific point of view, Churchill's early interest in flying had another important result. It brought him into contact with a young scientist named Frederick Lindemann, who was director of the Aeronautical Research Laboratory at Farnborough. Lindemann had a theory about tail-spin, which was causing a lot of trouble and many casualties. Theoretically he worked out a way to get out of a tail-spin. It was so much against current views that there seemed only one way to prove its value. Lindemann learned to fly in three weeks, took up a 'plane, put it into a spin, carried out the actions he had suggested and came out safely. This was just the kind of thing that appealed to Churchill and he became a close friend of the scientist. Frederick Lindemann became Professor Lindemann and a great admirer of Churchill. This friendship brought a working partnership of great value to Britain in World War II. As Lord Cherwell, Professor Lindemann supplied the link between Winston Churchill, the statesman who realized the immense importance of Science, and the many scientists who lacked Lord Cherwell's own gift of being able to make highly technical matters and statistics quickly intelligible to a man of Churchill's disciplined intellect.

It is not without significance that for the first time in history a British premier has had a scientist as one of his closest advisers. Detractors have sometimes spoken of Churchill as a "statesman of the eighteenth-century pattern". Nothing could be further from the truth. Churchill is the first premier who has attempted to introduce into Government at its highest level something of the scientific method. William Pitt is supposed to have rejected the first submarine and torpedo with moral dislike of a "secret weapon" and practical fear because, he thought, they would mean the end of British naval power. I cannot see Churchill rejecting any weapon as "too scientific" and his reaction would have been that the weapon must be developed for use if necessary and the Navy given defences against its power. If, because of the balance of military force at the moment, some new weapon seemed to give advantage to the enemies of Britain, he would have done what he did with "Window" during the war—kept it in reserve until the advantage came to Britain.

Window,[1] incidentally, was another great invention which, in a sense, we owe to Churchill. Churchill did not invent it—the idea was Professor Lindemann's in 1937. But it was Churchill who pressed it on the Air Defence Research Committee. The "experts" were doubtful and, in fact, the idea was never tested until four years later when Churchill was in a position to order the necessary experiments. The idea was developed by Dr. Jackson and others, but as with so many inventions that proved of vital importance, we are conscious always of the figure in the background writing minutes to the effect that difficulties are known but must be overcome. Pluto, Mulberry, Oboe, Gee, H_2S[1]—none of these and many other inventions were conceived by Churchill. But in each case he was able to grasp the principles, appreciate possibilities and put behind the scientists all the weight of his authority, sometimes spurring them to achieve the "impossible".

In an article written before the war, Churchill said: "On reading that a certain invention has been made many scientists can say how it works. They can see at once that it is useful, but it never entered their heads to design that particular thing. In war, particularly, the soldiers and sailors do not know what it is they want done for them." His ability to see "what's wanted" and to express the need in simple language has been of great importance.

It would be wrong to suppose that Churchill has always backed winners or that all the ideas that have come from his scientific stables have been successful. When some scheme has a fundamental defect, the doggedness, optimism and confidence that technicians can do anything, provided they have faith and sufficient facilities, has been, perhaps, apt to result in experiment and research being pushed beyond the point where it was clear that the result would be barren. His political opponents have made the most of these mistakes and the consequent "waste" of money. But on balance there is no question that Churchill's interest in science and his ability to grasp technicalities has been of inestimable value. His attitude towards science in defence has always

---

[1] "Window" = The dropping of strips of tin foil to simulate a bomber and confuse enemy radar. "Oboe" = A radio device to guide bombers to their targets. "Pluto" = "Pipe Line Under The Ocean", an invention to supply oil to the Allies' invading forces in Normandy. "Mulberry" = An artificial harbour which was floated across the Channel and joined to the French coast. "Gee" = A device for guiding bombers. H_2S = "A blind bombing device".

been the exact opposite of the negative Baldwin, who was certain "that some of the bombers would always get through".

Advised by Professor Lindemann, his view before the last war was that science might be harnessed to make it impossible for any of the attacking bombers to reach their target. That hope proved too optimistic, but in due course radar, the proximity fuse and other inventions came near to sealing England against successful raids. How would the course of history in Britain have been changed if, during those vital nineteen-thirties, Churchill had been in a position to initiate and press scientific research?

The continual accumulation of knowledge at an ever-increasing rate means that it is now more difficult for one man to keep pace with developments in all branches of even one science, much less of all. The key men are no longer like Lord Kelvin. The "all-rounder" is highly suspect. This is the age of the expert, and the less he is expert about, the higher he is rated. Churchill would not claim to be skilled in any branch of science. But he knows how to use experts, and that quality can result in contributions as valuable in their way as are those of the originators themselves.

Using specialists does not necessarily mean accepting everything they say. There have been occasions when Churchill has flatly contradicted his advisers. In a speech some years ago he quoted Gladstone, who said, "Expert knowledge is limited knowledge," and there was his classic retort on one occasion to the specialist who had examined his throat, "I entirely disagree with your diagnosis." The expert is apt to think there is only one way to do anything and that is his way. Ten minutes' conversation with Sir Winston Churchill has sometimes provided an astonishing number of alternatives. The alternatives that have sprung fully armed from the fertile Churchill brain have not, of course, always been perfect, but at least they have always been stimulating. That is why scientists, even those with whom he has entirely disagreed, have found listening to Churchill so educative.

Sir Winston Churchill's mind ranges not only forwards but backwards. Faced with finding a solution to a problem, he likes to consider all that has been done in search for a solution in the past and his mind is astonishingly well stocked with a remarkable amount of varied knowledge, which, when the occasion arises, he supplements by demanding all the facts. And then, as Guy Eden has put it, "he will look back over it all, judging where the last lot of experiments or inquiries went wrong or were incomplete or reasoning was fallacious, suggesting a new line of examination in the light of better knowledge. This done, he will order new research, fitting bits of the old into place, until something quite new emerges." It is this combination of qualities —curiosity, imagination, great reasoning power, administrative ability—that is unusual and has enabled Churchill to play his unique part in the encouragement of scientific progress. That this progress has been mostly in the realm of military science has been due to the accident and misfortune that Churchill has had real authority only at times of national danger.

Yet it is quite fallacious to suppose that Churchill is interested in science only as it affects military matters. In his message to the International Conference of Scientists organized by the British Association in 1941, he said:

"One of our objects in fighting this war is to maintain the right of free discussion and interchange of ideas. In contrast to the intellectual darkness which is descending on Germany, the freedom that our scientists enjoy is a valuable weapon for us, for superiority in scientific development is a vital factor in the preparation of victory. . . . It will take a long time for the civilized powers to repair the trail of material and moral havoc which the Germans leave behind them. It will require all the resources of science. But I look forward to the day when the scientists of every nation can devote all their energies to the common task and I wish you every success in the work you are undertaking now."

A series of articles written by Churchill before the Second World War revealed that even if Churchill's formal scientific education ended when he passed into Sandhurst, he had continued to keep abreast of the extraordinary scientific developments that had taken place during his riper years. He described many of these developments, especially from the philosophical point of view, describing in rich but clear language the scientific principles involved and deducing their possible future effect upon mankind. Today the unleashing and harnessing of

P

atomic energy has made debates on the "moral" aspects of science a commonplace. This aspect has always interested Churchill and he has pointed out that "without an equal growth of Mercy, Pity, Peace and Love, Science herself may destroy all that makes human life majestic and tolerable. There never was a time when the hope of immortality and the disdain of earthly power and achievement were more necessary for the safety of the children of men." He expressed his innate revulsion against the possibilities of biological developments that might lead to a race of supposed "supermen".

It is clear that, far more than most scientists, he was aware of the immense implications of the advance of science in certain directions. When the time came, he gave great thought to the question of research directed towards the atom bomb, and we sense that he decided in favour of necessity and not of choice—he knew that Germany was engaged on this research and that however fearful might be the results, it was his duty to urge Britain to the race with all his power. In 1945 he was to say, "There are those who consider that the atomic bomb should never have been used at all. I cannot associate myself with such ideas." But we may suspect he would not have been disappointed if the scientists of *all* nations had failed to unlock the key to this weapon.

Sir Winston Churchill, perhaps more than any other statesman of our age, honours science and has encouraged its exponents. But he is also deeply convinced of the limitations of the technical scientist. He does not believe that because a man makes a discovery or an invention he is necessarily fitted to become a statesman or to have the last word on what should be done with the products of his labour. Particularly is he opposed to the popular notion that a world ruled by scientists would be any happier. Application of the scientific method to the art of politics —yes. But scientists, as scientists in politics—no. As he put it in 1945: "It is now suggested we should have a scientistic—not a scientific— Government. It is the duty of scientists, like all other people, to serve the state and not rule it because they are scientists." As a scientist he has himself served the state, but the many qualities that have made him so great a statesman are very different.

CHURCHILL THE MASTER OF WORDS

Ivor Brown

Ivor Brown, Editor of the Observer *from 1942 to 1948 and Associate Editor since then, has written eight books about Words, their history and meaning, their humour and beauty.*

IT is well known that Master Winston Churchill, of Harrow School, was never a ready or resourceful Latinist. "The boys learn enough Latin to detest it," he wrote in later life. For the imitation of ancient orators and poets, which in all the Public Schools was a substantial part of the "grand, old, fortifying curruculum", he had no affection. He preferred his own language and he preferred to be himself. A classical education is based largely on mimicry of old models. The pupil must try to be a semi-Cicero or a pseudo-Vergil. But the idea of Churchill, at any age, being "semi" this or "pseudo" that is ridiculous. He could recite English with fire and at length, and when he spoke of the Romans it was in Lord Macaulay's lays and not in their own tongue.

Yet in his use of words he has never been prejudiced against the shapely and sonorous terms of Latin origin. In English speech these, with their amplitude, usually supply the bulk, while the terser Anglo-Saxon element contributes the muscle. Neither speaking nor writing can live on muscle alone: there must be, on occasion, copiousness of size. Indeed, *copia*, plenty, was one of the qualities insisted on by the classical teachers of rhetoric. Sir Winston Churchill is well aware that plenty counts, and he can be cornucopious when he speaks or writes. In his fullest style he reminds one especially of Gibbon and also of the Roman orator Cicero, although presumably he never cared much about the latter in the original Latin.

I mention Cicero because that Roman pleader and politician had a peculiar trick; there was a routine ending to his weighty sentences, a recurrent tune of which the words *"esse videatur"* were typical. Pronounced with a long broad "a" in the second word, their ring is unmistakable and also stirring. Gibbon's parallel trick in English was to end a long sentence, time and time again, with an "of" clause. "Of a mighty people." "Of a Roman Empire." Reading his *Decline and Fall* one notices that he acquires a special rhythm, a special lift, that way. Churchill has always instinctively understood the value of such terminations. "To launch this cataract of horror." "New fields of slaughter, pillage, and despair." "The soft underbelly of the Axis." I say "instinctively" because poets and orators do not think out the technical devices which produce emotional effects. These effects spring out of natural genius.

It is fascinating to see how in Churchill's histories, just as much as in the speeches, this organ-music is present, and fascinating also to trace by what choice of word and by what arrangement of clauses it is achieved. This passage, for example, is not from a speech. It is from the first volume of the great history *Marlborough: His Life and Times* (Chapter IV):

> "No dreamer, however romantic, however remote his dreams from reason, could have foreseen a surely approaching day, when, by the formation of mighty coalitions and across the struggles of a generation, the noble colossus of France would lie prostrate in the dust, while the small island, beginning to gather to itself the empires of India and America, stripping France and Holland of their colonial possessions, would emerge victorious, mistress of the Mediterranean, the Narrow Seas and the Oceans. Aye, and carry forward with her, intact and enshrined, all that peculiar structure of law and liberty, all her inheritance of learning and letters, which are today the treasure of the most powerful family in the human race."

The "aye" may suggest the spoken word, though in this case it was in fact directed at the reader. But it must be remembered that this author is also, at the desk, a speaker: he dictates much and then revises; hence the oratorical cadences in his choice of vocabulary are natural. Then there is the alliteration which would cause Churchill to write "the plenitude of power" instead of using the simpler "fullness of power". Amplitude asks for plenitude and Churchill has both at his command.

The greatest writers are masters of two styles, the ample and the brief; they can vary the sonorous and rhetorical with the quiet and the poignant. Shakespeare, who became as polysyllabic as any in order to raise a hurricane, calling on

> You sulphurous and thought-executing fires,
> Vaunt-couriers to oak-cleaving thunderbolts . . .

could, in the same tragedy of *King Lear*, end on a miraculous stream of monosyllables:

> So we'll live
> And pray and sing and tell old tales and laugh
> At gilded butterflies, and hear poor rogues
> Talk of court news; and we'll talk with them too,—
> Who loses and who wins; who's in, who's out;—
> And take upon's the mystery of things,
> As if we were God's spies.

There are few authors who have not valued the power of a sudden change in vocabulary, and Churchill, both as writer and as speaker, has proved his full comprehension of this sovereign quality of varied words.

Quite early in his political career he had shown a humorous interest in the fascinations of prolixity. In 1906 he was Under-Secretary of State for the Colonies in the Liberal Government. To a question about the alleged slavery of the indentured labour of Chinese workers in South Africa he replied, "It cannot in the opinion of His Majesty's Government be classified as slavery in the extreme acceptance of the word without some risk of terminological inexactitude." "Lie" has one syllable; Churchill, with a sly humour, employed eleven. Verbosity was never more adroit.

So constantly, in reading his essays and papers as well as his speeches, we find a relish for a similar rolling music of the classical term. For example, in his Oxford University Romanes Lecture of 1930 on "Parliamentary Government and the Economic Problem", he said: "In the present period the House of Commons is engaged in digesting and assimilating a large new party founded, in theory at any rate, upon the basis of manual labour. It is a very heavy meal and the process of deglutition must take time." Who else would have chosen "deglutition"?

The dictionaries maintain that the word means swallowing, not absorption. Therefore it would have been simple to write "swallowing" instead of "deglutition". But Churchill likes an occasional Latinity of this kind, especially when the word, by its rarity, strikes hard at our attention. He does not, however, let the habit be his master: he knows that we could not "deglute" a series of deglutitions.

One of his favourites is "decrepitude". This word, sounding more impressive than "decay" and yet not so cruelly definitive in meaning, has a rich smack of age; it gives weight and dignity to any sentence in which it appears; it has the pathos, too, of a noble tree whose end the next storm may ordain. "Spain was in decrepitude," he announced in the beginning of his history of Marlborough instead of saying that a great Centre of Empire was now old and weak. In his charming little book which defends the pleasure of painting as a relief for the fatigued and the ageing he has explained, with a touch of rhetoric in his amplest style, that "Painting is a friend who makes no undue demands, excites to no exhausting pursuits, keeps faithful pace even with feeble steps, and holds her canvas as a screen between us and the envious eyes of Time or the surly advance of Decrepitude".

It is typical of the Churchillian word-usage that you always seem to hear what you read. "The surly advance of Decrepitude", with the sounding "of" clause which I previously noted as characteristic, might come across the air any evening; it is as much of the speaker as of the essayist. But he always has had that propensity for a vocal cadence to accompany the literary grace or descriptive power. You may dip anywhere into his great surveys of ancient and modern conflict and find emerging the "struggle-music", as theatre folk call the orchestral accompaniment to a stage fight or scuffle. In all that he has written of the two World Wars there is the march of verbs, the nouns go into battle, and the adjectives sound the flourish and alarm.

When the situation is more than ever critical, desperate and even tragical, he will, as Shakespeare did before him, turn back from the ample to the simple and cultivate an economy of syllables which beat, sharp, distinct and poignant, upon the listening ears and the attentive spirit. "Give us the tools and we will finish the job." What more compact or more compelling? The following passage from his speech in the House of Commons on June 4, 1940, will never be forgotten:

"We shall go on to the end, we shall fight in France, we shall fight on the seas and oceans, we shall fight with growing confidence and growing strength in the air, we shall defend our island, whatever the cost may be, we shall fight on the beaches, we shall fight on the landing grounds, we shall fight in the fields and in the streets, we shall fight in the hills; we shall never surrender."

Until the final roll of r's in "surrender" there is never a long word, and "confidence" and "surrender" are hardly to be called terminological monstrosities. Then the passage soars to its finish with a most effective change to the ampler style:

"And even if, which I do not for a moment believe, this island or a large part of it were subjugated and starving, then our Empire beyond the seas, armed and guarded by the British Fleet, would carry on the struggle, until, in God's good time, the new world, with all its power and might, steps forth to the rescue and the liberation of the old."

Once more we have the "of" clause to give pattern to the crescendo and finale.

There was a forceful curtness and wise avoidance of the voluble when, three weeks earlier, he had become Prime Minister by universal consent. It was then that he made his historic offer to the House, the offer of nothing but "blood, toil, tears, and sweat". Since that sentence, with the ordering of its nouns, is not always quoted correctly, it is perhaps worth noting that Churchill ended on the positive appeal to hard labour instead of stressing the melancholy and tear-compelling nature of the calamitous situation. That the gripping power of these short nouns was intuitively appreciated by the speaker is shown by their occurrence in the first chapter of his chronicle of the First World War, called *The World Crisis*. "Their sweat, their tears, their blood bedewed the endless plain."

The employment of a short term rendering a vivid picture is exemplified in his use of "claw them down", as applied to the activities of the R.A.F. "We have been clawing down three or four to one of our enemies," he claimed in May 1940, and I remember the effective use of this image in a later broadcast. There was a fine British film shown early in the war, *The Lion Has Wings*. Not many wings at that time, but what claws!

The English of the Bible is a natural ingredient of all great writing and of all great rhetoric in our tongue. Its strict austerity has often been notable in Churchill's praise and condemnations. For example, in one speech, after the German attack on Russia in 1941, he spoke of Hitler as "the blood-thirsty guttersnipe", which is far from the Churchillian best. Any public speaker might have said that. But when he calls Hitler quite simply, "this wicked man", how much more telling is the scriptural ring of it! When he speaks of "wickedness, enormous, panoplied, embattled", we see the plain, old ethical noun linked with one of those rows of adjectives which Churchill loves to enrol for action. Suddenly, just after that, he goes back to the Biblical: "Justice is cast from her seat."

Sir Winston Churchill, though he has worked in every kind of prose as well as enjoying his leisure with the paint-box and the easel, has never, I think, written a play. Yet drama is native to his vision of the world and to his experience of history in the making. He has lived amid huge conflicts and ridden the whirlwind. To the crash of conflict he fits his vocabulary. The contrasts that he makes are of light and darkness, not of light and shade. Good and evil are nothing but their tremendous selves: they are not qualified by the phrases which palliate crime, phrases now offered to us by modern psychology. One does not expect to find in Churchillian prose a description of Hitler as "that maladjusted man" or as "a victim carrying the traumas of juvenile frustration". He is "that wicked man", a judgment as final as it is just.

There is in Churchill a deep and genuine admiration for the ordinary man who bears the brunt while the Ruperts lead their charges. He has given to the unknown warrior, the common hero, some of his finest prose. At the close of the First World War he wrote, in tribute to the civilized man's "reserves of plain fortitude", words which were more than ever justified in the ensuing struggle of 1939–45, when the millions of non-combatants were submitted to ordeal by fire on a scale hitherto unknown. This is how he described the abiding courage of the ordinary citizen. "Again and again to the hideous bombardment, again and again from the hospital to the front, again and again to the hungry submarines, he strode unflinching. And withal, as an individual he preserved through these torments the glories of a reasonable and compassionate mind."

The use of the word "glories" is fascinating. It is unusual to apply so romantic a noun to a mental process. But to show consideration, tolerance, and mercy is not to Churchill an arid form of conduct. To use reason with sympathy is more than right; it has the quality of glory. And the rolling sound of "glory", as any student of words knows, is always victorious. "Glory of warrior, glory of orator. . . ." Tennyson's praise, ending with "the glory of going on and still to be", is especially well suited to Churchill's employment of language as well as to the great practice of his life.

CHURCHILL THE MAN OF TALENT

George Bernard Shaw

What did George Bernard Shaw think of his brilliant and talented contemporary, Winston Churchill? Some years ago I asked Shaw to write an article about Churchill in reply to the one Churchill had written about Shaw which was included in his book Great Contemporaries. *Shaw had by that time ceased writing articles but nevertheless he agreed to write this particular contribution, though he was careful to point out to me that he did not look upon it as "a professional job".*

CHURCHILL is the most brilliantly talented Minister on the Treasury Bench.

The moment we got a good fright, and had to find a man who could and would do something, we were on our knees to Winston Churchill, making him Prime Minister almost by violence, and booting out all those we had formerly preferred to him.

Mark that his talents and character were no new discovery: they were as obvious as they are now years ago, when, after a military career as distinguished as his famous ancestor had achieved at the same age, he entered Parliament when I was a youth of fifty and marked himself out for Cabinet rank from the beginning.

And then, on the verge of the scriptural three score and ten years and when he should have been in a well-earned retirement, he found himself shoved violently into the Premiership because there was a war on and the men who were preferred to him during all those years were evidently no match for a live wire of Herr Hitler's voltage.

Why were they so preferred?

Obviously, because they could be depended on to do nothing but keep the Party machine going in the House of Commons.

Nothing terrifies us so much as a threat of any sort of upset in our arrangements or any increase in Government interferences with us.

That terror was at its height after the 1918 Armistice.

Young men of action, with that up-to-date knowledge of the modern world which is carefully excluded from the curricula of our Public Schools, and replaced by a fool's paradise based on the feudal system of 1066 with adulterations from 1484, 1649, and 1832, were upsetting capitalist prosperity all over Europe.

The Kaiser, Lenin, Ataturk, Reza Khan, Mussolini and Hitler were kicking parliaments into the gutter and making the revolutionary social changes attributed to God in the Magnificat.

Our hearts were bursting with our desire for rulers who could be depended on to do nothing but call for their pipes and call for their pots and call for their fiddlers three.

When it was found that the ex-revolutionary Socialist Ramsay Mac-Donald had finally given up international Socialism for the Treasury Bench at Westminster, and that nevertheless he had the disturbing Labour Movement still in his pocket, his former intransigence was forgotten, he became Prime Minister of the Conservative and Labour Parties alike.

His only rivals were Stanley Baldwin and the Chamberlains, who were equally "safe".

Had it not been for the resumption of the war, Churchill would not have had a dog's chance of crowning his parliamentary career as Prime Minister; for he had always been suspected of wanting to do something; and he was known to be capable of crossing the floor of the House on the merits of a parliamentary measure instead of invariably voting on the one question that is ever before the House in one disguise or another: to wit, whether the Party Government is to remain in power or to be ousted by the Opposition.

Even now, when we dare not in the face of the new Napoleons go on with Right Honourable Do-Nothings, we take care to balance him in the Cabinet with reactionary forces strong enough to keep his Tory Democracy active in its Toryism and paralysed in its Democracy.

What I want Churchill to tell us is whether if he had his life to live over again he would waste it in the British House of Commons as it has been wasted by the Party System.

He could have done far more as Mayor of one of the provincial cities, where there are Parties but no Party System.

His real career has been as a soldier and an author.

His recreations are civilized: painting and bricklaying, not hunting and shooting.

There was a time when I was invited to contest parliamentary seats which I could not possibly win.

I should not have accepted even if the seats had been safe for me. It was better to be "The Amazing Shaw" than to put my head under the Westminster extinguisher.

Was I not right, O Winston?

CHURCHILL AND RACING

Geoffrey Gilbey

Geoffrey Gilbey has been one of Britain's leading writers on horse-racing for thirty-three years. Besides being a regular contributor to the National Press and the author of several books about racing, he was a member of the deputation which tried to persuade Churchill, then Chancellor of the Exchequer, to put a tax on betting. Geoffrey Gilbey broadcast the B.B.C.'s first running commentaries on the Derby and the St. Leger in 1927.

Q

S IR WINSTON CHURCHILL'S interest in racing did not develop until very late in his life. It is more than twenty-five years ago since I sat in a room with him for the express purpose of discussing the sport and the strong impression I received was that he was not in the least interested in racing, except as a possible means to an end.

At that time he was Chancellor of the Exchequer and I was a member of the deputation which was suggesting to him that it would benefit the country, and also benefit racing, if a betting tax was imposed. He received the distinguished members of the deputation— and those of us who were undistinguished—with great courtesy, but he seemed anxious to impress on us that it was very doubtful whether he would adopt the suggestion.

It was the first time I had been close enough to study the distinguished politician. Nowadays, thanks to pictures and television, we know Sir Winston intimately. As I watched him I felt certain that, in spite of what he was saying, it was long odds on his trying out the tax.

As most of us remember, the tax was tried out in 1926 and it failed. The reason why I personally was so in favour of it was because I have always longed to see betting legalized, and I imagined the powers that be could not tax anything which was not legal.

My next meeting with him was of a very different sort. It was not such a personal meeting as the first one, when, as far as I can remember, I was one of a dozen, but it was a much happier occasion. In the second meeting I was one of hundreds who, at Ascot on Thursday, September 22, 1949, flocked to the unsaddling enclosure at four minutes past five, to cheer him and Colonist II after the grey three-year-old had cantered home to win the Ribblesdale Stakes by eight lengths. It was not the first victory of Colonist II. He had won at Salisbury in August and at Windsor earlier in September, but in both

467

these races he had not had much to beat. His distinguished owner did not see his first victory because he was in the South of France suffering from a chill, but his son, Randolph, telephoned the news of the victory and he chuckled over the 'phone and said: "That news has cheered me up no end. I feel a lot better already." He was back in England in time to see his second victory, at Windsor, and there for the first time in his life he entered the weighing room and saw the successful rider weigh in, saying to a friend, "This is something new for me."

It is inevitable in dealing with Sir Winston's interest in racing that much of what one writes must necessarily concern Colonist II—a great and courageous animal; and, as I shall explain later, there are certain similarities between the horse and the owner.

It is remarkable in racing that there are always crowds of people who take a delight in running down a horse. When I said, "He seems to have a pretty good colt," there were many who replied: "He has beaten nothing. You wait until he meets anything that can go." Before he won that Ascot race these critics were quite sure that Colonist II had no chance of beating a useful colt called Sardonyx II ridden by the champion jockey, Gordon Richards. I happened to watch the race between two of my colleagues who had been running down Colonist II. When the colt had a good lead at half-way and seemed to be going easily, they said, "You wait, he'll come back to them." There have been races when I have been so excited that I have taken down my glasses, being unable to watch. This was one of them. As Colonist II came into the straight I was very frightened that Gordon Richards might be able to overhaul him. Gordon got to work, but Hawcroft, on Colonist II, called for an extra effort and he left Sardonyx II standing still. I have often heard cheering start when a horse, which the public has longed to see win, draws out to the front, and there have also been many times when I have heard the cheering turn to groans as the leader has been overhauled. But this was not one of them. Colonist II drew further and further away to win with his ears pricked. I ran, with many others, to the unsaddling enclosure to greet the return of the colt who had scored the most popular victory I had ever seen on any racecourse. As we all cheered and congratulated his owner, it really seemed too good to be true that Churchill's first race-horse should be a champion. There was obviously

CHURCHILL AND RACING

Churchill and his most famous racehorse, Colonist II

nothing fluky about his Ascot race; he had won in the style of a brilliant colt. Even those who had run him down had to admit that he was better than they had thought.

So thrilled were many members of the racing public with the new owner's successful entry into the sport that they went to Lingfield on the following Thursday for the sole purpose of being there to cheer Colonist II in the Tonbridge Plate. I expected to see him win by twenty lengths. It was a shock and a general disappointment when he went very wide coming into the straight and his jockey had difficulty in preventing him from running out altogether. Even then we thought he would have no trouble in overhauling the leader. He either couldn't or wouldn't and was well beaten. It was a semi-political joke at the time that even Churchill's horse would not turn *Left*. After the race there were stories told of how Colonist II had gone mad on Epsom Downs. There were many who were quite certain that he would never win another race, and when he lost his next two races we Churchill supporters very reluctantly had to admit that Colonist II was not the horse we thought he was.

The general public was most interested in Churchill's racing enterprise, and it is not surprising that much was written and published about Colonist II during the winter months. I hope Sir Winston did not read one writer who went so far as to say that one of the few certainties in racing was that Colonist II would never win another race.

I was reminded of that prediction in 1950 when Colonist II was going from victory to victory and my thoughts also went back to a book I had once read. I will not mention the name of the book or the author—any more than I would mention the name of the journalist who was so certain that Colonist II would never win again—but I recall that on page 170 of the book there was a reference to Churchill in these words: "The only thing he is unable to command—and never will—is confidence. . . . It is precisely this Parliamentary and public attitude to Winston which convinces me that, whatever changes this nation may see, there can never again be a high place in the State for this most distinguished statesman." The unfavourable predictions relating both to Churchill and Colonist II were certainly as wide of the mark as they could possibly have been.

After two defeats at the start of the 1950 season, Colonist II won easily at Kempton and again at Hurst Park, but when he finished fourth in the Gold Cup at Ascot once again his detractors got to work and said we should not see him in the winners' enclosure again that year.

However, the horse had six more races that season and we saw him in the winners' enclosure every time. In every one of those six races Colonist II gave racegoers a magnificent thrill.

And now about the "Churchill receptions". My colleagues on the racing Press are not usually given to gross exaggeration, but the one exception is when they write that some horse, when he came back to the unsaddling enclosure, got a "great reception". The "great reception" in fact usually consists of not more than a dozen people clapping rather half-heartedly. When King George VI won a race everyone was delighted, but when the horse was led in, the reception was what might be called a dignified one. Hats were raised and one saw the great affection everyone had for their King. On July 14, 1950, the race before the Eclipse Stakes at Sandown was won by the King's two-year-old Norwester. The usual dignified reception was given. The race after the Eclipse was won in gallant style by Colonist II. The public went mad with excitement and Colonist II and Churchill got a terrific reception. By this time everyone had to admit that we had never seen a gamer colt.

At the end of the season Churchill was shown in the list of winning owners as having won nine races, value £7,447, with two horses. Colonist II had won all of that amount except £241 8s., won by a two-year-old, Canyon Kid, a horse which he subsequently had the misfortune to lose.

Colonist II's last appearance on a racecourse was in the Bentinck Stakes at Goodwood in 1951. Unfortunately he lost a plate in this race and, gamely as he tried, he was third.

Colonist II won thirteen races with prize money totalling £13,000 and he was then sold. Many people were surprised when they heard he was going to be sold, but men ten or more years younger than Sir Winston have told me that much as they would have liked to own a stud they have felt they were much too late in life to do so. Probably he felt the same way. Colonist II was bought by Captain P. G. A. Harvey. We shall all look forward to seeing his stock running on our racecourses and we hope they will follow in father's footsteps. Churchill joined the Thoroughbred Breeders Association in his first year as an owner and in the following year he was elected a member of the Jockey Club.

From what I have written it must not be thought that Sir Winston Churchill's interest in racing was confined to one horse. He takes the greatest interest in all his horses, and considering the comparatively few horses he has had, he has been wonderfully successful. When we look at the small book *Horses In Training* at the end of a season we see that the percentage of horses listed as winners of even one race is small. In 1952 Sir Winston had five horses in training and won a race with all five of them. They were Pol Roger, Loving Cup, Non-Stop, Gibraltar III and Prince Arthur, all trained by Walter Nightingall.

Those of us who, much as we like flat racing, love the sport under National Hunt rules even more, were delighted when we heard that the Prime Minister's horses were to be seen out in hurdle races. Saturday, November 29, 1952, was one of the most miserably cold and unpleasant days on which I have ever been racing. During the afternoon my brother remarked to me, "Anyone who has come here today and didn't *have* to be here, ought to have his head examined." Before the last race of the day I was told that Churchill's Non-Stop had shaped well over hurdles at Epsom and was thought to have a great chance of winning here. I said, "What a pity he is not here to see him run," and, in view of the weather, I was amazed when I was told that the Prime Minister was in fact present. This indeed confirmed the words of Walter Nightingall when he told me that Churchill has the greatest affection for all his horses. If the weather was good enough for one of his horses to run and jump hurdles, it was good enough for Churchill to go and see him do it. Non-Stop ran a good race but could only finish second.

On Boxing Day in the following month Pol Roger, a three-year-old by Rienzo, the sire of Colonist II, won the first jump race for a Prime Minister in the history of racing. Fortunately he was there to see it and the National Hunt crowd showed him that his popularity with them was just as great as with the flat-racing followers.

I have left until now the one question which I have not seen answered before, but which is the question almost anyone would ask first in connection with Sir Winston Churchill and racing. It is, of course, "What caused Churchill to become a racehorse owner so late in life when he had previously shown such small interest in the sport?" Like so many other things in life his latest enterprise had a small beginning. On January 12, 1948, a mare twenty years old, by Peter Pan, was knocked down to the bid of Mr. S. Marsh for forty guineas. She had been bought for Churchill's son-in-law, Captain Soames. She was sent to Sir Winston's Chartwell Farm. In 1949 she foaled a bay filly foal by Holywell, called Loving Cup. Churchill took such a fancy to this foal that he decided to have a mare of his own. So Captain Soames bought him Poetic, from the late Mr. James V. Rank, and a filly foal by Vigorous out of Gallant Girl, which was later named Moll Flanders. Some months later the veterinary surgeon, Major Carey Foster, bought Colonist II in France for Walter Nightingall, who passed him on to Churchill, and that started his serious interest in the sport.

It is curious that Sir Winston Churchill did not take a personal interest in racing much earlier in life, because his father, Lord Randolph Churchill, owned horses in partnership with the Earl of Dunraven in the 'eighties of last century. When Churchill took to the sport he registered his father's old colours—chocolate, pink sleeves and cap—as his own, but he had to change them to avoid a clash with the colours of the Newmarket trainer, J. L. Jarvis, and switched to pink, chocolate sleeves and cap.

Many years ago I was told that dogs get like their owners. It would appear that some horses can also do so. If we were asked for the name of the most courageous Englishman of all time, many of us would say without a moment's hesitation—Winston Churchill. If the racing public were asked for the name of the most courageous horse of all time, there would be a great many who would also say without hesitation—Colonist II. Walter Nightingall's training of the horse will go down in racing history as a most brilliant performance. We must also not forget Tommy Gosling, Colonist II's partner in most of his triumphs. Gosling has always been a good jockey, but when riding in Churchill's colours he seemed to be inspired. The Prime Minister has never interfered with his trainer and jockey in the handling of his horses. Gosling once declared that Sir Winston really understands horses and is a good judge of form but gives both trainer and jockey a free hand. Every lover of racing in this country hopes that his colours will be first past the post many times under both rules for many years to come. A racing crowd loves the chance to shout, "Good old Winnie!"

CHURCHILL THE PHILOSOPHER

Dr. C. E. M. Joad

Can Sir Winston Churchill, supreme man of action as he surely is, also be regarded as a philosopher? His writings and speeches leave no doubt about it. In this chapter, the late Dr. C. E. M. Joad, Head of the Department of Philosophy, Birkbeck College, University of London, from 1930 until his death this year, discusses Churchill's philosophy of life as revealed in his published works, and points to his strange contrasts of pessimism and hope.

During the War, Dr. Joad achieved remarkable fame as a member of the radio feature "The Brains Trust", and few speakers on the wireless have ever equalled the interest he won at that time with millions of listeners. As an author, newspaper columnist, farmer, sportsman and traveller, Dr. Joad experienced a full and varied life, but it was as a writer and lecturer on philosophy that he made his greatest reputation and became one of the most provocative personalities of the day.

THERE are two senses in which a man can be said to be a philosopher. There is the strict sense, the sense in which a philosopher is one who makes it his business to enquire into the nature of this puzzling universe in which our lives are set, with a view to throwing light in the course of his enquiry on the status and purpose of human life. Is the universe a dance of material particles and human life a by-product of their collision, a merely temporary passenger travelling across an alien and brutal environment? If so, the whole scheme of space and time is a bad joke beyond our understanding, an empty laugh braying across the centuries.

Or has the familiar world in which we live and move a meaning in the sense that it was created for a purpose? If so, reality must consist of a mind, a mind which created and planned, which means that there lies at the heart of things something akin to ourselves. These are the sort of questions to which philosophers in all ages have devoted their attention; they belong to philosophy proper.

The word "philosopher" is also used in a looser sense, the sense in which a man who has touched life at many points may comment at large upon men and things, distilling in aphorisms and epigrams, in maxims and exhortations, the ripe fruits of his mellow experience. The philosopher so conceived is akin to the sage or wise man of the East; experience has ripened in him a faculty of insight which enables him to see farther into things than his fellows, and to embody what he has seen in pregnant observations. In this rôle the philosopher is the dispenser of wisdom crystallized in memorable thoughts and sayings on a vast variety of topics of eternal interest—on money, God, love, marriage, desire, death, ambition, chance—a wisdom which in the great majority of cases springs from and is informed by the philosopher's general view of the nature of the universe as a whole.

Plato and Aristotle were philosophers in both senses; Descartes and Kant and Locke in the first; while King Solomon, Samuel Johnson, Goethe, Lincoln and Winston Churchill belong predominantly in the second. Philosophers of this second group must not only formulate their philosophy but practise and apply it in public. But then for all of us, philosophers or not, life is like that; it is as if one were giving a public performance on the violin when one has to learn to play the instrument as one goes along.

Churchill, indeed, does not at first sight belong to any type of philosophic man. He is to all appearances the supreme extrovert; his gaze has almost from the first been determinedly focused upon external things—"From the beginning of 1895," he writes in 1929, "down to the present time of writing I have never had time to turn round. I could almost count on my fingers the days when I have had nothing to do"—and these external things, in his case, have been so engrossing—affairs, as he would put it, of "so great a moment"—that whenever he has felt disposed to interest himself in the universe, or indeed the self, and turned in upon himself to report what he finds there, they have taken him up, as it were, by the scruff of the neck— if I may use so disrespectful a metaphor of so formidable a man; yet it exactly represents what seems to me to have happened—and insisted on his immersing himself in *them*. In a word, he has been far too busy talking, and talking to some purpose, to stop to listen; too preoccupied with thinking to have time to stop to think.

That is on the first view of him. But further investigation reveals, scattered up and down his speeches and his writings, many incursions into philosophy in its looser sense. Churchill is, among other things, a man of exceptional intelligence; he has had unexampled opportunities for studying men and affairs, and it goes without saying that whatever he has to tell us about life will be extremely well worth listening to.

Reading the books, studying the speeches, it seems to me that one can discern two different and, at times, incompatible strands in his thinking. The first is realistic—here is a man who strips away pretences and faces hard facts; pessimistic—he expects the worst and holds himself in constant preparation to meet it; cynical—detecting the hidden motives which are the springs of human action, he rates them low, and fatalistic—in that he sees human beings as puppets twitched into love or war by some invisible showman who pulls the strings, without the freedom to alter the course which chance or destiny has mapped for them.

Secondly, there is the man of action, sanguine and optimistic, confident in his power to meet and overcome circumstances, however untoward, and sustained by a strong spiritual conviction of the rightness of his cause. He is much given to hope and convinced that in the end the right will triumph. I think that the second point of view more nearly represents the man, but before we come to it, let me glance in some little detail at the first.

In the Preface to a volume entitled *Thoughts and Adventures*, a series of essays published in 1932, Churchill speaks of the two alternative "Infernos"—the word is his own—which may await mankind, the Inferno of destruction in modern war and the Inferno of Robotization, a condition in which man loses his birthright of human freedom and surrenders the ordering of his life to a government of scientists and planners. These alternatives are developed at length in two essays entitled respectively *Shall We Commit Suicide?* and *Fifty Years Hence*.

In the past, Churchill points out, man's destructive power was extremely limited. With the best will in the world to destroy his fellow men he was too feeble to achieve much success; but now for the first time science has given him the wherewithal to accomplish his own destruction. Now science is in itself neither a good thing nor a bad, it is ethically neutral; what it does is to enable men to satisfy their desires and to further their purposes. If their desires and purposes are on the whole good and make for human welfare, this added power of satisfaction, this increased ability to further, are also good; but if not, not.

Looking at human history as a whole, how is it possible to regard men's desires as collectively expressed in the policies of States as being good and making for human welfare? Is not Gibbon rather right when he describes history as a record of the crimes, follies and misfortunes of mankind? Hence the supreme importance, which is at the same time the supreme danger, of the age in which we live. "It is this power called Science," Churchill writes, "which has laid hold of us, conscripted us into its regiments and batteries, set us to work upon its highways and in its arsenals. . . . None of the generations of men before the last two or three were ever gripped for good and ill and handled like this." Man, in short, may well use science to destroy himself. Nor will his end be noble, for the qualities of valour, discipline and endurance which wars have called forth in the fighting men of the past will be of no avail when the weapons of science have reached their full development. Of what avail are strength of arm and fleetness of foot, what is the courage that never falters, what the determination to fight on when all seems lost, in the face of the hydrogen bomb? Contemporary science, in fact, is advancing along a corridor at the far end of which sits a blind, deaf and dumb cripple who, inspired by malignity, can, by pressing a button, encompass the destruction of a whole army corps of young, vigorous men, not to speak of the teeming populations of our great cities. As Churchill puts it in one of his memorable phrases, "The liberties of men are no longer to be guarded by their natural abilities, but by their dodges; and superior virtue and valour may fall an easy prey to the latest diabolical trick."

The same realism, the same pessimism, are evoked in Churchill's forecast of the possible future of man at peace. Following the thought of Karel Kapek's play *Rossum's Universal Robots* and anticipating Huxley's *Ape and Essence* and Orwell's *1984*, Churchill envisages the coming of a race of automata. A course of treatment which begins with the embryo, proceeds through the manipulation of the brain of the infant, and continues with the unremitting psychological conditioning of the child's responses, may well produce a race which is all brawn and no brain, or a race of docile, sheep-like creatures, or a race in whom the sentiment of loyalty overshadows all the rest—a race which, whatever the situation, can be trusted to do the dull and drudging work of the community and never on any occasion or for any reason to criticize the Government. "Our minds," as Churchill rightly comments, "recoil from such fearful eventualities." They do, indeed. Whatever may be man's ultimate destiny on this planet, he cannot, one feels, be fated to be transformed into a well-behaved automaton. Yet if the present disparity between the power of man and his intelligence, between the ever-increasing force of his weapons and his presumably stationary nobility, continues and grows more marked, it is difficult to see how one or other of these two eventualities, destruction in war or robotization in peace, can be avoided.

Nor let it be supposed—and here it is that the pessimism turns sour and the cynic speaks—that the time-honoured safeguards of the freedom and integrity of man will avail to prevent this development.

Democracy? There is in general no more stalwart champion of democratic institutions than Churchill, who, besides extolling democracy in a hundred speeches, has shown himself to be one of the greatest "House of Commons men" in practice. Nevertheless, when he is surveying our parliamentary institutions in the light of the impact of science upon human affairs, he sees how impotent they are to avert the development at which we have briefly glanced.

Democracies do not, he tells us—he is writing in the early 'thirties —confer power upon their ablest men, "or those who know most about their immediate affairs or even those who have a coherent doctrine". Democracies tend to take the line of least resistance and to approve and appoint those who promise the people easy things in "pleasant-sounding platitudes". The conclusion, that the system of universal suffrage results not so much in the election of the best but in that of the average man, has been urged in its disfavour by the critics of democracy in all ages, and is no doubt in part true. But the answer to it is not far to seek. It is that only the wearer knows where the shoe pinches, which, being applied, means that those who have to obey the laws should in the last resort be those who make them, a result which is most likely to be achieved if Parliament consists very largely of average men, precisely because average men tend to be representative men. Much of Churchill's own power has derived from the fact that when the crisis came he, too, turned out to be the average Englishman, but the average Englishman raised to the nth degree, with the result that he knew just how far the average Englishman was prepared to go in resistance to the Nazis, just how much he was prepared to risk and sacrifice. It was precisely this capacity for representing his countrymen that enabled him to touch their hearts and minds to high endeavour in the great speeches of the war: "It is not given to the cleverest and the most calculating of mortals to know with certainty what is their interest, yet it is given to quite a lot of simple folk to know every day what is their duty." Who, but an Englishman speaking to his fellow countrymen, could have hit their mood so surely as that? The democratic system, though at best a second best, is nevertheless better than any alternative system under which a group of self-appointed experts cut the legislative clothes of the community by some standard of assumed perfection, with the consequence of making all citizens uncomfortable and, if they are English citizens, insisting that an end be put to their discomfort.

But what of religion as a means of saving man from Robotization? In the essay *Shall We Commit Suicide?* Churchill treats religion not as the channel of man's communication with another order of reality, but as a form of institution within a society designed to justify that society's proceedings to its members. Thus of the Christian religion in its bearing upon the war of 1914–18 he writes, "Religion, having discreetly avoided conflict on the fundamental issues, offered its encouragement and consolations through all its forms impartially to all the combatants."

There is nothing in religion so conceived to save men from self-destruction through science.

But science, after all, is not only a destroyer; it is also a healer. It has relieved man's pain, eased his discomfort, lengthened his life. . . . Yes, but in war-time science restores broken bodies only in order that they may be offered a second time as sacrifices to the god of war. Reflect for a moment on the cynicism of "Healing and surgery, in their exquisite developments, returned them again and again to the shambles. Nothing was wasted that could contribute to the process of waste. The last dying kick was brought into military utility." Here, surely, we plumb the very depths of bitterness.

This brings me to what is, perhaps, the most disquieting of all the speculations with which Churchill's philosophy of man and his future is enriched—his insistence on the rôle of chance in human affairs.

In one of the most intriguing of his essays, entitled *A Second Choice*, Churchill considers whether he would like to live his life again and how far, if he were given the chance of doing so, it would be different from his life as actually lived. He begins by stressing our subservience to chance. Over and over again, looking back over his life, he notes how his successes were the result of miscalculation, while many of what appeared at the time to be his wisest decisions, had they been acted upon, would have meant disaster. He instances tobacco. His father wanted him to give it up, but he did not give it up. I give his comment in his own words: "How can I tell that my temper would have been as sweet or my companionship as agreeable, if I had abjured from my youth the goddess Nicotine?" But this is not all; he leaves his match-box in a dug-out in Flanders in the First World War and goes back for it. While he does so a shell bursts in the precise spot where he would have been had he not gone back for the matches. Instance after instance is given of the extent to which what happens to us in life is determined not by us but for us. This train of thought leads on to the question, how different would Churchill's life have been if at a comparatively late age he were taken back to his twenties and given one choice to make again. He deals with this very acutely, pointing out that the question is an improper one, since either (1) one goes back to one's twenties bringing with one the knowledge of all the events which have occurred since, together with such wisdom as one may have acquired, in which case, of course, one wouldn't be the same man—or (2) one goes back without memory of any of the events that have taken place in the succeeding years, in which event, of course, being precisely the same man as one was at twenty, one would have acted in precisely the same way.

But the first contingency brings another complication. Foreknowledge of the future based on past remembrance involves not only that the man in his twenties is a changed man, but also that the world in which he has to act is a changed world. For consider—I give Churchill's own example—on returning to his twenties he uses his foreknowledge to back the winner of the Derby; in point of fact, he backs him with such an enormous stake that several important bookmakers default, while one or two people heavily engaged in the fortunes of losing horses commit suicide. When therefore the Derby came to be run in the next year it would be run in different circumstances, perhaps with different horses, different betting expectations and different odds from what would have been had the Derby winner of the preceding year not been heavily backed as the result of Churchill's foreknowledge. Thus, in a year's time the world would already be different from what it was because of this one decision of Churchill's based upon knowledge abnormally obtained. As time went on the difference between the world as it actually was and the world as, in the circumstances supposed, it would have been, grows greater until the continually diverging train of circumstances begins in the end to affect Churchill's own immediate environment. Hence, given foreknowledge, not only would the young man of twenty be a different young man, but the world in which he lived and moved would be a different world.

I draw two conclusions. First, in any event chance rules. Secondly, this seems a strange conclusion for a man of Churchill's calibre to adopt. Indeed, it is perhaps because in the light of it that he ends his paper on the pessimistic note which I give in his own words: "When I survey, in the light of these reflections, the scene of my past life as a whole, I have no doubt that I do not wish to live it over again"—not even, apparently, if he *were* given the second choice.

I have summarized this argument not only because of the agreeable piece of philosophizing in which Churchill can, it shows, indulge if he feels so minded, as because it brings me to the question—Is this which I have called the realistic, pessimistic, cynical strand in Churchill's thinking the main one? Does it really represent the man as a whole? And here the answer must, I think, be decisively in the negative.

It is important in this connection to emphasize the *period* during which the book from which I have taken most of the foregoing was written. Published in 1932, it was compiled when Churchill was not only out of office but had, so far as any reasonable calculation went, very little chance of again holding office.

"Great nations," as he himself had put it in his bitter comment on democracy, "are no longer led by their ablest men"—at least they are not in quiet times. But it is hard not to believe that, had the paragraphs from which I have quoted been written ten years later, they would not have read very differently, and that so far from representing man as a mere puppet of circumstance, Churchill would have insisted on the contrary view, which is so much more in consonance with his own life and character, that man can, at least within limits, control circumstances.

For it is Churchill himself who has written—and here we pass to what I take to be the strain in his philosophy that essentially represents the man: "We have always to be on our guard against being thrown off our true course by chance and circumstance; and the glory of human nature lies in our seeming capacity to exercise conscious control of our own destiny." Now *that* is the philosophy of a man of action, of a man, moreover, whose true worth is shown in adversity, always provided that the adversity is not one which leaves him helpless but permits him to exhibit "the glory of human nature" by pulling out every stop of faculty and talent in his personality for the purpose of facing and, if so it may be, of overcoming circumstance.

Churchill, indeed, would make a shocking prisoner. Speaking of his short period of captivity in the Boer War, he tells us how he "hated every minute" of it "more than I have ever hated any other period in my whole life", and goes on to remark how the abiding memory of it led him, when Home Secretary, to try to introduce some mitigation in the awful monotony of the prisoner's lot, as he reflects that "a death sentence" may be "more merciful than a life sentence". It will be seen, then, that the proviso that Churchill should be able to be active in the meeting and overcoming of circumstance is essential. Given that proviso, of what sort are the reports that one has received so unanimously from those who were in contact with him, however briefly, during the War, that pieced together they bring to the eye of the imagination the picture of the man?

The hypothetical visitor, we will suppose, is ushered into the presence to find Churchill in a blaze of activity exerted in a situation apparently bordering on despair. From every side come reports of discouragement or disaster. That the ship of State escapes shipwreck from moment to moment is a miracle; that she should *finally* escape from the perils that beset her and come safely to port seems wholly beyond belief. Churchill is in his most ruthlessly realist mood; he shows no disposition to make light of the situation or to pass off ugly things with easy words. No man more conscious than he of the "grievous perils"—it is so likely that they would be his very words— by which the country is beset. But in and with all this he contrives to convey something else—that bad as things may be, he has yet the resources to match them, so that as long as he is there, an embodied will to face and deal with circumstance, circumstance, though it may be dangerous, can never be disastrous. Yet the contest is one that calls out every ounce of his resources of energy, intellect and will, so that observing him you could say, here is a man living out to the very widest extent of the full scope of his being; and if Aristotle is right, as

I think he is, in holding that happiness is to be found in the being used so utterly and completely in the service of a cause or an ideal which one deems worth while, that one has neither leisure nor disposition to wonder whether one is happy or not, then Churchill might, in those War years, have been accounted a happy man, because he was living a life that matched his philosophy.

Indeed, he has said so.

I have a theory that there are certain specific periods of our lives when we are at our best, in the sense of releasing most fully and distinctively the characteristics which distinguish our personalities—but that these periods vary from person to person. Some of us are at our best as young men, some in early middle age, some, late maturers, in late middle age, while others are at their most successful as old men. It is only as old men, so to say, that they really come into their own. Now Churchill I think of as a man whose true *floruit* was in his twenties. Whether these were the years in which he touched his best I have not the knowledge to enable me to say, but they were certainly the years when he most wholeheartedly enjoyed himself. "When I look back," he writes, "upon the years 1895 to 1900"—he was twenty-one in 1895—"I cannot but return thanks to the high gods for the gift of existence. All the days were good and each day better than the other."

"What a thing to say!" I hear somebody muttering under his breath. "Surely he must have touched wood when he said it, or made some gesture to appease the animosity of the jealous gods." My own voice has no part in such mutterings—for indeed I could say the same of myself at that age. But in Churchill's case there has been something else, a something in virtue of which he seems to break all the rules.

In the passage to which I have referred—it occurs in a book *My Early Life*, written in the late nineteen-twenties—he proceeds to make an eloquent appeal to other young men. "Come on now, all you young men, all over the world," he says to them. "Twenty to twenty-five! These are the years! Don't be content with things as they are. 'The earth is yours and the fullness thereof.'" Churchill proceeds to bid them take up their responsibilities, enter "life's fighting line", above all live out to the full scope of every side of their natures and being and enjoy themselves—enjoy themselves as he did, enjoy themselves as I, too, did. And a good philosophy it is—at any rate for a young man it is.

But—and here we come to the Churchill peculiarity—by some magic he has managed to retain precisely this outlook and zest of the young man throughout a long life; not always, of course—there have been periods and moods of discouragement and bitterness which have found expression in passages like those quoted earlier in this chapter —but for longer, far more continuously than most of us, as if there were in him some spring of ever-renewed vitality such as, for most of us, flows only in youth, a spring from which he perpetually recruits his energies and powers. Now it is in this extraordinary and continuous zest and energy for living as in a man continuously young that the outstanding Churchillian characteristics seems to me to consist. He breaks all the rules—smokes interminably, drinks, sits up late, won't go to bed—but still the vitality persists. It is as if his special excellence as a young man had extended itself to grace his life as a whole, so that after seventy-nine years I believe that he could still be found to say, as he did of his twenty-first, "When I look back upon them, I cannot but return my sincere thanks to the high gods for the gift of existence." Now this continued zest for living seems to me the essence of Churchillian philosophy. On reflection one cannot help but see that it is precisely the philosophy you would expect, for it is the philosophy *par excellence* of the man of action.

The Summing-up
CHURCHILL'S PLACE IN HISTORY

A. L. Rowse

In this final chapter, A. L. Rowse, Fellow of All Souls College, Oxford, and one of Britain's most distinguished historians, discusses the place Sir Winston Churchill will come to occupy in world history.

Mr. Rowse is a leading authority on the Elizabethan Age with his books The England of Elizabeth, Sir Richard Grenville of the "Revenge" *and* The English Spirit. *It is appropriate that this historian should pay tribute to the most Elizabethan of contemporary figures.*

NEARLY half a century ago, an able journalist, A. G. Gardiner, made a most interesting prognosis of the personality and career of the young Churchill then in his early thirties. "His future," Gardiner wrote, "is the most interesting problem of personal speculation in English politics." He singled out courage as the key to his character: courage first and foremost, but with strategic insight coming second. Then "he is a personal force and not a party instrument, and he will never be easily controlled except by himself". Generosity, candour, openness of mind come next: "he has no reserves and no shams. . . . He has that scorn of concealment that belongs to a caste which never doubts itself and to a personality that is entirely fearless. . . . More than any man of his time, he approaches an issue without mental reserves or the restraints of party caution or calculation. To his imperious spirit, a party is only an instrument." And then, as to the future: "the passion for humanity, the stern resolve to see justice done though the heavens fall and he be buried in the ruins, the surrender of himself to the cause—these things have yet to come. . . . Then it will be seen how far courage and intellectual address, a mind acutely responsive to noble impulses, and a quick and apprehensive political instinct will carry him in the leadership of men."

I quote that not only to show that journalists are not always wrong, but as a penetrating and just estimate of the young politician, remarkably suggestive and prescient as to the statesman he was to become. We have indeed seen, in a measure that neither A. G. Gardiner nor even Churchill himself can have dreamed of, where courage, intellectual ability, noble impulses have taken him and in what inconceivable circumstances. "Any private ambitions I may have cherished in my younger days," said Churchill in his Fulton speech after the war, "have been satisfied beyond my wildest dreams." The difficulty of attempting an estimate of his career and placing it in historical perspective is to be just without at the same time appearing to exaggerate; for it is indeed almost fabulous in its range and variety, in richness and fertility, in touching and affecting English life at so many points—starting as soldier and journalist, going on to become politician, orator, writer, painter, historian, statesman, and with such variety of experience in public life beginning with the Boer War, social insurance, the Admiralty, the war of 1914–18, the Colonies, the Irish Treaty, the Treasury, Prime Minister in the greatest war in our history, leader of Western opinion in the conflict between East and West in the post-war years, symbol of the unity of the English-speaking world in the dangers to come. And then there is the significance of it all historically: impossible to do full justice to it in brief.

But I think I shall not exaggerate when I say that it is a career going beyond the conventional bounds of "great statesmen", transcending the ordinary categories, that it is in its extent and range unique. Everyone will agree that Winston Churchill is among the greatest Englishmen known to history. Only one figure in the past offers a parallel to Churchill in the double capacity for action and writing it too: Clarendon, a greater writer but a less important career. The early kings had a deeper influence in shaping the English State—naturally they had an advantage in its formative phase: such men as the mighty Conqueror, or Henry II, or Edward I; or Henry VIII and Thomas Cromwell in laying the foundations of the modern State. Oliver Cromwell had a more shattering immediate impact, though his military dictatorship died with him and left nothing behind—except a distaste for the rule of saints.

Among modern statesmen, since the English State achieved maturity, the elder Pitt comes nearest in the essential nature of his achievement: the architect and director of the coalition in the struggle with France for North America and India, whose victory raised this country to the most dazzling (and dangerous) heights it ever achieved, with all North America within the Empire. That was too overwhelming to last. But Pitt was in possession of full power for only five years, 1756–61; most of his life he was out of power, and sometimes not in full possession of his faculties: with him genius was closely allied to madness. Nothing is more obvious about Winston Churchill's

genius than its profound sanity, soundly anchored in the common
sense and common experience, the good humour and fund of enjoyment, of normal humanity. Nothing could be more different from the
lofty remoteness, the arrogance, the stress and strain upon the spirit of
the "Great Commoner"—no one was less common than he. But there
are some qualities they share: imperiousness, a courage beyond
anything, a strategic eye and an overriding sense of responsibility for
the well-being of the State as such. "I know that I can save my country,
and that nobody else can," said Pitt amid the defeats of 1756. *There*
is the recognizable spirit. Of the shattering events of 1940 his distant
kinsman, taking over supreme responsibility, says:

> "As I went to bed at about 3 a.m., I was conscious of a profound
> sense of relief. At last I had authority to give directions over the
> whole scene. I felt as if I were walking with destiny, and that all
> my past life had been but a preparation for this hour and for this
> trial. I could not be reproached either for making the war or with
> want of preparation for it. I thought I knew a good deal about it
> all, and I was sure I should not fail."

How remarkably his past life was a preparation for this hour may
be seen from the extraordinary range of his administrative experience:
he had had active experience of all the key offices of state, except the
Foreign Office. (And no one can say that his inclinations and con-
victions in that sphere were not better than the dreary succession of
Foreign Secretaries—always excepting that Churchillian, Anthony
Eden—of the 1930s.) Starting with the paternal background of Lord
Randolph Churchill's Tory Democracy, he reacted against the static,
monumental Conservatism of the 'nineties, which had also revealed
its incompetence—and the need for drastic reform—in the Boer War.
As a consequence of the war, his sympathies—like a good many
Englishmen's—came to be with the Boers. He was himself captured
by Botha, and that was the beginning of a firm friendship with Botha
and Smuts which endured the shaking of the universe. His South
African sympathies had a large part in causing him to leave his own
Party, his ancestral Party, the Conservatives, to join the Liberals. The
Conservative Party never really forgave him for that, for over thirty

years, until they had to accept him as Prime Minister—forced on them by the disasters of 1940. This unconventional beginning to a political career, by leaving his own Party for another, portended something important for the far future: the man who was never circumscribed by Party could become the national leader above party in the crisis of his country's fate. And at the time, in introducing the Liberal grant of self-government for South Africa, as Under-Secretary for the Colonies, he could appeal to the Conservatives: "With all our majority we can only make it the gift of a Party. You can make it the gift of England." That too was a pointer to the future.

When Asquith's Ministry was formed in 1908—the ablest Government this country had had in a century, a Cabinet of Prime Ministers with Asquith, Grey, Haldane, Lloyd George and Churchill all in it— the young Winston refused to go to the Local Government Board: he declined, he said, "to be shut up in a soup-kitchen with Mrs. Sidney Webb". Going to the Board of Trade, he took a leading part in the developing social legislation which was the mark of that Government after the long Tory somnolence on the subject. In two years he introduced the Trade Boards Bill, established Labour Exchanges and initiated Unemployment Insurance—besides giving a great deal of advice all round to everybody else about their jobs too. (Sir Edward Grey once complained that "Winston, very soon, will become incapable from sheer activity of mind of being anything in a Cabinet but Prime Minister.") However, though one must not underestimate the constructive element in Churchill's work here, the intellectual interest in the subject of social services is rapidly exhausted—after all, anybody can spend public money: that does not require first-class ability. After a short spell at the Home Office, Churchill went to his vitally important work at the Admiralty.

The German naval challenge was upon us; the Germans were determined to rival us at sea—a matter of life and death for this country—in addition to having the most powerful army on the Continent. Haldane re-formed the British Army from top to bottom, incorporating all the lessons of the South African War, and made it an efficient, if small, fighting instrument. It was for Churchill to perform a similar service for the Navy, our first line of defence. This, in four remarkable years, 1911–15, he accomplished. The introduction of

Dreadnoughts had revolutionized the Fleet and the conditions of naval warfare. Churchill, with that flexibility of mind, that interest in new ideas and inventions, which goes so oddly with the old bulldog qualities, applied his mind to this new world of work. He encouraged the development of new types; he was an early believer in the value of air reconnaissance—with the result that when war came the British Fleet was the only one with 100 aircraft in being. Tanks developed out of a by-way of the Navy's exploratory activities in this extraordinarily inventive epoch. He was responsible for the new strategic disposition of the Fleet, the arrangement with the French in the Mediterranean, the concentration in the North Sea. In 1914 the Fleet was ready.

In the war itself, the idea of forcing the Dardanelles by a combined sea and land attack was Churchill's. It was a brilliant conception, and no one can doubt now that if it had been properly carried out it would have shortened the war, perhaps by a couple of years. It would have knocked Turkey and Bulgaria out of the war, given us a direct link with Russia and saved her from defeat. It is a fascinating speculation what would have happened if the Dardanelles expedition had succeeded and Tsarist Russia not been defeated: she would have gained Constantinople; on the other hand, the world might have been spared some of the malign and evil things that have happened, the threat to the foundations of civilization.

But the Dardanelles expedition was never given a fair chance. Many good men died on it, many good ships went down. The whole thing was bungled by the military command, essentially by Kitchener. However, Churchill was made to take the responsibility for it; and when Asquith formed his coalition with the Conservatives, they insisted on driving Haldane out of the War office and Churchill out of the Admiralty: the two men to whom the country owed its state of preparedness, the like of which did not exist in 1939 after nearly twenty years of Conservative rule. It was Kitchener who pronounced a generous epitaph upon the fallen Minister. "Well, there is one thing at any rate they cannot take from you. The Fleet was ready." A fellow soldier, Sir Ian Hamilton, fighting in the Dardanelles, made a more prescient comment: "How grievous this set-back is to one who has it in him to revive the part of Pitt, had he but Pitt's place." The demoted Minister joined up to fight with other men on the Western Front.

In 1917, after the fearful blood-drain of the Allied offensives, he came back to the House of Commons to speak against any further precipitate attacks until the full weight of the United States could be brought to bear in Europe. There is not only an instinctive sympathy with the soldier's point of view, but an indication of the prudence and self-restraint with which he resisted the clamour for a premature Second Front in 1941, 1942 and 1943. Surprisingly, for those people who always distrusted Churchill's impulsiveness, the war of 1939–45 was fought in a way far more economical of British lives than the war of 1914–18. The man of imagination and vision was found a safer guide through danger than dangerously safe men, the mediocrities from whom States may pray to be delivered. Lloyd George, a man of genius himself, called Churchill back to succeed him as Minister of Munitions; the experience he garnered there bore fruit in the Ministry of Supply which he advocated in the 'thirties, and which was established when Hitler's war was upon us, to organize and direct the whole productive effort of the country.

In 1919 he was moved to the War Office, with responsibility for the Air Force too. Here he found himself saddled with the Allied intervention in Bolshevik Russia, a policy for the origins of which he bore no responsibility. In 1917, at the crisis of the war, it was natural enough that the Western Allies should have done what they could to stiffen the Russian Front and keep Russia in the war against Germany. Lenin decreed otherwise. If it had not been for the continued effort of the Western Allies, Germany would have won and that would have been the end of Lenin and his Bolshevism. When Lenin made peace with the enemy, it was equally reasonable that we should attempt to extricate the immense military stores we had piled up at Archangel and to keep the oil of Batum and Baku from the Germans. Gradually we were led into collaborating with the White Russian forces in these areas, which proved themselves so inefficient and hopeless in the Russian manner. Lloyd George was all in favour of leaving the Russians to settle their own differences and then coming to terms with them. Undoubtedly Churchill's inclination was to see the malign thing riveted on Russia in 1917 ended; and who, looking at its consequences for humanity, the sickening tale of sufferings, the millions of lives sacrificed, the deformation of the human mind, the threat to civilization, can say that he was wrong?

In 1921 he was moved to the Colonial Office, where the critical problems were to be tackled. First, the Middle East, where the defeat and break-up of the Turkish Empire had left an inextricable tangle of Arab and Jewish claims, British interests and obligations and promises to both. Churchill—like Lloyd George, no enemy to genius—recruited T. E. Lawrence; and Lawrence tells us that Mr. Churchill "in a few weeks made straight all the tangle, finding solutions fulfilling (I think) our promises in letter and spirit (where humanly possible) without sacrificing any interest of our Empire or any interest of the peoples concerned".

After that first-hand introduction to the problems of the Middle East—in which he had always been interested since the days of Omdurman, in which he fought—there came the settlement of the secular Irish problem, which had degenerated into a grievous form: a murder campaign on one side, answered by Black and Tans on the other. In the settlement Churchill's rôle was a crucial one: once more with ex-enemies, as in South Africa, he was in favour of a generous grant of self-government, responsibility and complete trust. "Tell Winston we could never have done anything without him," was Michael Collins's last message to him: he was killed by his own people. One who worked with Churchill over this told me that no less important was his administrative follow-up: the necessary drive he supplied in the complex business of transferring the apparatus of government, whole Departments and consequent arrangements, financial and otherwise, to a new Government that had emerged out of the shadows of conspiracy, murder and rebellion. It too was revolutionary; but there is no need to gild the circumstances of the revolution.

Here was another head of offence that Conservatives found hard to forgive. It is fairly safe to say that it was only Churchill's enthusiastic and undeviating anti-Socialism that enabled him to "work his passage" when a purely Conservative administration was formed; and even so, it was after he had served a penitential period in the wilderness and Baldwin—no friend to genius—astutely popped him in the prison of

R

the Treasury. There, from 1924 to 1929, he could do—from Baldwin's point of view—no harm, or, from the point of view of the country, no good. For the Treasury, in that period of financial orthodoxy, was the only Department of State that turned out to be too much for him. Churchill had never been noted for financial orthodoxy; and, in fact, his unorthodox hunches were far more intelligent than the oracles of Montagu Norman and the Treasury pundits. If only Churchill had been able to follow his own instincts! His inner heart by no means shared their fatuous fixation on the gold standard, or regarded the par-value of sterling as the Ark of the Covenant. However, he was in a strait-jacket and kept there for five years: we were forced back on to the gold standard; there followed deflation, unemployment, the Coal Strike, the General Strike, and all the rest of the sequelae of the Baldwin —or rather Montagu Norman—epoch.

When, after the dreary intermission of a Labour Government 1929–31, the disastrous National Government was formed to "save the pound" and keep Labour out, Baldwin and MacDonald found it more convenient to keep the two men of genius the country possessed, Lloyd George and Churchill, out. The 'thirties were the heyday of the second-rate, and they all made hay while the sun shone; they made hay too with the country's interests—in fact, they came as near as anything to ruining it and destroying it for ever. For if, as the result of their wonderful conduct of our affairs, the Germans had managed to bring it off in 1940—as they so very nearly did—they would never have made the mistake of letting us recover again. Very early in this terrible decade—far worse to have lived through than the heroic 'forties, which had their inspiration and nobility along with the danger and the suffering—Churchill withdrew from the inner counsels of the Conservative leadership over India. It is arguable, it may even be probable, that on the specific issue of India Churchill was old-fashioned and wrong; though it must be said on his side that the arguments from the point of view of world-strategy were with him—the partial neutralization of India has left a dangerous vacuum in the conflict with Russian and Chinese Communism. There was also a more personal reason for Churchill's withdrawal: the incompatibility of such a mind, powerful, candid and true, with the hybrid phenomenon provided by Baldwin and his National Government.

We recall A. G. Gardiner's phrase about a "personality that is entirely fearless" belonging to "a caste that never doubts itself". Never till 1931, we may say; for in that year the caste lost confidence in itself and, undermined by fear, it lost not only confidence but conscience. Confused in mind about everything, except the main chance—its own preservation—it survived from year to year, from month to month, from day to day, by blurring the clarity of all issues, even the most dangerous—that of the nation's safety; it maintained its enormous majority by electoral trickery, it spoke and perhaps thought in the language of humbug, it hoped to stave off conflict with the enemies of civilization by offering appeasement. The end was 1940.

That was no place for Churchill, and indeed for a whole decade he was not only out of power, out of office, but out of any influence, unlistened to by his own Party, never capable of commanding a following of more than a score in the House, out of the enormous mass of Conservatives with their unexampled majority. It was like Pitt, during most of his life. We all know Churchill's record during those years:

> "Last time I saw it all coming and cried aloud to my own fellow-countrymen and to the world, but no one paid any attention. Up till the year 1933 or even 1935, Germany might have been saved from the awful fate which has overtaken her and we might all have been spared the miseries Hitler let loose upon mankind. There never was a war in all history easier to prevent by timely action than the one which has just desolated such great areas of the globe. It could have been prevented in my belief without the firing of a single shot, and Germany might be powerful, prosperous and honoured today; but no one would listen and one by one we were all sucked into the awful whirlpool."

We are bound to pay special attention to his proved judgment; but even at the time, I thought it more probable that Germany, after so nearly succeeding in 1914–18, would make a second attempt at world power; and that, in that event, we should keep a cordon of the powers around her so that the break, when it came, should come internally. We now know that that is what would have happened: if Hitler had not been *given* his successes, the Army would have bumped him off when he had fatally compromised himself and the country.

In addition to crying in the wilderness, trying to arouse the country to the increasing danger to it, demanding armaments, the maintenance of air-parity with Germany, tanks, a Ministry of Supply, a Grand Alliance, a coherent foreign policy that made sense—all the things we were without—on top of this he wrote in those years one of the historical masterpieces of our time. In his *Life and Times of John Churchill, Duke of Marlborough*, a vast panorama in which he surveyed the whole public life of that age, he was viewing, through the eyes of his great ancestor, the problems, political, diplomatic and military, of fighting a war of a coalition against an overwhelming aggressor. Marlborough had been not only the executive right arm of a Grand Alliance, but its indispensable connecting link. It was in the course of this prolonged, reflective study of the strategy of the Grand Alliance that Churchill came to maturity as a statesman: writing that book, too, was part of his preparation.

His deliberate exclusion from power—for it was no less—had immeasurable advantages for himself in the end, by the extraordinary fortuitous justice of politics. He bore no responsibility for the situation we found ourselves in in 1940; he was not associated in the public mind with any of the humiliating (and always senseless) gestures of the policy of appeasement: on the contrary, he had always attacked it, the one statesman who had dared to state the truth about Munich at the time, when everybody else hugged his illusions. So far from its being "Peace for our time", he described it by its proper name: the people

"should know that we have sustained a defeat without a war . . . they should know that we have passed an awful milestone in our history, when the whole equilibrium of Europe has been deranged, and that the terrible words have for the time being been pronounced against the Western democracies: 'thou art weighed in the balance and found wanting'. And do not suppose that this is the end. This is only the beginning of the reckoning. This is only the first sip, the first foretaste of a bitter cup which will be proffered to us year by year unless by a supreme recovery of moral health and martial vigour, we arise again and take our stand for freedom as in the olden time."

When that supreme recovery came with the mortal danger in which we stood in 1940, he was in consequence able to express the nation's will to resist as no one else could. All those of us who heard his immortal words at the time still thrill at the memory.

"We have before us an ordeal of the most grievous kind. We have before us many long months of struggle and of suffering. You ask, What is our policy? I will say: It is to wage war, by sea, land and air, with all our might and with all the strength that God can give us: to wage war against a monstrous tyranny, never surpassed in the dark lamentable catalogue of human crime. That is our policy. You ask: What is our aim? I can answer in one word: Victory—victory at all costs, victory in spite of all the terror, victory however long and hard the road may be; for without victory there is no survival. Let that be realized; no survival for the British Empire; no survival for all that the British Empire has stood for, no survival for the urge and impulse of the ages, that mankind will move forward towards its goal. But I take up my task with buoyancy and hope. I feel sure that our cause will not be suffered to fail among men. At this time I feel entitled to claim the aid of all, and I say, 'Come then, let us go forward together with our united strength.'"

And so he became the greatest leader in war this country has ever had. Everything had prepared him for it: he had been head of all the fighting Services and knew more about it as a whole than the Service chiefs. In the conduct of the war and in its over-all strategy, no Chiefs of Staff would have objected to his overruling their advice. In that respect he was in a far stronger position and had an easier task than Lloyd George in the first German war. Churchill had an absolutely united country behind him from beginning to end. The Labour Party accepted the leadership of the most uncompromising of anti-Socialists with complete confidence; for they knew that under him no sectional or private interest would be allowed to come before the safety of the nation. No war-time profiteers as in 1914–18. And indeed a complete war-time socialism at once came into being—the whole nation's and everybody's resources and efforts taken control of for the purpose of national survival. Historians in the future may come to see that from the point of view of the social revolution of our time, 1940 was far more important than 1945. No conventional peacetime Labour Government, in the ordinary rhythm of Party alternation, would have dreamed of the degree of social change brought about in this country. It was the war that did it: there really never has been any going back on 1940.

Churchill could therefore leave the Home Front, the organization of the total man-power of the country, of its industrial and war production and supplies, the rationing of food, the financing of it all, to his colleagues. In all this, the most Churchillian figure among Labour leaders, Ernest Bevin, played a part second only to Churchill in winning the war. The Prime Minister could devote all the energies of his mind to the war, both the whole sweep of its strategy and every detail of it. No place here for the detail; the strategy as a whole, political equally with the military, is what is important. Here Churchill's services were immeasurable, his rôle unexampled. In the circumstances of complete defeat on the Continent, he made himself and this country the leader of the European resistance. All those fragments of the beaten nations which represented their real will, their determination to continue to resist, their future—French, Dutch, Belgians, Norwegians, Danes, Czechs, above all the Poles—came to pivot upon the island and its bulldog figure. He was engaged in building a Grand Alliance out of the fragments.

Relations with America were even more important—as they must always be, for there is the more powerful half of the English-speaking world. And it was from there that the wherewithal of our resistance came: even before America came into the war—and it seemed an age before she did—we could not have gone on without her aid. President Roosevelt grasped all that depended on the struggle and was determined that at all costs and by all means he would do all he could no matter what happened to him. He ultimately fell in the struggle, the greatest of war casualties; but before he did, he saw victory certain. The comradeship that he established with Churchill made one of the most human and touching passages in all the dark scenes of human misery. Blood *is* thicker than water, and no doubt the fact of being half American was an instinctive help to the most John Bullish of Englishmen in establishing a special understanding with the great

President and the American people. He shared their uninhibited ardour, their unreserve, their boyishness and bounce, their vigour with an edge on it, their unquenchable optimism and confidence in the underlying goodness of humanity. Churchill has himself expressed that better than anyone: "There is a great tide of good nature and comprehension in civilized mankind which sweeps to and fro and washes all the pebbles against each other, cleans the beach of seaweed, strawberry baskets and lobster pots. Hurrah for the tide!" That is almost more an American way of putting it than it is English; but how different from the malign and sinister men, the cynicism and brutality, the consciencelessness, the insanity and evil of the men he and the President were up against.

The fundamental strategy of the war for us was that when the common interest of this country with America and Russia and the subjugated countries, against the aggressors, could be realized and brought into play, then the war could be won: it could hardly be lost. Meanwhile we had to endure and resist alone, and exploit the mistakes of our insane opponents. They were not too long in coming. Hitler's attack on Russia gave us our great strategic opportunity. Without a moment's hesitation Churchill grasped his chance and grappled the Russians—so lately willing to throw us to the wolves—as an ally. His readiness was all the more effective coming as it did from one who had never concealed his hostility to Communism: it rallied doubters. With the Japanese attack on Pearl Harbour—an example of hubris equal to Hitler's and bringing an equal nemesis—America was brought fully into the war. The Grand Alliance was complete: it remained for the war to be won.

Like his great ancestor, the Duke, two and a half centuries before, Churchill made himself the indispensable linchpin, the connecting link, in the Alliance. An older man than either Roosevelt or Stalin, he did most of the journeying necessary to confer and concert measures. Co-operating with the Russians was by no means a bed of roses, as his *War Memoirs* reveal; and most of the hard words and brickbats fell on him. The President, whose vanity was assiduously flattered by Stalin, did not give Churchill the support he expected in dealing with the Russians, either at Teheran or later. From that, from the weakness arising from our disaccord over our approach to Russia, flowed the worse consequences after the war; from the too good nature of the Americans, their trust in human nature, the President's belief that he alone could deal with Stalin. Churchill had the better informed prevision of the historian as to what to expect: he had been there before. We may specify the most grievous mistake in all this: our joint weakness in allowing Stalin to displace and destroy the accredited Government of Poland's national resistance, the embodiment of her will to survive as an independent power. We gave way—and all the rest followed: the Baltic States, East Prussia, Rumania, Hungary, Czecho-Slovakia, the Russians entrenched intolerably in the middle of Europe. We cannot blame Churchill for this, though he has to bear some share of responsibility for what happened: it remains a joint Anglo-American responsibility, an historic mistake for which we have to endure the gravest consequences.

It was a pointer to the whole conduct of Russia in the post-war period: the withdrawal from the war-time comradeship, the cynical exploitation of Anglo-Saxon goodwill (not ultimately wise: witness the example of Germany) to push forward the conquests of Stalinist Imperialism wherever and whenever it met with no resistance, the calculated plan of aggression that in the end—though all too slowly—united the free world to resist it.

As in the 1930's Churchill was the first to realize the significance of what was happening, to draw the correct conclusions and sound a warning. His famous Fulton speech on March 5, 1946, roused a storm of protests from people who preferred to cherish their illusions: he did not allow himself to be put off by that: it was a reaction he had often had to put up with before. We wonder now what all the fuss was about, for Churchill was only, as so often before, pointing out what was in front of people's noses. To do that in politics is the prerogative of genius, and it takes the simplicity of genius to do it. The third-rate are apt to be lost in the complexities of the unreal. Indeed the combination of common-sense realism with a lofty imagination, of a rock-like standing by tried traditional values with a readiness to try out new ideas and inventions, of a monumental endurance with a responsive flexibility of mind, of hard facts with a certain poetry: that is what is characteristic of the man. At Fulton he merely pointed out the obvious:

"I do not believe that Soviet Russia desires war. What they desire is the fruits of war and the indefinite expansion of their power and doctrines."

And the remedy?

"We cannot afford, if we can help it, to work on narrow margins, offering temptations to a trial of strength. . . . If the population of the English-speaking Commonwealths be added to that of the United States with all that such co-operation implies in the air, on the sea, all over the globe and in science and industry, and in moral force, there will be no quivering, precarious balance of power to offer its temptation to ambition or adventure."

It is indeed a most unusual phenomenon to find a statesman out of office and out of power who was more influential, in a way more powerful, than those who held power: for in those post-war years 1945–51 he was the real leader of Western opinion. His importance as such has been summed up from a useful vantage-point by the Dutch publicist, Mr. Huizinga:

"Who in this country—and indeed in the world—could more legitimately claim to have displayed these virtues [of leadership], at Fulton and after, than Churchill? Who had enough faith in the Western way of life, not merely to proclaim its superior merits, but to propose that something should be done to safeguard it, regardless of the threats and censure such self-protective measures would evoke from the enemies of liberty? Who showed enough originality of mind to break with the traditional conception of the 'quivering, precarious balance of power' and to plead for the replacement of 'such narrow margins offering temptations to such a trial of strength' by a new and infinitely more stable system of retaining a balance of power in hand? [I am bound as an historian to point out here that this is precisely what the traditional concept of the Balance of Power in our policy meant: a stable balance of power against would-be aggressors; a Grand Alliance being the means to maintain it. Nothing could be more traditional than

R*

Churchill's conception.] Who had enough vision, imagination and insight to realize as early as the beginning of 1946 that it was practical politics to count on the Americans making such a system possible? Who was not afraid to confront the British public as early as November 1945, when it was still flushed with the pride of victory, with the extremely unpalatable fact—and surely to none more unpalatable than to this proudest of Britons himself—that the leadership in such a novel system would inevitably pass to the Americans?"

Mr. Huizinga is only wrong in thinking that this fact is unpalatable to us. It is in truth only natural; it is in keeping with realities, and the English people are great realists: unlike the Germans, they do not waste time and wreck themselves struggling against the nature of things. The main burden of leadership has passed to the other, more powerful half of the English-speaking peoples. But they are ourselves, modified by new geographical circumstances and by European immigration; we are with them—and our resources, as Churchill pointed out in that speech, are not negligible: added to those of America, as they always will be in the dangers of the modern world, they make the balance safe.

For the dangers of the modern world are so great that our separate history as a people is coming to merge with that of the English-speaking peoples as a whole. Again Churchill's are the prophetic words in that same speech:

> "Eventually there may come—I feel eventually there will come—the principle of common citizenship, but that we may be content to leave to destiny, whose outstretched arm many of us can already clearly see."

It has been his providential good fortune that the climax of his historic career should have coincided with the apogee of our separate history as a people. The heroic years 1940–45 touched the highest point that this country has ever been able to achieve for others: it was the culmination of our secular struggles for the liberties of Europe, against Philip II, Louis XIV, Napoleon, the Germany of William II and Hitler. Now that this tradition of ours is becoming merged in the larger unity of the English peoples, is it not by an extraordinary propriety of history that the symbol of that unity should be the bearer of an historic English name who is half an American?

In the end, it is difficult not to exaggerate. For Winston Churchill sums up the whole first half of our century as no other statesman does. Coming into public notice before the end of the nineteenth century, he already took an important part—which might well have been more so—in the First World War. All the figures of that epoch have passed away: the Kaiser is gone, Lloyd George is gone; President Wilson and Lenin have long vanished from the scene. Now all the leading figures of the Second World War also are dead: Hitler and Mussolini, President Roosevelt and Stalin. Only Winston Churchill remains, incarnating how much of modern history in himself, a fabulous figure on the small stage of the modern world.

INDEX

(1) SIR WINSTON CHURCHILL

As Humorist

Parliamentary Career (*began in* 1900)

The Philosopher

And Racing

The Scientist

(2) GENERAL INDEX